THE COLLECTED WORKS
OF W. B. YEATS

VOLUME X

THE COLLECTED WORKS OF W. B. YEATS

Richard J. Finneran and George Mills Harper, General Editors

W. B. YEATS

Later Articles and Reviews

UNCOLLECTED ARTICLES, REVIEWS,
AND RADIO BROADCASTS
WRITTEN AFTER 1900

EDITED BY
Colton Johnson

Scribner

SCRIBNER
1230 Avenue of the Americas
New York, NY 10020

SCRIBNER and design are trademarks of Macmillan Library Reference USA, Inc.,
used under license by Simon & Schuster, the publisher of this work.

Designed by Jennifer Dossin
Set in Sabon

Manufactured in the United States of America

1 3 5 7 9 10 8 6 4 2

Library of Congress Cataloging-in-Publication Data

Yeats, W. B. (William Butler), 1865–1939.
Later articles and reviews: uncollected articles, reviews, and radio
broadcasts written after 1900/W. B. Yeats; edited by Colton Johnson.
  p.   cm.—(The collected works of W. B. Yeats; v. 10)
Includes bibliographical references and index.
  1. Books Reviews. I. Johnson, Colton. II. Title. III. Series:
Yeats, W. B. (William Butler), 1865–1939. Works. 1989; v. 10.
PR5900. A2F56   1989 vol. 10
[PR5902]
821'8 s—dc21
[828'.808]   99-16533
CIP

ISBN 0-684-80727-0

CONTENTS

EDITOR'S PREFACE

This volume of *The Collected Works of W. B. Yeats* contains fifty-four prose pieces published between 1900 and Yeats's death in January of 1939 and not collected subsequent to their original appearance by either Yeats or Mrs Yeats. Thirty-five of these pieces were included in the second volume of *Uncollected Prose by W. B. Yeats*, and nearly twice as many from this period in that volume are not included here. Some of the omitted items, such as the occasional theatre articles Yeats published in *Beltaine* and *Samhain*, are included elsewhere in *The Collected Works*, better to supply their context. Others, such as Yeats's letter of sympathy to the widow of Kevin O'Higgins (*UP2 476*), are more properly thought of as public letters and are left for inclusion in the appropriate volume of *The Collected Letters of W. B. Yeats*, which is appearing under the general editorship of John Kelly.

With a few exceptions, these pieces are occasional, reflecting both Yeats's freedom in the last half of his life from reliance for income on writing prose and his practice during this period of gathering and shaping much of his prose into integrated volumes. Manuscript and typescript material for many of these texts survives, but, as incidental works published usually only once and generally in journals, after submission they were frequently never seen by Yeats before publication. For many of these writings, as, for example, his notes on the 1902 productions in St Teresa's Hall of *Cathleen ni Houlihan* and AE's *Deirdre*, this edition relies primarily on a newspaper text, with often fragmentary typescript or manuscript material as supplement. In one instance, the 1917 letter-essay to the *Observer* on the controversy over Sir Hugh Lane's pictures, we have galley proofs partially edited by Yeats. This letter also was included by Alan Wade in his edition of Yeats's letters.

A few other pieces in this volume, such as Yeats's appreciation in 1915 of Thomas Davis or his remarks the previous year on the awarding of the Polignac prize, have similarly received editorial attention from, respectively in these instances, Denis Gwynn and Richard J. Finneran. I have drawn gratefully on these efforts where they have been available to me. Yeats's commentary on early Irish literature, 'An Ancient Conversation', appeared as an endnote to Lady Gregory's *Cuchulain of Muirthemne,* published in April 1902, and that text is included as Appendix 11 in Volume VI of this edition. The closely identical text from the *All Ireland Review* is included in this volume both because of the near-simultaneity of the two publications and to supplement the bibliographical record.

Six articles in this collection which appeared in the *United Irishman* between November 1901 and October 1903 were gathered together, probably by Yeats, under the tentative title 'Some Uncollected Essays and Notes from the *United Irishman:* 1901–1903'. The collection, among Yeats's papers (NLI Ms 30039, SUNY SB Box 20), was not published.

Ten of the writings in this volume are texts of radio programmes broadcast between 1931 and 1937. While these pieces present special editorial challenges, they are in some ways uniquely rewarding. They also constitute the largest previously uncollected body of Yeats's published work and, arguably, the most important one to remain largely unstudied.

We can clearly document Yeats's planning and participation in eleven radio programmes, all but one broadcast by the British Broadcasting Corporation. The text omitted from this volume, the lecture on modern poetry broadcast October 11, 1936, was published in *Essays 1931 to 1936* and is included in Volume V of *The Collected Works.* The text of another programme, broadcast from Belfast on March 17, 1934, appeared in the BBC publication the *Listener* the following month. The BBC has an incomplete file of the broadcast typescripts along with thorough notes of 'programmes as broadcast'. Not all of the broadcasts were recorded, and only parts of most of these recordings are extant; a complete recording of one programme, 'In the Poet's Pub', survives.

With the exception of the programme published in the *Listener,* textual authority for this body of work begins with Yeats's manuscripts, his typescripts, and his emendations, and incorporates information from the BBC file copies and notes on 'programmes as broadcast', as well as Yeats's notes on the file copies where it can be established that they were those from which he read. Wherever pos-

sible, the text is established from a recording of the actual broadcast. The interpolation of the several textual sources is indicated in
the notes to each programme. The text for one programme, the
broadcast from the Abbey Theatre on February 1, 1937, can be
established only from a set of recordings made in Dublin several
days after the actual public performance. Its restoration has been
aided by my access to Yeats's considerable correspondence relating
to the programme, most of which is at present unpublished. A
reconstruction of the several elements of another radio programme,
'My Own Poetry', broadcast on July 3, 1937, is included in Appendix C. The manuscript and typescript material in Yeats's papers for
several of the radio programmes was partially collected and put
into working order by the late Professor Curtis Bradford, and I
have benefited from that effort.

The order of the writings in this volume is chronological, according to the dates of their appearance before the public. As they are
often in response to very specific events or to other published views,
an initial note supplies, often with other information, the topical
setting as well as the source or sources of the text. Both when they
have been traced and when they have not, Yeats's references are
generally noted at their first occurrences; subsequent, unannotated
occurrences may be traced through the index. A listing of the copy-
texts for printed material is supplied as Appendix A.

As Yeats saw few of these writings through their publication, it is
reasonable to assume that the fair number of typographical errors and
simple misspellings in the copy-texts appear without his editorial intent.
This consideration has guided my emendation of the printed texts,
which I have altered sparingly, indicating each change with a dagger
in the text and providing the relevant information in Appendix B. For
example, the printed text of Yeats's letter to the *United Irishman* for
April 26, 1902, contains both the correct spelling of Edward Martyn's name and an incorrect one, 'Martin', which I have emended in
two instances, given ample evidence elsewhere that Yeats would not
have seen this misspelling through the press. The radio broadcasts offer
a particular challenge in this regard. For example, because the radio
broadcast of March 17, 1934, concluded with a musical performance of 'Down by the Salley Gardens', the programme's text was
reshaped for publication, presumably by Yeats. Thus the printed form
becomes the copy-text and the several variations in the broadcast ver-

sion are noted. In two successive typescripts, including the heavily annotated one from which he read during the broadcast, the name of Ballisodare in County Sligo appears as 'Ballysodare', a variant spelling used by Yeats in a note on 'Down by the Salley Gardens' when it was published in 1889 (see *VP* 90). In the *Listener,* a rare but accepted variant, 'Ballysadare', was substituted. As the early note establishes Yeats's preference, the place name is emended, and the variations are noted. However, the present text preserves the *Listener*'s inclusion of one of three of the radio text's indicated revisions by Yeats to 'The Song of the Old Mother', on the authority of his manuscript revision in the radio text and the assumption that he further revised the poem prior to its publication.

Although none of the other radio texts in this volume was printed, Yeats clearly saw many of the texts through several typescripts and, in some instances, through the reading copy and/or into the BBC archives. I have noted emendations in this material. Where either the script from which Yeats read or the recordings indicate he omitted material in the presumptive final text in his reading, this is noted, and his rare recorded interjections are included in the text in brackets. For the unpublished broadcasts, the format of Yeats's poems is regularised to conform with Volume I of *The Collected Works;* that of poems by other authors conforms to their first collected publication.

Commas and periods are uniformly placed after quotation marks, and British spelling conventions are observed in the editorial matter. In Yeats's texts, however, spelling variations are retained. The appearance of 'labor', for example, in Yeats's note on his translation of Sophocles, published in the *New York Times* in 1933, may arguably be the work of an American editor. But Yeats's practice was irregular—as, for example, in the remarks in 1908 to the British Association, edited by Yeats himself, where 'subsidized theatre' appears, along with 'specialising' further on and 'judgment' just a bit further—making precise determination of his intention in this matter impossible. I have not attempted to regularise Yeats's somewhat idiosyncratic placement of commas, much of which is supported in typescript or manuscript, and, also on the authority of typescript or manuscript, I have retained certain unorthodox locutions, such as 'logical deductions from a too narrow premises' and leisurely life long past away'. Plausible alternate forms—'Kathleen' and 'Cathleen' or 'BBC' and 'B.B.C.', for example—are preserved, and substantive errors of fact remain unchanged in the text but are noted where detected.

This volume adopts the following typographical and format conventions of *The Collected Works of W. B. Yeats:*

1. The presentation of headings is standardised. In this volume, the main headings are set in full capitals (capitals and small capitals for subtitles). Section numbers are in roman capitals. All headings are centered and have no concluding full point.

2. The opening line of each paragraph is indented, except following a displayed heading or section break.

3. All sentences open with a capital letter followed by lower-case letters.

4. British single quotation mark conventions are used.

5. A colon that introduces a quotation is not followed by a dash.

6. Quotations that are set off from the text and indented are not placed within quotation marks.

7. Except in headings, the titles of stories and poems are placed within quotation marks; titles of books, plays, long poems, periodicals, operas, statues, paintings, and drawings are set in italics.

8. Contractions (i.e., abbreviations such as 'Mr', 'Mrs', and 'St') that end with the last letter of the abbreviated word are not followed by a full point.

9. Abbreviations such as 'i.e.' are set in roman type.

10. In this volume, a dash—regardless of its length in the copy-text—is set as an unspaced em rule when used as punctuation.

11. Ampersands are expanded to 'and'.

12. Each signature of the author is indented from the left margin, set in upper- and lower-case letters, and ends without punctuation.

Capitalisation of the titles of French books in this volume follows the convention of that language.

I have relied on the assistance of friends, students, and scholars and on staff assistance from several libraries and other institutions during my work on the materials in this volume. I appreciate particularly the guidance both general and specific of Richard J. Finneran,

University of Tennessee, and also of George M. Harper, Florida State University. John Kelly, St John's College, Oxford, generously shared with me not only his extraordinary knowledge of Yeats but also the rich resource of the Yeats correspondence under his expert care. Michael B. Yeats and Gráinne Yeats aided me substantially, and I am particularly grateful to Senator Yeats for his discovery of the recordings of his father's radio programme broadcast in February of 1937.

Ronald Schuchard, Emory University; Colin Smythe, Gerrards Cross, Bucks.; and William M. Murphy, Union College, also gave generously of their knowledge. I am in addition grateful to David R. Clark, University of Massachusetts; Warwick Gould, Royal Holloway and Bedford New College, University of London; and, for his excellent precepts in other volumes of Yeats's prose in this edition, to William H. O'Donnell, University of Memphis.

Among the Vassar College students who have contributed to this volume, I particularly thank Marianne Merola for prodigious efforts she may have nearly forgotten. More recently, Anna Beaty, Cecelia Curran, Arcadia Haid, David Lavinsky, and Justin Ravitz have seen the project to its completion with care and splendid energy. The Vassar College libraries have been expert in their assistance, and among my Vassar colleagues, I especially wish to thank Robert DeMaria, Lucinda Dubinsky, Eamon Grennan, Richard Jones, Brian Mann, James Mundy, Robert Pounder, Christine Reno, Evert Sprinchorn, and Richard Wilson.

More generally, I wish to note the contributions of Patricia Boylan, Dublin; Margaret J. Cox, BBC Sound Archives; Tom Desmond, National Library of Ireland; Tara Doyle, RTE Reference and Illustrations Library; Catherine Fahy, National Library of Ireland; Christopher Fitzsimon, Dublin; Brendan Flynn, Clifden, County Galway; Jayne Herringshaw, National Gallery; Sgt Terry Hudson, Irish Military Archives; Norma Jones, BBC Sound Archives; John Jordan, BBC Written Archives Centre; Sarah McGrath, Scribner; Bobbie Mitchell, BBC Picture Archives Photography Library; Vicki Mitchell, BBC Rights Archive; Collette O'Flaherty, National Library of Ireland; Jim O'Shea, National Library of Ireland; Susan Rose, Department of Special Collections, Frank Melville, Jr., Memorial Library, State University of New York at Stony Brook; Noel Shiels, RTE Archives; Jeremy Silver, British Library National Sound

Archive, London; and Geoff Smyth, Dublin. While the errors, omissions, and opacities in the edition of the material in this volume are entirely mine, much of what may be useful in it is attributable to those named above, among others.

This book is dedicated to Jean, Augusta, and Olivia, the loves of my life, and I hope that, its faults my own, its merits may make it worthy of the memory of Richard Ellmann.

ABBREVIATIONS

The following abbreviations are used in the annotations to the texts in this volume.

Au	W. B. Yeats, *Autobiographies* (London: Macmillan, 1955)
Berg NYPL	Henry W. and Albert A. Berg Collection, New York Public Library, Astor, Lenox and Tilden Foundations
CL1	*The Collected Letters of W. B. Yeats,* vol. I, ed. John Kelly, associate ed. Eric Domville (Oxford: Clarendon Press, 1986)
CL3	*The Collected Letters of W. B. Yeats,* vol. III, ed. John Kelly and Ronald Schuchard (Oxford: Clarendon Press, 1994)
E&I	W. B. Yeats, *Essays and Introductions* (London and New York: Macmillan, 1961)
Ex	W. B. Yeats, *Explorations,* sel. Mrs W. B. Yeats (London: Macmillan, 1962; New York: Macmillan, 1963)
Hone	Joseph Hone, *W. B. Yeats, 1865–1939* (New York: St Martin's Press, 1962)
Kelly	Unpublished letter in possession of John Kelly, St John's College, Oxford
L	*The Letters of W. B. Yeats,* ed. Allan Wade (London: Hart-Davis, 1954; New York: Macmillan, 1955)
Mem	W. B. Yeats, *Memoirs,* ed. Denis Donoghue (London: Macmillan, 1972; New York: Macmillan, 1973)
NLI	Unpublished material in the National Library of Ireland, Dublin
OBMV	*The Oxford Book of Modern Verse, 1892–1935,* chosen by W. B. Yeats (Oxford: Clarendon Press, 1936)
O'Shea	Edward O'Shea, *A Descriptive Catalog of W. B. Yeats's Library* (New York: Garland, 1985)
P	W. B. Yeats, *The Poems,* revised edition, ed. Richard J. Finneran (New York: Macmillan, 1989; London: Macmillan, 1991)
SUNY-SB	Yeats Microfilm Archive, Frank Melville, Jr., Memorial Library, State University of New York, Stony Brook
UP1	*Uncollected Prose by W. B. Yeats,* vol. I, ed. John P. Frayne (New York: Columbia University Press; London: Macmillan, 1970)
UP2	*Uncollected Prose by W. B. Yeats,* vol. II, ed. John P. Frayne and Colton Johnson (London: Macmillan, 1975; New York: Columbia University Press, 1976)

VP   *The Variorum Edition of the Poems of W. B. Yeats,* ed. Peter
      Allt and Russell K. Alspach (New York: Macmillan, 1957)
VPl   *The Variorum Edition of the Plays of W. B. Yeats,* ed. Russell
      K. Alspach (London and New York: Macmillan, 1966)
Wade Allan Wade, *A Bibliography of the Writings of W. B. Yeats*
      (London: Hart-Davis, 1958)

I

NOBLE AND
IGNOBLE LOYALTIES

I have written a couple of letters to the Irish papers on the visit of
Queen Victoria to Ireland, but they have been very short, for I do
not find that I have much to say upon such matters.[1] Kings and
Queens come and go, and men wear emblems in their button-holes
and cannons fire; and we all grow excited, and forget how little
meaning there is in the cheers that such things buy. On the day after
the taking of the Bastille,† Louis XVI sent a message to the French
Assembly, saying that he would address it in person. The members
took council how the king should be received, and Mirabeau
advised that a 'mournful respect' best became that 'hour of grief',
for 'the silence of the people is the lesson of kings'.[2] But because the
desire to cheer a king lies deep in human nature, all cheered
the king; and everybody knows what followed those cheers. Did the
cheers that greeted Queen Victoria mean more than those that
greeted Louis XVI? But for her fleet and her soldiers, and her great
Empire, that watches over her, would she or any representative of
English rule sleep easy under an Irish roof? She was here before,
and was greeted with louder and more plentiful cheers, for I learn
from certain English papers that this time the poor kept silent. She
came in 1849, and though we had the great Famine to forget, and
though Mitchel and Meagher and Smith O'Brien[3] had been transported a few months before she came, she was met by cheering
crowds. The streets were as full as they were a couple of weeks ago,
and yet she had scarce gone when the Tenant League was founded
and the Land War in its modern shape began.[4] She came again in
1853 and opened an exhibition, amid cheering crowds, and five

years later the Fenian Organisation was founded.[5] In August, 1861, she paraded the streets again, amid cheering crowds, and two years, after she had gone, the *Irish People*[†] was founded,[6] and after that came State Trials, and insurrection, and suspension of Constitutional Law. Her visits to Ireland have indeed been unfortunate for English power, for they have commonly foreshadowed a fierce and sudden shaking of English power in Ireland. I do not think this last visit will be more fortunate than the others, for I see all round me, among the young men who hold the coming years in their hands, a new awakened inspiration and resolve. It is for the best that they should have the two loyalties, loyalty to this English Queen, loyalty to her we call Kathleen Ny Hoolihan, called up before them, that they may choose with clear eyes the harder way, for man becomes wise alone by deliberate choice and deliberate sacrifice. There is a commandment in our hearts that we shall do reverence to overflowing goodness, wisdom, and genius, and to the noble kinds of beauty, and to those immortal ideals that will accept none but arduous service, and to the Maker of these things; and that we shall do reverence to nothing else under Heaven. Was it for any of these that those thousands stood cheering by the roadway, and that those numberless children, in the stands, were brought together from all over Ireland, that they might some day tell their children what they had seen? It was to see a carriage with an aged woman, who is so surrounded by courtiers that we do not know with any certainty, whether she is wise or foolish, bitter or magnanimous, miserly or generous; and who, unlike the great kings and queens of a greater time, has certainly used her example and her influence to cherish mediocrity in music and in painting and in literature. In a few years crowds will gather, in as many thousands, to see a carriage with an elderly man, her son, who has used his example and his influence to make the love of man and woman seem a light and vulgar thing among great numbers in his islands.[7]

2

IRISH FAIRY BELIEFS

Some ten or eleven years ago, when I was compiling a little anthology of Irish fairy and folk tales, somebody asked an eminent authority to advise me.[8] He replied that there was little Irish folklore in print, that could be trusted as one could trust the books of Scottish folklore, and went on to moralise over the defects of Irish character. A couple of years ago this eminent authority described the works of the Irish folklorists as more exhaustive and valuable than the works of the Scottish folklorists. The truth is that moralising over defects and virtues of national character is for the most part foolish, for the world is shaped by habits of thought and habits of expression, and these, in young nations at any rate, can change with extreme swiftness. Ireland learned to do in about five years the work she had neglected for a century, and the intellectual awakening, which has given us so much, gave us Mr Larminie, Mr Curtin, Dr Hyde,[9] the most admirable of all that have translated out of the Gaelic of the country people, and some whose work is in magazines and newspapers. But because these writers, with the exception of Mr Curtin in one little book,[10] have devoted themselves to the traditional tales and rather neglected the traditional beliefs one has a quite unworn welcome for Mr Daniel Deeney, a National school teacher of Spiddal, in Western Galway, and a Gaelic speaker, who has got together a little bundle of tales of omens and charms and apparitions. He follows his masters wisely too, though here and there he shows a defect of the evil days of Croker and Lover,[11] and, while making some little incident vivid with characteristic dialogue, uses a word or phrase which has not come out of the life he is describing, but out of the life of some other place, or out of books. He should know the English dialect of Galway as few know it, and yet I am certain that 'indade' is out of some novelist. The Irish country people do not mispronounce, but rather over pronounce, the sound of the 'ees' in 'indeed', and surely 'till' for 'to' belongs to the north of Ireland, where Mr Deeney was born, I believe, and not to Galway. He has heard many of his stories in Irish, I should imagine, for the countrypeople where he lives talk Irish principally, and, concluding very rightly that literary English is not a natural equivalent for the Irish of the countrypeople, has translated them into a dialect which even those who know it perfectly must continue to write imperfectly until it is classified and examined by learned men, as English and Scottish dialect has been. No merely instinctive knowledge can quite overcome a convention which innumerable novelists and journalists have imposed upon the imagination. A safer equivalent would have been that English, as full of Gaelic constructions as the English of the countrypeople but without a special pronunciation, which Dr Hyde has adopted in *Beside the Fire*,[12] the one quite perfect book of Irish folklore. Once, too, in telling a very wild and curious story of the Cladagh of Galway, he allows himself to look through the clouds of a literary convention. Lily-white fingers and flowing golden hair cannot be typical of the Cladagh, though they are typical of the heroines of forty years ago.[13]

I point out these faults because Mr Deeney, living in the middle of a primitive people and with a real knack in story and dialogue and a perfect knowledge of Gaelic, has only to work carefully at his craft to be of great importance to the intellectual awakening of Ireland. As it is he has made a book which makes one understand better than any book I know of the continual communion of the Irish countrypeople with supernatural beings of all kinds. A man who lives not far from Mr Deeney once said to me, 'There is no man mowing a meadow but sees them one time or another'.[14] These country people have seen what a king might give his crown and the world its wealth to have seen, and the doubts and speculations, that are in our eyes so great a part of the progress of the world, would be in their eyes, could they understand them, but dust in the hollow of a hand. Already some that have devoted themselves to the study of the visions and the beliefs of such people are asking whether it is we, still but very few, or primitive and barbaric people, still a countless multitude, who are the exceptions in the order of nature, and whether the seer of visions and hearer of voices is not the normal and healthy man. It may be that but a few years shall pass before many thousands have come to think that men like these mowers and fishers of Mr Deeney's, who live a simple and natural life, possess more of the experience on which a true philosophy can be founded than we who live a hurried, troubled, unhealthy life. I am convinced, as I am convinced by no other thing, that this change will come; and it may be that this change will make us look to men like Mr Deeney, who are at the gates of primitive and barbaric life, for a great deal of the foundations of our thought.[15]

W. B. Yeats

3

IRISH WITCH DOCTORS[16]

The Irish countryman certainly believes that a spiritual race lives all about him, having horses and cattle, and living much the same life that he does, and that this race snatches out of our life whatever horse or cow, or man or woman it sets its heart on; and this belief, harmonised with Christianity by certain ingenious doctrines, lives side by side with Christianity and has its own priesthood. This priesthood, sometimes called 'faery doctors', sometimes 'knowledgeable men', and sometimes 'cow doctors', from its curing cows that have been 'swept', as the word is, has secrets which no folklorist may ever perhaps wholly discover, for it lives in terror of the spiritual race who are, it believes, the makers and transmitters of its secrets. I have questioned these men, and some of them have talked to me pretty freely, so freely, indeed, that they were afraid for themselves afterwards, but I feel that there is more to be known about them, and that I know less about them than about anything else in Irish folklore. I met one man, whom I will call Kirwan, on the Galway coast last year. I cannot tell his whereabouts more freely, for he is afraid of the priests, and has made me promise to tell nobody where he lives. A friend of mine, who knew I was curious in these matters, had asked some of the coast people if there was anyone who did cures through the power of the faeries, as I wanted a cure for a weakness of the eyes that had been troubling me. A man I will call Daly said, 'There's a man beyond is a great warrior in this business, and no man within miles of the place will build a house or a cabin or any other thing without going there to ask if it's a right place. He cured me of a pain in my arm I couldn't get rid of. He gave me something to drink, and he bid me to go to a quarry and to touch some of the stones that were lying outside it, and not to touch others of them. Anyway, I got well'.

The country people are always afraid of building upon a path of 'the Others', as they call the spirits, and one sometimes hears of houses being deserted because of their being 'in the way', as the phrase is. The pain in the arm was doubtless believed to be what is called 'the touch', an ailment that is thought to come from 'the Others', and to be the beginning of being carried away. The man went on to give another example of Kirwan's power, a story of a horse that seemed possessed, as we would say, or 'away' and something else put in its place, as he would say. 'One time down by the pier we were gathering in the red seaweed; and there was a boy there was leading a young horse the same way he had been leading him a year or more. But this day, of a sudden, he made a snap to bite him; and, secondly, he reared and made as if to jump on top of him; and, thirdly, he turned round and made at him with the hoofs. And the boy threw himself on one side and escaped, but with the fright he got he went into the bed and stopped there. And the next day Kirwan came, and told him everything that had happened, and he said, "I saw thousands on the strand near where it happened last night".'

The next day my friend went to see the wife of 'the great warrior in this business', to find out if he would cure my eyes. She found her in a very small cottage, built of very big stones, and of a three-cornered shape that it might fit into a crevice in the rocks. The old woman was very cautious at first, but presently drew her stool over to where my friend was sitting, and said, 'Are you *right*? you are? then you are my friend. Come close and tell me is there anything Himself can do for you?' She was told about my eyes, and went on, 'Himself has cured many, but sometimes *they* are vexed with him for some cure he has done, when he interferes with the herb with some person they are meaning to bring away, and many's the good beating they gave him out in the field for doing that. Myself they gave a touch to here in the thigh, so that I lost my walk; vexed they are with me for giving up the throwing of the cup'. She had been accustomed to tell fortunes with tea-leaves. 'I do the fortunes no more, since I got great abuse from the priest for it. Himself got great abuse from the priest, too, Father Peter, and he gave him plaster of Paris. I mean by that he spoke soft and humbugged him, but he does the cures all the same, and Father Maginn gave him leave when he was here'. She asked for my Christian names, and when she heard them went on, 'I'll keep that, for Himself will want it when he goes on his knees. And when he gathers the herb, if it's for a man, he must call on the name of some other man, and call him a King, *Righ*. And if it's for a woman, he must call on the name of some other woman, and call her a Queen. That is calling on the king or the queen of the plant'. My friend asked where her husband had got the knowledge, and she answered, 'It was from his sister he got the cures. Taken she was. We didn't tell John of it, where he was away caring horses. But he knew of it before he came home, for she followed him there one day he was out in the field, and when he didn't know her, she said, "I'm your sister Kate". And she said, "I bring you a cure that you may cure both yourself and others". And she told him of the herb, and the field he'd find it growing, and he must choose a plant with seven branches, the half of them above the clay and the half of them covered up. And she told him how to use it. Twenty years she's gone, but she's not dead yet, but the last time he saw her he said she was getting grey. Every May and November he sees her; he'll be seeing her soon now. When her time comes to die, she'll be put in the place of some other one that's taken, and so she'll get absolution. A nurse she has been all the time among them'.

May and November, the beginning and end of the old Celtic year, are always times of supernatural activity in Ireland. She is to be put back as a changeling to get absolution when she is too old to be any more use among 'the Others'. All, one is almost always told, are put back in this way. I had been told near Gort[17] that 'the Others' had no children of their own, but only children they stole from our world. My friend, hearing her say that Kirwan's sister was a nurse, asked her about this. She said, 'Don't believe those that say they have no children. A boy among them is as clever as any boy here, but he must be matched with a woman from earth; and the same way with their women, they must get a husband here. And they never can give the breast to a child, but must get a nurse from here'. She was asked if she had herself seen 'the Others', and if 'Himself' saw them often. She said, 'One time I saw them myself in a field, and they hurling. Bracket caps they wore, and bracket clothes of all colours. Some were the same size as ourselves, and some looked like gossoons that didn't grow well. But Himself has the second sight, and can see them in every place. There's as many of them in the sea as on the land, and sometimes they fly like birds across the bay. There is always a mistress among them. When one goes among them they would be all laughing and jesting, but when that tall mistress you heard of would tap her stick on the ground, they'd all draw to silence'.

The clothes of 'the Others' are always described as 'bracket', which is the Irish for variegated, but is explained to mean striped by the country people when talking of 'the Others'. The old inhabitants of Ireland who have become 'the Others', the people say, because they were magicians, and cannot die till the last day, wore striped clothes. The famous story of 'The Quest of the Bull of Cualgne',[18] preserved in a manuscript of the eleventh century, makes its personages wear 'striped' and 'streaked' and 'variegated' jackets of many colours.

It was arranged that I should go to Daly's house, and that Kirwan should go there to meet me after dark, that our meeting might not be noticed. We went to Daly's next evening, but found that Kirwan had been there earlier in the day to leave a bunch of herbs, which a botanist has since identified as the dog violet, for me to drink in boiled milk, which was to be brought to the boil three times; and to say that he could do nothing more for me, for what was wrong with my eyes 'had nothing to do with that business', meaning that it was not the work of spirits. We left an urgent message asking Kirwan to come and talk to us, and next day Daly, who had been very doubtful if he would come, brought us word that he would come as soon as it was dark. We reached the cottage amid a storm of wind, and the door was cautiously opened, and we were let in. Kirwan was sitting on a low stool in a corner of a wide hearth, beside a bright turf fire. He was short and broad, with regular features, and had extraordinary dark and bright eyes, and though an old man, had, as is common among these sea people, thick dark hair. He wore a flannel-sleeved waistcoat, cloth trousers, patched on the knees with darker stuff, and held a soft felt hat in his hands, which he kept turning and squeezing constantly. Unlike his wife he spoke nothing but Irish. Daly sat down near us with a guttering candle in his hands, and interpreted. A reddish cat and a dog lay beside the fire, and sometimes the dog growled, and sometimes the woman of the house clutched her baby uneasily and looked frightened. Kirwan said, stopping every now and then for Daly to interpret, 'It's not from *them* the harm came to your eyes. There's one of the eyes worse than the other' (which was true) 'and it's not in the eyes that the trouble began' (which was true). I tried to persuade him that it might be 'from them', to find out why he thought it was not, and I told him of a certain vision I had once, to make him feel that I was not a mere prying unbeliever. He said my eyes would get well, and gave me some more of the herb, but insisted that the harm was not 'from *them*'. He took the vision as a matter of course, and asked if I was ever accustomed to sleep out at night, but added that some might sleep out night after night and never fall into their power, or even see them. I asked if it was his friends among them who told what was wrong with anybody, and he said, 'Yes, when it has to do with their business, but in this case they had nothing to do with it'. My friend asked how he got his knowledge first, and he said, 'It was when I was in the field one day a woman came beside me, and I went on to a gap in the wall, and she was in it before me. And then she stopped me, and she said, "I'm your sister that was taken, and don't you remember how I got the fever first and you tended me, and then you got it yourself, and one had to be taken, and I was the one?" And she taught me the cure and the way to use it. And she told me she was in the best of places, and told me many things that she bound me not to tell. And I asked was it here she was kept ever since, and she said it was, but, she said, in six months I'll have to move to another place, and others will come where I am now, and it would be better for you if we stopped here, for the most of us here now are your neighbours and your friends. And it was she gave me the second sight'.

I asked if he saw 'them' often, and he said: 'I see them in all places, and there's no man mowing a meadow that doesn't see them at some time or other. As to what they look like, they'll change colour and shape and clothes while you look round. Bracket caps they always wear. There is a king and a queen and a fool in each house of them, that is true enough, but they would do you no harm. The king and the queen are kind and gentle, and whatever you'll ask them for they will give it. They'll do no harm at all, if you don't injure them. You might speak to them if you'd meet them on the road, and they'd answer you, if you'd speak civil and quiet, and not be laughing or humbugging—they wouldn't like that'.

He told a story about a woman we knew, who had been taken

away among them to nurse their children, and how she had come back after—a story that I am constantly hearing—and then suddenly stopped talking and stooped to the hearth, and took up a handful of hot ashes in his hand, and put them into the pocket of his waistcoat, and said he'd be afraid going home, because he'd 'have to tell what errand he had been on'. I gave him some whisky out of my flask, and we left him.

The next day we saw Daly again, and he said, 'I walked home with the old man last night, he was afraid to go by himself. He pointed out to me on the way home a graveyard where he got a great beating from them one night. He had a drop too much taken, after a funeral, and he went there to gather the plant, and gathered it wrong, and they came and punished him, that his head is not the better of it ever since. He told me the way he knows, in the gathering of the plant, what is wrong with the person that is looking for a cure. He has to go on his knees and to say a prayer to the king and the queen and to the gentle and the simple among them, and then he gathers it; and if there are black leaves about it, or white (withered) ones, but chiefly a black leaf folded down, he knows the illness is some of their doing. But for this young man the plant came fresh and clean and green. He has been among them himself, and has seen the king and the queen, and he says they are no bigger than the others, but the queen wears a wide cap, and the others have bracket caps. He never would allow me to build a shed beside the house here, though I never saw anything there myself'.

We found an old man on the borders of Clare and Galway who knew English,[19] and was less afraid of talking to us, from whom we heard a great deal. We went through a stony country, a good way from any town, and came at last to the group of poor cottages which had been described to us. We found his wife, a big, smiling woman, who told us that her husband was haymaking with their children. We went to the hay-field, and he came, very well pleased, for he knew my friend, to the stone wall beside the road. He was very square and gaunt, and one saw the great width of his chest through his open shirt, and recognised the great physical strength, supposed constantly to mark those who are in the service of 'the Others'. We talked of some relations of his, who were in good circumstances and tenants of my friend, and I think I told him some visionary experiences of my own. It was evident that he lived in great terror of 'the Others', but gradually he began to talk. We asked him where he got his power to work cures, and he replied, 'My uncle left me the power, and I was able to do them, and did many, but my stock was all dying, and what could I do? So I gave a part of the power to Mrs Merrick, who lives in Gort, and she can do a great many things'.

His stock died because of the anger of 'the Others', or because some other life had to be given for every life saved. We asked about his uncle, and he said, 'My uncle used to go away amongst them. When I was a young chap, I'd be out in the field working with him, and he'd bid me to go away on some message, and when I'd come back it might be in a faint I'd find him. It was he himself was taken, it was but his shadow or something in his likeness was left behind. He was a very strong man. You might remember Ger Kelly, what a strong man he was, and stout, and six feet two inches in height. Well, he and my uncle had a dispute one time, and he made as though to strike at him, and my uncle, without so much as taking off his coat, gave one blow that stretched him on the floor. And at the barn at Bunnahow he and my father could throw a hundredweight over the collar beam, what no other man could do. My father had no notion at all of managing things. He lived to be eighty years, and all his life he looked as innocent as that little chap turning the hay. My uncle had the same innocent look. I think they died quite happy'.

He pointed out to us where there was a lake, and said, 'My uncle one time told, by name, of a man that would be drowned there that day at 12 o'clock; and so it happened'. We asked him if his uncle's knowledge was the same kind of knowledge as the knowledge of a famous wise woman called Biddy Early; and he said, 'Surely I knew Biddy Early, and my uncle was a friend of hers. It was from the same they got the cures. Biddy Early told me herself that where she got it was, when she was a servant-girl in a house, there was a baby lying in the cradle, and he went on living for a few years. But he was friendly to her, and used to play tunes for her, and when he went away he gave her the bottle and the power. She had but to look in the bottle and she'd see all that had happened and all that was going to happen. But he made her give a promise that she'd never take more than a shilling for any cure she did, and she wouldn't have taken £50 if you had offered it to her, though she might take presents of bread and wine, and such things. The cure for all things in the world? Surely she had it, and knew where it was, and I knew it myself, too, but I could not tell you of it. Seven parts I used to make it with, and one of them's a thing that's in every house'.

He had only told us of one spirit he had himself seen. He was walking with another man on the road to Galway, and he saw 'a very small woman in a field beside the road, walking down towards us, and she smiling and carrying a can of water on her head, and she dressed in a blue spencer', and he asked the other man if he saw her, 'but he did not, and when I came up to the wall she was gone'. I have since heard, however, that he was 'away' among them himself. He would only talk of what his uncle or somebody else had seen. I showed him some water-colour drawings of men and women of great beauty, and with very singular halos about their heads, which had been drawn and painted from visions by a certain Irish poet[20] who, if he lives, will have seen as many wonders as Swedenborg; and rather to my surprise, for I had thought the paintings too idealised for a peasant to understand, he became evidently excited. 'They have crowns like that and of other shapes', he said, pointing to the halo. I asked if they ever made their crowns out of light, and he said, 'They can do that'. He said one of the paintings was of a queen, and that they had 'different queens, not always the same, and clothes of all colours they wear'. My friend held up a sapphire ring, and made it flash, and asked if their clothes were as beautiful. He said, 'Oh, they are far grander than that, far grander than that. They have wine from foreign parts, and cargoes of gold coming in to them. The houses are ten times more beautiful and ten times grander than any house in this world, and they could build one of them up in that field in ten minutes. Coaches they make up when they want to go out driving, with wheels and all, but they want no horses. There might be twenty going out together sometimes, and all full of them. Youngsters they take mostly to do work for them, and they are death on handsome people, for they are handsome themselves. To all sorts of work they put them, digging potatoes, and the like. The people they bring away must die some day, but as to themselves they were living from past ages, and can never die till the time when God has his mind made up to redeem them. And those they bring away are always glad to be brought back again. If you were to bring a heifer from those mountains beyond and to put it into a meadow, it would be glad to get back again to the mountain, because it's the place it knows'.

And he showed us a sign with the thumb that we were never to tell to anybody, but that we were to make if we ever felt 'a sort of shivering in the skin when we were walking out, for that shows that something is near'. If we held our hand like that we might go 'into a forth itself' and get no harm, but we were not to neglect that, 'for if they are glad to get one of us they'd be seven times better pleased to get the like of you. And they are everywhere around us, and now they may be within a yard of us on this grass. But if I ask you, What day's tomorrow? and you said Thursday, they wouldn't be able to overhear us. They have the power to go in every place, even on the book the priest is reading!'

To say, 'What day is to-morrow?' and be answered 'Thursday', or to say, 'What day is this?' and be answered 'Thursday', or to say, 'God bless them Thursday', is a common spell against being over-heard, but in some places the country people think that it is enough to be told what day the next day, or that day, really is. There is no doubt some old pagan mystery in Thursday, and if we knew more about the old Celtic week of nine nights we might understand it.

We went to see old Langan, as I will call him, another day, and found him hay-making as before, but he went with us into his house, where he gave us tea and home-made bread, both very good. He would take no money either that time or the time before, and his manner was very courteous and dignified. He told much more about 'the Others', this time. He said: 'There are two classes, the Dundonians, that are like ourselves, and another race more wicked and more spiteful. Very small they are and wide, and their belly sticks out in front, so that what they carry, they don't carry it on the back, but in front, on the belly, in a bag'.

The Dundonians are undoubtedly the Tuatha de Danaan, and Folk of the Goddess Danu, the old gods of Ireland, and the men with the bags on their stomachs undoubtedly the Firbolg, or Bag Men, as it is commonly translated, who are thought by M. de Jubainville an inferior Divine race, and by Prof. Rhys[21] an inferior human race conquered by the Celts. The old Irish epic tales associate the Megalithic ruins upon Aran with the Firbolg, and a friend, Mr Synge,[22] tells me that the people of Aran call the builders of the ruins belly-men. Bolg in Irish means bag or belly.

He went on: 'There are fools among them, dressed in strange clothes like mummers, but it may be the fools are the wisest after all. There is a queen in every regiment or house of them. It is of those they steal away they make queens for as long as they live, or that they are satisfied with them. There were two women fighting at a spring of water, and one hit the other on the head with a can and killed her. And after that her children began to die. And the husband went to Biddy Early, and as soon as she saw him she said, "There's nothing I can do for you. Your wife was a wicked woman, and the one she hit was a queen among them, and she is taking your children one by one, and you must suffer till twenty-one years are up". And so he did'.

We asked him if he ever knew anybody 'the Others' had given money to, and he said, 'As to their treasure, it's best be without it. There was a man living by a forth, and where his house touched the forth he built a little room and left it for them, clean and in good order, the way they'd like it. And whenever he'd want money, for a fair or the like, he'd find it laid on the table in the morning. But when he had it again he'd leave it there, and it would be taken away in the night. But after that going on for a time, he lost his son.

'There was a room at Cregg where things used to be thrown about, and every one could hear the noises there. They had a right to clear it out and settle it the way they'd like it'. Then he turned to my friend and said, 'You should do that in your own big house. Set out a little room for them with spring water in it always, and wine you might leave—no, not flowers, they wouldn't want so much as that, but just what will show your good will'.

A man at Kiltartan had told us that Biddy Early had said to him, 'There is a cure for all the evil in the world between the two mill-wheels of Ballylee', and I asked what cure that could be. He said, 'Biddy Early's cure that you heard of, between the two wheels of Ballylee, it was the moss on the water of the millstream. It can cure all things brought about by them, but not any common ailment. But there is no cure for the stroke given by a queen or a fool'.

We told him of an old man who had died a little time before, and how fighting was heard by the neighbours before he died. He said, 'They were fighting when Stephen Gorham died, that is what often happens. Everyone has friends among them, and the friends would try to save, when the others would be trying to bring you away. Youngsters they pick up here and there, to help them in their fighting or in their work. They have cattle and horses, but all of them have only three legs. The handsome they like, and the good dancers, and the straight and firm; they don't like those that go to right and left as they walk. And if they get a boy amongst them, the first to touch him, he belongs to her. They don't have children themselves, only the women that are brought away among them have children, but those don't live for ever like the Dundonians. They can only take a child, or a horse, or such a thing, through the eye of a sinner. If his eye falls on it, and he speaks and doesn't say "God bless it", they can bring it away then. But if you say it yourself in your heart, it will do as well. They take a child through the eye of its father, a wife through the eye of her husband'. The meaning was that if you look at anybody or anything with envy or desire or admiration, it may be used by 'the Others', as a link between them and the thing or person they are coveting. One finds this thought all over Ireland, and it is probably the origin of the belief in the evil eye. Blake thought that everything is 'the work of spirits, no less than digestion and sleep';[23] and this thought means, I think, that every emotion, which is not governed by our will, or suffused with some holy feeling, is the emotion of spirits who are always ready to bring us under their power. Langan had himself been accused once of giving a chicken into the power of 'the Others'. 'One time myself, when I went to look for a wife, I went to the house, and there was a hen and a brood of small chickens before the door. Well, after I went home, one of the chickens died. And what do you think they said, but that it was I overlooked it'.

This seems to have broken off the marriage for a time, but he married her in the end, and has had to suffer all kinds of misfortunes because of her. 'The Others' tried to take her first, the day after her marriage using, as I understand, his feelings about her as their link between her and them. 'My wife got a touch from them, and they have a watch on her ever since. It was the day after I married, and I went to the fair of Clarenbridge. And when I came back the house was full of smoke, but there was nothing on the hearth but cinders, and the smoke was more like the smoke of a forge. And she was within lying on the bed, and her brother was sitting outside the door crying. And I took down a fork from the rafters, and asked her was it a broom, and she said it was. So then I went to the mother and asked her to come in, and she was crying too, and she knew well what had happened, but she didn't tell me, but she sent for the priest. And when he came, he sent me for Geoghagan, and that was only an excuse to get me away, and what he and the mother tried was to get her to face death. But the wife was very stout, and she wouldn't give in to them. So the priest read mass, and he asked me, would I be willing to lose something. And I said, so far as a cow or a calf, I wouldn't mind losing that'.

Smiths are often associated with 'the Others', and with magic in Ireland, and so the room filled 'with the smoke of a forge'. St Patrick prayed against the spells of smiths. The question about the fork was to find out if she was in what we would call an hypnotic state, receptive to every suggestion. 'Well, she partly recovered, but from that day no year went by, but I lost ten lambs maybe, or other things. And twice they took my children out of the bed, two of them I have lost. And the others they gave the touch to. That girl there, see the way she is, and she is not able to walk. In one minute it came on her, out in the field, with the fall of a wall'. He told the girl to come out from where she sat in the corner of the chimney, with the dazed vacant look that one saw on the faces of the other children. She staggered for a foot or two, and then sat down again. From our point of view, her body was paralysed and her mind gone. She was tall and gentle-looking, and should have been a strong, comely, country girl. The old man went on: 'Another time the wife got a touch, and she got it again, and the third time she got up in the morning, and went out of the house and never said where she was going. But I had her watched, and I told the boy to follow her, and never lose sight of her. And I gave him the sign to make if he'd meet any bad thing. So he followed her, and she kept before him, and while he was going along the road, something was up on top of the wall with one leg. A red-haired man it was, with a thin face and no legs. But the boy got hold of him and made the sign, and carried him till he came to the bridge. At first he could not lift him, but after he had made the sign he was quite light. And the woman turned home again, and never had a touch after. It's a good job the boy had been taught the sign. It was one among them that wanted the wife. A woman and a boy we often saw coming to the door, and she was the matchmaker. And when we would go out, they would have vanished'.

He told us some other little odds and ends about a warning his uncle had given against cutting down a certain bush before his house, and how, when it was cut down twenty years after his uncle's death, a bullock died; and that 'Danes hate Irishmen to this day', and that 'when there is a marriage in Denmark', he has been told, 'the estates they owned in Ireland are handed down' (I have heard something like this in Sligo also); and then, evidently feeling that he was telling us a great mystery, he said, 'The cure I made with seven parts, and I took three parts of each, and I said, Father, Son, and Holy Spirit be on it, and with that I could go into a forth or any place. But as to the ingredients, you could get them in any house'.

We did not ask him for the ingredients, nor do I believe that any threat or any bribes would ever get them from him. When we were going, he said, and we were both struck by his dignity as he said it, 'Now I've told you more than ever I told my wife. And I could tell you more, but I'd suffer in my skin for it. But if ever you, or one belonging to you, should be in trouble, come to me, and what I can do to relieve you, I'll do it'.

Kirwan spoke of seeing his spirits, and Langan his, while in their ordinary state; but only those who are at times 'away', that is, who are believed to go away among the spirits, while their bodies are in a trance, are thought to be able to bring back those who are 'away'. In ancient Ireland it was only a *File* who had the knowledge of a certain ritual called the *imbas forosna,* or great science which enlightens, whereby he could pass as many as nine days in trance, who had the full knowledge of his order. It was long before we could find anyone who was 'away' and would tell us what it was like, for almost all who are 'away' believe that they must be silent. At last an old woman, whom I will call Mrs Sheridan, after telling many lesser things, told us what it was like. My friend had gone to see her one day, and been told a few curious things, but cautiously, for her daughter, who was afraid of such things, was there. She had said, 'Come here close, and I'll tell you what I saw at the old castle there below.[24] I was passing there in the evening, and I saw a great house and a grand one, with screens at the end of it, and windows open. Coole House is nothing to what it was for size or grandeur. And there were people inside, and a lady leaning out of the window, and her hair turned back, and she made a sign to me, and ladies walking about, and a bridge over the river. For they can build up such things all in a minute. And two coaches came driving up and across the bridge to the house, and in one of them I saw two gentlemen, and I knew them both well, and both of them had died long before. One was Redmond Joyce, and the other was the master's own father. As to the coach and horses, I didn't take much notice of them for I was too much taken up with looking at the gentlemen. And a man came and called out to me and asked, would I come across the bridge, and I said I would not. And he said it would be better for you if you did; you'd go back heavier than you came. I suppose by that he meant they'd give me some good thing. And then two men took up the bridge and laid it against the wall. Twice I've seen that same thing, the house and the coaches, and the bridge, and I know well I'll see it a third time before I die'.

This woman had never seen a drawbridge, and she had not read about one, for she cannot read. 'It would have cost a penny a week to go to school', she explains, and it is most unlikely that she has ever seen a picture of one. The peasants continually see in their visions the things and costumes of past times, and this can hardly be tradition, for they have forgotten the names of their own great-grandfathers, and know so little about ancient customs that they will tell you about Finn MacCool flinging a man over a haystack on his way to the assizes in Cork.

They had met another day on the road, and as they came opposite to a very big twisted thorn-tree, the old woman had curtsied very low to the bush, and said, 'And that's a grand bush we're passing by—whether it's a bush belonging to them I don't know, but wherever they get shelter, there they might be, but anyway it's a fine bush, God bless it'. But she had not said anything about being 'away'. At last, one day she came and sat with us and talked and seemed very glad to talk. She is one of the handsomest old country-women I have ever seen, and though an old woman, is vigorous in mind and body. She does not seem to know the cures that Kirwan and Langan know, and has not, I think, any reputation for doing cures. She says, however[25]—'I know the cure for anything they can do to you, but it's few I'd tell it to. It was a strange woman came in and told it to me, and I never saw her again. She bid me to spit and to use the spittle, or to take a graineen of dust from the navel, and that's what you should do if anyone you care for gets a cold or a shivering, or they put anything upon him.

'All my life I've seen them, and enough of them. One day I was with John Cuniff by the big hole near his house, and we saw a man and a woman coming from it, and a great troop of children, little boys they seemed to be, and they went through the gate into Coole, and there we could see them running and running along by the wall. And I said to John Cuniff, "It may be a call for one of us", and he said, "Maybe it's for some other one it is". But on that day next week he was dead'.

She has seen the coach-a-baur or deaf coach, as it is called from the deaf or rumbling sound it makes, in which they drive about.

'I saw the coach one night near the chapel. Long it was, and black, and I saw no one in it. But I saw who was sitting up driving it, and I know it to be one of the Fardys that was taken some time before. I never saw them on horses, but when I came to live at Martin Macallum's, he used to bring in those red flowers that grow by the road, when their stalks were withered, to make the fire. And one day I was out in the road, and two men came over to me, and one was wearing a long grey dress, and he said to me, "We have no horses to ride on, and we have to go on foot, because you have too much fire". So then I knew it was their horses we were burning'.

She seems to confuse red and yellow, and to have meant the yellow *bucalauns* or ragweeds, believed to be the horses of 'the Others'. Ragweed is given as a medicine to horses, and it may have got its association with the horses of 'the Others' through its use in witch medicine.

'One day I saw a field full of them, some were picking up stones to clear it, and some were ploughing it up. But the next day, when I went by, there was no sign of it being ploughed up at all. They can do nothing without some live person is looking at them, that's why they were always so much after me'.

One is constantly hearing that 'the Others' must have a mortal among them, for almost everything they do, and one reads as constantly in the old Irish epic tales of mortals summoned by the gods to help them in battles. The tradition seems to be that, though wisdom comes to us from among spirits, the spirits must get physical power from among us. One finds a modification of the same idea in the spiritualistic theory of mediumship. Mrs Sheridan went on: 'One time I went up to a forth to pick up a few sticks for the fire, and I was breaking one of the sticks on the ground, and a voice said from below, "Is it to break down the house you want?" and a thing appeared that was like a cat, but bigger than any cat ever was. And one time I was led astray in Coole, where I went to gather sticks for the fire. I was making a bundle of them, and I saw a boy beside me and a little dogeen with me, a grey one. And at first I thought it was Andrew Healy, and then I saw it was not. And he walked along with me, and I asked him did he want any of the sticks, and he said he did not, and as we were walking he seemed to grow bigger. And when we came to where the caves go underground he stopped, and I asked him his name, and he said, "You should know me, for you've seen me often enough". And then he was gone, and I knew he was no living thing.

'One day I was following the goat, to get a sup of milk from her, and she turned into the field and up into the castle of Lydican, and went up from step to step up the stairs to the top, and I followed, and on the stairs a woman passed me, and I knew her to be Ryan's wife that died. And when I got to the top I looked up, and there standing on the wall was a woman looking down at me, long-faced and tall, and with bracket clothes, and on her head something yellow, and slippery, not hair, but like marble. And I called out to ask her wasn't she afraid to be up there, and she said she was not. And a herd that used to live below in the castle saw the same woman one night he went up to the top, and a room and a fire, and she sitting at it, but when he went there again there was no sign of her or of the room.

'I know that I used to be away with them myself, but how they brought me I don't know; but when I'd come back, I'd be cross with my husband and with all; and I believe that I was cross with *them* when they wouldn't let me go. I met a man on the road one time, he had striped clothes like the others, and he told me why they didn't keep me altogether was because they didn't like cross people to be with them. The husband would ask me where I was, and why I stopped so long away; but I think he knew I was taken, and it fretted him; but he never spoke much about it. But my mother knew it well, but she'd try to hide it. The neighbours would come in and ask where was I, and she'd say I was sick in the bed, for whatever was put there in place of me would have the head in under the clothes. And when a neighbour would bring me in a drink of milk, my mother would put it by, and say, "Leave her now, maybe she'll drink it tomorrow". And, maybe, in a day or two I'd meet a friend, and she'd say, "Why wouldn't you speak to me when I went into the house to see you?" And I was a young, fresh woman at that time. Where they brought me to I don't know; nor how I got there; but I'd be in a very big house, and it round, the walls far away that you'd hardly see them, and a great many people all round about. I would see there neighbours and friends that I knew, and they in their own clothing, and with their own appearance, but they wouldn't speak to me, nor I to them, and when I'd meet them again, I'd never say to them that I saw them there. But the others had all long faces, and striped (bracket) clothes of blue and all colours, and they'd be laughing and talking and moving about. What language did they speak? Irish, of course; what else would they speak? And there was one woman of them, very tall, and with a long face, standing in the middle, taller than anyone you ever saw in this world, and a tall stick in her hand: she was the Mistress. She had a high yellow thing on her head—not hair—her hair was turned back under it, like the woman I saw at the window of the castle, and she had a long yellow cloak hanging down behind, and down to her feet'.

I showed her a picture of a spirit, by the seer I have already spoken of, and made her look at the halo, which is made up of rods of light, with balls of gold light upon their ends, and asked if she had anything like that on her head. She answered, 'It was not on her head, it was lower down here about the body', and by body she seemed to mean the waist. The old epic tales talk constantly of golden apples being used as ornaments. She looked at the brooch in the picture, a great wheel brooch, and said, 'She had a brooch like that in the picture, but hanging low down like the other'. I took up a different picture, a picture of a gigantic spirit, with the same rod-like head-dress, leaning over a sleeping man. It was painted in dull blue and grey, and very queer. She did not wait for me to question her, but said, 'And that picture you have there in your hand, I saw one like it on the wall. It was a very big place and very grand, and a long, long table set out, and grand food offered me, and wine, but I never would touch it. And sometimes I had to give the breast to a child; and there were cradles in the room. I didn't want to stop there, and I began crying to get home, and the tall woman touched me here on the breast with the stick in her hand; she was vexed to see me wanting to go away.

'They have never brought me away since the husband died, but it was they took him from me'. She has much fear of 'the Others', and tells of many mischiefs they have done her. She went on to tell of her husband's death. 'It was in the night, and he lying beside me, and I woke and heard him move, and I thought I heard someone with him. And I put out my hand, and what I touched was an iron hand, like knitting needles it felt. And I heard the bones of his neck crack, and he gave a sort of a choked laugh; and I got out of the bed and struck a light, and saw nothing, but I thought I heard someone go through the door. And I called to Honor, and she didn't come, and I called again, and she came; and she said she struck a light when she heard me calling, and was coming, and someone came and struck the light from her hand. And when we looked in the bed he was dead, and not a mark on him'.

They have taken also two of her children. 'There was a child of my own, and he but a year and a-half old, and he got a quinsy and a choking in the throat and I was holding him in my arms beside the fire, and all in a minute he died. And the men were working down by the river washing sheep, and they heard the crying of a child pass over them in the air, and they said, "That's Sheridan's child that's brought away". So I know, sure enough, that he was taken'.

Another fell under their power through being brought to Biddy Early by a neighbour. 'There was a woman, Mrs Merrick, had something wrong with her, and she went to Biddy Early, and nothing would do her but to bring my son along with her. And I was vexed—what call had she to bring him there? And when Biddy Early saw him she said, "You'll travel far, but wherever you go, you'll not escape". The woman he went up with died about six months after; but he went to America, and he wasn't long there, when what was said came true and he died. They followed him sure enough as far as he went. And one day since then I was on the road to Gort, and Macan said to me, "Your son is on the road before you". And I said, "How can that be and he dead?" But for all that, I hurried on. And on the road I met a little boy and I asked did he see anyone, and he said, "You know well who I saw". But I got no sight of him at all myself'.

They have injured her and annoyed her in all kinds of ways. 'Even when I was a child I could see them, and once they took my walk from me and gave me a bad foot. And my father cured me, and if he did, in five days after he died. But there's not much harm at all in them, not much harm'. She said there was not much harm in them for fear they might be listening. 'Three times when I went for water to the well the water was spilled over me, and I told Honor after that, they must bring the water themselves, I'd go for it no more. And the third time it was done there was a boy—one of the Healys—was near, and when he heard what happened me, he said, "It must have been the woman that was at the well along with you that did that". And I said, "There was no woman at the well along with me". "There was", he said: "I saw her there beside you, and she with two tin cans in her hand". One time after I came to live here, a strange woman came into the house, and I asked what was her name; and she said, "I was in it before you were in it"; and she went into the room inside, and I saw her no more. But Honor and Martin saw her coming in the door, and they asked me who she was, for they never saw her before. And in the night, where I was sleeping at the foot of the bed, she came and threw me out on the floor, that the joint of my arm has a mark on it yet. And every night she'd come, and she'd spite and annoy me in some way. And at last we got Father Boyle to come and to drive her out. And as soon as he began to read, there went out of the house a great blast, and there was a sound as loud as thunder. And Father Boyle said, "It's well for you she didn't have you killed before she went".'

And another time a man said to her in a forth, ' "Here's gold for you, but don't look at it till you go home". And I looked and saw horse-dung, and I said, "Keep it yourself, much good may it do you". They never gave me anything did me good, but a good deal of torment I had from them'. She is afraid that the cat by her hearth may be one of *them* in disguise, come to work her some evil. 'There's something that's not right about an old cat, and it's well not to annoy them. I was in the house one night, and one came in, and he tried to bring away the candle that was lighting in the candlestick, and it standing on the table. And I had a little rod beside me, and I made a hit at him with it, and with that he dropped the candle, and made at me, as if to kill me. And I went on my two knees, and I asked his pardon three times, and when I asked it the third time he got quiet all of a minute, and went out the door. But when you speak of them, you should always say the day of the week. Maybe you didn't notice that I said, "This is Friday", just as we passed the gate'.

I did not see her again, but last winter my friend heard she was ill, and went to see her. She said: 'It's very weak I am, and took to my bed since yesterday. *They* have changed now out of where they were, near the castle, and it's inside the demesne they are. It was an old man told me that; I met him on the road there below. First I thought he was a young man, and then I saw he was old, and he grew very nice-looking after, and he had plaid clothes. "We've moved out of that now", he said, "and it's strangers will be coming in it. And you ought to know me", he said.

'It's about a week ago, one night someone came in the room, in the dark, and I knew it was my son that I lost, he that went to America—Mike. He didn't die; he was whipped away. I knew he wasn't dead, for I saw him one day on the road to Gort on a coach, and he looked down and he said, "That's my poor mother". And when he came in here I couldn't see him, but I knew him by his talk. And he said, "It's asleep she is", and he put his two hands on my face, and I never stirred. And he said, "I'm not far from you now". For he is with the Others, inside Coole, near where the river goes down. To see me he came, and I think he'll be apt to come again before long. And last night there was a light about my head all the night, and no candle in the room at all'.

4

IRISH LANGUAGE
AND IRISH LITERATURE

I look upon the appearance of the *Leader*[26] as of importance, for it will express, I understand, and for the first time, the loves and hates, the hopes and fears, the thoughts and ideals of the men who have made the Irish language a political power. *Claidheamh*[†] *Soluis* and *Fainne an Lae*,[27] because of their preoccupation with the language itself, have been unable to make that free comment on the life about them, which the times require, if illusions that were, perhaps, truths in their day are not to cling about us and drown us. Ireland is at the close of a long period of hesitation, and must set out before long under a new policy, and it is right that any man who has anything to say should speak clearly and candidly while she is still hesitating. I myself believe that unless a great foreign war comes to re-make everything, we must be prepared to turn from a purely political nationalism with the land question as its lever, to a partly intellectual and historical nationalism like that of Norway, with the language question as its lever. The partial settlement of the land question has so limited the number of men on whom misrule presses with an immediate pressure, and ten years of recrimination have so tarnished the glory that once surrounded politics as a mere game, that the people of Ireland will not in our time give a full trust to any man who has not made some great spectacular sacrifice for his convictions, or that small continual sacrifice which enables a man to become himself Irish, to become himself an embodiment of some little of the national hope. We will always have politics of some kind, and we may have to send members of Parliament to England for a long time to come, but our politics and our members of Parliament will be moved, as I think, by a power beyond themselves, though by one which they will gladly obey, as they were moved by a power beyond themselves, which they gladly obeyed, in the recent debate on the report of the Commissioners of Education.[28] We need not feel anxious because the new movement has taken a firmer hold in the towns than in the country places, for very many of the priesthood are coming to understand that the Irish language is the only barrier against the growing atheism of England, just as we men of letters have come to understand that it is the only barrier against the growing vulgarity of England; and the priesthood can do what they like with the country places. In ten years or in fifteen years or in twenty years the new movement will be strong enough to shake governments, and, unlike previous movements that have shaken governments, it will give continuity to public life in Ireland, and make all other righteous movements the more easy.

I do not think that I am likely to differ very seriously from you and from your readers about this movement, and for the very reason that it is a national movement, a movement that can include the most different minds. I must now, however, discuss another matter, about which I have differed and may still differ from you and from many of your readers. Side by side with the spread of the Irish language, and with much writing in the Irish language, must go on much expression of Irish emotion and Irish thought, much writing about Irish things and people, in the English language, for no man can write well except in the language he has been born and bred to, and no man, as I think, becomes perfectly cultivated except through the influence of that language; and this writing must for a long time to come be the chief influence in shaping the opinions and the emotions of the leisured classes in Ireland in so far as they are concerned with Irish things, and the more sincere it is, the more lofty it is, the more beautiful it is, the more will the general life of Ireland be sweetened by its influence, through its influence over a few governing minds. It will always be too separate from the general life of Ireland to influence it directly, and it was chiefly because I believed this that I differed so strongly in 1892 and 1893 from Sir Charles Gavan Duffy and his supporters, who wished to give such writing an accidental and fleeting popularity by uniting it with politics and economics.[29] I believe that Ireland cannot have a Burns or a Dickens, because the mass of the people cease to understand any poetry when they cease to understand the Irish language, which is the language of their imagination, and because the middle class is the great supporter and originator of the more popular kind of novels, and we have no middle class to speak of; but I believe that we may have a poetry like that of Wordsworth and Shelley and Keats, and a prose like that of Meredith and Pater and Ruskin.[30] There will be a few of all classes who will read this kind of literature, but the rest will read and listen to the songs of some wandering Raftery,[31] or of some poet like Dr Hyde who has himself high culture, but makes his songs out of the thoughts and emotions he finds everywhere about him, and out of the circumstances of a life that is kept poetical by a still useful language, or they will go to perdition with their minds stuffed full of English vulgarity; till perhaps a time has come when no Irishman need write in any but his own language.

We can bring that day the nearer by not quarrelling about names, and by not bringing to literary discussion, which needs a delicate and careful temper, the exasperated and violent temper we have learned from a century of political discussion. You have decided, and rightly, considering your purpose, to call all 'literature concerning Ireland written in English', 'Anglo-Irish literature', and I shall certainly do the same when I would persuade a man that nothing written in English can unite him perfectly to the past and future of his country, but I will certainly call it Irish literature, for short, when I would persuade him that 'Farewell to Ballyshannon and the Winding Banks of Erne' should be more to him than 'The Absent-Minded Beggar',[32] or when I am out of temper with all hyphenated words, or with all names that are a mixture of Latin and English. Such things are governed by usage and convenience, and I do not foresee a day when there will not be Englishmen who will call Walt Whitman English literature, and merely because they like him, and Englishmen who will call him American literature, and merely because they dislike him. And I would be sorry to see a day when I should not find a certain beautiful sermon of St Columbanus, which compares life to a roadway on which we journey for a little while, and to the rising and falling of smoke, in accounts of Irish literature, as well as in accounts of the Latin literature of the Early Church.[33]

Whether we dispute about names or not, the temper of our dispute is perhaps of more importance than the subject, and it is certainly of especial importance when we discuss those among our writers who have any rank, however small, in that great household I have spoken of. Ruskin, Meredith, Pater, Shelley, Keats, Wordsworth, had all to face misunderstanding and misrepresentation, and sometimes contumely, for they spoke to an evil time out of the depths of the heart, and if England had been accustomed to use in literary discussion the coarse methods of political discussion, instead of descending to them in rare moments of excitement, she would not now have that remnant which alone unites her to the England of Shakespeare and Milton. In Ireland, too, it may be those very men, who have made a subtle personal way of expressing themselves, instead of being content with English as it is understood in the newspapers, or who see all things reflected in their own souls, which are from the parent fountain of their race, instead of filling their work with the circumstance of a life which is dominated by England, who may be recognised in the future as most Irish, though their own time entangled in the surfaces of things may often think them lacking in everything that is Irish. The delicate, obscure, mysterious song of my friend, 'A.E.', which has, as I know, comforted the wise and beautiful when dying, but has hardly come into the hands of the middle class—I use the word to describe an attitude of mind more than an accident of birth—and has no obviously Irish characteristics, may be, or rather must be, more Irish than any of those books of stories or of verses which reflect so many obviously Irish characteristics that every newspaper calls them, in the trying phrase of 1845, 'racy of the soil!'[34]

Now, sir, you and I have paid each other a very pretty compliment, for when you wrote to me for a letter, you must have thought that I would not be influenced by the many attacks you have made upon me and upon the movement I represent,[35] while I, on my side, have written this letter because I am convinced from what I have read of your writings, that you are one of the few in Ireland who try to go down to the root of public events and who seek the truth with earnestness and sincerity. For you and me, as for all others, it may be wholesome to dispute about a real issue, but if we dispute about misunderstandings or about names we can only destroy that clear ardour of life which is as necessary to your cause as to mine, and never long exists without precision and lucidity. I have, therefore, dealt at length with the public issues which lie between us, and must say some few words on a purely personal issue. You have been mis-led, doubtless, by reading what some indiscreet friend or careless opponent has written, into supposing that I have ever used the phrases 'Celtic note' and 'Celtic renaissance' except as a quotation from others, if even then, or that I have quoted Matthew Arnold's essay on Celtic literature, 'on a hundred platforms' or elsewhere in support of the ideas behind these phrases, or that I have changed my opinions about the revival of the Irish language since a certain speech in Galway. I have avoided 'Celtic note' and 'Celtic renais-sance' partly because both are vague and one is grandiloquent, and partly because the journalist has laid his ugly hands upon them, and all I have said or written about Matthew Arnold since I was a boy is an essay in *Cosmopolis*,[36] in which I have argued that the charac-teristics he has called Celtic, mark all races just in so far as they pre-serve the qualities of the early races of the world. And I think I need not say after the first part of this letter, that I still believe what I believed when I made that speech in Galway; but none of these mat-ters are likely to interest your readers. I will, therefore, close this long letter with a hope that the *Leader* may enable you to complete the powerful analysis of Irish life which you have begun in the *New Ireland Review.*[37]

5

A POSTSCRIPT
TO A FORTHCOMING
BOOK OF ESSAYS BY
VARIOUS WRITERS[38]

When I have stood before some Irish crowd, speaking of something, that seemed to me an immediate duty, if the popular hope, the life of all our hopes, as I think, was not to be weakened, I have said to myself 'how bewildered, how angry, perhaps, everybody would be if any thoughtful person on any platform spoke out all his mind'. Though it may well be that no man can ever speak out all his mind, for the mind is half silence and even the subtlest[†] words lay their bonds on truth, a work like this helps men, who spend much of their lives in the midst of a movement of enthusiasm, where one can but speak as if one wrote upon the dark with a burning stick, to tell what permanent quarrel, as of good and evil angels, has thrown upward what may seem to[†] the indifferent and the weary but a passing clamour.[39] Though I doubt not that all but all one's convictions go deeper than reason, I think that our Irish movements have always interested me in part, because I see in them the quarrel of two traditions of life, one old and noble, one new and ignoble. One undying because it satisfies our conscience though it seemed dying and one about to die because it is hateful to our conscience, though it seems triumphant throughout the world. In Ireland wherever the Gaelic tongue is still spoken, and to some little extent where it is not, the people live according to a tradition of life that existed before the world surrendered to the competition of merchants and to the vulgarity that has been founded upon it; and we who would keep the Gaelic tongue and Gaelic memories and Gaelic habits of our mind would keep them, as I think, that we may some day spread a tradition of life that would build up neither great wealth nor great poverty, that makes the arts a natural expression of life that permits even common men to understand good art and high thinking and to have the fine manners these things can give. Almost every one in Ireland on the other hand, who comes from what are called the educated and wealthy classes, that is to say, every man who has read a little Homer for the grammar, and many vulgar books for his pleasure, or who thinks his stable of more importance than all libraries, seeks, and often with fervour, to establish a tradition of life perfected and in part discovered by the English speaking peoples, which has made great wealth and poverty and which would make the arts impossible were it not for the self-sacrifice of a few who spend their lives in the bitterness of protest, and has already made the understanding of the arts and of high thinking impossible outside of a small cultivated class. They do this because they are entangled in the subtle net of bribery, which England has spread among us by courts, and colleges and Government offices, and by a social routine, and they fold† and unfold their net before us that they make us like themselves, and we have answered by discovering an idea, by creating a movement of intellect, whose ever growing abundance, whose ever deepening energy, would show their education its sterility, their wealth, its raggedness. There has been no notorious self-seeker these twenty years, no seller of causes for money down, but he has arisen amongst them; and there has been no man that has lived poorly that he might think well, no master of lofty speech, no seeker of subtle truth, but he has arisen among us; and abundance in these things comes now as always from the hand of the Future already half lifted in blessing.

Part of the power of this movement is that unlike the purely political movement, it can use every talent and leave every talent in freedom. It has need of the violence of the mob that it may sometimes tear that subtle net, and it has need of every delicate talent for it would discover, as would all such movements, the form of the nation made perfect, the fiery seed as upon the divine hand, in the ideas and passions of the nation, and as all religions have built upon hope and desire and terror of death, changing them to sacraments that are like flames rustling up into one white point; it would build upon their ideas and passions an idea, a passion, as little to be reasoned over, as little to be doubted or analysed as any simple love or hate though it is that form of perfection, that fiery seed, as in a mirror.

6

JOHN EGLINTON[40]

When I got *Two Essays on the Remnant*[41] some years ago, I am ashamed to say that I read but a few pages and threw it aside, irritated by superficial characteristics, and that although I afterwards tried to make people read it, I did not do so until somebody else had written in its praise.

And now, again, I have been irritated by superficial characteristics and have let months go by before I discovered that *Pebbles from a Brook* was all but as beautiful and as weighty. I do not, indeed, agree with John Eglinton about, perhaps, the most important matters, but to differ from a writer of so much precision is to discover a truth for oneself, to enrich one's conscience. A single argument is to be found in all these essays, and in spite of their curious, furtive style, this argument is so formidable that if a few thousand people believed in it and tried to arrange their lives as it would have them, they would become like the foxes that dragged the torches into the Philistines' corn.[42] He thinks that States and every other institution of man begin by fostering men's lives, and then gradually perfect themselves at the expense of men's lives, becoming more and more separated from life, until at last they become fixed as by a kind of frost, so that men, if they would keep alive and not be frozen, must fly from them as the Children of Israel fled from Egypt.[43] He imagines that the children of Israel, the idealists, are now wavering between Egypt, comfort, civilisation, as they call it, and the wilderness, the unworldly life; and he would persuade them to hesitate no longer.

He looks at this thought from many sides, and he looks at books and men under its light. He is now eloquent and now ironical about it. He often seems to have forgotten it, and then in a moment he is in the midst of it again. He describes in beautiful words the youth of States when 'the young men exercise in the fields, the old men sit in council, and at sunset the daughters leap down the street to the dance',[44] and how the faculties and works of men perfect themselves until, 'as the rosebud becomes a rose', 'its expanded petals fall away in a shower of dramas and epics',[45] and how at last the flower withers and the State dies. He writes—'The test of the state of civilisation is therefore quite simple, whether in assisting it the individual is astride of his proper instincts. If in gratifying his deepest and truest inclinations he is subserving the general end, then of that civilisation it may be said it is growing and prospering, and that nature is in it. When, on the other hand, a man does some violence to his nature[46] in adhering to the parent bulk, when its character and aspirations are not repeated in him, when his duty to himself runs counter to his outward obligations; when the component parts of the State, its institutions, must have mainstays passed round them to hold them together; when the family is no longer the State in miniature, and woman demurs to what is expected of her; when the populace breaks over its natural barriers; when the faculty of building ceases; when the ideal and the practical seem mutually antagonistic, and the youth must crush his genius into his cleverness if he will catch on as a citizen—then of that State it may be said that its day as a State is over; that nature is no longer in it, and that endless disintegration is its portion'.

When this day has come, patriotism changes its nature, for the State has accomplished its purpose, which is 'to enrich the life of each with the life of all; to form, fashion, educate and finally to liberate an individual', and henceforth the patriot must be a giver instead of a receiver, and ever readier to drink the hemlock than to carry a sword. He must honour his nation, 'parent and nurse of men', but he must live his own life, for she is about 'to die, being full of wisdom as of days'.[47]

He often speaks of Wordsworth and of devout readers of Wordsworth who live a tranquil country life, unmindful of most things that men care for, when he would tell us how these 'liberated individuals' should live their own lives.

II

Nobody can write well, as I think, unless his thought, or some like thought, is moving in other minds than his, for nobody can do more than speak messages from the spirit of his time. Thoughts, not all unlike these of John Eglinton, passed through my mind when I was growing up; some of them I wrote out a few years later in a lecture for the National Literary Society, though not with the beauty and precision of these essays;[48] but that which has made John Eglinton turn from all National ideas and see the hope of the world in individual freedom, in 'the individual grown wiser than his institutions', has made me a Nationalist and has made me see the hope of the world in re-arrangements of life and thought which make men feel that they are part of a social order, of a tradition, of a movement wiser than themselves. Perhaps I might think as he does had I not lived more than he has among those 'liberated individuals' and come to understand that their life never seems natural and seldom seems happy to them. He would not deny the name of 'the Remnant'[49] to the men and women I have in mind. They certainly refused to crush their genius into their cleverness, and they have almost all been outcasts of some kind. One, whom I know very well, lived for a long while on bread and shell conch to escape from hack work, and another, a very fine scholar whom I know slightly, spent some ten years selling matches in the Strand; while another, worn out by the bitterness of a struggle not to live, but to live and work finely, and by some of the bad habits of the miserable, died of starvation because he had ceased to care enough for life to be at the trouble to buy sufficient food. Then, too, I have known two or three men of philosophic intellect like Wilde or Beardsley[50] who spent their lives in a fantastic protest against a society they could not remake. Huysmans has once and for all summed up the life of such men in a famous novel.[51] He tells of a man whose 'Individual freedom' has been increased by great wealth and who is more miserable than a squirrel in a cage, because the society he lives in is too far towards its death to send a living stream into his intellect and his heart: 'None of us liveth to himself and no man dieth to himself'.[52] I have known but two that were certainly happy men and yet were men of the Remnant—William Morris,[53] who believed that society was about to be remade according to his heart's desire, and that his own hands were helping to remake it; and a rather vulgar lad, who found in the East what he calls wisdom, but might call with perhaps greater accuracy a society that is still simple and joyous. He was in bad health and very poor, and his friends sent him to Ceylon for his health, and in a little while he wrote home a beautiful letter, of which I have made a copy, to tell them that he was dressed in white clothes and sitting at a little table two feet high in a Buddhist monastery, saying his prayers before an offering of white flowers. He described in words of simple piety the beautiful life, full of pity and reverence, he was now a part of, and seemed in everything a new man, except that he still spelled 'veranda' with an 'r' at the end. When I knew him he was full of the restlessness of poverty, and I have no doubt a good deal despised by neighbours and relations, but now that he had found a welcome amongst the heathen, his letters were full of merry and beautiful conversations with children and old men and with the wise men of the villages.[54]

III

If John Eglinton had found any one of these people of the Remnant I can imagine what they would have said to one another. He would have begun perhaps with: 'You and I should be singularly happy, for the State has been put to a lot of trouble making us. We are perfected individualities, and ever since Hengist and Horsa[55] it has been making imperfect ones. Indeed, it has been put to so much trouble that it is all but dead'. The other, fresh from a walk down Tottenham Court-road, would answer: 'How can I be happy when I see nothing that is pleasant or comely all day long. If one lived in the age of Chaucer, when people were handsomely dressed and had handsome houses, and sang charming songs and had not to work very hard, that might be different'. John Eglinton would answer: 'But Chaucer's individuality must have been very imperfect. I know what is wrong with you. You should go into the wilderness. You will be happy when you are in the wilderness'.

'But what is the wilderness?'
'The wilderness is a country life'.
'And when I get into the country what am I to do?'
'Why! read Wordsworth'.

'But I can read all the Wordsworth I think good poetry in a couple of days, and besides I am of an active disposition, I haven't a country clergyman among my ancestors for ten generations, nothing but soldiers. There was one of them that—'

'You can fish?'

'But I don't want to fish. I want to pull down Tottenham Court-road, and to build it nearer to the heart's desire'.[56]

Then as likely as not he would go on, for the Remnant is not prejudiced: 'If I belonged to your country I could do something. There one has a chance. Your national life is not old and decadent as it is with us. One might help to build a better civilisation over there. But you must get rid of the English first. We are the makers of all vulgarity'.

'The sword is really quite obsolete, but one should always be ready to drink the hemlock. I have always admitted that'.

'Oh, the hemlock is a sedentary drink. I have just been hearing Prince Kropotkin[57] lecture; he, too, is for the Remnant, and I am for the sword'.

The truth is that John Eglinton is too preoccupied with English literature and civilisation to remember that the decadence he has described is merely the modern way, because it is the English way, because it is the commercial way. Other countries only share it in so far as they are commercial. Here and there over Europe there are countries that preserve a more picturesque and elastic life. He forgets, too, that in the East, where civilisation is older than recorded history, and where there have always been 'liberated individuals', there have been, perhaps, other kinds of decadence, but not his kind.

I believe him right in thinking that the great movement of our time is a movement to destroy modern civilisation, but I cannot but believe him wrong in thinking that it will be ended by 'liberated individuals' who separate themselves from the great passions, from the great popular interests, from religion, from patriotism, from humanitarianism. The movement against it takes the form now of collectivist, now of anarchist, now of mystical propagandas, now of groups of artists who labour to make the things of daily life, plates and candlesticks and the like, be dutiful again; now of the awakening of the smaller nations who preserve more of the picturesque life of the ancient world than do the big nations. 'The Remnant', the men and women who have learned whatever modern life has to teach and grown weary of it, should be the leaders of these movements. They are a small body, not more than one in five thousand anywhere, but they are many enough to be a priesthood, and in the long run to guide the great instinctive movements that come out of the multitude. They should be, as Walter Pater said of Leonardo da† Vinci, like men 'upon some secret errand',[58] and in sharing in a great passion, should look beyond the passion to some remote end; and they must be as ready to sacrifice themselves as those are who have never seen beyond the passion. Their labour must be to live as the blind do for the most part, to live as if they had but one idea, who have so many; but there will be times when they may have to bear witness for the end for some far-off thing, and seemingly against the passion itself, the idea itself, and John Eglinton may call this being ready to drink the hemlock. I think that if they have not this simplicity, this singleness of mind, they may do many beautiful things, write madrigals and the like, and be good critics, but they will not, while the world remains what it is to-day, make the most weighty kind of literature, or give the world the impulse it is waiting for.

John Eglinton tells how, when Rome was decadent, when there was no longer an elastic and vigorous 'civic life', the new impulse came from the early Christians. That impulse is coming to-day from the seemingly contradictory propagandas and persons I have described, and though the external forms of their activities are doubtless as mortal as the social and religious experiments of the early Christians, I cannot doubt that they are about to make the world change its image like a cloud.

IV

I was kept from reading Eglinton's essays for many months by certain petulances which are strange in so scrupulous a writer. In Ireland, where we have no mature intellectual tradition, and are in imperfect sympathy with the mature tradition of England, the only one we know anything of, we sometimes carry with us through our lives a defiant dogmatism like that of a clever schoolboy. I remember sitting all day in a Dublin garden trying to persuade myself that Walter Pater was a bad writer, and for no better reason than that he perplexed me and made me doubtful of myself. Keats, who was a sensitive, brooding man, says in one of his letters: 'When I am among women I have evil thoughts, malice and spleen. I am full of suspicion, and, therefore, listen to nothing; I am in a hurry to be gone'.[59] We approach the great masters and the great things of the world when they are a little difficult to us in just this spirit: we listen to nothing, we are in a hurry to be gone. Exaggerate this spirit a little and you have Shakespeare's Jack Cade, who wanted to hang everybody who could read and write because he had once put his name to a bond and was never his own man after.[60] We learn more slowly than other people to understand that everything that has ever interested large numbers of men is very worthy of study and reverence. A journalist must be content often with opinions that have no importance beyond some controversy of the hour, but a writer like John Eglinton, who must know that his words will outlive him and us, has no business writing such a phrase as 'vulgarity ritual', 'and all that riff-raff', or writing a too notorious sentence about the crucifix, or declaring that philosophy takes only a 'pathological and perfunctory' interest in a certain kind of poetry, which he defines as Belles Lettres, and which was certainly the kind that was written by Keats, or in writing that Wagner and Shelley 'saw in art a refuge from the squalid reality', an inaccuracy which implies in his system of thought an equally careless condemnation, or in describing a certain book, which decides by perfectly logical deductions from a too narrow premises that Shakespeare and the Greek tragedians are bad art and Mrs Beecher Stowe is good art, as 'a formidable book, the doom of the cliques'.[61] He does not believe these things. He does not even want us to believe that he believes them. He is merely irritated. He sees a great complicated tradition which weighs upon his spirits, and is full of that kind of defiant timidity which some of us never get over when we are among strange people whose life we do not understand.

W. B. Yeats

7

LITERATURE AND
THE CONSCIENCE[62]

A phrase in my letter to the *Freeman's Journal* about the proposed clerical censorship of the National Theatre has caused a good deal of misunderstanding. 'Irial', for instance, objects to my description of literature as 'the principal voice of the conscience', and himself defines literature as 'any piece of writing which in point of form is likely to secure permanence'. If 'Irial' will recall the names of a few masterpieces he is much too intelligent not to see that his description is inadequate. Let him recall to mind *Don Quixote*, or *Hamlet*, or *Faust*, or Tolstoi's *War and Peace* and *Anna Karenina*, or almost any novel by Balzac or Flaubert, or any play by Ibsen, his *Enemy of the People* let us say. If he will do so, he will understand why literature seems to me, as indeed it seems to most critics of literature, to be the principal voice of the conscience. A great writer will devote perhaps years, perhaps the greater part of a lifetime, to the study of the moral issues raised by a single event, by a single group of characters. He will not bemoralise his characters, but he will show, as no other can show, how they act and think and endure under the weight of that destiny which is divine justice. No lawgiver, however prudent, no preacher, however lofty, can devote to life so ample and so patient a treatment. It is for this reason that men of genius frequently have to combat against the moral codes of their time, and are yet pronounced right by history. 'Irial' will recall many examples, of which the most recent is Ibsen. A play or a novel necessarily describes people in their relation to one another, and is, therefore, frequently concerned with the conscience in the ordinary sense of that word, but even lyric poetry is the voice of what metaphysicians call innate knowledge, that is to say, of conscience, for it expresses the relation of the soul to eternal beauty and truth as no other writing can express it. That apparently misleading sentence of mine was, indeed, but an echo of a sentence of Verhaeren's,[63] the famous Belgian poet. He says that a masterpiece is a portion of the conscience of the world. An essay on poetry by Shelley and certain essays by Schopenhauer are probably the best things that have been written on the subject by modern writers, but Mr George Santayana has written a book called *The Sense of Beauty*,[64] which deals profoundly with the whole philosophy of aesthetics. 'Irial' should read it. He can buy it for half-a-crown if he is lucky.

Now, another matter. I am doing an historical note on the various versions of the Diarmuid and Grainne legend, of which there are many.[65] The critics who have objected to Mr Moore's treatment and mine only seem to know one version and that a late literary form of the story, and this version they misunderstand. They have not even consulted so obvious a source as J. G. Campbell's book, *The Fions*,[†] which gives several Highland folk-lore versions of the legend which are also current in Ireland. I may send my note to you when I have time to finish it, but, in any case, if Mr Moore consents, as I have no doubt he will, it shall go with the printed text of the play.[66]

W. B. Yeats

P. S. I must add a sentence or two to what I have said about the conscience. It is made sensitive and powerful by religion, but its dealings with the complexity of life are regulated by literature. 'Irial' spoke of a book[67] which discusses problems of the hour and yet seems to him at once literature and iniquitous. He is certainly mistaken. Literature, when it is really literature, does not deal with problems of the hour, but with problems of the soul and character.

8

EGYPTIAN PLAYS

The Egyptian Society, whose object is to illustrate the life and thought of Ancient Egypt by plays and lectures, gave two plays at the Victoria Hall on Monday night and on Tuesday afternoon.[68] The plays, which are the work of Miss Florence Farr and of Mrs Shakespear,[69] interested me by being an attempt to do a new thing. They are not only new in their subject, but in the rigorously decorative arrangements of the stage, which imitated the severe forms of Egyptian mural painting. The plays themselves are less plays than fragments of a ritual—the ritual of a beautiful forgotten worship. The characters are priests and priestesses of Ancient Egypt, and the names and mysteries of a religion that was one with magic are perpetually in their mouths. Their tribulations are the unearthly tribulations of the weavers of enchantments and of the moulders of talismans, and when the Ka, or double, of a priestess stands beside her in the sanctuary we do not find its manifest flesh and blood too earthly for a spirit, as we so often do upon the stage, for flesh and blood itself have begun to seem unearthly. This effect was, indeed, to me the chief merit of the plays, and it came, I think, more from the scenic arrangements, which did not grossen the imagination with realism, and from the symbolic costumes and from the half-chanting recitation of phrases of ritual, than from anything especially dramatic. If I except one final dramatic moment when a priestess, who has just been shrinking, in terror before her god, the Golden Hawk, dances in ecstasy before his image, neither play stirred in me a strictly dramatic interest. The too realistic acting was to blame for this in the second play, but *The Beloved of Hathor* was not ill-acted, and yet it irritated me from time to time by its chaos of motives and of motiveless incidents. When the irritation was over one listened contentedly enough. One understood that something interesting was being done—not very well done, indeed—but something one had never seen before, and might never see again.

Miss Farr and Miss Paget[70] played often picturesquely, and sometimes with sweetness and gravity, and always with that beauty of voice, which becomes perhaps the essential thing in a player when lyrical significance has become the essential thing in a play. They spoke their sentences in adoration of Heru, or Hathor, copied or imitated from old Egyptian poems, as one thinks the Egyptian priestesses must have spoken them. They spoke with so much religious fervour, with so high an ecstasy, that one could not but doubt at times their Christian orthodoxy. Miss Paget has, in addition to a beautiful voice, still a little lacking in the richness of maturity, the beauty of extreme youth, and a fluent charm as of one who had put on womanhood and not yet put off childhood. If they had had 'The Shrine of the Golden Hawk' to themselves, with a couple of priests who would have been content to speak and not to act, I might feel that an interesting thing had not only been done, but done well, or well enough. Some imperfections one must always expect in work out of the ordinary track, for there the worker finds nothing ready to his hand. He has to make everything afresh.

W. B. Yeats

9

AWAY[71]

I

There is, I think, no country side in Ireland where they will not tell you, if you can conquer their mistrust, of some man or woman or child who was lately or still is in the power of the gentry, or 'the others', or 'the fairies', or 'the sidhe', or the 'forgetful people', as they call the dead and the lesser gods of ancient times. These men and women and children are said to be 'away', and for the most part go about their work in a dream, or lie all day in bed, awakening after the fall of night to a strange and hurried life.

A woman at Gort, in County Galway,[72] says: 'There was an old woman I remember was living at Martin Ruanes, and she had to go with them two or three hours every night for a while, and she'd make great complaints of the hardships she'd meet with, and how she'd have to spend the night going through little boreens, or in the churchyard at Kinvara, or they'd bring her down to the sea shore. They often meet with hardships like that, those they bring with them, so it's no wonder they're glad to get back; this world's the best'. And an old pensioner from Kiltartan, a village some three miles from Gort, says: 'There is a man I knew that was my comrade after, used to be taken away at nights, and he'd speak of the journeys he had with them. And he got severe treatment and didn't want to go, but they'd bring him by force. He recovered after, and joined the army, and I was never so astonished as I was the day he walked in, when I was in Delhi'. There are a boy near Gort and a woman at Ardrahan close at hand, who are 'away', and this same man says of them: 'Mary Flaherty has been taken, and whenever she meets old Whelan the first thing she asks is for his son. She doesn't go to see him in the house, but travelling of nights they meet each other. Surely she's gone. You have but to look in her face to see that. And whatever hour of the night she wants to go out, they must have the horse harnessed to bring her wherever she likes to go'.

The commonest beginning of the enchantment is to meet some one not of this earth, or in league with people not of this earth, and to talk too freely to them about yourself and about your life. If they understand you and your life too perfectly, or sometimes even if they know your name, they can throw their enchantment about you. A man living at Coole near Gort says: 'But those that are brought away would be glad to be back. It's a poor thing to go there after this life. Heaven is the best place, Heaven and this world we're in now. My own mother was away for twenty-one years, and at the end of every seven years she thought it would be off her, but she never could leave the bed. She could but sit up, and make a little shirt or the like for us. It was of the fever she died at last. The way she got the touch was one day after we left the place we used to be in, and we got our choice place on the estate, and my father chose Kilchreest. But a great many of the neighbours went to Moneen. And one day a woman that had been our neighbour came over from Moneen, and my mother showed her everything and told her of her way of living. And she walked a bit of the road with her, and when they were parting the woman said: "You'll soon be the same as such a one". And as she turned she felt a pain in the head. And from that day she lost her health. My father went to Biddy Early, but she said it was too late, she could do nothing, and she would take nothing from him'. Biddy Early was a famous witch.

If you are taken you have always, it is said, a chance of return every seven years. Almost all that go 'away' among them are taken to help in their work, or in their play, or to nurse their children, or to bear them children, or to be their lovers, and all fairy children are born of such marriages. A man near Gort says: 'They are shadows, and how could a shadow have power to move that chair or that table? But they have power over mankind, and they can bring them away to do their work'. I have told elsewhere[73] of a man who was 'away' with Maibh Queen of the western Sidhe as her lover, and made a mournful song in the Gaelic when she left him, and was mournful till he died.

But sometimes one hears of people taken for no reason, as it seems, but that they may be a thing to laugh at. Indeed, one is often told that unlike 'the simple' who would do us an evil, 'the gentle' among 'the others' wish us no harm but 'to make a sport of us'.

And a man at Gort says: 'There was one Mahony had the land taken that is near Newtown racecourse. And he was out there one day building a wall and it came to the dinner hour, but he had none brought with him. And a man came by and said, "Is it home you'll be going for your dinner?" And he said, "It's not worth my while to go back to Gort, I'd have the day lost . . ." And the man said, "Well, come in and eat a bit with me". And he brought him into a forth and there there was everything that was grand, and the dinner they gave him of the best, so that he eat near two plates of it. And then he went out again to build the wall. And whether it was with lifting the heavy stones I don't know, but with respects to you, when he was walking the road home he began to vomit, and what he vomited up was all green grass'.

You may eat their food, if they put it out to you, and indeed it is discourteous to refuse and will make them angry, but you must not go among them and eat their food, for this will give them power over you.

II

Sometimes one hears of people 'away' doing the work of the others and getting harm of it, or no good of it, but more often one hears of good crops or of physical strength or of cleverness or of supernatural knowledge being given and of no evil being given with it except the evil of being in a dream, or being laid up in bed or the like, which happens more or less to all who are 'away'. A woman near Craughwell says: 'There's a boy now of the Lydons, but I wouldn't for all the world let them think I spoke of him. But it's two years since he came from America and since that time he never went to Mass, or to Church, or to market, or to fair, or to stand at the cross roads, or to the hurling. And if anyone comes into the house, it's into the room he'll slip not to see them. And as to work, he has the garden dug to bits and the whole place smeared with cowdung, and such a crop as was never seen, and the alders all plaited that they looked grand. One day he went as far as Peterswell Chapel, but as soon as he got to the door he turned straight round again as if he hadn't power to pass it. I wonder he wouldn't get the priest to read a mass for him or some such thing. But the crop he has is grand, and you may know well he has some that help him'.

Indeed, almost any exceptional cleverness, even the clever training of a dog may be thought a gift from 'the others'. I have been told of a boy in Gort 'who was lying in the bed a long time, and one day, the day of the races, he asked his father and mother were they going to the course, and they said they were not. Well, says he, "I'll show you as good sport as if you went". And he had a dog and he called to it and said something to it, and it began to take a run and to gallop and to jump backwards over the half door, for there was a very high half door to the house. "So now", says he, "didn't you see as good sport as if you were on Newtown racecourse?" And he didn't live long, but died soon after that'. And the same man whose mother had been away for twenty-one years says: 'There was one of the Burkes, John, was away for seven years, lying in his bed but brought away at nights. And he knew everything. And one Kearney up in the mountain, a cousin of his own lost two hoggets and came and told him. And he knew the very spot where they were and told him, and he got them back again. But *they* were vexed at that, and took away the power, so that he never knew anything again, no more than another. There was another man up near Ballylee could tell these things too. When John Callan lost his wool he went to him, and next morning there were the fleeces at his door. Those that are away know these things. There was a brother of my own took to it for seven years, and he at school. And no one could beat him at the hurling and the games. But I wouldn't like to be mixed with that myself'. The wool and perhaps the hoggets had been taken by 'the others' who were forced to return them.

When you get a 'touch' you feel a sudden pain, and a swelling comes where you have felt the pain. I have been told that there is a fool and a queen 'in every household of them', and that nobody can cure the touch of the fool or the queen, but that the touch of anyone else among them can be cured. A woman at Kiltartan says: 'One time a woman from the North came to our house, and she said a great deal of people is kept below there in the lisses. She had been there herself, and in the night time in one moment they'd be all away at Cruachmaa, wherever that may be, down in the north I believe. And she knew everything that was in the house, and told us about my sister being sick, and that there was a hurling match going on that day, as there was, at the Isabella Wood in Coole. And all about Coole house she knew, as well as if she spent her life in it. I'd have picked a lot of stories out of her, but my mother got nervous when she heard the truth coming out and bid me be quiet. She had a red petticoat on her, the same as any country woman, and she offered to cure me, for it was that time I was delicate and her ladyship sent me to the salt water. But she asked a shilling, and my mother said she hadn't got it. "You have", says she, "and heavier metal than that you have in the house". So then my mother gave her the shilling and she put it in the fire and melted it, and says she, "After two days you'll see your shilling again", but we never did. And the cure she left I never took it—it's not safe, and the priests forbid us to take their cures, for it must surely be from the devil their knowledge comes. No doubt at all she was one of the Ingentry, that can take the form of a woman by day and another form by night. After that she went to Mrs Finnegan's house and asked her for a bit of tobacco. "You'll get it again", she said, "and more with it". And sure enough that very day a bit of meat came into Mrs Finnegan's house'.

The people of the North are thought to know more about the supernatural than anybody else, and one remembers that the good gods of the Celts, the children of Danu, and the evil gods of the Celts, the Fomor, came from the North in certain legends. The North does not mean Ulster, but any place to the north, for the people talk of the people of Cruachmaa, which is but a little north of Galway, as knowing much because they are from the North—one cannot tell whether the woman from the North in this tale was a mortal or an immortal. People 'away', like people taken by 'the others' from their death-beds, are confounded with the immortals, the true children of Danu, or the Dundonians, as I have heard them called in Clare. I have never heard the word 'Ingentry' for 'the others' at any other time.

Sometimes people who are 'away' are thought to have, like the dead who have been 'taken', that power of changing one thing into another, which is so constantly attributed to the Children of Danu in the Gaelic poems. The Children of Danu were the powers of life, the powers worshipped in the ecstatic dances among the woods and upon the mountains, and they had the flamelike changeability of life, and were the makers of all changes. 'The others', their descendants, change the colours of their clothes every moment, and build up a house 'in the corner of a field' and 'in ten minutes', 'finer than any gentleman's house'. An Irishwoman from Kildare that I met in London told me: 'There was a woman used to go away at night, and she said to her sister, "I'll be out on a white horse, and I'll stop and knock at your door as I pass", and so she used to do sometimes. And one day there was a man asked her for a debt he owed, and she said, "I have no money now". But then she put her hand behind her, and brought it back filled with gold, and then she rubbed it in her hand, and when she opened her hand again, there was nothing in it but dry cow-dung, and she said, "I could give you that, but it would be of no use to you".'

Those who are 'away' have sometimes, too, it seems, the power of changing their size and of going through walls as 'the others' themselves do. A man on Inisheer says: 'There was a first cousin of mine used sometimes to go out of the house through the wall, but none could see him going. And one night his brother followed him, and he went down a path to the sea, and then he went into a hole in the rocks that the smallest dog wouldn't go into. And the brother took hold of his feet and drew him out again. He went to America after that, and is living there now, and sometimes in his room they'll see him beckoning and laughing and laughing, as if some were with him. One night there, when some of the neighbours from these islands were with him, he told them he'd been back to Inishmaan, and told all that was going on, and some would not believe him. And he said, "You'll believe me next time". So the next night he told them again he had been there, and he brought out of his pocket a couple of boiled potatoes and a bit of fish, and showed them; so then they all believed it'. And an old man on Inisheer, who has come back from the State of Maine, says of this man: 'I knew him in America, and he used often to visit this island, and would know what all of them were doing, and would bring us word of them all, and all he'd tell us would turn out right. He's living yet in America'.

It often seems as if these enchanted people had some great secret. They may have taken an oath to be silent, but I have not heard of any oath, I am only certain that they are afraid or unable to speak. I have already told of Whelan[74] and his nightly rides. I got a friend, with whom I was staying, to ask Whelan's father, who is a carpenter, to make a box and send it by his son. He promised to 'try and infatuate him to come', but did not think it would be of any use. It was no use, for the boy said, 'No, I won't go, I know why I am wanted'. His father says that he did not tell him, but that 'the others' told him, when he was out with them.

A man said to a friend of mine in the Abbey of Corcomroe among the Burren hills in County Clare: 'There was one O'Loughlin that lies under that slab there, and for seven years he was brought away every night, and into this Abbey. And he was beat and pinched, and when he came home he'd faint. He told his brother-in-law, that told me, that in that hill beyond, behind this Abbey, there is the most splendid town that ever was seen, and grander than any city. Often he was in it and ought not to have been talking about it, but he said he wouldn't give them the satisfaction of it. He didn't care what they'd do to him. One night he was with a lot of others at a wake, and when he heard them coming for him he fainted on the floor. But after he got up he heard them come again and he rose to go, and the boys all took hold of him, Peter Fahey was one of them, and you know what a strong man he was, and the arms of those that were holding him were near pulled out of their sockets'.

And a woman near Loughrea says: 'My mother often told me about her sister's child, my cousin, that used to spend the nights in the big forth at Moneen. Every night she went there, and she got thin and tired like. She used to say she saw grand things there, and the horses galloping and the riding. But then she'd say, "I must tell no more than that or I'll get a great beating". She wasted away, and one night they were so sure she was dead they had the pot full of water boiling on the fire to wash her. But she recovered again and lived five years after that'.

And an old man on the north isle of Arran says: 'I know a good many on the island have seen *those,* but they wouldn't say what they're like to look at, for when they speak of them their tongue gets like a stone'.

The most of what the country people have to tell of those who have been 'taken' altogether, and about the ways and looks of the 'others', has come from the frightened and rare confidences of people upon whom 'the others' cast this sleepy enchantment.

A man in the Burren hills says: 'That girl of the Connors that was away for seven years, she was bid tell nothing of what she saw, but she told her mother some things, and told of some she met there. There was a woman, a cousin of my own, asked was her son ever there, and she had to press her a long time, but at last she said he was. And he was taken too, with little privication, fifty years ago'.

And a woman near Ardrahan says: 'There was a girl near West-port was away, and the way it came on her was she was on the road one day, and two men passed her, and one of them said, "That's a fine girl", and the other said, "She belongs to my town". And there and then she got a pain in her knee, and she couldn't walk home but had to be brought home in a cart, and she used to be away at night, and thorns in her feet in the morning, but she never said where she went. But one time the sister brought her to Kilfenora, and when they were crossing a bog near to there she pointed to a house in the bog and she said, "It's there I was last night". And the sister asked did she know anyone she met there, and she said, "There was one I knew that is my mother's cousin", and told her name. And she said, "But for her they'd have me ill-treated, but she fought for me and saved me!" She was thought to be dying one time, and my mother sent me to see her, and how she was. And she was lying on the bed, and her eyes turned back, and she was speechless, and I told my mother when I came home she hadn't an hour to live. And the next day she was up and about and not a thing on her. It might be the mother's cousin that fought for her again then. She went to America after'.

This girl fell under the power of 'the others' because the two men looked at her with admiration, 'overlooked her', as it is called, and did not say 'God bless her'. 'The others' can draw anything they admire to themselves by using our admiration as a bond between them and it.

III

In some barbarous countries no one is permitted to look at the king while he is eating, for one is thought to be less able to drive away malicious influence when one is eating, and most mortal influence must be malignant when one is the representative and instrument of the gods. I have sometimes been told that nobody is ever allowed to see those who are 'away' eating. A woman near Gort says of Whelan the carpenter's son, 'He's lying in bed these four years, and food is brought into the room but he never touches it, but when it's left there it's taken away'. And a man at Coole says: 'I remember a boy was about my own age over at Cranagh on the other side of the water, and they said he was away for two years. Anyhow, for all that time he was sick in bed, and no one ever saw bit or sup pass his lips in all that time, though the food that was left in the room would disappear, whatever happened it. He recovered after and went to America'.

They are sometimes believed to hardly eat our food at all, but to live upon supernatural food. An old man from near Loughrea says: 'There was Kitty Flannery at Kilchreest, you might remember her. For seven years she had everything she could want, and music and dancing could be heard round her house every night, and all she did prospered. But she ate no food all that time, only she'd take a drink of the milk after the butter being churned. But at the end of the seven years all left her, and she was glad at the last to get Indian meal'.

But often one hears of their fearing to eat the food of 'the others' for fear they might never escape out of their hands. An old man on the Gortaveha mountain says: 'I knew one was away for seven years, and it was in the next townland to this she lived. Bridget Kinealy her name was. There was a large family of them, and she was the youngest, a very nice-looking fair-haired girl she was. I knew her well, she was the one age with myself. It was in the night she used to go to them, and if the door was shut she'd come in by the keyhole. The first time they came for her she was in bed between her two sisters, and she didn't want to go, but they beat her and pinched her till her brother called out to know what was the matter. She often spoke about them, and how she was badly treated because she wouldn't eat their food, and how there was a red-haired girl among them that would throw her into the river she'd get so mad with her. But if she had their food ate, she'd never have got away from them at all. She got no more than about three cold potatoes she could eat the whole time she was with them. All the old people about her put out food every night, the first of the food before they have any of it tasted themselves. She married a serving man after, and they went to Sydney, and if nothing happened in the last two years they're doing well there now'.

IV

The ancient peoples from whom the country people inherit their belief had to explain how, when you were 'away', as it seemed to you, you seemed, it might be, to your neighbours or your family, to be lying in a faint upon the ground, or in your bed, or even going about your daily work. It was probably one who was himself 'away' who explained, that somebody or something was put in your place, and this explanation was the only possible one to ancient peoples, who did not make our distinction between body and soul. The Irish country people always insist that something, a heap of shavings or a broomstick or a wooden image, or some dead person, 'maybe some old warrior', or some dead relative or neighbour of your own, is put in your place, though sometimes they will forget their belief until you remind them, and talk of 'the others' having put such and such a person 'into a faint', or of such and such a person being 'away' and being ill in bed. This substitution of the dead for the living is indeed a pagan mystery, and not more hard to understand than the substitution of the body and blood of Christ for the wafer and the wine in the mass; and I have not yet lost the belief that some day, in some village lost among the hills or in some island among the western seas, in some place that remembers old ways and has not learned new ways, I will come to understand how this pagan mystery hides and reveals some half-forgotten memory of an ancient knowledge or of an ancient wisdom. Time that has but left the lesser gods to haunt the hills and raths, has doubtless taken much that might have made us understand.

A man at Kiltartan, who thinks evil of 'the others', says: 'They have the hope of heaven or they wouldn't leave one on the face of the earth, and they are afraid of God. They'll not do you much harm if you leave them alone, it's best not to speak to them at all if you should meet them. If they bring anyone away they'll leave some good-for-nothing thing in its place, and the same way with a cow or a calf or such things. But a sheep or a lamb it's beyond their power to touch, because of our Lord'. And a woman near Ardrahan says: 'There was a cousin of my own was said to be "away", and when she died I was but a child, and my mother brought me with her to the house where she was laid out. And when I saw her I began to scream and to say, "That's not Mary that's in it, that's some old hag". And so it was, I know well it was not Mary that was lying there in the bed'. And a woman from near Loughrea says: 'Sure there was a fairy in a house at Eserkelly fourteen years. Bridget Collins she was called, you might remember Miss Fanny used to be bringing her gooseberries. She never kept the bed, but she'd sit in the corner of the kitchen on a mat, and from a good stout lump of a girl that she was, she wasted to nothing, and her teeth grew as long as your finger, and then they dropped out. And she'd eat nothing at all, only crabs and sour things. And she'd never leave the house in the daytime, but in the night she'd go out and pick things out of the fields she could eat. And the hurt she got, or whatever it was touched her, it was one day she was swinging on the Moneen gate, just there by the forth. She died as quiet as another, but you wouldn't like to be looking at her after the teeth fell out'.

And a man from Cahirglissane says: 'There was one Tierney on the road to Kinvara, I knew him well, was away with them seven years. It was at night he used to be brought away, and when they called him he should go. They'd leave some sort of a likeness of him in his place. He had a wart on his back, and his wife would rub her hand down to feel was the wart there before she'd know was it himself was in it or not. Himself and his pony used to be brought up into the sky, and he told many how he used to go riding about with them, and that often and often he was in that castle you see below. And Mrs Hevenor asked him did he ever see her son Jimmy that died, among them, and he told her he did, and that mostly all the people that he knew that had died out of the village were amongst them now. And if his wife had a clutch of geese they'd be ten times better than any other one's, and the wheat and the stock and all they had was better and more plentiful than what anyone else had. Help he got from them of course. But at last the wife got in the priest to read a mass and to take it off him. And after that all that they had went to flitters'.

And a girl at Coole says of a place called 'The Three Lisses', where there are three of those old clay remnants of ancient houses or encampments so much haunted by 'the others': 'There must in old times have been a great deal of fighting there. There are some bushes growing on them, and no one, man or woman, will ever put a hand to cut them, no more than they would touch the little bush by the well beyond, that used to have lights shining out of it. And if anyone was to fall asleep within in the Liss, himself would be taken away, and the spirit of some old warrior would be put in his place, and it's he would know everything in the whole world. There's no doubt at all but that there's the same sort of things in other countries, sure *these* can go through and appear in Australia in one minute, but you hear more about them in these parts because the Irish do be more familiar in talking of them'.

The chief way of bringing a person out of this state of dream is to threaten the dead person believed to have been put in his place. A man from county Clare says: 'I heard of a woman brought back again. It was told me by a boy going to school there at the time it happened, so I know there's no lie in it. It was one of the Lydons, a rich family in Scariff, whose wife was sick and pining away for seven years. And at the end of that time one day he came in, he had a drop of drink taken, and he began to be a bit rough with her. And she said, "Don't be rough with me now, after bearing so well with me all these seven years. But because you were so good and so kind to me all the time", says she, "I'll go away from you now, and I'll let your own wife come back to you". And so she did, for it was an old hag she was. And the wife came back again and reared a family. And before she went away she had a son that was reared a priest, and after she came back she had another that was reared a priest, so that shows a blessing came on them'.

The country people seldom do more than threaten the dead person put in the living person's place, and it is, I am convinced, a sin against the traditional wisdom to really ill-treat the dead person. A woman from Mayo who has told me a good many tales and has herself both seen and heard 'the royal gentry', as she calls them, was very angry with the Tipperary countryman who burned his wife, some time ago, her father and neighbours standing by. She had no doubt that they only burned some dead person, but she was quite certain that you should not burn even a dead person. She said: 'In my place we say you should only threaten. They are so superstitious in Tipperary. I have stood in the door and I have heard lovely music, and seen the fort all lighted up, but I never gave in to them'. 'Superstitious' means to her 'giving in' to 'the others', and 'giving in' means, I think, letting them get power over you, or being afraid of them, and getting excited about them, and doing foolish things. One does hear now and then of 'the dead person' being really ill-treated, but rarely. When I was last in Western Galway a man had just been arrested for trying to kill his sister-in-law, because he thought she was one of 'the others' and was tempting him to murder his cousin. He had sent his cousin away that she might be out of his reach in case he could not resist the temptation. This man was merely out of his mind, and had more than common reasons for his anger besides. A woman from Burren tells a tale more like the Tipperary tale. 'There was a girl near Ballyvaughan was away, and the mother used to hear horses coming about the door every night. And one day the mother was picking flax in the house and of a sudden there came in her hand an herb with the best smell and the sweetest that ever anyone smelled. And she closed it into her hand and called to the son that was making up a stack of hay outside, "Come in Denis, for I have the best smelling herb that ever you saw". And when he came in she opened her hand and the herb was gone, clear and clean. She got annoyed at last with the horses coming about the door, and some one told her to gather all the fire into the middle of the floor and to lay the little girl upon it, and to see would she come back again. So she did as she was told, and brought the little girl out of the bed and laid her on the coals, and she began to scream and to call out, and the neighbours came running in, and the police heard of it, and they came and arrested the mother and brought her to Ballyvaughan, before the magistrate, Mr Macnamara, and my own husband was one of the police that arrested her. And when the magistrate heard all, he said she was an ignorant woman, and that she did what she thought right, and he would give her no punishment. And the girl got well and was married, and it was after she married I knew her'.

I was always convinced that tradition, which avoids needless inhumanity, had some stronger way of protecting the bodies of those, to whom the other world was perhaps unveiling its mysteries, than any mere command not to ill-treat some old dead person, who had maybe been put in the room of one's living wife or daughter or son. I heard of this stronger way last winter from an old Kildare woman, that I met in London. She said that in her own village, 'there was a girl used to be away with them, you'd never know when it was she herself that was in it or not till she'd come back, and then she'd tell she had been away. She didn't like to go, but she had to go when they called to her. And she told her mother always to treat kindly whoever was put in her place, sometimes one would be put and sometimes another, for, she'd say "If you are unkind to whoever is there, they'll be unkind to me".'

Sometimes the person is thought to be brought back by some one who meets him on his wanderings and leads him home. A woman near Kinvara says: 'There was a child was dying in some house in Burren by the sea, and the mother and all around it, thinking to see it die. And a boy came in, and he said when he was coming through a field beyond the house he heard a great crying, and he saw a troop of them and the child ran out from among them, and ran up to him and he took hold of its hand, and led it back, and then he brought it safe and well into the house. And the thing that was in the bed he took up and threw it out, and it vanished away into the air'.

An army pensioner says: 'My family were of the Finns of Athenry. I had an aunt that married a man of the name of Kane, and they had a child was taken. So they brought it to the Lady Well near Athenry, where there's patterns every 15th of August, to duck it. And such a ducking they gave it, that it walked away on crutches, and it swearing. And their own child they got back again, but he didn't live long after'. I have one tale in which a visit to Knock, the Irish Lourdes, worked the cure.[75] 'There was a girl was overlooked got cured at Knock, and when she was cured she let three screams out of her, it was a neighbour of mine saw her and told me. And there are a great many cures done at Knock, and the walls thick with crutches and sticks and crooked shoes. And there was a gentleman from America was cured there, and his crutch was a very grand one, with silver on it, and he came back to bring it away, and when he did, he got as bad as ever he was before'. It was no doubt the old person who gave the three screams.

And sometimes a priest works the cure. A piper who wanders about county Galway says: 'There was a girl at Kilkerran of the same name as my own, was lying on a mat for eight years. When she first got the touch the mother was sick, and there was no room in the bed; so they laid a mat on the floor for her, and she never left it for the eight years, but the mother died soon after. She never got off the mat for anyone to see, but one night there was a working man came to the house and they gave him lodging for the night. And he watched her from the other room, and in the night he saw the outer door open, and three or four boys and girls come in, and with them a piper or a fiddler, I'm not sure which, and he played to them, and they danced, and the girl got up off the mat and joined them. And in the morning, when he was sitting at breakfast, he looked over to her where she was lying, and said, "You were the best dancer among them last night".'

Many stories of the old Gaelic poems and romances become more fully intelligible when we read them by the light of these stories. There is a story about Cuchullain in *The Book of the Dun Cow*, interpreted too exclusively as a solar myth by Professor Rhys,[76] which certainly is a story of Cuchullain 'away'. The people of Uladh, or Ulster, were celebrating the festival of the beginning of winter that was held the first day of November, on the days before and after. A flock of wild birds lighted upon a lake near where Cuchullain and the heroes and fair women of Uladh were holding festival, and because of the bidding of the women Cuchullain caught the birds and divided them among them. When he came to his own wife Emer, he had no birds left, and promised her the finest two out of any new flock. Presently he saw two birds, bound one to the other with a chain of gold, and they were singing so sweetly that the host of Uladh fell in a little while into a magic sleep. Cuchullain cast a stone out of a sling, but missed them, and then another stone, but missed them, and wondered greatly, because he had not missed a cast from the day when he took arms. He threw his spear, and it passed through the wing of one of the birds, and the birds dived out of his sight. He lay down in great sorrow, because of his bad casting, and fell asleep and dreamed that two women, one dressed in green and one dressed in red, came to him and first one and then the other smiled and struck him with a whip, and that they went on beating him until he was nearly dead. His friends came while he was still dreaming, but only saw that he slept and must not be awakened, and when at last he awoke, he was so weak that he made them carry him to his bed. He lay in his bed all through the winter, the time of the power of the gods of death and cold, and until the next November Eve, when those who watched beside him suddenly saw a stranger sitting upon the side of his bed. This stranger was Ængus, perhaps that Ængus, the master of love, who had made four birds out of his kisses, and he sang that Fand, the wife of Mannannan, the master of the sea, and of the island of the dead, loved Cuchullain, and that, if he would come into the country of the gods, where there was wine and gold and silver, she would send Leban, her sister, to heal him. Having ended his song, the stranger vanished as suddenly as he had come. Cuchullain having consulted with his friends, went to the place where he had seen the swans and dreamed his dream, and there the woman dressed in green came and spoke with him. He reproached her, and she answered that she wished him no harm, but only to bring him to her sister Fand, who had been deserted by Mannannan, and who loved him passionately, and to bring him to help her own husband Labraid of the Swift Hand on the Sword in a one-day's battle against his enemies. After hearing what another mortal who had been to the country of Labraid had to tell, Cuchullain mounted into his chariot, and went to the country of Labraid, and fought a one-day's battle, and had Fand to wife for a month. At the month's end he made a promise to meet her at a place called 'The Yew at the Strand's End', and came back to the earth. When Emer, his mortal wife, heard of the tryst, she went with other women to the Yew at the Strand's End, and there she won again the love of Cuchullain. When Fand saw that she had lost his love she lamented her happy days with Mannannan when their love was new. Mannannan heard and came swiftly and carried her away to his own country. When Cuchullain saw her leaving him his love for her returned, and he became mad and went into the mountains, and wandered there a long time without food or drink. At last the King of Uladh sent his poets and his druids to cure him, and though he tried to kill them in his madness, they chanted druid spells, so that he became weak. He cried out for a drink in his weakness, and they gave him a drink of forgetfulness; and they gave Emer a drink of forgetfulness, so that she forgot the divine woman.

Mr Frazer discusses in, I think, the second volume of *The Golden Bough*—I am writing in Ireland and have not the book at hand and cannot give the exact reference—the beating of the divine man in ancient religious ceremonies, and decides that it was never for a punishment but always for a purification, for the driving out of something.[77] I am inclined, therefore, to consider the beating of Cuchullain by the smiling women, as a driving out or deadening, for a time, of his merely human faculties and instincts; and I am certain it should be compared with the stories told by the country people of people over whom 'the others' get power by striking them (see my article in the *Nineteenth Century* for January, 1898, p. 69, for one such story);[78] and with countless stories of their getting power over people by giving them what is called 'the touch'—I shall tell and weigh a number of these stories some day—and perhaps with the common habit of calling a paralytic attack a 'stroke'. Cuchullain wins the love of Fand just as young, handsome country-men are believed to win the love of fair women of 'the others', and he goes to help Labraid as young, strong countrymen are believed to help 'the others' who can do little, being but 'shadows' without a mortal among them, at the hurling and in the battle; and November Eve is still a season of great power among the spirits. Emer goes to the yew at the Strand End just as the wife goes to meet her husband who is 'away' or has been 'taken', or the husband to meet his wife, at midnight, at 'the custom gap' in the field where the fair is held, or at some other well known place; while the after madness of Cuchullain reminds me of the mystery the country people, like all premature people, see in madness, and of the way they sometimes associate it with 'the others', and of the saying of a woman in the Burren hills, 'Those that are away among them never come back, or if they do they are not the same as they were before'. His great sorrow for the love of Fand reminds me of the woman told of in Arran, who was often heard weeping on the hill-side for the children she had left among 'the others'. One finds nothing in this tale about any person or thing being put in Cuchullain's place; but Professor Rhys has shown that in the original form of the story of Cuchullain and the Beetle of Forgetfulness, Cuchullain made the prince who had come to summon him to the other world, take his place at the court of Uladh.[79] There are many stories everywhere of people who have their places taken by Angels, or spirits, or gods, that they may live another life in some other place, and I believe all such stories were once stories of people 'away'.

Pwyll and Arawn in the Mabinogian change places for a year, Pwyll going to the court of the dead in the shape of Arawn to overcome his enemies, and Arawn going to the court of Dyved. Arawn said, 'I will put my form and semblance upon thee, so that not a page of the chamber, not an officer nor any other man that has always followed me, shall know that it is not I . . . And I will cause that no one in all thy dominions, neither man nor woman, shall know that I am not you, and I will go there in thy stead'.[80] Pwyll overcomes Arawn's enemy with one blow, and Arawn's rule in Dyved was a marvel because of his wisdom, for in all these stories strength comes from among men, and wisdom from among gods who are but 'shadows'.

Professor Rhys has interpreted both the stories of Cuchullain and the story of Pwyll and Arawn as solar myths, and one doubts not that the old priests and poets saw analogies in day and night, in summer and winter; or perhaps held that the passing away for a time of the brightness of day or of the abundance of summer, was one story with the passing of a man out of our world for a time. There have been myth makers who put the mountain of the gods at the North Pole, and there are still visionaries who think that cold and barrenness with us are warmth and abundance in some inner world; while what the Aran[†] people call 'the battle of the friends' believed to be fought between the friends and enemies of the living among the 'others', to decide whether a sick person is to live or die, and the battle believed to be fought by 'others' at harvest time, to decide, as I think, whether the harvest is to stay among men, or wither from among men and belong to 'the others' and the dead, show, I think, that the gain of the one country is the other country's loss. The Norse legend of the false Odin that took the true Odin's place, when the summer sun became the winter sun, brings the story of a man who is 'away' and the story of the year perfectly together. It may be that the druids and poets meant more at the beginning than a love story, by such stories as that of Cuchullain and Fand, for in many ancient countries, as even among some African tribes to-day, a simulated and ceremonious death was the symbol, or the condition, of the soul's coming to the place of wisdom and of the spirits of wisdom; and, if this is true, it is right for such stories to remind us of day and night, winter and summer, that men may find in all nature the return and history of the soul's deliverance.

W. B. Yeats

MR YEATS'S† NEW PLAY[81]

My subject is Ireland and its struggle for independence. The scene is laid in the West of Ireland at the time of the French landing.[82] I have described a household preparing for the wedding of the son of the house. Everyone expects some good thing from the wedding. The bridegroom is thinking of his bride, the father of the fortune which will make them all more prosperous, and the mother of a plan of turning this prosperity to account by making her youngest son a priest, and the youngest son of a greyhound pup the bride promised to give him when she marries. Into this household comes Kathleen Ni Houlihan herself, and the bridegroom leaves his bride, and all the hopes come to nothing. It is the perpetual struggle of the cause of Ireland and every other ideal cause against private hopes and dreams, against all that we mean when we say the world. I have put into the mouth of Kathleen Ni Houlihan verses about those who have died or are about to die for her, and these verses are the key of the rest. She sings of one yellow-haired Donough in stanzas that were suggested to me by some old Gaelic folk-song:[83]

> I will go cry with the woman,
> > For yellow-haired Donough is dead,
> With a hempen-rope for a neck-cloth,
> > And a white cloth on his head.
>
> I am come to cry with you woman,
> > My hair is unbound and unwound;
> I remember him ploughing his field
> > Turning up the red side of the ground.

> And building his barn on the hill,
>> With the good-mortared stone;
> Oh, we'd have pulled down the gallows,
>> Had it happened at Enniscrone.

And just before she goes out she sings:

> Do not make a great keening
>> When the graves have been dug to-morrow;
> Do not call the white-scarfed riders
>> To the burying that shall be to-morrow;
> Do not spread food to call strangers,
>> To the wakes that shall be to-morrow,

And after a few words of dialogue she goes out crying:

> They shall be remembered for ever;
> They shall be alive for ever;
> They shall be speaking for ever,
>> The people shall hear them for ever.

I have written the whole play in English of the West of Ireland, the English of people who think in Irish. My play, *The Land of Heart's Desire,* was, in a sense, the call of the heart, the heart seeking its own dream; this play is the call of country, and I have a plan of following it up with a little play about the call of religion, and printing the three plays together some day.[84]

I I

AN ANCIENT
CONVERSATION[85]

This conversation,† so full of strange mythological information, is an example of the poetic speech of ancient Ireland. One comes upon this speech here and there in other stories and poems. In the poems attributed to Aibhe, daughter of Cormac MacArt, and quoted by O'Curry in *MS. Materials,* one finds an allusion to the story of Baile and Aillinn:

> The apple tree of high Aillinn;
> The yew of Baile of little land;
> Though they are put into lays
> Rough people do not understand them.[86]

One finds it, too, in the poems which Brian, son of Tuireann, chanted when he did not wish to be wholly understood: 'That is a good poem, but I do not understand a word of its meaning', said one of the kings before whom he chanted; but the obscurity was more in a roundabout way of speaking than in mythological allusion.[87] There is a description of a banquet quoted by Professor Kuno Meyer;[88] there hens' eggs are spoken of as 'Gravel of Glenn Ai', and leek as 'a tear of a fair woman', and some eatable seaweed, dulse, perhaps, as 'a net of the plains of Rein', that is to say, 'of the sea', and so on. He quotes also a poem that calls the sallow 'the strength of bees', and the hawthorn, 'the barking of hounds', and the gooseberry bush, 'the sweetest of trees', and the yew, 'the oldest of trees'.

This poet speech somewhat resembles the Icelandic court poetry, as it is called, which certainly required alike for the writing, understanding of it and a great traditional culture. Its descriptions of shields and tapestry, and its praises of kings, that were first written, it seems, about the tenth century, depended for their effects on just this heaping up of mythological allusions, and the Eddas were written to be a granary of allusions for the makers of such poems.[89] But in the fourteenth and fifteenth centuries they had come to be as irritating to the new Christian poets and writers who stood outside the tradition, as are the more esoteric kinds of modern verse to unlettered readers. They were called 'obscure' and 'speaking in riddles' and the like.

It has sometimes been thought that the Irish poet speech was indeed but a copy of this court poetry, but Professor York Powell contradicts this, and thinks it is far more likely that the Irish poems influenced the Icelandic, and made them more mythological and obscure.[90]

I am not scholar enough to judge the Scandinavian verse, but the Irish poetic speech seems to me at worst an over abundance of the esotericism which is an essential element in all admirable literature, and I think it is a folly to make light of it, as a recent writer has done.[91] Even now verse no less full of symbol and myth seems to me as legitimate as, let us say, a religious picture full of symbolic detail, or the symbolic ornament of a cathedral. Nashe's[†]

> Brightness falls from the air
> Queens have died young and fair
> Dust hath closed Helen's eye.[92]

must seem as empty as a scald's song or the talk of Cuchulain and Emer, to one who has never heard of Helen, or even to one who did not fall in love with her when he was a young man. And if we were not accustomed to be stirred by Greek myth, even without remembering it very fully, 'Berenice's ever burning hair' would not stir the blood, and especially if it were put into some foreign tongue, losing those resounding *b*'s on the way.[93]

The mythological events Cuchulain speaks of, give mystery to the scenery of the tales, and when they are connected with the Battle of Magh Tuireadh, the most tremendous of mythological battles, or anything else we know much about, they are full of poetic meaning.[94] The hills that had the shape of a sow's back at the coming of the children of Miled, remind one of Borlase's convictions that the pig was the symbol of the mythological ancestry of the Firbolgs, which the children of Miled were to bring into subjection, and of his suggestion that the magical pigs that Maeve numbered were some Firbolg tribe that Maeve put down in war.[95] And everywhere that esoteric speech brings the odour of the wild woods into our nostrils.

The earlier we get, the more copious does this traditional and symbolical element become, the more precise, the more artistic, even. Till Greece and Rome created a new culture, the sense of the importance of man, all that we understand by humanism, nobody wrote history, nobody described anything as we understand description. One called up the image of one thing by comparing it with something else, and partly because one was less interested in man, who did not seem to be important, than in divine revelation, changes among the heavens and the Gods which can hardly be expressed at all and only by symbols and enigmas—one was always losing oneself in the unknown and rushing to the limits of the world. Imagination was all in all. Is not poetry, when all is said, but a little of the habit of mind of a time when the imagination was all in all, caught in the beryl stone of a wizard?

W. B. Yeats[96]

THE ACTING AT
ST TERESA'S HALL[97]

The acting of *Deirdre* delighted me by its simplicity. It was often a little crude, it showed many signs of inexperience, but it was grave and simple. I heard somebody say 'they have got rid of all the nonsense', the accumulated follies of the modern stage. An amateur actor, as a rule, delights even more than a professional actor, in what is called 'business', in gesture and action of all kinds that are not set down in the text. He moves restlessly about, he talks in dumb show with his neighbours, and so on. He wishes to copy at every moment the surface of life, to copy life as he thinks the eye sees it, instead of being content with the simple and noble forms the heart sees. The result is that he, like the professional actor, can act modern comedy, but he cannot act any kind of drama that would waken beautiful emotions. Beautiful art is always simpler and graver and quieter than daily life, and, despite many defects, the acting of *Deirdre* has left to me a memory of simplicity and gravity and quietness. The actors moved about very little, they often did no more than pose in some statuesque way and speak; and there were moments when it seemed as if some painting upon a wall, some rhythmic procession along the walls of a temple had begun to move before me with a dim, magical life. Perhaps I was stirred so deeply because my imagination ignored, half-unconsciously, errors of execution, and saw this art of decorative acting as it will be when long experience may have changed a method into a tradition, and made Mr Fay's company, in very truth, a National company, a chief expression of Irish imagination.[98] The Norwegian drama, the most important in modern Europe, began at a semi-amateur theatre in Bergen, and I cannot see any reason in the nature of things why Mr Fay's company should not do for Ireland what the little theatre at Bergen did for Europe.[99] His actors, now that he has set them in the right way, need nothing but continuous experience, and it should be the business of our patriotic societies to give them this experience. The audience is there, for an audience that could be moved by the subtleties of thought and sentiment of a play like 'A.E.'s' *Deirdre,* that could take pleasure in a beauty that was often as imponderable as the odour of violets, cannot be less imaginative than the men of the Renaissance.[†] Victor Hugo said somewhere: 'It is in the Theatre that the mob becomes a people',[100] and it is certain that nothing but a victory on the battlefield could so uplift and enlarge the imagination of Ireland, could so strengthen the National spirit, or make Ireland so famous throughout the world, as the creation of a Theatre where beautiful emotion and profound thought, now fading from the Theatres of the world, might have their three hours' traffic once again.

W. B. Yeats

P.S. I have said nothing of the acting of *Kathleen Ni Houlihan,* for though altogether excellent of its kind, it was not of a new kind. The play tried to give the illusion of daily life, and the actors therefore acted it in the usual way, and quite rightly. That they did so well in two so different plays is a good promise for the future.

13

THE ACTING AT
ST TERESA'S HALL II[101]

I

I partly agree with you that the 'laughter' that Mr Martyn[†] says 'greeted every word however serious that fell from Peter Gillane's lips' was due on the night of the first production to the relaxation of tension to which the audience had been brought by *Deirdre*,[102] but there were other causes. Many phrases that have a tragic meaning in Connacht have no meaning or even a comic meaning in Dublin. 'He looks like somebody that has got the touch' is, for instance, tragic in Connacht. In Dublin it means somebody that is not right in his head. The stroke of the fairy wand and the touch of a fairy hand are only remembered where folk tradition lingers, though we still talk everywhere of 'a stroke of paralysis' and of being 'touched'. Another reason for the laughter was that Mr Fay has so long delighted Dublin audiences with excellent humorous acting that they are ready to laugh even before he speaks, as they did on the first night. I do not write to you, however, to argue with Mr Martyn, but to say that if he had been in the theatre on Friday he would have seen Mr Fay again and again rob himself of the laughter and applause that is the legitimate reward of the actor lest the play as a whole might suffer. Instead of trying to make points, he tried with admirable self-sacrifice to make his effect as subdued as possible.

I need hardly say that I do not agree with Mr Martyn[†] as to the acting of *Deirdre*. I think the difference between us comes from the difference of our arts. Mr Martyn likes a form of drama that is essentially modern, that needs for its production actors of what is called the 'natural school', the dominant school of the modern stage. The more experience an actor has had of that stage the better he is for Mr Martyn's purpose, and almost of a certainty the worse for mine. English actors or Irish actors trained in England, for years to come, must serve his turn far better than Irish-trained Irish actors who are likely to be extravagant, romantic, oratorical, and traditional, like Irish poetry and legend themselves. I can only repeat that I was delighted with the acting of Mr Fay's company, that I cannot see any reason in the nature of things why it should not be the foundation for a National Drama. I have plans for a somewhat elaborate essay on the Theatre, and am also lecturing on the subject at Oxford next month, and I shall probably speak of that acting in both lecture and essay as the first example of right method that I have come upon.[103] Its defects were the defects of inexperience and of all new things. A poet, or painter, or actor who is trying to make his art afresh is always more imperfect than one whose art is founded upon the current art of his time. One sees it in the imperfect drawing of the imaginative painters of a time when painting, like acting, has come to be founded upon observation rather than upon imagination. Until the stream of the world has begun to flow in a different direction, a Rossetti[†] will always draw worse than a Millais.[104]

II

When Mr Fay's company have the time and money, and it will need little of either, I hope that they will apply the same principles that they have applied to acting to the scenery and the stage itself. The scenery of a play as remote from real life as *Deirdre* should, I think, be decorative rather than naturalistic. A wood, for instance, should be little more than a pattern made with painted boughs. It should not try to make one believe that the actors are in a real wood, for the imagination will do that far better, but it should decorate the stage. It should be a mass of deep colour, in harmony with the colours in the costumes of the players. I was, I think, the first to commend this kind of scenery, and now Mr Gordon Craig has used it to make certain old English operas the most beautiful sight that has been seen upon the modern stage.[105] I do not think that he was influenced by me; but the reaction against the scientific age is setting decorative art in the stead of naturalistic art everywhere and it was bound to come upon the stage.

I would try and make a theatre where realism would be impossible. I am not at all certain, but I think I would bring the floor out in front of the proscenium, as it was in the old theatres before the 'natural school' drove out poetry. All the great poetical dramatists of the world wrote for a theatre that was half platform, half stage, and for actors that were, at least, as much orators as actors. William Morris once said to me of an eminent dramatist of our time, 'He will never understand any art because he does not understand that all art is founded upon convention'. It has been our pride, hitherto, to destroy the conventions of the Stage, and until we have restored them we will never have a dramatic art which the Englishman of the time of Shakespeare and the Greek of the time of Sophocles and the Spaniard of the time of Calderon[106] and the Indian of the time of Kaladasa[107] would have recognised as akin to their own great art.

W. B. Yeats

14

THE FREEDOM
OF THE THEATRE

In my play, *Where There is Nothing* I have put my stick into so many beehives that I feel a little anxious.[108] Someone is sure to say I have written a mischievous attack upon the Law, upon Church and State, upon Sobriety, upon Custom and even upon the Sun in his strength. I have some reason to expect this, for ingenious theatre-goers both in London and America have found my poor little *Land of Heart's Desire* to be both clerical and anticlerical; and when *The Countess Cathleen* was acted, the opinions of my demons were said to be my own opinions, and there was thought to be something dangerous and demoralising in the spectacle of a woman so intoxicated with compassion that she sold her own soul that she might give the money to the poor. It was thought that she was setting a dangerous example. I was described as unpatriotic, too, because I pictured Irish men and women selling their souls to keep death from their houses. It was well-known, I was told, that they had never done such a thing, and yet I think that I have known some few Irish men and women who sell their souls daily for a much smaller price.[109]

Then, too, I cannot keep from thinking of the experience of other dramatists, for the drama has always been a disturber. The plays of Shakespeare and his contemporaries had to be acted on the Surrey side of the Thames to keep the Corporation of London from putting them down by law. The Corporation of London represented in those days that zealous class who write and read the *Freeman's Journal*, and the *Independent* and the *Irish Times* in our day. I myself can remember when Wagner was the worst of those that had fallen from heaven, when people used to ask one another how could an audience who had witnessed *Tristan and Isolda* resist temptation. And even the youngest of my readers will remember the indignant noise when Ibsen's *Ghosts*[110] was played in London.

I hope nobody will think that I am comparing my powers with those of these great men. I am trying to show that it is impossible to write plays in a spirit of sincerity without sometimes putting one's stick into the beehives. The reason is that drama is a picture of the soul of man, and not of his exterior life. We watch Coriolanus with delight, because he had a noble and beautiful pride, and it seems to us for the moment of little importance that he sets all Rome by the ears and even joins himself to her enemies. Shakespeare makes a wise hearer forget everything except what he wants him to remember. But those citizens of the Corporation, hungry to have the law of him, saw nothing it may be but a bad example. They saw the exterior life plainly enough, for their little petty businesses taught them that, but they could not see clearly any picture of the soul. It is the same with all tragedies, we watch the spectacle of some passion living out its life with little regard for the trouble it is giving.

Drama describes the adventures of men's souls among the thoughts that are most interesting to the dramatist, and, therefore, probably most interesting to his time. Shakespeare's age was interested in questions of policy and kingcraft, and so he and his contemporaries played shuttlecock with policy and kingcraft. We are interested in religion and in private morals and personal emotion, and so it is precisely out of the rushing journey of the soul through these things that Ibsen and Wagner get the tumult that is drama. Doubtless, the character must always have something of the dramatist when it is a character that is pictured from within. It has been said that Shakespeare could not have written the part of Iago unless he had something even of Iago in him. If he had given himself up to his amorous emotions he would have been Romeo, if to his hatred of the world he would have been Timon, if to his Philistinism he would have been Henry the Fifth, and if to the near ally of his wit he would have been King Lear.

Some of our idealists have thought to help their cause by crying out lately that certain English plays are immoral. If they had only cried out that they were vulgar and stupid we would have all joined in the cry. But immoral? That is a dangerous cry.

If one wants to know what is vulgar and stupid one can turn to certain admirable writers. There is a recognised criticism. But every newspaper man, every crossing-sweeper, thinks himself a moralist. The reign of the moralist is the reign of the mob, or of some Jack-in-office. It is always either one or the other, or both of them. I have just read in the morning paper that the Turkish Censor has altered *Othello* beyond recognition, because among other reasons, the play speaks of Cyprus 'as if it was not an integral part of the Turkish Empire'. There you have them both. Jack-in-office appeals to the patriotism of the mob.

Ireland is, I suppose, more religious than any other European country, and perhaps that is the reason why I, who have been bred and born here, can hardly write at all unless I write about religious ideas. In *The Land of Heart's Desire,* a dreamy girl prefers her own dreams and a wandering voice of the night to the priest and his crucifix. In *The Hour Glass,* which is soon to be acted, it is the proud spirit that is defeated by the belief that has seemed folly to the wise. And in *The Countess Cathleen* the commandment of mercy is followed to the forgetting of all else. In *The Shadowy Waters* human love, and in *Cathleen ni Houlihan* love of country, become through their mere intensity a cry that calls beyond the limits of the world. In *Where There is Nothing,* Paul, because he is a seeker after God, desires the destruction of all things. So far as I am a dramatist, so far as I have made these people alive, I watch them with wonder and pity, and I do not even ask myself were they right to go upon that journey.

W. B. Yeats

P.S. *Where There is Nothing* is founded upon a subject which I suggested to George Moore when there seemed to be a sudden need of a play for the Irish Literary Theatre; we talked of collaboration, but this did not go beyond some rambling talks. Then the need went past, and I gradually put so much of myself into the fable that I felt I must write on it alone, and took it back into my own hands with his consent. Should he publish a story upon it some day, I shall rejoice that the excellent old custom of two writers taking the one fable has been revived in a new form. If he does I cannot think that my play and his story will resemble each other. I have used nothing of his, and if he uses anything of mine he will have so changed it, doubtless, as to have made it his own.[111]

15

A CANONICAL BOOK[112]

Sometimes I have made a list of books for some friend who wanted to understand our new Irish movement, but the list has seldom been much to my mind. One book would show the old poetry through the dark glass of a pompous translator, and another's virtue was in a few pages or even in a few lines. There was, however, one book that was altogether to my mind, *The Love Songs of Connacht,*[113] for it was all about beautiful things, and it was simply written; and now I know of two other books, which will be always a part of our canon, Lady Gregory's *Cuchulain of Muirthemne,* which it is no longer necessary to praise, and this new book of hers, *Poets and Dreamers* (Dublin: Hodges and Figgis; London: John Murray). It is not as important as *Cuchulain of Muirthemne,* but it should be read with it, for it shows the same spirit coming down to our own time in the verses of Gaelic poets and in the stories of the country people. Her chapters on Raftery, the wandering poet of some ninety years ago, on Irish Jacobite ballads, and old country love songs and on the spells that are in herbs and the like, are necessary to anybody who would understand Ireland. She translates the ballads and love songs into prose, but it is that musical prose full of country phrases, which is her discovery and Dr Hyde's; and her own comments, for all their simplicity and charm, cannot hide from discerning eyes an erudition in simple things and a fineness of taste in great things, that are only possible to those who have known how to labour.

The towns, for our civilisation has been perfected in towns, have for a long time now called the tune for the poets, even as, I think, for the Lake poets. And because one is not always a citizen there are moods in which one cannot read modern poetry at all; it is so full of eccentric and temporal things, so gnarled and twisted by the presence of a complicated life, so burdened by that painful riddle of the world, which never seems inexplicable till men gather in crowds to talk it out. I could not imagine myself, though I know there are some who feel differently, reading modern poetry when in love or angry or stirred by any deep passion. It is full of thoughts, and when one is stirred by any deep passion one does not want to know what anybody has thought of that passion, but to hear it beautifully spoken, and that is all. Some seventeenth century lyric, where the subtleties are of speech alone, or some old folk tale that had maybe no conscious maker, but grew by the almost accidental stringing together of verses out of other songs, commingle one's being with another age, or with the moods of fishers and turfcutters. Sometimes, indeed, being full of the scorn that is in passion, one is convinced that all good poems are fruit of the Tree of Life, and all bad ones apples of the Tree of Knowledge. I find in this book many fruits of the Tree of Life, and am content that they offer me no consolation but their beauty.

A friend of mine[114] once asked some Irish-speaking countrymen, who were learning to write and read in Irish, what poem they liked the best out of a bundle that had been given them. They said, 'The Grief of a Girl's Heart', an Aran poem, which is among those Lady Gregory has translated, and they added that the last verse of it was the best. This is the last verse: 'You have taken the east from me; you have taken the west from me; you have taken what is before me and what is behind me; you have taken the moon, you have taken the sun from me; and my fear is great that you have taken God from me'. A few years ago, before the modern feeling for folk-thought on the one hand, and for certain schools of esoteric poetry on the other hand, had brought a greater trust in imagination, a verse like that would have seemed nonsense to even good critics, and even now a critic of the school represented by most of the writing in, let us say, the *Spectator*,[115] would probably call it vague and absurd. The poet who made it lived when poetry, not yet entangled in our modern logic, a child of parliaments and law courts, was contented with itself, and happy in speaking of passions almost too great to be spoken in words at all. The poet had bitten deeply into that sweet, intoxicating fruit of the tree that was in the midst of the garden, and he saw the world about him with dim, unsteady eyes. Another verse of the Aran song, and all the song is lovely, would seem, I think, more wicked than foolish. The girl would give everything to her lover, and at last cries out: 'O, aya! my mother[116] give myself to him; and give him all that you have in the world; get out yourself to ask for alms, and do not come back and forward looking for me'. A critic to whom the hidden life of the soul is of less importance than those relations of one person to another that grow in importance as life becomes crowded would find it hard to sympathise with so undutiful a daughter. He might, indeed, if he had learnt his trade in that singular criticism of Shakespeare, which has decided that *Hamlet* was written for a warning to the irresolute, and *Coriolanus* as a lesson to the proud, persuade himself that the poem was written to show how great passion leads to undutifulness and selfishness. He could hardly come to understand that the poet was too full of life to concern himself with that wisdom, which Nietzsche has called an infirmary for bad poets,[117] that if he had known of it he would have scorned it as deeply as any true lover, no matter how unhappy his love, would scorn the wizard drug, that promised him easy days and nights untroubled by his sweetheart's eyes. I would send any man who wants to be cured of wisdom to this book, and to *Cuchulain of Muirthemne,* and to books like them. The end of wisdom is sometimes the beginning of heroism, and Lady Gregory's country poets have kept alive the way of thinking of the old heroic poets that did not constrain nature into any plan of civic virtue, but saw man as he is in himself, as an amorous woman has seen her lover from the beginning of the world. Raftery, the peasant poet, praises one man, 'because he had pleasantness on the tops of his fingers',[118] 'because in every quarter that he ever knew he would scatter his fill and not gather. . . . He would spend the estate of the Dalys, their beer and their wine';[119] and he praises another because 'He did not lower himself or humble himself to the Gall, but he died a good Irishman, and he never bowed the head to any man'.[120] In the presence of thoughts like these two aristocracies have passed away. The one, hearing them sung in its castles, perished fighting vainly against the stranger, and the other, hearing them in the praise and dispraise of the Celtic poor, felt without understanding what it felt, the presence of a tribunal more ancient and august than itself, and became spendthrift, and fought duels across handkerchiefs, and at last, after a brief time of such eloquence that the world had hardly seen its like, passed away ignobly.

Lady Gregory finishes her book with translations of Dr Hyde's little plays. These plays, which are being constantly acted throughout Ireland, are typical of the new movement, so far as it is a movement in Irish. Acted for peasants, and sometimes by them, and full of the peasant mind, they show how it keeps to-day the thoughts of Raftery and his predecessors back to the beginning of history. One play is about Raftery himself, one is about an imaginary poet, Hanrahan, one is about an old saint, one is a very beautiful Nativity.[121] They have an impartial delight in the sinless wandering saint, and in the drunken wandering poet with his mouth full of curses. Are not both of them fine creatures, and what does it matter if one has hard claws and the other carries no burdens? Is it not an illusion that man exists for man? Was he not made for some unknown purpose, as the stones and the stars and the clouds, or made, it may be, for his Maker's pleasure? I think the old poets thought that way, and the Irish countryman, who is prosaic enough in himself, is the clay where one finds their footsteps even yet.

W. B. Yeats

16

THE IRISH NATIONAL THEATRE AND THREE SORTS OF IGNORANCE

Much that has happened lately in Ireland has alarmed Irishmen of letters for the immediate future of the intellectual movement.[122] They would sooner do their work in peace, writing out their speculations or telling the stories that come into their heads without being dragged into a battle, where the worst passions must of necessity be the most conspicuous for perhaps a long time. I have listened of late to a kind of thought, to which it is customary to give the name 'obscurantism', among some who fought hard enough for intellectual freedom when we were all a few years younger. Extreme politics in Ireland were once the politics of intellectual freedom also, but now, under the influence of a violent contemporary paper, and under other influences more difficult to follow, even extreme politics seem about to unite themselves to hatred of ideas.[123] The hatred of ideas has come whenever we are not ready to give almost every freedom to the imagination of highly-cultivated men, who have begun that experimental digging in the deep pit of themselves, which can alone produce great literature, and it has already brought the bad passions, when we accuse old friends and allies of changing their policy for the sake 'of the servants of the English men who are among us', or when we pervert their work out of all recognition or split hairs to find a quarrel. It will save some misunderstandings in the future if I analyse this obscurantism.

1st There is the hatred of ideas of the more ignorant sort of Gaelic propagandist, who would have nothing said or thought that is not in country Gaelic. One knows him without trouble. He writes the worst English, and would have us give up Plato and all the sages for a grammar. 2nd There is the obscurantism of the more ignorant sort of priest, who, forgetful of the great traditions of his Church, would deny all ideas that might perplex a parish of farmers or artisans or half-educated shopkeepers. 3rd There is the obscurantism of the politician and not always of the more ignorant sort, who would reject every idea which is not of immediate service to his cause. He lives constantly in that dim idol-house I described last week.[124] He is more concerned with the honour and discipline of his squad than with the most beautiful or the most profound thought, and one has only right to complain when he troubles himself about art and poetry, or about the soul of man. One is under the shadow of his darkness when one refuses to use, even in the service of one's own cause, knowledge acquired by years of labour, when that knowledge is an Englishman's and is published in a London paper. Nor is one out of that shadow when one complains that someone has found a Cleopatra in the villages. Everyone knows who knows the country-places intimately, that Irish countrywomen do sometimes grow weary of their husbands and take a lover. I heard one very touching tale only this summer. Everyone who knows Irish music knows that 'The Red-haired Man's Wife'[125] is sung of an Irish woman, and I do not think anybody could gather folk-tales along the Galway coast without coming on the ancient folk-tale (certainly in no way resembling the Widow of Ephesus as it is told by Pogius of Florence) which Mr Synge has softened in his play.[126] These things are inconvenient one thinks when one is under that heavy shadow, for it is easier to go on believing that not only with us is virtue and Erin, but that the virtue has no bounds, for in that way our hands may not grow slack in the fight. It will be safer to go on, one says, thinking about the Irish country people, as if they were 'picturesque objects', 'typical peasants', as the phrase is, in the foreground of a young lady's water-colour.

Now, I would suggest that we can live our national life without any of these kinds of ignorance. Men have served causes in other lands and gone to death and imprisonment for their cause without giving up the search for truth, the respect for every kind of beauty, for every kind of knowledge, which are a chief part of all lives that are lived, thoughtfully, highly, and finely. To me it seems that ideas, and beauty and knowledge are precisely those sacred things, an Ark of the Covenant as it were, that a nation must value even more than victory.

W. B. Yeats

17

EMMET THE APOSTLE OF IRISH LIBERTY[127]

One nation is bound to another by all kinds of subtle threads and no two nations are bound more closely together than Ireland and America. In this present century every Irish movement has had to look to America for a principal means of its support and every Irishman looks to Irish-Americans for a principal encouragement. And even before emigration had made a second Ireland the example of America was of great importance to Ireland. When the Irish Parliament won its freedom in 1782 it was encouraged and strengthened by the example of America. Indeed it is doubtful if Grattan could have accomplished that great task if he had not had the example of America before him—so powerful is any great achievement for liberty, even far off. And when we think of the whole history of Ireland for the last seven hundred years, there is perhaps only one epoch that we look upon with entire joy and pride—the ten or fifteen years after the declaration of the independence of the Irish Parliament.[128]

During that brief period the manufactures of Ireland awoke; prosperity began to come upon the land. Lord Clare,[129] no friendly witness, said that no country in Europe became so prosperous during so short a period. The Irish gentry suddenly cast off their irresponsibility and became a great class, creating an eloquence whose like has not been in any modern nation. There arose in Dublin a brilliant social life. Many books were published. Many beautiful houses were built—public buildings and great country houses. The nation was growing to greatness and it was precisely because it was so growing that England became afraid and decided to overthrow it. She fomented a rebellion by quartering the soldiers upon the people, and then when the land was struck with terror by that rebellion and by the means that had been used to crush it, she bribed with tithes and with money till she was able to extinguish our Parliament and to cut off all that splendid, growing life. So desolate was the land made, so many atrocities were committed, so many thousands were killed and left unburied by the roadside, that I have read that in that day people feared to eat bacon for fear the hogs might have fed on human flesh.

But more criminal than the crimes that were committed to bring about the extinction of our nationality, was that extinction itself. The day will some day come when the world will recognize that to destroy a nation, a fountain of life and civilisation, is the greatest crime that can be committed against the welfare of mankind. An old Dutch traveler has said of the Elizabethan Englishmen that they were witty, boastful and corrupt.[130] Alas! how they have changed. They are no longer witty. They still, however, understand how to use the most corrupt means in their public life, and how to boast. I have seen in the parlors of an English inn a cartoon of the year 1800 representing Ireland and England as clasping hands in an eternal friendship and prosperity descending upon Ireland pouring her gifts out of a cornucopia. And in the English Parliament of that time a common theme was the prosperity which England in her wisdom and her greatness had conferred upon Ireland.

Out of that self-complacency the rebellion of Robert Emmet awoke the English people. Just when it seemed that they had bribed all that mattered in Ireland, this young man came and he laid down his life. He showed that there was something in Ireland which not all the wealth of the world could purchase. He seemed to say to England: How can you permanently triumph? What can you offer to us if we do not fear to leave even life itself?

But England had always another weapon against Irish national-ity besides bribery. She knows how to slander. As the greatest preacher of Emmet's ideals, John Mitchel, says, England has the ear of the world.[131] She says, as it were, to our young men: If you only will serve me, this will be done for you. You will find preferment, if[†] you go to the bar; maybe you will rise to be a judge. If you serve me well against the interests of your country, wealth will come to you in some shape or other. But if that young man go against her and unite himself to the Irish people, then England will follow him with every kind of slander. Her representatives in Ireland, the class who depend upon her, will whisper against him all kinds of subtle accusations; or it may be he may have to meet some charge such as that Parnell had to meet when the *Times* newspaper accused him of recommending assassination.[132] Like all tyranny, she knows how to make what she admires seem great and what she fears seem despicable. She has tried to persuade us that Robert Emmet was but a wild, hare-brained,[†] vain young man, and some of our own people out of weakness have repeated the slander.

It is well, therefore, that we should examine and find out why Ireland has placed him foremost among her saints of nationality; why she honors him most of all those who have laid down their lives to serve her. The Catholic Church has a curious ceremony which precedes the canonization of a saint. One states all that can be said against him and then another refutes these accusations. The saint's life is carefully examined, and so I would have you examine with me the life of Emmet.

When the rebellion of 1798 was stirring Ireland he was a youth of nineteen, an undergraduate of Trinity College, and we have still the opinions of his contemporaries about him. They tell us that when he stood up to debate in the College Debating Society all thronged in to hear him; and one, the most famous of his admirers, the poet Thomas Moore, has spoken of the greatness of his eloquence, saying that he had heard no eloquence since then that seemed to him loftier or purer than the eloquence of that boy of nineteen, and he adds: 'He was altogether a noble fellow and as full of imagination and tenderness of heart as of manly bearing'.[133]

And another famous contemporary has said of him: 'He was gifted with abilities and virtues that rendered him an object of universal esteem and admiration. His mind was fed from the pure fountain of classic literature, and he lived not so much in the scenes around him as in the society of the illustrious and sainted dead. The poets of antiquity were his companions, its patriotism his methods, and its republics his admiration'.[134]

And another who knew him well has written: 'So gifted a creature does not appear in a thousand years'.[135] Indeed, all that knew him speak of him in what would seem an extravagant eulogy.

'Were I to remember', Moore has said, 'the men among all I have ever known who appear to me to contain in the greatest degree pure moral worth and intellectual power, I should among the highest of the few place Robert Emmet'.[136] And many of those who speak of him praise his great modesty and speak of a diffidence that was curiously mingled with self-reliance. In any other land he would have risen to the highest position and have lived honoured by all men. But in Ireland he was expelled from his college without a degree because of his treasonable opinions.

He went to France and was almost immediately in communication with Napoleon and Talleyrand. He was then but twenty-four, and yet these men, the mightiest in Europe, listened to his plans and discussed with him the liberation of Ireland. Napoleon was then the most victorious conqueror the world had ever seen. No check had come to his power. He had conquered many European nations and had their power mingled with his own and he was turning all this great power against England. He had just collected an enormous fleet for the invasion of England; 360,000 men were to be flung on the English coast. Emmet returned to Ireland to raise there a rebellion which was to strike at Dublin Castle when Napoleon struck at England. He acted in consultation with others, with the survivors of the rebellion of 1798, and it is manifest that his plan was their plan. The organization of the United Irishmen had been immense, but its very size had been a difficulty in its way, for it had been full of spies.[137] The hardest and strongest fight had been made in Wexford, where the United Irishmen organization was very weak, and Emmet and his friends decided to do without any such organization, to substitute surprise for great numbers. They believed that all Ireland was so disaffected to English rule that if they could suddenly seize the centre of government in Dublin all Ireland would rise to help them.

Emmet established in Dublin two depots for the manufacture of pikes and for the storing of ammunition almost under the walls of the Castle. He set to work in March, 1803, and was to strike in the autumn, when he expected Napoleon's fleet to disembark its troops upon the English coast. All, however, went wrong almost from the beginning. An explosion in one of the depots forced him to make his attempt before all his plans were ready, and then by what was either an extraordinary succession of accidents or treachery, nothing happened as it was expected to happen. Large bodies of men were to have been assembled on Saturday night, July 23d, in

Thomas Street, Dublin—so many hundred from Wexford, so many hundred from Kildare, so many hundred from Wicklow. The Wicklow men under Michael Dwyer did not come because a messenger had turned treacherous or cowardly. The Kildare men came but were met with a rumor that all was postponed and went home again. Some eighty men alone answered the call. The officers who should have led them—young men of fashion whose names have not come down to us—failed him at the last moment. The crowd became a disorderly mob and was dispersed by the soldiers. Emmet took refuge in the mountains with Michael Dwyer.

And yet he might have easily escaped to France had he not waited for a last interview with his sweetheart, Sarah Curran. That was a weakness more touching than any strength. He was taken and put upon his trial and at his trial spoke those words that are a part of Irish imagination for ever. He had the eloquence of the great generation he belonged to.

On the day of his execution a coach was seen waiting near the prison. In it was a lady with her face buried in her handkerchief; it was Sarah Curran. When he ascended the scaffold he had a braid of her hair pleated over his heart. But others who were bound to him by no such passionate ties were almost as deeply moved by his fate. It has been recorded that as he went to execution he passed the turnkey in whose care he had been, a man accustomed to the tragedies of a prison. The tears were streaming down the man's cheeks. Robert Emmet's hands were pinioned, but he leaned forward and touched him on the cheek with his lips. The turnkey fell fainting to the ground. When he awoke from his faint Robert Emmet's life had been snatched away.

I need not remind you of how Anne† Devlin was tortured by the soldiers who sought to make her reveal his hiding place, and how she kept silent through it all.[138]

This young lad of twenty-five had certainly won the confidence of all, the love of all. Old men and men of middle life obeyed him and served him unquestioningly. In one thing only was he foolish. He was a very young man. He had not that distrust of human nature which is the bitterest part of wisdom and only comes to men by long experience. He trusted too easily. Men failed him through weakness, through idleness, through all kinds of little petty weaknesses. Some, too, perhaps, were treacherous. His mind was in flame with his own thoughts, with his own purposes. But such men, though they see often less into human nature than others until the world has schooled them, have often been the very masters of the world.

Nor did his scheme lack historical precedents. He took few men into his counsel. He had no great army. But Portugal won her freedom from Spain in 1640 by the help of only two-score men. Two score of conspirators spent the night praying in the cathedral, and then seized the Vice-Queen of Portugal, the representative of Spain, and the whole country rose about them and became free.[139] It may well have seemed to Robert Emmet that Ireland could do as much. He showed, too, by the details of his plan that he had studied military science very deeply. He had indeed mastered everything but human nature.

And when he failed he did not repine. Our age has seen no loftier courage. In letters that he wrote, in the speech that he made, there is no regret for his own death, no sorrow for the loss of the beautiful world and the loss of love. He goes to his death full of a kind of ecstasy[†] of self-sacrifice and all the time his mind is as athletic, is as clear, as if he were sitting quietly in his study. The man who reported his death scene for an English paper—a hostile witness—said that he had not thought any man could die so.[140] Emmet had hoped to give Ireland the gift of a victorious life, an accomplished purpose. He failed in that, but he gave her what was almost as good—his heroic death. The fear and malice of his enemies followed him even after death. The English authorities denied him a last known resting place. His burial place, like the burial place of the great French orator, Mirabeau, remains unknown. His enemies seemed to have wished that his dust might mingle with the earth obscurely; that no pilgrimages might come to his tomb and keep living the cause he served. And by so doing they have unwillingly made all Ireland his tomb.

And out of his grave his ideal has arisen incorruptible. His martyrdom has changed the whole temper of the Irish nation. England celebrates her successes. She celebrates her victorious generals. Her music halls have sung the praises of the victors of Omdurman and South Africa. They have not sung of the noble sacrifice of Gordon.[141] In Ireland we sing the men who fell nobly and thereby made an idea mighty. When Ireland is triumphant and free, there will yet be something in the character of her people, something lofty and strange, which shall have been put there by her years of suffering and by the memory of her many martyrs. Her martyrs have married her forever to the ideal. When the poetry of Young Ireland came some forty years after Emmet's death, his memory was one of its principal inspirations.[142] And in a little while it came about that his picture hung in thousands of Irish cottages beside the picture of St Patrick and the picture of the Mother of God.

There is a street ballad that always sounds very touching to my ears. It was made by no professing poet, but by some obscure rhymer of the streets, written immediately after the exile of John Mitchel, the greatest disciple of Emmet in the last century. His name comes in at the end of nearly every stanza, but it seems to one as if that latest tragedy moved the writer of the poem too deeply for him to give it many words.

(Then Mr Yeats read the old song with the refrain: 'Here's the memory of the friends that are gone'.)[143]

Sometimes in our Irish politics we have forgotten for a brief period the example of our martyrs, and in the end we have always suffered for that forgetfulness. Sometimes we have become so absorbed in the politics of the hour, in the pursuit of some great political measure, that we have forgotten the more eternal and ideal elements of nationality.

When I was a young lad all Ireland was organized under Parnell. Ireland then had great political power; she seemed on the verge of attaining great amelioration, and yet when we regret the breaking up of that power—and we may well regret it—we must remember that we paid for that power a very great price. The intellect of Ireland died under its shadow. Every other interest had to be put aside to attain it. I remember the *Freeman's Journal* publishing an article which contrasted the Parnell movement with the movement that had gone before it by saying: 'The last movement was poetry plus cabbage garden' (meaning poetry and the failure of Smith O'Brien)[144] 'but this movement is going to be prose plus success'. When that was written Ireland was ceasing to read her own poetry. Ireland was putting aside everything to attain her one political end.

I sometimes think that O'Connell was the contrary principle to Emmet.[145] He taught the people to lay aside the pike and the musket, the song and the story, and to do their work now by wheedling and now by bullying. He won certain necessary laws for Ireland. He gave her a few laws, but he did not give her patriots. He was the successful politician, but it was the unsuccessful Emmet who has given her patriots. O'Connell was a great man, but there is too much of his spirit in the practical politics of Ireland. That great Parnellite movement tried now to bully England by loud words and now to wheedle England by soft words, and Ireland herself, her civilisation and her ideals, were forgotten in the midst of it all. She was ceasing to have her own thoughts, to speak her own language, to live her own life. Idealists and poets had once been of importance to her, but I can remember some verses in a daily paper which gave the prevailing feeling of that time. They were addressed to the poet and they wound up by saying:

> 'Take a business tour through Munster;
>   Shoot a landlord; be of use.

We poets were expected to be of use. The day had come when Ireland was to be content with prose plus success; but then it turned out to be not prose plus success but prose plus Committee Room Number 15.[146]

Then suddenly Parnell fell. The new school of practical and ecclesiastical politicians sold him to the enemy for nothing. Let us mourn his tragic fall, but let us remember that it brought, besides much evil, also a new life into Ireland. To you Irishmen in America what followed must have seemed a time of sheer desolation, of mere ignorable quarrelling. To us it was the transformation of the whole country. We saw that the imaginations of our young men would be directed away from the politics of the hour; that a time had come when we could talk to them of Davis, and of Emmet, when we could talk to them of Irish history and Irish culture, when we could make them think of Ireland herself. We would take up the work of Young[†] Ireland; and direct the imaginations of our young men towards Irish nationality, as Thomas Davis and the Young[†] Irelanders understood Irish nationality. Then we founded the Irish Literary Society of London and the National Literary Society of Dublin.[147]

In a few years great numbers of books were published about Ireland—more books, it has been said, with but little exaggeration than during the whole hundred years that went before. We appealed to the people as Davis had appealed to the people. But it was not that movement which was destined to rouse the people. They were not to be roused by any words spoken in English.

One day the man whose name will mark this epoch, Dr Douglas Hyde, went to a little country town bringing with him certain friends and he urged that all who had the Irish language should keep it living and all that had lost it should learn it. He told them that while Ireland had been agitating for a single necessary political measure, she had been giving up the battle in all else. The little country town had sent its member of Parliament to Westminster, but it had sent also a man or woman to London to bring back to the little local shop the latest London fashions. We were even giving up our own cloth; we were dressing like Englishmen in all things; and what was true of our clothes was true of all our thoughts. We were reading little English papers—the *Police News,* vulgar English story papers and comic papers. We were no longer reading Irish history; no longer reading the Young Irelander.[†] We had become too practical for all that. We did, indeed, read the debates at Westminster to know what our vigorous members of Parliament were doing there and that only absorbed us the more in what was taking place beyond the channel.

Some of the politicians who had been most active in that struggle had even Anglicized their names; had given up their old Gaelic names that had a place in the history of Ireland. Dr Hyde gave long lists of such names. He told the people that the native culture of Ireland was in the Irish language; that the history of Ireland could only be understood through that native language; that the Irish nation would die if it lost its language. His appeal had an immediate and wonderful success. What could have seemed more impracticable than that the people should begin to learn a language in which no business of the modern world is transacted, in which no thought peculiar to the modern world is expressed? And yet his movement succeeded with the most amazing rapidity. And after all, is not that always so? Is it not the impracticable dreamer that conquers the world? Is it not the impracticable dreamers who take the world up out of its course and turn it from one way to another? Who else are the founders of schools of philosophy? The founders of religions?

Ireland is being transformed from end to end by that impracticable dream. In every county† now there are held what are called Feises—assemblies little and big for the singing of Irish poems, for the telling of Irish stories, for the playing of Irish plays, and these Feises are centres for the re-awakening of the national life. There comes very vividly before my mind the picture of the Galway Feis of last year and of an old man 104 years of age, repeating there his own poems in the high shrill voice of age. He had been found in the workhouse and had been brought out of it to be honored and cherished by his countrymen in his old age.

But I need not waste many words to prove to you that this language movement has become a great power in Ireland, a great moral power. Last spring the Gaelic League decided to hold its procession to collect money for the language cause on St Patrick's Day. They decided that the public houses must close. They invited them to do so. At first they were scornful. Then girls waited outside the different houses, each distributing leaflets telling the people to pass by. On the morning of St Patrick's Day there were streams of publicans outside the doors of the Gaelic League, come there to make their submission and to receive the little cards announcing that they had closed by order of the Gaelic League. As the result of this there were not six public houses open in all Dublin.[148]

A movement that stirs the people deeply while those people have ancient culture like the Irish, can hardly fail to produce memorable poetry. Ireland in the old time was celebrated among the nations for her poets and the revival of the Gaelic language has brought with it a new living poetry. If I were asked to choose a poem in which Ireland's hate of English tyranny had found its most memorable expression, I would not choose a poem that came out of any of our professedly political movements but a certain poem written in Irish the other day by an anonymous writer. I know no expression of political hatred quite so splendid and passionate. I am a man of letters. It is difficult for me to hate anything very deeply. My life is too quiet for that. But I know that a nation cannot be powerful, cannot be ready for necessary battle, unless it has hatred as well as love in its heart. A nation is like a great tree and it must lift up its boughs towards the cold moon of noble hate no less than to the sun of love, if its leaves are to be thick enough to shelter the birds of heaven. Nor can its fruit be worthy to be eaten by men unless it have a harsh as well as a sweet savour.

(Mr Yeats here read a translation from the Irish of the poem referred to.)[149]

When this great movement appeared in Ireland, it looked for a time as if there was nothing for men like myself to do. We had learned English in the nursery. We thought in English. A man can only write well in the language he thinks in. We might learn Irish, but we would never learn it well enough to write good poetry or good prose in it. It seemed at first as if there was nothing for us to do except tell everyone to learn Irish. And then it became clear to us that when we experienced any beautiful emotion or saw any truth, it was right for us to tell others about it in whatever language we could use the best. And then we discovered the theatre. We found that we could reach our people[†] through the theatre. One of the most powerful instruments for the Anglicizing of Ireland was the English theatre in Ireland. It was no use merely denouncing it. It was necessary to put something in its place. A young artisan, Mr William Fay, whose name will some day be known in the history of Irish drama, got together a company of young men and women and he has taught them to act very beautifully and very simply, so beautifully and so simply that one of the most celebrated dramatic critics in England has said of them that they have given him more pleasure than anything he has seen in the regular theatre for a long time.[150] They perform every month now in Dublin and are drawing appreciative audiences and all their plays are taken from the history of Ireland or from the heroic age of Ireland or are satires or comedies on contemporary Irish life. This little theatre fears nothing and the doctrines of Emmet have found upon its stage a vivid expression. We are producing in Ireland a school of dramatists writing both in Irish and in English. Three years ago we produced a play in Irish by Dr Douglas Hyde. It was called *The Twisting of the Rope*. It was immediately taken up through the country in many places and from that has risen a whole vigorous dramatic literature in Irish. One day I was going through a street in London when two tall lads and a big tall country girl came up to me. They began speaking all at once. I could not make out anything of their story, except that they were manifestly from County Cork. I brought them into a little restaurant and got them to speak one at a time, and then they told me that they had recognized me; that they had seen me once at a meeting, and that they had stopped me to tell me the latest theatrical news from Ireland. Father Peter O'Leary, their parish priest, had turned playwright at the age of seventy. The whole countryside was excited about his play. It was about a rogue who had lived in that parish forty years before and one reason why the people were so excited was that the descendants of the rogue were there and the descendants of the man he cheated were there, and the descendants of the rogue had taken it so badly that poor Father Peter O'Leary had been compelled to change his name in the play.

There are now many Gaelic playwrights and many little companies performing their plays. A year ago a little company came up from Ballinadereen with a play of Dr Hyde's and another little company came up from County Cork with a play of Father Peter O'Leary's and they performed in the round room of the Rotunda for a week, filling that great hall which holds some three thousand people, night after night.[151] Instead of the metropolis sending travelling companies to the country to Anglicize the country, we have now little companies coming up from the villages to the town to make the town Irish. It is as though the very sods had begun to sing to us.

None of these actors or these dramatists are paid anything for their work. They give to their art a disinterested service which they would hardly be ready to give if Ireland had not been trained in self-sacrifice by her political martyrs. Some of them have their sufficient reward, for it is no light thing to become a part of the proudest aristocracy upon earth, the aristocracy of the artists, the only aristocracy which has never oppressed the people and against which the people have never arisen.

But it is not only intellectual movements that have been created by this new moral fervor that has come into the country with the revival of the Irish language. When a man believes in his own nation, in the culture of his own nation, in the products of his own nation, his belief very soon has a practical outlet in many directions. Wherever the Gaelic League goes you will find in the shop windows, in out of the way country towns even, printed notices saying that goods of Irish manufacture can be got there. These printed notices are all the work of the Gaelic League. A somewhat celebrated sentence puts the doctrine of the Gaelic League upon this subject very briefly: ' "Ireland can never be conquered", said a certain orator. Ten thousand hats made in England were lifted to applaud that sentiment'.[152]

Side by side with the work of the League, created out of the enthusiasm which has been mainly inspired by the League, has grown a most vigorous industrial movement. The cloth mills of Cork, for instance, have doubled their product in the last five or six years. The paper mills of Sagart have increased their business sixfold. They are employing, I believe, six times as many hands as they did before the rise of this movement. The movement for the organization of agriculture upon scientific principles goes forward side by side with the League, helped by its organizers and helping its organizers. Ten years ago Irish butter was being beaten from the market. Today the societies organized by this movement are alone exporting $10,000,000 worth of butter every year, which means a profit of $3,000,000 to Irish farmers. Two hundred and fifty co-operative banks have been established in the country places to rescue the farmer from the money lender, and it is certainly a tribute to the moral worth of the people of Ireland that not one of these banks has ever lost a shilling. There have been no bad debts.

But I need not speak further upon this side of the movement, for my friend Father O'Donovan[153] has already spoken to many of you upon it, and my friend Mr Patrick Hannon[154] is here in America now and will also, I have no doubt, speak to you most eloquently and convincingly upon it.

But most interesting of all to me, an artist, has been the rise of a school of ecclesiastical art in Ireland. One of the papers of the movement discovered that the Irish priests and parsons sent $150,000 every year to Munich to buy the worst possible stained glass. We have no good maker of stained glass in Ireland, but a certain very well known Irish artist opened there a workshop, and got the most famous maker of stained glass of the time to come and to superintend the work and to send then his best pupil, and now, really beautiful stained glass is being made in Dublin for the new Cathedral of Loughrea and for many other churches throughout Ireland.[155]

And this is only a part of the work. Beautiful windows are being made; young Irish sculptors are at work; and surely the people of Ireland will not be the less devout because the windows of their cathedrals celebrate in beautiful colors saints who lived their lives in Ireland and for the people of Ireland and because the artists of Ireland sculptured for them St Patrick or St Brendan with Irish hands. Nor will the church be less powerful if it became again, as it was everywhere in the middle ages, a patron of the arts.

This new movement has touched the moral life, the intellectual life, the material life of the country. If I were asked to put into a single sentence what it has done, I would say that it has made Irish intellect occupy itself with Ireland. I began by telling you how England bribed the Irish Parliament, but that bribery did not cease with the Irish Parliament. It has gone on all the while. England by an elaborate system of preferment of offices drew away the intellect of Ireland, hypnotized it as it were, and turned it to her own purposes. She keeps up a vast legal establishment, to take but one instance, far greater than the nation needs, and that is but a bribe to Irish intellect to occupy itself with anything rather than with Ireland. This new movement that I speak of, has brought back Irish intellect to Ireland.

An intense intellectual activity has arisen throughout the whole country. The old books of Ireland have been translated into beautiful and simple English. Surely it is no exaggeration to say that the last ten or twelve years—years which to the merely political observer have been years of defeat and desolation—have produced in Ireland an intellectual and moral activity the like of which has not been seen there for a century. Ireland is thinking about herself, is living her life within her own borders. A political movement can only give occupation to some two or three thousand of the people of a nation. The others can only join some organization and subscribe a little money. But a movement like that of Irish Ireland and the intellectual awakening of the people gives occupation to every man and woman and child in the country. The activity of such a movement is continuous. It has been one of the curses of Irish public life that we have had but an intermittent activity. We have had a period of intense life—Fenianism, Parnellism, whatever it may be— and then it dies down again. But once you have an organization of the whole people, you give to every man some occupation that suits him, to one man the awakening of an industry, to another man the learning of a language, you prepare for a political activity so powerful, you create leaders so full of resource, that one may say without fear that such a nation will be master of its own destiny; that no power outside itself will ever be able to check its development; that if it desires complete nationality it will attain it at the last, for it will be full of an inflexible power, full of an unconquerable energy, and for the future of my nation now that its new life has come, I feel entirely confident. Man's life is short, but the life of the nation is long. Even a century of failure need not discourage it; this is but a moment in the life of a nation.

The nations of the world are like a great organ. A little while ago, the organ pipe that we call the Empire of Spain was sounding and it had filled the world with its music; and then that life fell silent and the divine hand moved to another stop of the organ and the pipe that we call the Empire of England began to sound. And we need not doubt that the divine hand will move again and that the pipe that is called Ireland will once more begin to sound and that its music will fill the world.[156]

18

AMERICA AND THE ARTS[157]

The other day I was dining with some friends in a little restaurant in Soho and somebody asked me what I thought of America, where I had been lecturing for some four months. I spoke of America as the best educated country I had met with, of its clean, well-dressed people, so unlike the people of London or Dublin; of charming houses where one saw the tradition of William Morris commingled with a native tradition, come down from Colonial days; of Western college buildings where one saw the architecture of the old Spanish Mission House adapted to new purposes; of colleges that led their districts in all intellectual things; of women who were not argumentative, although they had been to college; of all that vivid life where everything is more intense than elsewhere—a thirst for money, for ideas, for power, beyond our understanding. I had come back, I said, believing as never before in the future of the world, not merely the remote future when beauty and leisure shall have returned to men, but the immediate future of labour and disorder.

Everything, I said, had been a delight to me except American poetry, which had followed the modern way of Lowell, who mistook the imaginative reason for poetry, not that ancient way Whitman, Thoreau and Poe had lit upon.[158]

Presently, an Englishman who was there said: 'You and I would soon quarrel, for I am a good Englishman'. And he got up and went away. I had forgotten I was speaking of a civilization that has influenced my country so constantly, that it is as natural for an Irishman to like it as it seems natural for an Englishman to dislike it, or to like it with something of condescension. Friends had said to me that in America I should of a certainty find nothing likable, and I had set out thinking that for me at any rate—an artist—there would be nothing. And yet I found there what is surely the root of all pleasure to an artist, many cultivated people in every town, with whom one could discuss the most interesting things. In England one finds hardly such people anywhere but in London. One sometimes comes upon some charming town with an old cathedral in the midst of it and some fragment of the old wall that once kept it in safety, and for a moment one thinks that it had been a better place to winter in than in London. Then one remembers that one could not live there where the only intellectual preoccupation would be, whether it was the church-goer or the chapel-goer that is lost. But everywhere in America—Indianapolis, Minneapolis, Chicago, St Louis, New York and far western San Francisco—one finds people who are of one's own tribe, liberated souls, partakers of the mysteries as it were. The words of Morris and of Ruskin have found hearers who have listened better because of Thoreau and Emerson;[159] and everywhere one finds one's own table of values. A man could set up house without fear wherever the skies are bluest and the shadows deepest. I had got to think it a necessary part of modern life that my tribe should be very small and that I should look at most men with a little hostility because of their hatred for what I love and their love for all that I hate. Half of the beauty of old romance is that it made men to be of one kind and so could find a worthy adventure behind every wall. I once indeed knew a romantic looking Hindu poet who lived in London as it were Bagdad or Samarkand† or ancient Delhi, and he would speak of his life there, and very eventful it was, with the same emotion I have heard him put into the words: 'There was a princess of Delhi, and she had a purple parrot'; but he had not our thoughts and one thing was like to another where all were strange.

Perhaps the absence of an hereditary aristocracy has something to do with this intellectual curiosity. An American will boast to you of the seven generations of his fathers that have been to college, as an Englishman of relations in the peerage. He has even invented the words 'college-bred' and one can see that education opens to man or woman doors that only birth or wealth would open here. Education is a national passion, and everywhere one finds some college having its own distinct life, differing from that of other colleges and getting its endowments out of its own countryside. And everywhere quite poor people pare and save to send their children to college, understanding that their country offers all forms of wealth and power to the disciplined mind. I was in many colleges, and I went to them expecting to find vigorous teaching of whatever leads to professional success, but not expecting to find imaginative teaching. And yet here also the lack of an hereditary order had brought fire and vigor. A teacher must interest his pupils, for if he bore them no unassailable tradition will keep them to listen. In many places I found students who are set to analyze the modern novel for the whole of their first year in literature, and in one great school the pupils read nothing but the Norse Sagas for a long time, for the Sagas, the headmaster told me, stirred their blood the most. The principal of a college said to me, 'The English have sent out a Commission to find out how we teach Science, thinking that our commercial success depends upon that, but I told them it came from all our life and that the Imagination was more than Science'. The men are for the most part too busy to show their imaginative side outside their business, but one finds the women, just in so far as they have been well educated, according to the accepted meaning of the word, imaginative, impulsive, and curious about ideas. I spoke at many Women's Colleges and I met few women who had not been to some college or other, and yet I never met that typical argumentative woman of the English college, who was meant, it may be, to have a happy natural charm but has learned an unhappy pose. Ever censorious, ever doing battle for the commonplace, her mind,[†] fashioned for joy and triumph, is full of virulent peevish negation; one would as soon sit down to supper with a host who dropped tin tacks into the soup tureen as converse with her; but these American women are as charming, as well-educated in all necessary things, as if they had spent their youth in the impulsive laborious ignorance of the studio. By what secret have these teachers learned so to enlarge the imagination and the sympathies of those who have been born to no creative art, and to make them as human as if they had held the paint brush and the chisel. The principal of a great college for women said to me, 'I have noticed the difference between the English educated women and ours, and it is because they teach them to teach in England and we prepare them for life'.[160] Certainly it was a great joy to speak before so many fair heads that are learning and yet not unlearning life, about the queens of old Irish romance who were fitted to be the perfect mistress and the perfect wife, and yet when the need called for it to carry a bow through the wilderness.

One wonders why America has not created more beautiful art. It is not, as I think, that she lacks the emotion of antiquity. Is not England for all practical purposes but of yesterday? If one leave but a few buildings here and there, is not London as new as Baltimore or even as New York? Indeed, one finds throughout America a sense of an immediate stirring past that should arouse the imagination as much as an age of romance, from which an early Victorian deluge divides us. In the Capitol at Washington there is a dome painted for four-fifths of its circle with historical frescoes, while one-fifth is but bare wall. It was felt that but one event, the Civil War, was important enough to fill that space, but that it was not right to commemorate civil war. A country that did not feel imaginatively about its past would have filled it with some state ceremony, some trivial noisy event.[161]

America has made many charming houses and some good novels, and there is Poe and Thoreau and Whitman, and there is Emerson, who seems to me of a lesser order because he loved the formless infinite too well to delight in form, and there is Whistler. But New England has passed away, and Whistler was shaped far from America.[162] One cannot think that this new America which has robbed culture of its languor and yet kept its fineness has found an adequate expression. Is it because it is an America of women, and women have not yet been abundant creators of the arts? Is it because, as several university teachers said to me, America has to assimilate with herself millions of immigrants who not only come with alien traditions but speak English coldly and unimaginatively because it is still a foreign tongue? Or is it that America has flung herself into the private wars of commerce and must be silent till they are over, as England was during the Wars of the Roses? I was in some beautiful and quiet towns, but I stayed in one town where a railway train went up and down the main street ringing a bell once every hour or so through the day and night. Perhaps the arts await until some Apollo slay that python. Yet here and there one could almost hear the footsteps of the Muses: in that beautiful San Francisco, for instance, under a sky of untroubled blue, by the edge of that marble Greek theater at Berkeley College, or in those ornamental gardens a little southward where the policemen ride among the pepper trees and the palm trees with lassoes before them on the saddle. Perhaps it was only the enchantment of a still sea, of a winter that endured the violets, and of a lovely book of verses from Petrarch, sent me by a young writer, that made me fancy that I found there a little of that pleasure in the Arts, which brings creative art and not scholarship, because it is delight in life itself.[163]

When life grows beautiful and joyful, when men are ready with a blow and women dream extravagantly, the Muses come in secret under the shadows that they may hurriedly consume upon their treacherous altar what many generations have gathered. The scholar and the connoisseur are friends of the artist indeed, but he is of a different race, for are not we artists but soldiers, merchants, malcontents and lovers who have turned from life because she has nourished us in desires that she cannot satisfy. Nobody can tell where life is going to catch fire and become art, and all our prophecies are but as a child's make-believe; but certainly should it come into those half Latin places that will be well, for the Northern voices of the world seem to be getting a little fainter and they do not, it may be, delight us as they did.

19

BRITISH ASSOCIATION VISIT TO THE ABBEY THEATRE[164]

THE ABBEY THEATRE

The movement out of which the Abbey Theatre and The Abbey Theatre Company were born began in 1898. A few Irish writers, among whom were Lady Gregory and myself, wrote or collected a certain number of Irish plays, and brought over English actors to play them. There was not at that time any Irish Company, but in 1901 performances were given by a little company of Irish amateurs, who did what amateurs seldom do—worked desperately. They had only their evenings for rehearsals; and at first playwrights and players formed a single body, deciding on everything together, and paying the expenses amongst them. Meanwhile new playwrights had joined us, one of these, J. M. Synge, has since become a very well-known dramatist. We gave our plays in various Dublin lecture halls, where the level floor of the auditorium made it difficult to see the stage, and as neither Player nor Playwright received any money, considered ourselves very wealthy. In 1904 Miss Horniman, who had seen us playing in London, where critics told us that we had found out a new, simple and sincere art of the stage, rebuilt for us the Abbey Theatre, and gave us the free use of it; and a little later, finding that the double work was becoming too hard for our principal players, gave us a small annual subsidy.[165]

We are the first subsidized theatre in any English-speaking country, the only theatre that is free for a certain number of years to play what it thinks worth playing, and to whistle at the timid. We make a concession now and then, but grant to ourselves for a compensation joyous defiance a little later on; and if we are not popular we can at any rate say that what support we have is from the shilling and sixpenny seats, and not from a coterie in the stalls. The stalls are generally empty, but again and again we have not sixpenny seats for all that come and I think that in spite of some complaints, which are not lacking in energy, our following likes us the better because we know our own mind. When we are anxious for a change, and would see the dearer seats as full as the cheap ones we go to the most intellectual places, where dramatic literature is a serious study, and fill a house in London, Oxford and Cambridge. Our Patent, for as the laws in Ireland are frequently old-fashioned, we come under the patent system, confines us to plays by Irishmen or upon Irish subjects, or to foreign masterpieces (and among these we may not include anything English). This limitation was put in at the request of the other theatres that we might not be their rival, the counsel for one of them being particularly anxious to keep us from playing Goldsmith and Sheridan who were, he believed, Englishmen.[166] It does not inconvenience us, however, for we believe that good art, whether in acting, playwriting, or anything else, arises from the shock of new subject-matter. We are trying to put upon the stage in playing as in playwriting the life of this country, not a slavish copy of it as in a photograph, but a joyous, extravagant, imaginative image as in an impressionist painting.

In Japan there are some who believe very erroneously that we are a great success, and even making money, and one of their distinguished critics uses our example to urge upon his countrymen the support of their native drama; and the Transvaal has begun to pirate us.[167]

W. B. Y.

THE ABBEY THEATRE—ITS AIMS AND WORK

To some of you, who may perhaps have heard of the Abbey Theatre for the first time, it is necessary that I should tell a little how it all came about.

Some years ago a group of Irish writers, among whom were Lady Gregory and myself, noticing that the Irish people cared more for oratory than for reading (for a nation only comes slowly to the reading habit) resolved to express ourselves through a Theatre. At first we brought over English Actors, because there was no Irish

Company in existence; but there was always something incongruous between Irish words and an English voice and accent. Presently with the help of a very able actor, who has lately left us, an electric light fitter by occupation, we got together a group of young men and young women here in Dublin, who were prepared to give their entire leisure to the creation of an Irish Theatre.[168] They worked for their living during the day, and for their art during the evening. At first we played in little inconvenient halls, but after a few years a generous friend gave us the use of this Theatre, and, finding that our people were becoming overworked, gave us enough money to free them from their shops and offices. In this way, quite apart from the traditions of the ordinary Theatre, we had built up an art of acting which is perhaps peculiar to ourselves; our players, instead of specialising, as most other actors do to represent the life of the drawingroom, which is the same all over the world, have concentrated themselves upon the representation of what is most characteristic in one nation. I think I can say with perfect sincerity that, until our people learnt their business, what is most characteristic in Irish life had never been set upon the stage at all. I doubt if the Irish accent had ever been accurately spoken there. It does not seem to us any drawback that we have limited ourselves, with the exception of a few foreign masterpieces, to the expression of the life of our own country.[169] Art has, I believe, always gained in intensity by limitation, and there are plenty of other Theatres for the other things. In rehearsing our Plays we have tried to give the words great importance; to make speech, whether it be the beautiful and rhythmical delivery of verse, or the accurate speaking of a rhythmical dialect, our supreme end, and almost all our play-wrights in the same way give to the vividness and picturesqueness of their style a principal consideration. We believe words more important than gesture, that voice is the principal power an actor possesses; and that nothing may distract from the actor, and what he says, we have greatly simplified scenery. When we wish to give a remote poetical effect we throw away realism altogether, and are content with suggestion; this is the idea of the Japanese in their dramatic art; they believe that artificial objects, the interior let us say of some modern house, should be perfectly copied, because a perfect copy is possible; but that when you get to sea and sky you should only suggest, and when they wish to suggest a sea they are content to put before you merely a pattern of waves. Good realistic scenery is merely bad landscape painting, an attempt to do something which can only be done properly in an easel painting; but if you are content to decorate the stage, to suggest, you create something which is peculiar to the stage, for you put before your audience a scene that only wakes into life when the actors move in front of it. *The Hour-Glass*[†] was our first experiment of this kind and our simplest; but I think the effect of the purple dresses against the green may have interested you.[170] This play, by the by, is one of our very earliest, and I notice, somewhat to my alarm, that it means one thing to myself, and often quite a different thing to my audience. To me it is a parable of the conscious and the sub-conscious life, an exposition of ideas similar to those in Ernest Myers's[†] great book; but the other day it converted a music hall singer, and kept him going to Mass for six weeks, after which he relapsed, and was much worse than before.[171]

But we are not always so orthodox. We have been denounced at one time or another by every party in Ireland. One of the plays which we give to-night, *The Rising of the Moon*, has roused the enmity of two parties.[172] A daily paper described it as a slander upon the police, for it represented a policeman letting off a Fenian prisoner, whereas some nationalist friends of mine were equally indignant because they said it was an unpatriotic act to represent a policeman as capable of any virtue at all. How could the Dublin mob fight the police, I was asked, if it looked upon them as capable of any patriotic act, and, Are not morals more than literature? At another time we were offered support from what are called 'the classes', and at a time we greatly needed it, if we would withdraw my own play, *Kathleen ni Houlihan*. We have always refused to listen to any of these demands, for we claim always the entire independence of the artist from everything except the high traditions of his craft. And our trouble has not always come from Ireland.

Any of you who have heard of us at all will have heard how a year and a half ago some hundreds of police were called out to quell a riot over one of our plays. We brought that play to London, and a little while before we produced it there we received a letter from your Censor—(we have no official censor in Ireland)—saying that as the play, though harmless in itself, was likely to raise a riot, he was consulting the Home Office as to whether it should be forbidden. Now your English Censor is a very much worse person than our

Irish censors are, for your man has got the police on his side. However, actors and authors consulted together, and after calculating ways and means and raising sufficient capital, we decided, if necessary, to give an illegal performance in London, and all go to prison. However, the Home Office had more sanity than your Censor, and we were allowed to give our play, which was taken very peaceably.[173]

That play has been our 'Belfast Address';[174] for just as history has shown that you are not the peaceable people you look, we are not either. No matter what great question you take up, if you are in earnest about it, you come to the great issues that divide man from man. Everything is battle. All the highest business of man is to do valiantly in some fight or other, and often when one looks into it, battles that seem fought about the most different things change their appearance and become but one battle.

When I was coming up in the train the other day from Galway, I began thinking how unlike your work was to my work, and then suddenly it struck me that it was all the same.[175] A picture arose before my mind's eye: I saw Adam numbering the creatures of Eden; soft and terrible, foul and fair, they all went before him. That, I thought, is the man of science, naming and numbering, for our understanding, everything in the world. But then I thought, we writers, do we not also number and describe, though with a difference? You are chiefly busy with the exterior world, and we with the interior. Science understands that everything must be known in the world our eyes look at; there is nothing too obscure, too common, too vile, to be the subject of knowledge. When a man of science discovers a new species, or a new law, you do not ask the value of the law, or the value of the species before you do him honour; you leave all that to the judgment of the generations. It is your pride that in you the human race contemplates all things with so pure, so disinterested an eyesight that it forgets its own necessities and infirmities, all its hopes and fears, in the contemplation of truth for the sake of truth, reality for the sake of reality.

We, on the other hand, are Adams of a different Eden, a more terrible Eden perhaps, for we must name and number the passions and motives of men. There, too, everything must be known, everything understood, everything expressed; there, also, there is nothing common, nothing unclean; every motive must be followed through all the obscure mystery of its logic. Mankind must be seen and understood in every possible circumstance, in every conceivable situation. There is no laughter too bitter, no irony too harsh for utterance, no passion too terrible to be set before the minds of men. The Greeks knew that. Only in this way can mankind be understood, only when we have put ourselves in all the possible positions of life, from the most miserable to those that are so lofty that we can only speak of them in symbols and in mysteries, will entire wisdom be possible. All wise government† depends upon this knowledge not less than upon that other knowledge which is your business rather than ours; and we and you alike rejoice in battle, finding the sweetest of all music to be the stroke of the sword.

2 0

THE ART OF THE
THEATRE[176]

I would answer your second question first, and say that managers
and producers in this country are certainly not using to the full 'the
advantages offered by the modern studio', nor is it desirable that
they should do so. We should use in every art but that which is
peculiar to it, till we have turned into beauty all things that it has,
and cease to regret the things that it has not. That which the stage
has, as distinguished from easel painting, is real light and the moving figures of the players. We should begin our reform by banishing
all painted light and shadow, and by clearing from round the stage
and above the stage everything that prevents the free playing of
light. Once we have done this, and it may mean a re-shaping of the
theatre, we shall discover a something very startling and strange—
the beauty of the moving figure. We shall no longer dwarf them as
Mr Tree does and Mr Trench[177] does, and every other popular producer, with a vast meretricious landscape, which has everything the
easel painting has except its subtlety and distinction. We shall have
abolished realism except in interiors, which can be exactly reproduced, and created a new art—the art of stage decoration.

I will answer your first and third questions together. Only two
artists have done good work upon the English stage during my
time, Mr Craig[178] and Mr Ricketts,[179] and the first of these is the
originator throughout Europe of almost every attempt to reform
the decoration and mechanism of the stage, and all that these artists
have done has had beauty, some of it magnificent beauty. I cannot
judge of the work done in France by Fortuny† and Appia,†,[180] but
what work I have seen in England by artists, other than those I have

named, has but increased the confusion between the stage and easel painting, for we gain nothing by substituting modern touch and handling for the touch and handling of the landscape painters of fifty years ago still in use among commercial scene-painters, and we lose by seeming to gain.

2 I

THE THEATRE OF BEAUTY[181]

One day when I was watching a player, a leading character in Lady Gregory's *Canavans*,[†,182] I made a discovery. I said to myself, 'That is beautiful comedy. He is displaying the fear of death, that is the subject of the play in all its forms, and yet it is all comedy, a game, all like a child's game'.

Then I said to myself, that because he was really never in fear of death—he was passionless. The discovery filled me with excitement; I had discovered a new thing about comedy. Presently I was producing Molière's *Miser*,[183] and there also I saw it was all a child's game. Those persons did not really love and hate. I began puzzling myself to find out what comedy had if it left the passion to tragedy, and I saw it was character. Then I found in a letter of Congreve's the statement that humour was that which one man had as distinguished from all other men. Humour was with him clearly the same thing as character. He said, too, that you could not give character to the young women in a play, because they had too much passion. It was clear that he saw the antithesis.[184] I realized that when I watched Falstaff on the stage; I said to myself, 'How unlike all other men he is! I would know him if I met him in the street'. But when I saw one of Shakespeare's tragic characters in a supreme moment—Hamlet, let us say, when he says to his friend: 'absent thee from felicity awhile'; or Antony when he names 'of many million kisses the poor last'; or Timon when he orders his tomb—at such times I do not say: 'How like that man is to himself', but rather: 'That man is myself'. All humanity is there in one man. Shakespeare expresses something that is common to all, something that is like a liquid that can be poured into vessels of every shape; whereas writers of comedy (and in all but his supreme moments Shakespeare is a writer of comedy) were occupied with the shape of the vessel. Corneille and Racine, who, like Shakespeare, were tragedians alone, substitute for character different motives—one man is jealous, another man hates, another loves. The persons of their plays are but contrasted or opposing passions, and with a right instinct they generalize the surroundings of these passions. To express character, which has a great deal of circumstance, of habit, you require a real environment; some one place, some one moment of time: but in tragedy, which comes from that within us which dissolves away limits, there is a need for surroundings where beauty, decoration, pattern—that is to say, the universal in form—takes the place of accidental circumstance.

The practical workers of the European theatres are at this moment seeking to create a method of representation that will make the theatre more beautiful, and some are striving to make possible there a stately unreal scenery; because they would find adequate staging for musical drama, which, like tragedy, is all passion, or because they desire to bring poetry on the stage again. If one would work honestly in any art, it is necessary to ask oneself what that art possesses as distinguished from all other arts. If you are going to decorate a plate you do not put upon it something which would look better in an easel painting. You think of the color, surface, shape, and use of the plate, and set something upon it which will look well there and nowhere else. It is the same if you were asked to put a great painting in a public building. You remember that this is to be seen from far away by people in many different moods, and that it is a part of the architecture. You avoid detail and a painted perspective that would make a hole in your wall—at least you do if you are Puvis de Chavannes.[185] Now the art of the stage has three things which the easel painting has not. It has real light and shade, it has real perspective, and it has the action of the player. It is absurd when you have these things to use a painting of light and shade with painted perspective, and a landscape so elaborate that your players are reduced to a picturesque group in the foreground of an old-fashioned picture. It is absurd to paint and set before an audience a meretricious easel painting, a bad academy picture which is so full of fussy detail that the players do not stand out in a clear outline against it, and that takes to itself also some of the attention which should be given to their actions and to their words. I have seen painted shadows again and again in the theatre contradict the real light; but even when they did not contradict it—when by some surprising conjuring trick the real light comes from the same point as the painted light does, or, as is more general, from all points—you have lost one of the most beautiful dramatic effects: change of light. We should banish all those painted shadows, and light the stage, as far as possible, as Nature does: from a single point. Very often a reflecting surface will give one, as it does in Nature, all the effusion of light one needs.

Nothing alarms the ordinary producer so much as a real shadow, yet it may be an infinitely expressive thing. In a play I am writing at this moment I shall represent the passing crowd by a row of huddled shadows on the wall.[186] Professor Reinhardt, one of the men of the New Movement, in a production that he brought to London the other day, brought certain of his players down a raised platform through the auditorium, and before they reached the stage one saw there their shadows of an immense size.[187] It was the finest thing in a production that a little disappointed me. In the same way you can use light and compose with it. You have a great, bare wall that seems to you monotonous. Instead of painting a commonplace window upon it, you can cast a shaft of light across it and so have something living and changing, which is all delightful to watch.

Easel painting is no natural part of the theatre. It was imposed upon it at the end of the Renaissance by the graphic genius of Italy. Up to that moment the theatre had used its real perspective and its real light almost wholly. For a time all art dwindled before painting, but now that the proportions have returned, we have restored the theatre to its normal state. This in the end will bring about a change in the shape of the building, for our theatrical architecture is at present arranged for effects of painting and does not admit of free play of light. If we are to get either ideal beauty or reality in our stage landscapes, we should change its shape. At present, narrow strips of painted canvas arranged in lines parallel to the footlights hang from the gridiron of the theatre to prevent the audience observing that gridiron, and on this the sky is painted, or the branches of trees. These borders are the ugly, obvious convention. They have no beauty and they create no illusion, and, what is worse, they make natural lighting—light from one point, as in Nature—impossible. The lights must be hung in rows between them; so, too, we have to fill up the sides of the stage that the audience may not see the walls of the building, and so we use there what are called 'wings': three or four frames of canvas on each side, one behind the other, from the proscenium to the back drop. They can hardly represent anything but trees—and what trees! Is there a picture gallery in the world that would accept such a painting? Every open place must be a bare place in a forest and lit by streaks of light from every direction.

Synge gave up his intention of showing upon the stage a fight in a plowed field between 'The Playboy' and his father, because he would not have six large trees, three on each side, growing in the middle of a plowed field. The stage directors of Europe have tried various experiments to amend this. One method would be to extend the platform behind the proscenium to a great distance on each side, until the shape of the building would be that of an immense T. I heard this discussed by a great stage director. It would have the advantage that any spectators sitting toward one side in the first rows would be prevented from seeing the side walls of the stage. No wings would be necessary, nothing but the back drop would be visible. We could get rid not only of our side wings, but of all those built-up scenes which make the stage so expensive. I am told that Herr Kemendy,[188] of Budapest, has carried out something like this scheme. He has bent the back wall of the top of his stage, a T, into an arc that brings it almost around the ends of the proscenium opening and gives it a curve. There are two opinions as to whether such a curve (which a friend of mine says makes him feel as if he were sitting in the middle of a balloon) better represents Nature than the flat surface or straight line which we are ready to accept as a simple convention. Herr Reinhardt and Mariano Fortuny have adopted another scheme that has much the same effect, and at the same time gives the arc of the sky instead of the canvas borders. They use a great hood of canvas, a half-dome, that curves from one side of the proscenium to the other, and from the back of the stage to the top of the proscenium arch. Nothing is visible but a great curved surface, much like the dome of the sky, upon which lights in color may be thrown. Monsieur Fortuny's lighting arrangements are very curious. He does not use painting at all, I understand, when he has everything in his own hands, and is applying his methods in his own way. He creates color by the throwing of colored light upon the object, and he shows his audience a clear or cloudy day by throwing into the hood, through a curved slot in the floor that goes around the base of the hood, lights reflected from rolls of colored silks. Monsieur Fortuny is very ingenious. His dome folds up like the hood of a perambulator, but in the opposite direction, from the bottom. The chief difficulty about this method is that, owing to the rolling of the canvas, creases soon appear across the sky.

All of these methods based upon the curved-back scene aim, I think, to give one a beautiful, realistic effect, reproducing as exactly as possible the sense of the open air—they aim to do what the Japanese theatre has always considered an impossibility. In Japan an interior will be exactly represented, because it can be reproduced on the stage so as to be indistinguishable from what it is in a house; but an exterior is only suggested. For instance, the Japanese will represent the sea by surrounding not only the stage but the auditorium with the well-known Japanese wave pattern. Being a writer of poetic drama, and of tragic drama, desiring always pattern and convention, I would like to keep to suggestion, to symbolism, to pattern like the Japanese. Yet realism, too, is a legitimate thing, and a necessary thing for all plays that seek to represent the actual environment of a man, and to reflect the surface of life in words and actions. We should not stage Galsworthy[189] and Shakespeare in the same way. Realism also may be beautiful, but it is well that its mechanism be made perfect.

2 2

THE STORY OF
THE IRISH PLAYERS[190]

When the idea of giving expression on the stage to the dramatic literature of Ireland was about to be carried out in 1899 it was found that no Irish actors were to be had. So we brought an English company to Dublin and Irish plays were presented by them for a short period. This method, however, did not produce the results we had hoped for; the English actors lacked the proper feeling for the Irish spirit. In 1902 there was a nearer approach to a realization of a truly national Irish theater, for a company of amateurs produced Irish plays in small halls in Dublin. The players received nothing, nor did they ask remuneration. Since they had to gain a living by another work to carry on the work they were interested in the double burden told heavily on them.

When it looked as if all might have to be given up my friend Miss Horniman arranged for a little theater in connection with the Mechanics' Institute and after a struggle the idea of a national Irish theater became an assured fact. The National Theater Society now has the Abbey Theater in Dublin and it is entirely independent and paying its way. But this does not mean that we did not have a hard fight. Our great difficulty was that in our first years our income was mostly from six-penny and one shilling seats in the gallery and pit. Clerks, shop boys, shop girls and workmen—audiences of much enthusiasm but little money—came to see our plays, which appealed to them. Our theater had its beginnings not among the rich, as did the New Theater in New York,[191] but right in the masses of the people. The working people showed the way and now that all classes come to us we constantly fill the Abbey Theater.

With us the Irish peasant is predominant for the moment, as was the peasant in the Norwegian movement. During the youth of Ibsen and Bjørnson their phrase was 'To understand the peasant by the saga and the saga by the peasant'. Our whole movement could apply to itself the same phrase. Lady Gregory, the author of our most amusing comedies, is also the author of the standard translation of the Irish epic stories, which she has translated into the speech of the Irish peasant. Synge, too, when he put an old heroic tale into dramatic play made use of dialect.[192]

Speaking of Synge, we have two opposite types of characters in Ireland that both seem peculiarly national. One is the gentle, harmless—you might call it saintly—type, that knows no wrong, and goes through life happy and untroubled, without any evil or sadness. Goldsmith was an Irishman of that type, a man without any real knowledge apparently of sadness or evil. And that kind of Irishman is common in Ireland, chiefly among the better-off people, but among the country people you find it too. There are a surprising number of constitutionally happy people in Ireland.

The other type that is also so characteristically Irish is represented by Swift. It is true he had little or no Irish blood, but in bringing up he was an Irish product. And that type is terribly bitter, hostile, sarcastic.[193]

Now Synge belonged to this bitter, sarcastic type in so far as he was a satirist. He was no incarnation of Goldsmith, but rather the opposite.[194] Yet his personality, his emotions were remarkably sane and healthy, even though they were not placid. Only the other day I heard a paper read in which he was described as the embodiment of a healthy mentality.

That was the truth, and I agreed with it. But the strange part was that Synge gained his healthiness from living for years facing death. He faced death in his own body, for he was constitutionally weak. And in going to the Aran Islands he found a people that faced death, and he lived with them. The islanders are all the time being picked off by the sea, from which they make their livelihood, yet they are a strong healthy people. And so, in his life facing death, Synge in the end gained a wonderful mental healthiness, though only after a struggle.

When I first met Synge in 1897 I found that he wanted to write about French literature. He had been studying Molière, Corneille, and Racine. I told him that if he was to write for the English papers he would find that they demanded something about modern French literature. Of the latter he knew nothing. If he was influenced by French writers they were of the pre-Molière period, and about them there was certainly nothing decadent.

He was a nationalist, but he never spoke of politics. Nothing interested him but the individual man. It was no malice, no love of mischief, that made him imagine, instead of colleens of the old sort and the good young men of Boucicault,[195] blind Martin and his wife, in *The Well of the Saints,* the erring wife in *The Shadow of the Glen,* the fantastic mistaken hero-worship of the people in his *Playboy of the Western World.* Dublin for a time saw but one-half his meaning and rejected him, rioting for a week after the first performance of his greatest play, rejecting him as most countries have rejected their greatest poets.[196] But Dublin has repented sooner than most countries have repented, and today *The Playboy* is played constantly in Dublin to good houses, drawn from all political and social sections.

23

THE POLIGNAC PRIZE[197]

We have awarded to Mr James Stephens the Polignac prize because of his book, *The Crock of Gold*. The conditions of the bequest required that the prize should be awarded for some book published in the twelve months that closed with December of last year, and that we should take into consideration the promise of the writer— that is to say, that we should give it rather to a young writer than to an old one. I can only speak of the reasons that made me propose *The Crock of Gold* and give that book my vote. It has given me more pleasure, I think, than it could give to another man, wise and beautiful though it is, because it is a proof that my native city has begun to live with a deeper life. Mr James Stephens has passed all his life in Dublin. He has been educated by the literary discussions, by the books and critical standards he has met. No matter how much we seem to create ourselves in solitude, wren or eagle, we proclaim the twigs we have sprung from. I think if he had grown up in Dublin any time before these last twenty years he would have found it hard to escape from rhetoric and insincerity. I hope he will not be offended if I say that even his rich soul might not have saved him from being, like some writers of young Ireland, but a gallant journalist.

During these last years, the Dublin that reads and talks has begun to interest itself in the ancient legends and in the living legends of Connaught and Munster, and here in this book it discovers them weighty with new morals, lofty and airy with philosophy. The town has begun to make, it seems also, in Mr Stephens's mouth new legends, new beliefs, new folk-lore, and instead of the rhetoric, the

hard-driven logic—natural wherever the interest was political—
there is a beautiful, wise, wayward phantasy, which an Aran
Islander or Blasket Islander would take pleasure in, though not
wholly understanding its new meanings, a phantasy that plays with
all things, that reverences everything and reverences nothing, an
audacious laughter, a whimsical pity. That is the thing I have loved
most in Ireland. 'Improvement makes straight roads', wrote Blake,
'but the crooked roads are roads of genius', and who would not
love that crooked fancy?[198] But until I read this book I had thought
the country alone had it, that a townsman had nothing for my love.

Mr Stephens has made an extravagant language, an extravagant
world which enables him to speak and to symbolize his emotions
and hidden thoughts, almost as fully as if he were an Elizabethan
dramatist with the mediaeval gag but just taken out of his mouth.

We can say so little without an extravagant speech, a vast symbolism. We of the Academic Committee are much wiser than we
seem. You will listen to us for an hour, and you will be surprised at
how little we shall have said, and even if you do not admire our
books very much, you will go away wondering that we could have
written them. That is because we (unlike the characters in Mr
Stephens's[†] book, 'The Grey Woman of Dun Gartin' and 'The Thin
Woman of Innis McGrath', and the two philosophers, and the God
Pan and Aengus Oge) have but our common speech. Mr Stephens
has invented all that phantasmagoria of eloquent people who have
an infinite leisure for discussion that he may express the things
which Mr Benson and Mr Newbolt and Mr Gosse and Lord Haldane and the rest of us are longing to say but are compelled to keep
hidden within us.[199] He is able, having escaped from sobriety and
moderation, to express everything: a mischievous candour like that
of a school-boy, humour like that of a cattle-drover, a passion for
life like that of a girl of sixteen, and the phantasy of a lyric poet.

Our prize is given for general promise and not merely for one
book, and that, I think, justifies me in saying that Mr Stephens had
perhaps deserved our award for certain of his poems—for passages
in 'A Prelude and a Song', for instance, had his prose been lacking.
When I first met with his name I was not interested; reviewers had
quoted violent verses about God and the devil that seemed too easy
in their defiance. Besides, I had noticed that when a man of middle
life writes his first poem, he invariably writes it about God, for he

thinks there is no other subject worthy to occupy the whole of his attention, but I had expected from youth a more original delight. Now I am ashamed that because of these quotations so little characteristic of his rich genius, I permitted others of my country-men to be before me with their praise. I have learned to repeat to myself again and again such lines as that where he describes the sea tramping with banners on the shore, or the little poem which is very simple and very gracious, and not less personal, not less 'crooked' and whimsical because it has inherited a cadence from William Blake.

> A woman is a branchy tree
> And man a singing wind,
> And from her branches carelessly
> He takes what he can find:
> Then man and wind go far away
> While winter comes with loneliness,
> With cold and rain and slow decay
> On woman and on tree till they
> Droop down unto the ground and be
> A withered woman, a withered tree;
> While wind and man woo undismayed
> Another tree, another maid.[200]

24

THOMAS DAVIS[201]

Fifteen or twenty years ago, when I was helping at the foundation of the Irish Literary Society in London, we were violently disparaged by newspapers and private persons for having praised Oliver Cromwell and the Danes, while we dispraised Thomas Davis. Was it possible to be a good Irishman and not remember the curse of Cromwell and churches the Danes had burnt? And how could it serve one's country to deny that Thomas Davis was the first among lyric poets? I cannot reproach myself for any liking for Oliver Cromwell or the Danes, but I believe that it was I alone who found certain flaws in Thomas Davis.[202] I was of a new generation, and the new generation is but little merciful to the old. To-day I have no thought but for his virtue and his service. He was not indeed, a great poet, but his power of expression was a finer thing than I thought. Yesterday as I turned over his pages I noticed how many thoughts could not have found more concise expression or in a more immediately telling way. He had poetical feeling, but saw that he had a work to do which would not set him in that road, and he made himself the foremost moral influence of our politics. One ballad of his, however, moves me always, and by its poetical feeling, 'The Lament for Owen Roe'. It has the intensity of the old ballads and to read it is to remember Parnell and Wolfe Tone, to mourn for every leader who has died among the ruins of the cause he had all but established, and to hear the lamentations of his people. When I compare it with 'O'Hussey's Ode to the Macguire', or with any good poem of Allingham's, the best poet of our next generation, I see at once that Mangan could have given it a more personal rhythm, and that Allingham would not have used those words of newspaper rhetoric 'living death', but that neither could have been so poignant.[203] Davis is mourning, not as poet, but as man over the sorrows of Ireland. Had he been born in the time of Elizabeth, he would, I believe, have been a great poet, for while the common language was still so little spoilt that deep emotion created its own speech, a man visibly moved could not but speak nobly. Men of the camp and of the council board, like Raleigh and like Sidney,[†] could be great poets, but when the language is worn down to mere abstraction by perpetual mechanical use, nobody can write tolerably, unless by some momentary accident, without exhausting continuous sedentary labour. He may have soldier or statesman in his blood, but all must be put away, for his work is to make a laborious personal language that the heart may still speak. I know, indeed, one Irish poem that seems to be the emotion of a gallant unsedentary man and has yet an altogether living style. It begins 'On the deck of Patrick Lynch's boat', and it had two men for its making—one an exile who gave all his thought to life itself, and a bookish man who turned it from Gaelic into English.[204] Nobody, no not Sir Walter Raleigh, could have beaten that. It seems as much alive, body and soul, as a mountain hare.

One understands the work Davis set his hand to when one remembers that he began it in the meridian hours of O'Connell. The policy of O'Connell had brought great reforms, but his personal influence had been almost entirely evil. His violent nature, his invective, his unscrupulousness, are the chief cause of our social and political divisions. He was accustomed to defend his manners by saying that such means alone could put spirit into a race dispirited by penal law; everybody knows his saying, 'The verdict is the thing', but his exaggeration and his hectoring have corrupted client and jury after the verdict has been given. When at the Clare election, he conquered the patriots of a previous generation by a slanderous rhetoric, he prepared for Committee Room No. 15 and all that followed.[205] In his very genius itself, there was demoralisation, the appeal—as of a tumbler at a fair—to the commonest ear, a grin through a horse-collar. We have copied all that, but have not copied his simplicity, his deep affectionate heart.

The first public event of Davis's life showed how different was his nature. The Royal Dublin Society was in trouble with government and people. Founded by the Irish Parliament, it had done much to develop the material resources of Ireland, but more and more it became a party club. Nationalists were refused admission, and it was accused of spending its money upon a political newsroom and library for the opponents of the national cause. An English government sympathetic to Ireland, that is to say sympathetic to the party of O'Connell, was in power and thought to please Ireland by compelling the Royal Dublin Society to put off the partisan, and this it attempted roughly and brusquely, dealing as it believed with a provincial assembly. Davis led a movement in favour of the Society. Mischievous as he thought its political activities, he would not have its services forgotten nor see it reformed by foreign law instead of Irish opinion. He asked in letters to the Press and carried public opinion with them, would England deal so with any of its own institutions or would an Irish government? Dublin was a capital and could not renounce the rights of a capital. To affirm national right, he gave up a party advantage. He had taught the like in songs and in ballads and would teach it in the few years of life that were yet to come. All who fell under his influence took this thought from his precept or his example; we struggle for a nation, not for a party, and our political opponents who have served Ireland in some other way may be the better patriots. He did not, as a weak and hectic nature would have done, attack O'Connell, or parade with a new party; no venomous newspaper supported his fame or found there its own support. When the quarrel came it was O'Connell's doing and his only, and the breach was so tragical to Davis that in the midst of the only public speech he ever made, he burst into tears.[206] It is these magnanimities, I believe, that have made generations of our young men turn over the pages of an old newspaper as though it were some classic of literature, but when they have come as some few have, to dream of another 'Nation' they do not understand their own lure and are content to copy alone his concentration and his enthusiasm. During the thirty years that have passed since my boyhood I have seen five or six movements founded by young men who might have changed their generation had they copied his magnanimity.

His writings whether in prose or verse, are little, indeed, but commentary on what he did in the matter of the Dublin Society, or upon what he felt in that quarrel with O'Connell, or one may turn it about the other way and say that he expressed in two or three simple unmistakable actions and in a small book of verses, tuned for the largest number of ears, certain, necessary, virtues.

Sometimes when I am discouraged by our quarrels, our jealousies, the intemperance of our speech, I remember this man who was so empty of peacock talent, having neither wit nor oratory, who put money into no man's pocket, whose only achievements were in the moral nature; and that his generation dimly understood and mourned him as conquerors are mourned. Those who mourned him and understood him have had, however choked the channel was, a capacity like his own. Lady Wilde once told me in that darkened room of hers where no ray of light was admitted to shew where time had withered, that once when she was a young girl and walking through some Dublin street, she came upon so great a crowd that she could go no further. She waited in a shop that it might pass, but it seemed unending. She asked of the shopman what brought so many people into the streets and he said: 'It is the funeral of Thomas Davis'. And when she answered, 'Who was Thomas Davis, I have never heard of him'; he said, 'He was a poet'. She was so struck to find so many people honouring a poet, and one she had never heard of, that she turned Nationalist and wrote those energetic rhymes my generation read in its youth.[207] It was not personal charm, though charm he had, that made thousands that had not spoken with him mourn for him. John O'Leary has told in his memoirs how once when he was sick and bedridden, somebody changed his life by putting into his hand the poems of Davis.[208] It was their influence, he believed, that made him endure his years of unrewarded dangerous work, his five years in prison, his fifteen years in banishment, neither repining nor looking backward.

Davis could shew forth the service of Ireland as heroic service worth a good man's energy, because he had in his words and in his actions a moral quality akin to that quality of style which can alone make permanent a picture and a book. Two men will paint a country scene or write out a story or expound an argument, and both may be alike as to their facts and all but alike in thought and yet the work of one is immediately forgotten while that of the other seems everlasting. The arguments in Milton's pamphlet on divorce may no longer help us in the controversies of the hour, but there is something in the motion of his sentences, or in his few brief moments of self-expression, that has made us live with a deeper and a swifter life.[209] But certainly it is not style for all its likeness that gave permanence to what Davis said or did. If O'Connell had a greater practical gift, Mitchel had a more vivid, more musical style, and yet the political influence of Mitchel, as I see it, has been almost wholly mischievous. The temper of his books, mixed with the habits that were settled by O'Connell, together with the denial of University education to the majority of the Irish people, is the cause why there has not arisen in Irish public life a tradition of restraint and generosity that would have made impossible the ignominy of public manners which in our own generation has weakened national feeling among the generous and the young. Mitchel played upon international suspicion and exalted the hate of England above the love of Ireland that Davis would have taught us, and his gaping harpies are on our roof-tree now. How could we learn from the harsh Ulster nature, made harsher still by the tragedy of the famine, and the rhetoric of Carlyle, a light that is the discovery of truth, or a sweetness that is obedience to its will?

I might have spared myself the trouble when I was so anxious to show what was lacking in the gift of Davis. I should have remembered that Reaction is a good ploughman, who never waits long before he readies the field for a new crop, and that he would not have failed to bring out his old tackle while I slept. To-day it is easy to understand all that and not merely because I am older, but it seemed then as if our new generation could not do its work unless we overcame the habit of making every Irish book, or poem, shoulder some political idea; it seemed to us that we had to escape by some great effort from the obsession of public life, and I had come to feel that our first work must be to close, not knowing how great the need of it still was, the rhymed lesson book of Davis. I might have remembered Goethe's phrase that great care is taken that the trees shall not grow up into the sky.[210] The folk poetry of the Gaelic revival (for the folk mind is never really political), the work in English and Irish of the new generation, was bound to find once more a speech for our private griefs and sorrows. When the other day I read *The Demi-Gods*† of Mr James Stephens, I felt that he alone by himself—and he has the Abbey Players to help him, the early lyrics of AE and much else—could take care of the future of Irish literature, till the next reaction comes.[211]

25

SIR HUGH LANE'S PICTURES[212]

I

It is important from the outset to weigh the moral weight of the will of 1913, leaving Sir Hugh Lane's French pictures to the National Gallery of London. I will show that so far as we can ever know another man's mind, we know he made it in 'momentary irritation' and when he was deceived about essential facts, and that Mr MacColl is wrong in supposing that he ever abandoned his Dublin work.[213] For some years before 1913 a project had been discussed between him and his friends for a temporary exhibition of the French pictures in the London National Gallery. On July 27, 1913, he wrote to Sir Charles Holroyd: 'These pictures are complementary to the collection I have already given them (the Dublin Corporation) and the other pictures given and subscribed for by others . . . I think if they were hung in the National Gallery or the Tate Gallery it might encourage the Corporation to fulfil my conditions'.[214] A little later, when it had become probable that the Dublin Corporation would refuse the building upon a bridge over the Liffey that he had asked for, he got a letter from one of the London Trustees asking if there was any chance of the National Gallery receiving a gift of the pictures, 'or would the loan, if accepted, be a loan in reality for the aid of Dublin'. A gift of the pictures to London would have implied the foundation of some kind of international gallery to contain them, for neither the National Gallery nor the Tate can, by their constitution, permanently exhibit modern Continental works of art.

It must have been about this date (I have no means of fixing the exact date) that Lord Curzon proposed to him the foundation of such a gallery.[215] There was always someone at his elbow in moments of despondency to suggest that he should give to England so rich in pictures what he had promised to Ireland in her poverty. He replied on August 8: 'As I still hope that my work in Dublin will not prove a failure, I cannot think of giving them to any other gallery at present, but the gallery that, not having such, refused the loan of them for one or two years would appear to be quite unworthy of them as a gift. I confess to being quite out of sympathy with the English National Gallery'. On August 12 the secretary of the National Gallery replied, unconditionally accepting loan of the pictures. A few days later came the Dublin refusal, and this refusal was aggravated by a disgraceful Press attack. In a cautious interview in the *Manchester Guardian* he spoke of a possible international gallery.[216] He took his French pictures from Dublin, sent them to the National Gallery, where they are still in the cellars, and changed his will. He had left everything he possessed to the Dublin Municipal Gallery, but now, with the exception of these pictures left to London, he gave all to the Dublin National Gallery. Dublin was still, it is plain, his chief interest.

Yet in letters to Lady Gregory, who always pleaded for Ireland and the work there, he spoke of Ireland with great bitterness. We were all very angry, less, indeed, with the Corporation than the newspapers, and some of us thought that only the sale of the pictures in the open market would prove their value. I myself printed, as a pamphlet, *Poems Written in Discouragement, 1912–1913,* and certainly these poems are as bitter as the letters Mr MacColl has quoted.[217] That is the manner of our intemperate Irish nature (and I think the Elizabethan English were as volatile); we are quick to speak against our countrymen, but slow to give up our work. I once said to John Synge, 'Do you write out of love or hate for Ireland?' and he replied, 'I have often asked myself that question'; and yet no success outside Ireland seemed of interest to him. Sir Hugh Lane wrote and felt bitterly, and yet when the feeling was at its height, while the Dublin slanders were sounding in his ears, he made a will leaving all he possessed, except the French pictures, to a Dublin gallery. A few days after writing that Ireland had so completely 'disillusioned' him that he could not even bear 'to hear of his early happy days in Galway', he had bequeathed to Dublin an incomparable treasure. I think Mr MacColl by quoting these intimate letters has but proved how stable the subconscious purpose was.

II

Dr Haydn Brown has given evidence to prove the will no final decision.[218] Mr MacColl would put this evidence aside, because the consultations were before the Dublin decision. Well, I offer him a document he cannot put aside. I saw Sir Hugh Lane at Lady Gregory's request on November 4—that is to say, a few days after the writing of the will—and I have before me a careful record of our conversation posted to Lady Gregory the following day. I asked him to offer the pictures to Ireland once more, perhaps after the establishment of the Home Rule Government that seemed coming so quickly, and pointed out that the disgraceful attack upon his pictures and himself had come from ignorant men in accidental power. Generous and irascible beyond any man I have known, he seemed without bitterness, and I[†] will now quote the words of my letter.

> 'All should be allowed to rest for the present'; he wanted 'time to recover his enthusiasms . . . but you may be very sure', he said, 'I have no desire to leave the present Dublin collection to represent me'.

Lady Gregory was to write privately to her subscribers, who had given her many thousands (all returned on the Dublin refusal) for the building of the Dublin gallery,[219] that we hoped to carry through our Dublin plan, 'though we have been defeated for the moment through the passing conditions of economic strife'.

III

Now a wonderful thing happened which certainly did not incline his mind to London. The Trustees, after they had accepted his loan unconditionally, after they had hung his pictures, after he had announced in Dublin (he was still thinking of Dublin) the day when they were to be first shown to the public, decided to make conditions. They would only hang a small collection chosen by themselves; fifteen pictures which they considered 'well worthy of temporary exhibition in the national collection', and they would not hang even these fifteen, unless he promised to bequeath them to the Gallery in his will. The selection was capricious or careless; it rejected, for instance, Daumier's 'Don Quixote', according to the mind of some of us a master work surpassing all the rest in beauty.[220] Sir Hugh Lane, though his new will was only some three months old, refused both conditions.

It became exceedingly difficult to get any reparation made to him for the Dublin Press attack; all his enemies were heartened. The rumour ran: 'The National Gallery in London has refused the Lane pictures because they are not good enough'. He considered himself abominably treated, and remained, so far as I know, of this mind to the end. On November 12, 1914, he wrote to an official of the National Gallery: 'I will leave the pictures at the National Gallery as you wish. I understand that my distinguished friends who are responsible for their being at the National Gallery are hoping to arrange to exhibit them at the Tate Gallery. It was this suggestion that induced me to refrain from publishing the particulars of the annoying affair . . . I cannot even return the pictures to Dublin without removing the slur that has been cast upon them'.

IV

From early in 1914 his London friends tried once more to secure the pictures for London and certainly at first they had heavy work, for the Trustees had not been ingratiating; he was once more 'quite out of sympathy with the English National Gallery'. Mrs Shine[221] remembers a conversation on March 3 or 4 when he flatly refused. Mr Witt, Mr MacColl, and Mr Aitken do, however, claim that they did get in the end a conditional promise, but they have not claimed and cannot claim that the condition was fulfilled.[222] 'He was prepared', says Mr Aitken in the *Morning Post,* 'to give at any rate his French pictures to whichever city seemed first ready to show some appreciation'. And Mr MacColl says that on March 5, 1914, he promised 'to wait and see what appreciation of them was shown, the test being the foundation of a gallery'.

These sentences are vague. There was clearly nothing in the nature of a compact. It was plain that he reserved for his own judgement what constituted 'some appreciation'. The only document cited by Mr MacColl in support of these memories is a letter written in February to an official of the National Gallery saying that if his pictures could lead to the establishment of an international gallery in London—'a crying want'—he would 'be greatly tempted to give them', but added 'I refuse to give any definite promise, as I do not intend to act hastily'. I will assume that he was ready, or at the moment ready or half ready to give his French pictures to an international gallery, but I do not believe that this man whom I know to have been even more tenacious than excitable, would have given a single picture but that he believed he could buy as good or better for the gallery that was created from his fancy as his lasting monument.

The matter is one of merely biographical and psychological interest now. Mr Witt and his friends may believe that if he had lived, he would have liked their present plan and have endowed it, but Parliament will only concern itself, I believe, with intentions while he lived. 'He told me', said Mr Aitken, 'that he intended altering his will in favour of Dublin if his French pictures were not to be exhibited in London'; and they were not exhibited.

V

His interest in Dublin was returning; he had become Director of the National Gallery there.[223] Dublin became as little distasteful to him as any place can be to a man whose nerves are kept upon edge by bad health and the desire to achieve more than the public opinion of his time permits of. He took a keener interest in his Municipal Gallery, and began to give it gifts once more, adding to it, for instance, a fine bust by Rodin. After all, Dublin had founded a gallery for him, and exhibited his French pictures for years, and that gallery was well attended, and among the rest by working people. His most vehement years had been expended in its service; it could but remain his chief work, his monument to future generations, and lacking important pictures that he had gathered for it, that noble monument would lack a limb. Was it not more natural to wish to leave behind him a small perfect thing with the pattern of his own mind than to be half remembered for a bequest soon lost in the growing richness of a London gallery? More than all the rest, he was Irish and of a family that had already in their passion and in their thought given great gifts to the people.

VI

In January, 1915, he told his sister that he was about to make a new will; and in February, 1915, he wrote the codicil, leaving the

French pictures once more to the Municipal Gallery in Harcourt Street. He wrote it so carefully that his sister is convinced that he must have made several drafts. It was well written, and he was accustomed to write even a letter with difficulty. He had always a prejudice against lawyers, and had dictated his two previous wills to his sister, and it was to her now that he addressed the envelope in which the codicil was sealed. It was signed but it was not witnessed, and she has testified that neither of his previous wills, neither that which left all he possessed to the Municipal Gallery, nor that leaving the French pictures to London, would have been witnessed but for her persistency. When he made the second will, he had forgotten all that she had said at the making of the first. He was a man of no business habits in the ordinary sense of the word, and though he never forgot any detail about a picture that once interested him, nothing else seemed to stay in his mind. If he remembered anything she had told him about the need of a witness, he perhaps thought that a postscript to an already witnessed will needed no new formality. Being signed and in his own handwriting, even as it is, it would be legal in Scotland or the trenches. If he had not gone down in the *Lusitania,* he would have spoken about it to someone and have learnt his mistake, and I cannot believe that a great English institution would wish to benefit by a German act of war. When he wrote, he expected to start for America, not in seven or eight weeks as he did, but in three or four, and he felt the danger of the journey so acutely that at first he had refused to go unless those who invited him would insure his life for 50,000 pounds to clear his estate of certain liabilities in case of death. For what purpose could that codicil have been written if he did not believe it to be legal, and certainly it was written with the thought of death in his mind?

VII

Mr Aitken says that he told Sir Hugh Lane shortly before he left for America that there was at last some real likelihood of the international gallery, and that Sir Hugh Lane said that he would decide the ultimate destination of the pictures, as Mr MacColl puts it, 'according to the action of the authorities in London and Dublin respectively'. A vague sentence that committed him to nothing even if he lived (especially as he was about to withdraw his claim for the bridge site, his one serious difficulty with the Corporation), and the codicil was a provision for his death. Mr Witt thinks that by leaving it unwitnessed he meant to keep 'the question of a change of destination' for the French pictures in suspense. We can put aside all such speculation. The day before he left Dublin and two days before he left England (for he spent but a day in London, I believe) he told Mrs Duncan, Curator of the Dublin Municipal Gallery, that he was about to take the French pictures from London, where 'they were not even seen', and rehang them in Dublin, and that he was content if the Corporation gave him a gallery on a site of their own choice.[224] He had not decided merely, as he might well have done, that because if he died now he would have no chance of endowing both galleries, his own gallery must have all he had collected for it. It was plain that even if he lived he would wait no longer, negotiate no more. He was very delicate and had already explained, in conversation with a Dublin alderman, the impatience which had caused some of his Dublin troubles by saying that he wanted to see his gallery finished as he would not live long. He told his friend, Mr Martin, who travelled with him to Liverpool, that he was giving the pictures to Dublin.[225] He had found waiting him in London as a last exasperation a bill of some pounds for mending his frames, damaged on their journey from Dublin to the cellars in Trafalgar Square, and his language was sufficiently definite.

Just before the *Lusitania* sailed from America he told Mr John Quinn, a well-known lawyer and one of the governing body of the Metropolitan Museum of New York, that 'if they would make some provision for a gallery . . . not necessarily the bridge site, he would give them (the pictures), as he always meant them to go there'.

VIII

The clause in the will of 1913 leaving the French pictures to London was founded upon a misunderstanding of the intentions of the London Trustees and in 'momentary irritation', and has no moral weight. The codicil has as much moral weight as any such document ever had or could have, and I believe that Parliament will give it the effect of law. Dublin is prepared to build for the pictures a suitable gallery. Even on Mr Aitken's own test Dublin has shown 'some appreciation' first. I gave evidence some twelve months ago before what I believe to be the Finance Committee of the Dublin Corporation, and the Lord Mayor, at my request, renewed the promise, already upon the books of the Corporation, of a suitable building. The Lord Mayor and the Corporation and representatives of all the principal learned and educational societies in Dublin and such distinguished men as Mr William Orpen, Sir Horace Plunkett, Mr George Russell, and Mr George Bernard Shaw have asked the Trustees for an act of generosity and of justice, and we shall ask Parliament to make that act possible.[226]

W. B. Yeats

P. S. Lady Gregory has asked me to say that she regrets that Mr MacColl, carried away by the excitement of discussion, should have published certain intimate letters of Sir Hugh Lane which she gave him 'after much hesitation for biographical purposes alone'. They were written 'in a dark transitory mood' and cannot be understood apart from the life and letters in their entirety. She adds, 'of course I do not imagine that Mr MacColl did this with the knowledge or consent of the National Gallery Trustees. It was certainly done without mine'. Mr MacColl points out that in a letter, published in *The Times*, certain letters were wrongly dated. I had found out the error immediately and written to withdraw the letter and to substitute another which I enclosed. *The Times* promised to make the substitution, but the political crisis was at its height, and after a considerable delay the original uncorrected letter was published.[227]

There is a misunderstanding in Mr Konody's sympathetic letter.[228] The pictures given by him and others to the Dublin Municipal Gallery are still there. They are not involved in the present dispute.

MAJOR ROBERT GREGORY[229]

A NOTE OF APPRECIATION

I have known no man accomplished in so many ways as Major Robert Gregory, who was killed in action a couple of weeks ago and buried by his fellow-airmen in the beautiful cemetery at Padua. His very accomplishment hid from many his genius. He had so many sides: painter, classical scholar, scholar in painting and in modern literature, boxer, horseman, airman—he had the Military Cross and the Légion d'Honneur—that some among his friends were not sure what his work would be. To me he will always remain a great painter in the immaturity of his youth, he himself the personification of handsome youth. I first came to understand his genius when, still almost a boy, he designed costumes and scenery for the Abbey Theatre. Working for a theatre that could only afford a few pounds for the staging of a play, he designed for Lady Gregory's *Kincora*† and her *Image* and for my *Shadowy Waters* and for Synge's *Deirdre of the Sorrows* decorations which, obtaining their effect from the fewest possible lines and colours, had always the grave distinction of his own imagination.[230] When he began to paint, accustomed to an older school of painting, I was long perplexed by what seemed to me neglect of detail. But in a few years I came to care for his paintings of the Clare coast, with its cloud shadows upon blue-grey stony hills, and for one painting of a not very different scenery by his friend, Innes, more than for any contemporary landscape painting.[231] A man of letters may perhaps find in work such as this, or in old Chinese painting, in the woodcuts and etchings of Calvert and Palmer, in Blake's woodcuts to Thornton's Virgil, in the landscape background of Mr Ricketts's† *Wise and Foolish*

Virgins,[232] something that he does not find in the great modern masters, and that he cares for deeply. Is it merely that these men share certain moods with great lyric poetry, with, let us say, the 'Leech[†] Gatherer' of Wordsworth;[233] or that their moods, unlike those of men with more objective curiosity, are a part of the traditional expression of the soul? One always understood by something in his selection of line and of colour that he had read his Homer and his Virgil and his Dante; that they, while giving something of themselves, had freed him from easy tragedy and trivial comedy.

Though he often seemed led away from his work by some other gift, his attitude to life and art never lost intensity—he was never the amateur. I have noticed that men whose lives are to be an ever-growing absorption in subjective beauty—and I am not mainly remembering Calvert's philosophy of myth and his musical theory, or Verlaine's sensuality, or Shelley's politics—seek through some lesser gift, or through mere excitement, to strengthen that self which unites them to ordinary men. It is as though they hesitated before they plunged into the abyss. Major Gregory told Mr Bernard Shaw, who visited him in France, that the months since he joined the Army had been the happiest of his life.[234] I think they brought him peace of mind, an escape from that shrinking, which I sometimes saw upon his face, before the growing absorption of his dream, the loneliness of his dream, as from his constant struggle to resist those other gifts that brought him ease and friendship. Leading his squadron in France or in Italy, mind and hand were at one, will and desire.

27

THE IRISH
DRAMATIC MOVEMENT[235]

A LETTER TO THE STUDENTS
OF A CALIFORNIAN SCHOOL

I. THE PRELUDE

Twenty years ago I was entertained at dinner by certain monks or friars in a Californian village that I forget the name of.[236] I was to lecture to their students, who were all of Irish descent, and as I walked to the hall under moonlight, through a quadrangle of palm-trees, I felt some anxiety. I had been given home-brewed wine, and thinking it as harmless as the raisin-wine or ginger-wine of Ireland or England, had drunk incautiously, and it had gone to my head. I felt slightly stupid, and wondered if it would spoil the lecture; but I had not spoken for five minutes before I felt at my ease.

I quoted some fragment of Young Ireland poetry, and there was just that immediate applause that would have welcomed it at home. As I went on speaking I felt that those lads, not one of whom had, it may be, seen Ireland, did not differ from Dublin lads of the same age in imagination or in literary knowledge. It pleases me to think that school has changed in nothing, except that it is no longer per-mitted to brew its own wine; and I will therefore—being a little chilled by the vast audience our editor has promised me—address my letter to its students. I will suppose that my letter is being read out, and that all students under fifteen years of age will be sent to bed before the reading begins, and that those who remain know the Ireland of history, while they are ignorant of modern Ireland.

II. THE LETTER

Some twenty-four years ago, Lady Gregory, who was near her fiftieth year, and I, who was in my early thirties, planned the foundation of an Irish Theatre, and we were soon joined by John Synge, who was in his late twenties. Lady Gregory had spent most of her life between two great houses in South Galway, while Synge had wandered over half Europe with his fiddle, and I had gone to and fro between Dublin and London. Yet Synge and I—like Lady Gregory —were people of the country; I because of my childhood and youth in Sligo, and he because of his in Wicklow. We had gone, all three, from cottage to cottage, collecting stories and hearing songs, and we thought that in these we had discovered that portion of the living mind of Ireland that was most beautiful and distinguished, and we wished to bring what we had discovered to Dublin, where, it seemed to us, the popular mind had grown harsh and ugly. We did not think that the Irish country lacked vice; we were even to be denounced because we insisted that they had the brutalities of country people elsewhere; but we were certain of the beauty of the songs and stories.

Lady Gregory had taken down a song in Irish—'The Grief of a Girl's Heart' it is called—and one day she showed it to a Gaelic-speaking man at her door, and asked what were the best verses. He picked just those verses that I would have picked—those that are most wild and strange, most unlike anything that is called 'popular poetry':

> My heart is black as the blackness of the sloe, or as the
> coal that is left on the smith's forge; or as the sole of a
> shoe left in white halls; it was you put that darkness over
> my life.

> You have taken the East from me; you have taken the
> West from me; you have taken what is before me and
> what is behind me. You have taken the moon, you have
> taken the sun from me; and my fear is great that you
> have taken God from me![237]

Amid your semi-tropical scenery, you think of Ireland as a far-off country of romance, and you will find it hard to understand one very prosaic reality. If a man is creating some new thing he has to question the taste of others, and that makes those others angry, and all the more if that new thing is a part of something they have long looked down upon as ignorant or foolish or old-fashioned. Then, too, even if he does not openly question the taste of others, it will be a long time before they can see the beauty that he has seen. I think it was George Henry Lewes[†] who said that at first he could see no merit in the Elgin Marbles;[238] and I remember an essay by Andrew Lang, in which he apologised for some attack on the poetry of my generation saying that when he first met with the poetry of that very great poet, Paul Verlaine, he thought it no better than the rhymes in some country newspaper.[239] George Henry Lewes and Andrew Lang had much taste and great erudition. We had to convince average men and women, and to do this by an art that must blunder and experiment that it might find some new form.

If any of you become artists or poets, do not ask a welcome from great crowds, but write at first for a few friends, and always for a comparatively few people—not because you scorn the crowd, but because you think so well of it that you will offer it nothing but your best. In a few generations—but a short time in the history of a masterpiece—that crowd will speak of you with respect, if you are a great artist or poet, and a sufficient number will study what you have made with pleasure and profit.

We thought that Irish drama would be historical or legendary, and in verse or romantic prose; neither Synge nor Lady Gregory had written plays nor had indeed thought of doing so; so it was I—my head full of poetical drama—that gave the theatre its first impulse. After an experiment with English actors, we began our real work in 1902 in a little temperance hall in a back street, and chose our players from boys and girls, whose interests were, with a couple of exceptions, more political than literary. For the next two or three years we moved from hall to hall making some reputation among students of literature, and among young patriots who thought a theatre with Irish plays might strengthen national feeling, but much derided by the newspapers. One night I came in front of the curtain and asked the audience to support us against our enemies. I quoted from a leading article in one of the morning newspapers, which had said: 'Mr Yeats proposes to perform foreign masterpieces'—that was part of our project at the time—'Foreign masterpieces are very dangerous things'.[240] I was angry; I should, perhaps, have remembered that the Elgin Marbles are 'foreign masterpieces', and that some of the figures are very unclothed. Among my audience was an English friend, Miss Horniman. I had been hoping—she had made one or two hints—that she would give us a subscription, and as she was rich, I had fixed upon twenty pounds as the amount. She came up to me the moment I had finished, and said: 'I will buy or build you a theatre'. In the next few months she bought and rebuilt a little old theatre that had been part of a Mechanics' Institute, and we opened there in the winter of 1903–04.

Our obscurity made it possible to create a new kind of acting, for it gave us time to prepare and experiment. If our players had been stage-struck young men and women of the usual kind, they would have developed much more quickly; but their art would have been the ordinary stage art of their time. I had once been asked, at the end of a lecture, where we would get our players, for at that time there were neither Irish players nor Irish plays. I answered with the first thing that came into my head: 'I will go into a room where there are a lot of people, and write all the names on slips of paper and drop them into a hat, shake them up, and take out twelve slips. I will ask those twelve people to act our plays'.[241]

Certainly William Fay, an electric light fitter, who was also an actor of genius, had some experience, for he had toured Ireland in a company with a negro actor-manager; and his brother, Frank Fay, was learned in the history of the stage, and fond of reciting poetry. But our women players were almost chosen at hazard. They all belonged to a political association, 'The Daughters of Erin', that described itself as educating the children of the poor, but was described by its enemies as teaching a catechism that began with the question: 'What is the origin of evil?' and the answer was—'England!' From this Association we got two actresses of genius—Miss Sara Allgood, and Miss Máire[†] O'Neill.[242] They grew but slowly to skill and power because, acting at first more from patriotism than ambition, they were never tempted to copy some popular favourite. They copied, under the guidance of William Fay, the life they had seen in their own homes, or saw during some country visit; or they searched, under the guidance of Frank Fay or of myself, for some traditional measured speech to express those emotions that we feel, but cannot observe.

I soon saw that their greatest success would be in comedy, or in observed tragedy; not in poetical drama, which needs considerable poetical and general culture. I had found an old Dublin pamphlet about the blind beggar, 'Zozimus'[†,243] and noticed that whereas the parts written in ordinary English are badly written, certain long passages in dialect are terse and vivid. I pointed this out to Lady Gregory, and said if we could persuade our writers to use dialect, no longer able to copy the newspapers, or some second-rate English author, they would become original and vigorous. Perhaps no one reason ever drives one to anything. Perhaps I do not remember clearly after so many years; but I believe it was that thought that made me write, with Lady Gregory's help, *The Pot of Broth,* and *Cathleen ni Houlihan.* The dialect in those two plays is neither rich nor supple, for I had not the right ear, and Lady Gregory had not as yet taken down among the cottages two hundred thousand words of folklore. But they began the long series of plays that have given our theatre the greater portion of its fame.

I once said to John Synge, 'Why is it that an early Renaissance building is so much more beautiful than anything that followed?' And he replied 'Style is from the shock of new material'. It was the shock of new material that gave our plays and players their admirable style. I insist on the word 'style'. When I saw Miss O'Neill play the old drunken woman in *The Tinker's Wedding,* at the Birmingham Repertory Theatre a few years ago, I thought her performance incredibly distinguished—nothing second-hand, nothing from the common stock of the stage; no *cliché,* no recognition of all that traditional humour about drunken women.[244]

Lady Gregory's little farces are the only farces of modern times that have not only humour but the beauty of style; and her tragedy, *The Gaol Gate,* is a classic, and not because of its action, for it has no action, but because of its style. One need not commend the style of John Synge's famous plays—*The Well of the Saints,* or *The Playboy, The Riders to the Sea, Deirdre of the Sorrows.*[245] Should our Abbey Theatre come to an end, should our plays cease to be acted, we shall be remembered, I think, because we were the first to give to the English-speaking Ireland a mastery of style by turning a dialect that had been used hitherto with a comic purpose to a purpose of beauty. If I were your professor of literature (I must remind myself that *you* hear me, while others but overhear) and were compelled to choose examples of fine prose for an Irish reading book, I would take some passages from Swift, some from Burke, one perhaps from Mitchel[†] (unless his mimicry of Carlyle put me off) and from that on find no comparable passages till *The Gaol Gate* and the last act of *Deirdre of the Sorrows*. I would then set my pupils to show that this strange English, born in the country cottages, is a true speech with as old a history as the English of Shakespeare, and that it takes its vocabulary from Tudor England and its construction from the Gaelic.

The dialect drama in the hands of Mr Fitzmaurice, Mr T. C. Murray, Mr Lennox Robinson, Mr Boyle, Mr Daniel Corkery, and Mr Sean O'Kelly, and of Mr Padraic Colum in one of his plays, took a new turn.[246] Synge and Lady Gregory were as little interested in social questions as the old men and women whose stories they had heard and copied; but our new dramatists were, in imagination and sympathy, mainly of the city. The countryman is much alone, and if, as happened through all the Middle Ages, when the most beautiful of our stories were invented, he is of a violent and passionate nature, he seeks relief from himself in stories or in songs full of delicate emotion: he delights, perhaps, in Arthur and his Court. In the cities, however, men who are in continual contact with one another have for their first need not the beauty but, as I think, the truth of human life. They suffer much from irritation, anger, jealousy; and in their hearts they desire to be shown that, though capitalist and labourer, Nationalist and Unionist, Republican and Free Stater, even honest men and bribed, differ in one thing, they are alike in a hundred. They wish to see themselves and the enemy of their working hours explained, derided or bantered, with at least occasional good humour, though they are not philosophic enough to know that art is the chief intellectual form of charity. When some play of this kind is acted, they are startled, sometimes angry, sometimes incredulous; but they are not bored. They cannot be shown too many such plays if we are not to murder or be murdered because we have given or received some partisan name. Such plays, in the hands of the writers I have named, have dealt with the life of the shop and workshop, and of the well-off farmer, more often than of those small farms of Connaught where there is so much folklore; and the scene is laid, as a general rule, in or near some considerable town, and their speech comes close to modern English. Except in the plays of Mr Lennox Robinson, however, where some character is introduced whose speech has no admixture of dialect, characterisation becomes conventional and dialogue stilted. They introduce such characters so often that I wonder at times if the dialect drama has not exhausted itself—if most of those things have not been said that our generation wants to have said in that particular form. Perhaps, having created certain classics, the dramatic genius of Ireland will pass on to something else.

What new form shall we invent? Or shall we but find new material, and so give the old form new interest? Perhaps on the whole it is likely that we shall but find new material. Ireland is full of tragedy and ruin; and though at the moment we have to reject the few new plays that deal with it, because they are full of the distortion of party feeling, that phase will pass. In a year or two there will be personal narratives, separate incidents which detach themselves. Motives will become apparent; we shall be able to see it all separated from our own fears and hopes, as if upon the luminous table of a *camera obscura*. We have to make peace among so many passions that are the most violent Ireland has known in modern days—violent not only because there has been so much suffering, but because great intellectual questions are involved. When should we distinguish between political and private morality, or is there only one morality? What is the part of the Catholic Church in public life? How far must the State respect humanitarian emotion? As all these things have been fought out in country districts, or, if in towns, by those classes which still use a language that has in some degree what is 'dialect'—that is to say, elements peculiar to Ireland—I have a little hope that I shall not be compelled, as one of the readers for the Abbey Theatre, to read through a great number of plays in ordinary English, where all is bookish and pedantic, or full of humourous or sentimental *clichés*.

Yet perhaps my first thought is correct, and that we are about to create a new form, and that this form will deal more with those classes who have lost almost every distinctive Irish form of speech. The other day a strange Irish novel was published—*Ulysses,* by Mr James Joyce—which is certainly a new form.[247] You are too young to read it—your master would rightly take it from you. It would cost you some pounds to buy a copy, and if you bought it you would be too startled by its incredible coarseness to see its profundity.

Every other successful Irish novel—certainly every other whose name I can recall at the moment—resembles our plays in dealing with some simple story of public or private life by the light of a morality which everyone accepts without hesitation. Great works of art have been written in that way—the comedies of Oliver Goldsmith, and nearly all the comedies of Molière, for instance. But there are other works which are also, as a famous Belgian poet said a masterpiece must be, a portion of the conscience of mankind, and which judge all by the light of some modern discovery.[248] Something which has been there always—more constantly there, indeed, than Tony Lumpkins or the miser[249]—but which has not been noticed, is brought out into the light that we may perceive it is beautiful or good, or most probably evil or ugly. The plays of Strindberg or Tchekof are of this kind, and it is such works, whether novels or plays, that are most characteristic of intellectual Europe to-day.

We have already two such plays in Mr Lennox Robinson's *Round Table* and his *Crabbed Youth;* and it looks as if the audience that welcomed his *Whiteheaded Boy*[†] and the other plays in his old manner will give them a sufficient welcome.[250] It is wavering; the shorter play it has delighted in, but the longer, which more openly calls in question a traditional point of view, leaves it a little cold. Mr Robinson has taught us to laugh at, and therefore to judge, a certain exaggeration of domesticity, a helpless clinging to the one resolute person that we had all perhaps noticed in some Irish house or other without knowing that we had noticed it.

He has not made his characters speak in dialect, for he is describing a characteristic that, though it may exist among peasants, needs a certain degree of leisure for its full display; one of those tragedies almost that only begin, as Maeterlinck said, when we have closed the door and lighted the lamp—almost a malady of contemplation.[251] Should some other of our dramatists use the same form, he will have spent many years, like Mr Joyce or like Mr Lennox Robinson, in the education of his judgment, and not only that he may keep his dialogue pure without the protection of a particular form of speech, but that he may judge where judgment has hitherto slept. Then he must be ready to wait—his audience may be slow to understand—for a long time, it may be, to do without all that pleasant companionship that belongs to those who are content only to laugh at those things that everybody laughs at.

He will have to help him a company of players who, though they are still masters of dialect alone, love work and experiment, and so constantly surprise us by some unforeseen success, and a theatre that, having no director or shareholder to pay, uses the profits on its more popular plays to experiment with plays that may never make a profit at all. The audience, though it has coarsened under the influence of public events and constant political discussion, is yet proud of its intelligence and of its old hospitality, and may be won over in time. Yet it may be a bitter struggle—one can never tell; as bitter as any Synge had to endure. And you, perhaps, walking among your palm trees under that Californian sunlight, may well ask yourself what it is that compels a man to make his own cup bitter?

2 8

NOBEL PRIZE ACCEPTANCE[252]

I have been all my working life indebted to the Scandinavian Nation. When I was a very young man, I spent several years writing in collaboration with a friend the first interpretation of the philosophy of the English poet Blake.[253] Blake was first a disciple of your great Swedenborg and then in violent revolt and then half in revolt, half in discipleship. My friend and I were constantly driven to Swedenborg for an interpretation of some obscure passage, for Blake is always in his mystical writings extravagant, paradoxical, obscure. Yet he has had upon the last forty years of English imaginative thought the influence which Coleridge had upon the preceding forty; and he is always in his poetry, often in his theories of painting, the interpreter or the antagonist of Swedenborg.[254] Of recent years I have gone to Swedenborg for his own sake, and when I received your invitation to Stockholm, it was to his biography that I went for information. Nor do I think that our Irish theatre could have ever come into existence but for the theatre of Ibsen and Bjørnson. And now you have conferred upon me this great honour. Thirty years ago a number of Irish writers met together in societies and began a remorseless criticism of the literature of their country. It was their dream that by freeing it from provincialism they might win for it European recognition. I owe much to those men, still more to those who joined our movement a few years later, and when I return to Ireland these men and women, now growing old like myself, will see in this great honour a fulfillment of that dream. I in my heart know how little I might have deserved it if they had never existed.

29

MISS SARA ALLGOOD[255]

Miss Sara Allgood is a great folk-actress. As so often happens with a great actor or actress, she rose into fame with a school of drama. She was born to play the old woman in *The Well of the Saints*,[256] and to give their first vogue to Lady Gregory's little comedies. It is impossible for those of us who are connected with the Abbey management to forget the night in December, 1904, when for the first time she rushed among the stage crowd in *Spreading the News*,† calling out, 'Give me back my man!'[257] We never knew until that moment that we had, not only a great actress, but that rarest of all things, a woman comedian; for stage humour is almost a male prerogative.

It has been more difficult in recent years to supply her with adequate parts, for Dublin is a little tired of its admirable folk-arts, political events having turned our minds elsewhere. Perhaps the Spaniard, Sierra, who in his plays expounds a psychological and modern purpose through sharply defined characters, themselves as little psychological and modern as Mrs Broderick herself, may give her the opportunity she needs.[258] I am looking forward with great curiosity to seeing her in his *Two Shepherds,* which is now just going into rehearsal, and one of our Irish dramatists, Mr Casey, has, in his new play, *Juno and the Paycock,* given her an excellent part.[259]

Miss Allgood is no end of a problem, and the sooner our dramatists get that into their heads and write for her the better for them and us. If we knew how to appreciate our geniuses, they would not have wasted her so scandalously.

A MEMORY OF SYNGE[260]

A correspondent has sent me the following little essay with the comment 'A short time ago I read Synge's life, and it seemed to me rather lacking in the personal touch, so I wrote down these few memories'.[261] Where we have so little with that 'touch', I am grateful as an old friend of Synge's, and I have asked the *Irish Statesman* to put the essay into print that it may remain for some future biographer. John Synge was a very great man, and in time to come every passing allusion that recalls him, whether in old newspaper articles or in old letters, will be sought out that historians of literature may mould, or try to mould, some simple image of the man. Even before the war, invention had begun, for a tolerably well-known American journalist, who had never been under the same roof with Synge, or even set eyes upon him, published scenes and conversations, that were all, from no malicious intention but because of his gross imagination, slander and travesty.[262] He based all upon what he supposed the inventor of so many violent and vehement peasants must be like, knowing so little of human character that he described, without knowing it, Synge's antithesis. I have left my correspondent's notes as they came from her unpractised hand, trivial and important alike. That praise of Wordsworth, for instance, is nothing in itself. To say that 'Wordsworth is more at one with Nature' than some other, is too vague to increase our knowledge, but it recalls some early work of Synge's, certain boyish reveries, that I excluded from his collected edition but not from material that his biographers might use, in which he described minutely brook or coppice—I have forgotten which—a shadowed, limited place, such as children love.[263] I had not known of his passion for Wordsworth, and to know it completes the image. Then again, his liking for Patrick Street has reminded me that a little before his death he planned to make it the scene of a play. I remember that 'little house' in Paris; it was one room which cost him two or three francs a week, yet was not in a slum, but had its own front door and even, I think, some kind of little hall between the front door and room door, and was at the top of a decent house full of flats near the Luxembourg.[264] Paris, as an old astrologer said to me once, is a good town for a poor man, or so it was twenty years ago. I do not know why I have not crossed out that allusion to *Dana*, 'a very short-lived but delightful paper . . . too remote from the world of thought',† except that it might give pleasure to *Dana*'s embittered editor.[265] C. H. H. has lent me the photograph she speaks of, but the *Irish Statesman* has no means of publishing such things. It shows a face less formed and decisive than the face of later years.

W. B. Yeats

COMPULSORY GAELIC[266]

Persons: Peter, a Senator
　　　　 Paul, a Deputy
　　　　 Timothy, an elderly student

PETER.

We will catch nothing, so I may as well listen to you. They have dynamited the fish, and several seasons will pass before there are enough trout to make a day's fishing. Let us put our rods against a tree and eat our lunch. I see Timothy coming along the river path, and I do not suppose he has had any better luck. While I am making the fire, you can explain that incredible doctrine of yours.

PAUL.

Which doctrine, for I have a number which you consider incredible.

PETER.

I mean what you said in the train, when you told me that you were about to vote scholarships or something of that kind for Gaelic speakers.

PAUL.

Our general culture cannot be better than that of the English-speaking world as a whole, and is more likely to be worse. We are on the banks of a river that flows through an industrial town and bathe in its waters. But visit certain small nations—one of the Scandinavian nations, let us say—and you will notice at once that not only education, but general well-being are better distributed there, and when you ask how they manage it, somebody says 'our people are so few that we can reach everybody'. Everybody you meet speaks several languages well enough for commercial purposes and travel, but only one well enough for intimacy. Kings, nobles, farmers, professional men, socialists and reactionaries, novelists and poets grow up with a common life, from which nothing can separate them. Their rich or able men seldom drift away permanently, for if they find themselves in London or New York or Paris, they feel but strangers there. They may perhaps be less rich than men of equal ability, who belong to some English-speaking nation, and so manipulate greater resources, material or living, but their ability or their riches create in their own country a habit of energy and a tradition of well-being. No bond constrains, because no man compels; they but accept a limitation like that imposed upon a sculptor by the stone in which he works. Would not Ireland have gained if Mr Bernard Shaw and Oscar Wilde, let us say, and the various Ryans and O'Briens who have enriched America, had grown up with such a limitation, and thought they were strangers everywhere but in Ireland?[†] Then, too, I could discover with a little research the names of actors and singers who might at this moment be performing in some Dublin State Theatre or State Opera House, but for the damnable convenience of the English tongue.

PETER.

If we have no State Theatre or State Opera House, we have the Abbey Theatre, and have all commended *Juno and the Paycock*.

PAUL.

We may keep the author of the play, but how long shall we keep the players that give it so great a part of its life? A great Empire buys every talent that it can use and for the most part spoils what it buys. If we keep a good comedian, it is generally because his art, being an art of dialect, interests few but ourselves. A play called *Peg o' my Heart*—a stage mechanism without literary value—because it contained one dialect part, robbed the Abbey Theatre of four actresses, and almost brought it to an end.[267] If they had been bound to Ireland by a separate language, they would not have gone, they would not have desired to go.

PETER.

You mean that if enforced bonds make hatred those that are obeyed though not enforced, make love.

PAUL.

Norway could never have created the greatest dramatic school of modern times if it had spoken a world-wide language.

PETER.

But surely a nation like Ireland or Norway should be able to pay an actress enough to keep her at home in comfort.

PAUL.

World-wide commercial interests exploit whatever form of expression appeals to the largest possible audience; that is to say, some inferior form; and will always purchase executive talent. The chief actress of Norway, some few years ago, had to threaten to stop acting altogether to get her salary raised from £200 a year.[268] If she had spoken English she could have earned more than that in a week, at some English or American music-hall.

PETER.

Your point seems to be that no nation can prosper unless it uses for itself the greater portion of its talent.

PAUL.

I am not thinking only of talent. The greater part of its creative life—that of the woman of fashion, not less than that of the founder of a business or of a school of thought, should be the jet of a fountain that falls into the basin where it rose.

PETER.

That may or may not be true, but what has it to do with practical affairs? I have heard a man discuss for an hour what would have happened if the library of Alexandria had never been burnt, and another bored me through a windy day on an outside car by describing what Europe might have been if Wilde had never fallen. The Irish language can never again be the language of the whole people.

PAUL.

Why not?

PETER.

Because the Irish people will not consent that it should, having set their hearts on Glasgow and New York.

PAUL.

We shall have to go slowly, making our converts man by man, and yet Ireland should become bilingual in three generations.

PETER.

Those three generations may be the most important since the foundation of Christianity. Architecture, and all the arts associated with architecture are being re-born as though to express a new perception of the inter-dependence of man. Drama and poetry are once more casting out photography, becoming psychological and creative. The experimental verification of a mathematical research—research made possible by the Irishman Rowan Hamilton[269]—has changed the universe into a mathematical formula, and a formula so astounding that it can but alter every thought in our heads. Psychical research interpreted by that formula in thirty years will once more set man's soul above time and change, and make it necessary to reconsider every secular activity. Nations are made neither by language nor by frontier, but by a decision taken in some crisis of intellectual excitement like that which Italy took at the Renaissance, Germany at the Reformation, moments of fusion followed by centuries of cooling and hardening. The whole world draws to such a crisis, and you would cut Ireland off from Europe and plunge it into a controversy that will be incredibly bitter, because it can be fought without ideas and without education.

PAUL.

I see no reason why the Gaelic movement should cut Ireland off from Europe, and I have never spoken a bitter word about an opponent.

PETER.

I know a man who, after certain years of dependence in a great house, has set up as a picture-framer in a country town. He employs a young man, poverty-stricken like himself at the same age, and though this young man is as well educated as himself, compels him to take his meals in the kitchen with the servants. The great house had not driven him to the kitchen, but his offended dignity has demanded an offering. Spinoza thought that nations were like individuals, and that it was no use pulling down a tyrant, for a tyrant is what he is, because of something in the nation. 'Look at the people of England', he said, or some such words. 'They have pulled down Charles, but have had to push up Cromwell in his place.'[270] Can you read an Irish propagandist newspaper, all those threatenings and compellings, and not see that a servitude, far longer than any England has known, has bred into Irish bones a stronger subconscious desire than England ever knew to enslave and to be enslaved? There is no public emotion in the country but resentment, and no man thinks that he serves his cause who does not employ that emotion. If we praise, the praise is unreal, and but given to some reflection of ourselves, but our vituperation is animated and even joyous. We think it effeminate to trust in eloquence and patience, and prefer to make men servile, rather than permit their opinions to differ from our own, and if there is a man notable for intellect and sincerity, we fit some base motive to his every act that he may not prevail against us. We had eloquence some hundred years ago, and had, it seems, when we spoke in Gaelic, popular poetry, but now we have neither—possessing indeed every quality of the negro but his music. We were a proud people once, but have grown so humble, that we have no method of speech or propaganda that the knave cannot use and the dunce understand.

PAUL.

There are a great many people in this country who neither threaten nor impute base motives, and besides what you say, in so far as it is true, describes half the democracy of Europe.

PETER.

Yes, all those who have pulled down a tyrant and would put another in his place.

PAUL.

All this passion means, I suppose, that you object to our teaching Gaelic to those who do not want it.

PETER.

I object to every action which reminds me of a mediaeval humorist compelling a Jew to eat bacon. Especially as in this case Jew compels Jew.

PAUL.

Yet, if a Government can enforce Latin it has a right to enforce Gaelic.

PETER.

I do not deny the right, but I deny that it should be employed in this country except within the narrowest limits.

PAUL.

Ruskin once contended that reading and writing should be optional because what a fool reads does himself harm, and what a fool writes does others harm.[271] That may be a convincing argument, but as our Government accepts the modern theory, I do not see why Gaelic should not be compulsory also. I have had nothing to do with that, however. My work, if I have a work, is to keep it from stupefying. I want the Government to accept the recommendation of the Senate and spend £5,000 a year on Gaelic scholarship; to train a small number of highly-efficient teachers of the living tongue, who should have general European culture; to found scholarships for the best pupils of those teachers; to endow a theatre with a Gaelic and English company, and to make Gaelic an instrument of European culture.[272] There is already a Gaelic company performing Tchekov,[†, 273] and there is much European literature, especially that of countries like Spain and Italy which have a long-settled peasantry that would go better into Gaelic than into English. After all, Sancho Panza is very nearly a Munster farmer.[274] I want the Government to find money for translation by ceasing to print Acts in Gaelic that everybody reads in English.

PETER.

As soon as a play or book is translated, which goes deep into human life, it will be denounced for immorality or irreligion. Certain of our powerful men advocate Gaelic that they may keep out the European mind. They know that if they do not build a wall, this

country will plunge, as Europe is plunging, into philosophic speculation. They hope to put into every place of authority a Gaelic
speaker, and if possible, a native speaker, who has learned all he
knows at his mother's knee.

PAUL.

I have always opposed the making of Irish obligatory for any
post not connected with the language. I want everywhere the best
man with the knowledge appropriate to his post.

PETER.

Once you make Gaelic a political question you are helpless. They
have made it obligatory, and will continue to do so.

PAUL.

That will last a few years. We are all new to public life, but the choice
between wisdom and fanaticism will be good for our intelligence.

PETER.

We are agreed that the future of Ireland depends upon the
choice.

PAUL.

If Gaelic cannot become as I would make it, a disturbing intellectual force, it means . . .

PETER.

A little potato-digging Republic.

PAUL.

No, but Ireland a dull school-book, consequent apathy and final
absorption in the British Empire.

PETER.

You are ready to chance all that?

PAUL.

I believe in the intellectual force created by years of conflict as by
a flint and steel.

[They are joined by Timothy]

TIMOTHY.

I see that you have the kettle boiling.

PAUL.

Had you any luck?

TIMOTHY.

Not a rise, but I saw some good fish floating with their bellies up. I am glad to sit down, for I am old enough to grow tired standing with a useless rod in my hand. What were you disputing about? Peter, you looked a moment ago as if you would fling the kettle into Paul's face, and Paul's face is red.

PETER.

At present we speak English and Gaelic is compulsory in the schools, but Paul wants us to speak Gaelic and make English compulsory in the schools, and I am not sufficiently attracted by the change to plunge the country into a permanent condition of bad manners.

TIMOTHY.

Whatever imagination we have in Ireland to-day, we owe to Gaelic literature or to the effect of Gaelic speech upon the English language. Think of the dialect plays of Synge and of Lady Gregory—of Lady Gregory's translations of the stories of Fionn and of Cuchulain, which have given new classics to the English tongue. I can read a little Gaelic, but I often think I would give some years of life if I could read in the original one of those old poems translated by Kuno Meyer, and the lamentations of *Deirdre*, and read well enough to feel the quality of their style. We can only feel the full beauty of a poem in another language when we can understand without translating as we read, when we can become for the time being a Frenchman, a German, or a Gael, and I sometimes wonder if that is really possible. Those lamentations of *Deirdre* have a poignancy unlike anything in any other European tongue. Surely, there must be something in the vocabulary, in the cadence, corresponding to it, and when I think that these poems were written in this country and by and about its people, it seems to me unbearable that I should be shut out, or partly shut out, from it all.

PAUL.

Then you want to make Gaelic the language of the country?

TIMOTHY.

But, Paul, I am so uncertain about everything, and there is so much to be said upon every side. English literature is, perhaps, the greatest in the world, and I am not in politics. If I were in politics, I would have to be certain, whereas I am an elderly student. I cannot even call myself a scholar, for I know nothing properly. Politics are a roulette wheel with various colours, and if a man is to take a part in the game, he must choose. If he prefers some colour that is not there, or if he be quite undecided, he must put that away and bang down his money firmly. So Peter must oppose the Gaelic movement and you must defend it.

PAUL.

If Ireland gives up Gaelic, it will soon be a suburb of New York.

PETER.

Like somebody in Shakespeare, I think nobly of the soul and refuse to admit that the soul of man or nation is as dependent upon circumstance as all that.

TIMOTHY.

I have held both opinions in the same hour, perhaps in the same minute. It sometimes seems to me, too, that there must be a kind of politics where one need not be certain. After all, imitation is automatic, but creation moves in a continual uncertainty. If we were certain of the future, who would trouble to create it?

PAUL.

I cannot see any means whereby a Parliament can pass uncertainty into law.

TIMOTHY.

I have no practical experience, but perhaps it might be possible to choose a schoolmaster as we choose a painter or a sculptor. 'There is so-and-so', we would say, 'who thinks that Ireland should be Gaelic-speaking, and because he is a very able, cultivated and learned man we will give him a school and let him teach. We ourselves think that he may be wrong, but after all, what does anybody know about it?' I think the knowledge of the Greek language must have come to Renaissance Italy in much that way. No two men, perhaps, would have agreed about its future. To some it meant a better knowledge of the New Testament, and to others—some at the Platonic Academy of Florence, for instance—a re-established worship of the Homeric gods.[275] I am not sure that I like the idea of a State with a definite purpose, and there are moments, unpractical moments, perhaps, when I think that the State should leave the mind free to create. I think Aristotle defined the soul as that which moves itself, and how can it move itself if everything is arranged beforehand?

PETER.

Do you mean to say that you would appoint a schoolmaster, not only to teach Irish, but that it must be the living language of Ireland, although you thought what he attempted neither desirable nor possible?

TIMOTHY.

Perhaps neither desirable nor possible, but remember I would not appoint him if I did not like him, and because I have always liked Peter, if he wanted to teach that English was the only proper language for the Irish people, I would appoint him also. I generally dislike the people of Ulster, and want to keep them out—when I was in Belfast a few years ago they had only one bookshop—but I am told the Government wants to bring them in, so it might be well to give a school to some likeable Orangeman and let him teach Orangeism there.[276] In fact, I am almost certain that the Education Office that would please me best, would choose schoolmasters much as a good hostess chooses her guests. It should never invite anybody to teach who is a bore or in any way disagreeable.

PETER.

Timothy, you have not shed any light upon the subject.

PAUL.

None whatever.

3 2

ROYAL IRISH SOCIETY AWARDS
AT THE TAILTEANN FESTIVAL

The awards are quite different from those given last Friday at the
Abbey Theatre to writers who sent in work for competition.[277] It
was inevitable that there should be writers who would not enter
any competition, and it seemed to the committee of Aonach Tailteann that authors should be crowned irrespective of competition.
The task of the adjudicators was simply to pick out the best writers
of the last three years resident in Ireland. They selected for the
awards a book of scholarship, a work of fiction, and two books of
verse, one of these which is by a very young writer, more for its
promise than for its achievement. When we came to consider the
books of scholarship, seeing that we are not learned men but creative artists, it seemed to us but right that we should give the award
to some book that united scholarship to great beauty of form.
There, perhaps, we have a little right to be heard, whereas upon a
work of pure learning we have no right.

We have, therefore, awarded the prize to Mr Stephen MacKenna[†]
for volume two of his noble translation of Plotinus.[278] No one, to our
knowledge, within the period fixed, united scholarship to a prose style
so austere and beautiful as that Mr MacKenna has fashioned to his
purpose, a style which at its best recalls the greater masters of English. The prose in which the Enneads are rendered enables us to
appreciate the intellectual passion of Plotinus; and to be able to
communicate to us his own love for his original may be held to be
one of the great virtues of a translator. The scholar who is not also
a man of letters rarely conveys character or atmosphere, and what
is noble in style in the original becomes undistinguished in the trans-

lation. So some sacred books, and poetry, which is half sacred liter-ature, have become secular and lost their divinity, or the poetry has evaporated because the translator has not the gift of style. The learning displayed by Mr MacKenna has been praised by many, yet the highest praise we can give is to say that this translation in its beauty, dignity and lucidity affects us as if it had been an original work of genius. When he translated Plotinus on 'Beauty' we may say of it in Milton's words, 'mine author sung it me'.[279] 'And one that shall know this vision—with what passion of love shall he not be seized, with what pang of desire, what longing to be molten into this, what wondering delight'.[280] We feel when we close the passage that he, too, has been seized by longing 'to fly to the beloved Fatherland', and the emotion in the words is that of one who has himself seen the vision.

In making the award for a book of fiction we have not thought well on this occasion, to consider dramatic literature. By far the greater part of the dramatic work produced in Ireland has been pro-duced at the Abbey Theatre, and with that theatre two of us are so intimately connected that it would be difficult for us to judge dis-passionately between play and play.

Having ruled plays out of our award, we have, therefore, only to consider the work of our novelists. We need not consider Mr Padraic Colum's *Castle Conquer* nor Mr James Joyce's *Ulysses,* nor Mr George Moore's *Conversations in Ebury Street,* as they are excluded by our definition, which requires that an author shall be domiciled in Ireland.[281] We feel, however, that it is our duty to say that Mr James Joyce's book, though as obscene as 'Rabelais', and therefore forbidden by law in England and the United States, is more indu-bitably a work of genius than any prose written by an Irishman since the death of Synge.[282] Lord Dunsany has created a strange and beau-tiful world, but he has only succeeded in imposing upon that world form and discipline in a few short plays and in a few scattered pages, and none of these were published in our period. We have anxiously considered his *Chronicles of Rodriguez* and his *King of Elfland's Daughter,* and set them aside with regret.[283] We admit the great merit of Mr Michael Ireland's phantasy and humour, of Mr Liam O'Fla-herty's grimness, of Mr Brinsley MacNamara's pitiless realism, but are unanimous in awarding the prize to Mr James Stephens for his *Deirdre.*[284] The story of Deirdre has always attracted the imagination of our writers, and the tale has been told and told again in poem and play and story. We rejoice that it captured Mr Stephens's[†] imagination. He has created a work of art that is vivid and original. His genius, which is so sympathetic and tender, so happy in its choice of word and phrase, has found a subject entirely after its own heart. Deirdre lives again in this book, and as there are very many people in Ireland who are not scholars and who read neither poetry nor plays, the beautiful story might have remained unknown to them if Mr Stephens had not retold it with such vividness and beauty. The book is one which Ireland should feel proud of having created.

In selecting among the writers of verse a certain historian's consideration seemed thrust upon us. The great Victorian poets wrote long poems, and touched upon many topics, and though they wrote many beautiful lyrics, these seemed almost an accident, something apart from the ambition of their lives. It was so, too, to an even greater extent, with the great Elizabethans, and just as the Elizabethan age was followed by the Jacobean with its lyricism, its perfection of detail, the Victorian age was followed by the poetical age in which we live. During the last twenty years poems have grown very short, and instead of touching upon many topics poets have celebrated life at its crisis, when it seems caught up into what Patmore calls the integrity of fire.[285] Irish poets have felt the general movement, but have not seemed to do so because, until lately, they have translated from the Gaelic, like Mr James Stephens, or chosen their subject matter from Gaelic antiquity. But for the last three years, the period that we are concerned with, they have been suddenly freed from historical prepossession, and written only out of themselves. It may prove in the end that they are not the less Irish because not obviously Irish at all.

One book seemed at once pre-eminent, *An Offering of Swans* by Dr Oliver Gogarty. A wit Dr Gogarty has always been, but in the midst of our civil war he created style and music and became a poet.[286] Like Henry James, he discovered his genius in contemplating with the eyes of a stranger, and so with clear eyes, what seemed most beautiful in the life of England; a beauty of great houses; and this beauty once seen he discovered also Rome, and the nobility that is inseparable from power. Though his genius, like that of Henry James, reminds us that the god came to Danae in a shower of gold,[287] it can sing finely of death.

Our friends go with us, as we go
Down the long path where Beauty wends,
Where all we love foregather, so
Why should we fear to join our friends?

Who would survive them to outlast
His children; to outwear his fame—
Left when the Triumph has gone past—
To win from Age not Time a name.

Then do not shudder at the knife
That death's indifferent hand drives home;
But with the strivers leave the strife,
Nor, after Caesar, skulk in Rome.[288]

When we came to consider the poetry of men under thirty, work more of promise than of achievement, we thought of the poems of Mr Robert Wilson, of Mr Austin Clarke, of Mr F. R. Higgins, of a moving poem by Miss Kaftannikoff, who is Irish-born, though partly of Russian extraction, and the poems of other writers. But in the case of all with one exception, we found but two or three noticeable poems or passages. One writer, however, Mr Harry Stuart, has made a little book called *We Have Kept the Faith*, where, though one finds no perfect poem, one finds constant beauty of metaphor and strangeness of thought, and so no lucky accident but a personality.[289] Will his expression clarify, his music grow strong and confident, or will his promise remain unfulfilled? That will probably depend upon his critical capacity, upon his intellect, and of these we have no means of judging. His genius, if genius it be, is the opposite of Dr Gogarty's, for he desires all that is faint, cold, and shadowy. He is drawn not to Rome, but to the Moon, for it is the Moon that he addresses when he cries:

Oft have I thought and troubled not my head,
My eyelids heavy with thy mystery,
Death would but blow me from the feathery dead
One heart-throb nearer thee.[290]

And it is to the Moon that he cries, 'O wound thyself and be for ever rid of the drug, the opium that dulls thy veins'.[291] He has found but pale Muses, and they have given him a song that is like themselves, and yet it may be worth his while to leave much that men value for its sake and to endure the hardest labour.

33

AN UNDELIVERED SPEECH[292]

I shall vote against the resolution sent up to us by the Dáil, not because I am interested in the subject of divorce, but because I consider the resolution an act of aggression. We have the right to assume—it was indeed declared in so many words at a meeting of the Catholic Truth Society[293]—that no Catholic would avail himself of opportunities for divorce; and President Cosgrave had before him the example of Quebec, where, though the proportion of Catholics is greater than in Ireland, facilities of divorce are permitted to the minority, but he had preferred to impose his Catholic convictions upon members of the Church of Ireland and upon men of no church.[294] I know that at the present stage of the discussion a large part of the Irish public, perhaps a majority, supports him, and I do not doubt the sincerity of that support—the sincerity that has heard only one side is invariably without flaw—and I have no doubt even that if he and they possessed the power they would legislate with the same confidence for Turks, Buddhists, and followers of Confucius. It is an impressive spectacle, so quixotically impressive, indeed, that one has to seek its like in mediaeval Spain. I wonder, however, if President Cosgrave and his supporters have calculated the cost—but no, I am wrong to wonder that, for such enthusiasm does not calculate the cost. This country has declared through every vehicle of expression known to it that it desires union with the North of Ireland, even that it will never be properly a nation till that union has been achieved, and it knows that it cannot bring that union about by force. It must convince the Ulster Protestants that if they join themselves to us they will not suffer injustice. They can be won, not now, but in a generation, but they cannot be won if you insist that the Catholic conscience alone must dominate the public life of Ireland. The Catholic Church fought for years against the Unity of Italy, and even invited recruits from this country to help it in that fight, and though it had the highest motives, history has condemned it, and now it is about to fight against the Unity of Ireland. But there is another cost which I will remind you of, though I am sure the Irish Bishops and President Cosgrave, whether they have calculated it or not, are prepared to pay it, and I shall speak of it, not to influence them, but because various journalists have charged those who favour divorce with advocating sexual immorality. The price that you pay for indissoluble marriage is a public opinion that will tolerate illegal relations between the sexes. Some time ago I was talking to an Italian of an illustrious Catholic house, from which have come Cardinals and, I believe, one Pope, and he spoke of what he considered the extreme harshness of American public opinion to illicit relations between the sexes, and explained it by the ease of divorce in America, which made such relations seem inexcusable. He thought that Italy was wiser, and said that the indissoluble marriage of Italy, of which he approved, caused great tolerance towards such relations. In describing Italy, he described, I think, every country where marriage has been indissoluble, Spain, France of the eighteenth century, and all mediaeval Europe. I will call Balzac as evidence, and not merely because he was the greatest of French novelists, but because he prided himself in recording the France of his own day. He was writing about aristocratic France which, though divorce was permitted since the French Revolution, was ardently Catholic, and did not recognise the laws of the Revolution. One of the most charming of his heroines is about to be married, and her mother takes her aside that she may speak these words: 'Remember, my child, that if you love your husband that is the most fortunate of things, but if you do not, you will no doubt take a lover. All I say to you is, do nothing against the family'. Then Balzac uses these remarkable words: 'She went to the altar with the words of that noble woman ringing in her ears'. I have just read the book in which my friend Mr Chesterton puts the Catholic case with so much ability, and I find nothing incompatible with the advice of that French mother; he is too wise an advocate of indissoluble marriage not to base it upon the family and the family only.[295] It is a protection to the family, a protection to the children, or it is believed to be so, and its advocates think that the price is worth paying. I am certainly not going to reason against that conviction, I certainly do not think that I have anything to say that can affect an issue that has been debated by men of the greatest sincerity and intellect for generations. I shall merely put another point of view, that we may understand each other the better, a point of view which is held with passion by men who follow the teachings of some Church that is not under Rome, or like myself, believe as little in an infallible book as an infallible Church. For a long time there has been a religious truce in Ireland, men like myself have kept silent about all those matters that divide one religion from another, but President Cosgrave has broken that truce, and I will avail myself of the freedom he has given me. Marriage is not to us a Sacrament, but, upon the other hand, the love of man and woman, and the inseparable physical desire, are sacred. This conviction has come to us through ancient philosophy and modern literature, and it seems to us a most sacrilegious thing to persuade two people who hate one another because of some unforgettable wrong to live together, and it is to us no remedy to permit them to part if neither can re-marry. We know that means the formation of ties which are commonly unhappy because transitory, and immoral because separated from the rest of life, and which, if there are children, may send the wrong into the future. We believe, too, that where such ties are not formed the emotions and therefore the spiritual life may be perverted and starved. The Church of Ireland permits the remarriage of such persons, and the Head of the Church of England has accepted the present Divorce Law of England. Neither would, perhaps, extend that law, but it will be extended in the future, for no nation which dates its public life from the Reformation will permanently compel a man or woman to remain solitary if husband or wife has been condemned to life-long imprisonment or has been certified as an incurable lunatic. We do not think that children brought up in a house of hatred, where the parents quarrel perpetually, are the better for it, and we are certain that a stepmother is better than no mother, even if the real mother is but in gaol or mad or bad beyond reformation, or estranged beyond recall, and we put our faith in human nature, and think that if you give men good education you can trust their intellects and their consciences without making rules that seem to us arbitrary. Some rules there have to be, for we live together in corporate society, but they are matters of prac-

tical convenience, and we think that they should be made by statesmen and not by a celibate clergy, however patriotic or public-
spirited.

I do not think that my words will influence a single vote here,
nor am I thinking of this House, I am thinking only of a quarrel
which I perceive is about to commence. Fanaticism having won this
victory, and I see nothing that can prevent it unless it be proved to
have overstepped the law, will make other attempts upon the liberty
of minorities. I want those minorities to resist, and their resistance
may do an overwhelming service to this country, they may become
the centre of its creative intellect and the pivot of its unity. For the
last hundred years Irish nationalism has had to fight against England, and that fight has helped fanaticism, for we had to welcome
everything that gave Ireland emotional energy, and had little use for
intelligence so far as the mass of the people were concerned, for we
had to hurl them against an alien power. The basis of Irish nationalism has now shifted, and much that once helped us is now injurious, for we can no longer do anything by fighting, we must
persuade, and to persuade we must become a modern, tolerant, liberal nation. I want everything discussed, I want to get rid of the old
exaggerated tact and caution. As a people we are superficial, our
Press provincial and trivial, because as yet we have not considered
any of those great political and religious questions which raise some
fundamental issue and have disturbed Europe for generations. It
must depend upon a small minority which is content to remain a
minority for a generation, to insist on those questions being discussed. Let us use the weapons that have been put into our hands.

34

DIVORCE[296]

I have no doubt that the party in this House which desires to prevent divorce will prevail. I do not think that this was the first intention of members of this House, nor that it represents the opinion of the country. We are a tolerant nation and the circumstances are very special that urge us to interfere with one another's rights or liberties. Left to themselves, Dáil and Senate would have found an easy solution.

I know, from many private conversations, that many members would gladly have seen a matrimonial bill concerning Protestants alone or persons of no church left to a purely Protestant vote, or to some committee appointed by that vote. It was certainly in the interests of this nation to have found some such solution.

If the profound desire of the Irish people for unity between North and South is ever fulfilled,[†] if North and South are ever to enter into some political association, the North will certainly not abandon any right which it already possesses; and it seems to me clear that if you show that Southern Ireland is to be governed on Catholic ideas alone, if you pass laws that the Protestant minority consider oppressive, you must give up all thought of unity, and I think that in the next few years it will have become perfectly plain to the whole people of North and South alike that the minority does consider oppressive the denial of a right which it has possessed since the 17th century, a right won originally under the leadership of John Milton and other great men and by struggles that are a famous part of Protestant history.[297]

This question came before the Committee that drew up the Irish Constitution. That Committee was urged to make marriage indissoluble and it refused. By that refusal it expressed the political mind of Ireland. Now you are urged to reverse the decision of that Committee by men whose minds are not political but religious. You are urged to it by men whom, I admit, it must be exceedingly difficult for the Catholic members of this House to resist.

In the long warfare of this country with England the Catholic clergy took the side of the people, and thereby attained to an authority they have not elsewhere in Europe, and when they speak through the mouth of their Archbishop, the Most Rev. Dr Byrne,[298] it is hard, I think, for any Irish Catholic to submit his arguments to that careful analysis to which all arguments should be submitted that claim to influence legislation.[299] Addressing the Catholic Truth Society in October last, Dr Byrne used these words:

> No power on earth can break the marriage bond until death. . . . That is true of all baptised persons, no matter what the denomination may be. To be sure, we hear that a section of our fellow countrymen favour divorce. While with nothing but respect and sympathy for all our neighbours, we have to say that we place the marriage of such people higher than they do themselves, for their marriages are unbreakable before God, and we cannot disobey God by helping to break them.

That is to say, you are to legislate on purely theological grounds, and you are to force your theology upon persons who are not of your religion. It is not a question of finding it legally difficult to grant to a minority what the majority does not wish for itself, for you are to insist upon members of the Church of Ireland, or members of any Church, taking a certain view of biblical criticism or of the authority of the text upon which that criticism is based, which they obviously do not take.

If you legislate upon such grounds, there is no reason why you should stop there. There is no reason why you should not forbid civil marriages altogether, seeing that civil marriages are not marriage in the eyes of the Church, and that it is just as much immorality according to that view as the remarriage of divorced persons is according to men like Dr Byrne. Nor do I see why you should stop at that, for we teach in our schools and print in our books many things which your Church condemns; in fact, once legislate on

purely theological grounds and there is no form of religious perse-
cution which cannot be justified, and I am not entirely certain that
there are not men in Ireland today who will urge you to it.

I have nothing but respect for Dr Byrne. I am told that he is an
accomplished and courtly man and the speech from which I have
made an extract, though I think it an unwise speech, was charitable
in form. But what am I to say to the following extract from an
article by Father Peter Finlay?

> The refusal to legalise divorce is no denial of justice to any
> section of our people; it is no infringement of the civil and
> religious liberties which our Constitution grants to all. As
> well say that prohibition of 'Suttee' is a denial of justice to
> an Indian widow. The Indian widow had a far clearer right
> to do herself to death on her husband's funeral pyre (her
> religion imposes it upon her as a duty) than any member of
> a Christian community can have to put away his wife and
> enter into a state of public legalised adultery. England acted
> justly and in fulfillment of a plain and grave moral obliga-
> tion when she forbade Suttee in India; the Irish Free State
> will act justly and in fulfillment of a plain and grave moral
> obligation in refusing to legalise absolute divorce and re-
> marriage among ourselves.

In a previous part of the essay he compares divorce to polygamy,
robbery and murder. I know little or nothing of Father Peter Finlay's career.[300] It may have been eminent and distinguished; but I do
not think that any member of this House will follow with pleasure
the leadership of a man who uses words of such a monstrous dis-
courtesy in describing the practice approved by the most civilised
nations of the modern world: by Germany, by England, by France,
by America and by the Scandinavian nations. He must know that,
judged by every kind of statistics, by every standard except the narrowest, these nations, by the greatness of their work, show that
they exceed us in virtue.

Father Peter Finlay has been supported by an ecclesiastic of the
Church of Ireland, the Bishop of Meath,[301] who has even excelled
him in invective; perceiving no doubt that indissoluble marriage
which he insists upon, for the guilty parties at any rate, has in other
countries made men and women exceedingly tolerant of certain

forms of sexual immorality, he declares that every erring husband or erring wife should be treated as a forger or a murderer; he hesitates, as it seems, between execution or a long term of imprisonment.

But, whereas the opinion of various Catholic ecclesiastics has probably influenced that of members of this House, I say with perfect confidence that the opinion of the Bishop of Meath has not affected a single vote. It is the glory of the reformed Churches that in all matters affecting legislation, even where religion is itself involved, the clergy carry merely the weight of their individual knowledge and capacity.

The right of divorce and many other rights were won by the Protestant nations in the teeth of most bitter opposition from their clergy. The living, changing, discovering, advancing human mind cannot base its legislation, as its clergy would have it, upon some doubtful interpretation of some doubtful passage in the Gospels.

The ecclesiastics who have spoken upon this question have all quoted a passage in St Matthew upon divorce and marriage.[302] There is not a scholar of any eminence in the world who considers the Gospels historical documents in the strict sense of those words. Their importance is devotional, not historical. They were written long after the events which they record; probably two generations after, and certainly where there was no living man who had heard the words or seen the events recorded, and they contradict one another on essential points. For an ecclesiastic to ask a statesman to base his legislation upon the assumption that any particular passage possesses historical validity is to appeal to public ignorance.

Possibly the majority of persons who advocate indissoluble marriage are under the impression that it preserves sexual morality. I wonder whether they have made an attempt to discover whether it preserves it in Spain, in Italy, or in South America. I notice that we do not propose to copy these nations in our economics, in our agriculture, or in our technical education. It is only in this matter that we propose to copy them. I think, before adopting their marriage law, we should discover if they exceed the rest of the world in sexual morality.

I have gone to what sources were available, and I find that they have suppressed some of the evidence of immorality; there are several instances not reported of divorce proceedings in the newspapers and the usual number of children are born in wedlock.

There is sometimes considerable uncertainty as to who their fathers are, but then public opinion discourages curiosity upon that subject and nobody need inquire very closely into the emotional relationship of men and women. However, all nations are immoral in some way or other.

There is a demand for happiness, which increases with education, and men and women who are held together against their will and their reason soon cease to recognise any duty to one another. You are going to permit separation. You cannot help yourselves there. You must permit young people who have found life impossible together, because of some indelible wrongs, to part; but they must never re-marry.

Do you imagine that men and women in the prime of life will accept the law of the cloister, and that this country can achieve what the rest of the world has failed to do in some 2,000 years? A great English lawyer, speaking out of his immense experience has stated that separation without divorce is the most potent imaginable cause of irregular unions.[303]

I would, however, urge those who take my view of this matter to avoid undue excitement. Father Peter Finlay and the Bishop of Meath and other fellow ecclesiastics will have but a short victory. It is not worthwhile quarreling with icebergs in warm weather. I have said that the Irish people are a tolerant people, yet remembering that we have in our principal street monuments of their tolerance and intolerance alike—the monuments of those great men of virtue, Nelson, Parnell and O'Connell—I think that I should have said that they are hesitating.[304] I have no doubt, however, that as the icebergs melt their tolerance will gain the day.

There has never been any trouble about O'Connell. His morals were Latin and his opinions orthodox. It was said of him that you could not fling a stone over any workhouse wall without hitting one of his children, but he always supported indissoluble marriage, and his heart is very properly preserved in some Roman church in an urn of bronze or marble.[305]

We do, however, differ about Parnell, and when, after the divorce proceedings, he married the woman who became thereby Mrs Parnell, he did what was his plain duty in the eyes of all Protestant gentlemen in the country; but Catholic ecclesiastics, with clear logic from their point of view, declared that his marriage doubled his offence, and now they are pressing to make such marriage impossible. They may, perhaps, interpret correctly that passage in St Thomas which lacks historical validity, but they deeply offend the consciences of an important minority of their fellow countrymen.[306]

I wish to draw the attention of the Protestant Bishop of Meath to the third monument. The English people honour the memory of Nelson and teach their children to honour that memory; but the Bishop of Meath thinks that he should have been hung or transported. A proposal has lately been made for the removal of this monument, on the ground that it obstructs the traffic. I suggest that the Bishop of Meath should urge this removal upon moral grounds, that we may have the whole matter out, and judge whether the view of certain ecclesiastics of all denominations is correct or that of the people of England, or of the members of the Church of Ireland who erected that monument. The Bishop of Meath would have preferred a gallows.

I think it unfortunate that, within three years of the establishment of this State, the Catholic Church should impose its law in this most vital matter upon a minority who regard that law as oppressive. Yet there are compensations. I am proud to consider myself a typical man of that minority. We have been a great stock. There are few more famous stocks in Europe. We are the people of Burke and of Swift, of Grattan, of Emmet, of Parnell. We have created nearly all of the literature of modern Ireland and most of its political intelligence. I shall now discover, or my children will discover, whether our stamina is impaired.

You have defined our position and given us a popular following, and if our stamina is, indeed, not impaired, your victory will be brief, your defeat final, and at its coming this nation may be transformed.

35

THE CHILD AND THE STATE[307]

Perhaps there are some here, one or two, who were present some thirty-six years ago at a meeting in my house, at which this society was first proposed. I think that meeting was the beginning of what is called the Irish Literary Movement. We and Dr Hyde and his movement, which began three or four years later with the foundation of the Gaelic League, tried to be unpolitical, and yet all that we did was dominated by the political situation. Whether we wrote speeches, or wrote poems, or wrote romances or wrote books of history, we could not get out of our heads that we were somehow pleading for our country before a packed jury. And that meant a great deal of strain, a great deal of unreality, and even a little hysteria. Now there is no one to win over, Ireland has been put into our hands that we may shape it, and I find all about me in Ireland to-day a new over-flowing life. To this overflowing life I attribute that our audiences at the Abbey Theatre have doubled, that the interest in music is so great that the Royal Dublin Society, which a few years ago was content with a hall that held seven hundred people, finds its new hall that holds some fifteen hundred so much too small, that every after-noon concert has to be repeated in the evening. Nor is it only appre-ciation that has grown, for where there is the right guidance and the right discipline, young men are ready for the hardest work. Colonel Brasé does not find it hard to get his young men to practise many hours a day, his difficulty is sometimes to get them to cease work.[308]

I know no case where the best teaching has been brought to Ireland in vain, and to-day there is a greater desire than ever before for expression, I think I may also say for discipline. The whole nation is plastic and receptive, but it is held back, and will be held back for some time to come by its lack of education, education in the most common and necessary subjects.

For that reason I put so much reliance in your patriotism and your patience that I am going to talk to you about education in the Primary Schools. Perhaps, indeed, I but speak of it because it is so running in my head that I would speak badly of anything else. I have been going round schools listening at a school attendance committee, talking to schoolmasters and inspectors. Many of you have influence in Ireland, influence through the Press, or through your friends, and I want to impress upon you that the schools in Ireland are not fit places for children. They are insanitary, they are out of repair, they are badly heated, and in Dublin and Cork they are far too small. The Government inherited this state of things, this old scandal; they want to put it right, but they will not be able to do so unless public opinion is with them, above all perhaps, unless just the kind of people who are here to-night are prepared to defend them and support them. The Government is introducing a Compulsory Education Bill, but we have all our individual responsibility, and we must see to it that compulsory education does not come into force—I do not say does not pass—until those schools are fitted for their work.[309] And if the children are going to be forced to school you must not only see that those schools are warm and clean and sanitary, but you must do as other countries are doing more and more, and see that children during school hours are neither half-naked nor starved.

You cannot do this by money alone, you must create some body of men with knowledge, that can give enough attention to see that all does not go to ruin again. Many of us think that you can only accomplish this by having a county rate struck, and by having county committees to supervise the spending of the money. No one proposes to interfere with the present manager's right to appoint and dismiss teachers. That right is cherished by the clergy of all denominations, but the ablest managers would, I believe, welcome popular control if confined to heating, housing, clothing, cleaning, etc. The old system has broken down, and all know that it has.

Only when the schools have been made habitable will the question arise that most interests us—what are you going to teach there? Whether Gaelic be compulsory or voluntary, a great deal of it will be taught. At present Gaelic scholars assure me that there is nothing to read in modern Irish except for very young children who love fairy-tales. You must translate, you must modernise. A committee of the Senate, of which I was chairman, has made a recommendation to the Government asking it to endow research into old, middle and modern Irish.[310] Nothing is decided, but I think the Government will make this grant. Probably most of the books so produced will be in middle or ancient Irish, and in any case unsuitable for young children. They will, however, supply the material from which in some degree a vivid modern literature may be created. I think the Government should appoint some committee of publication and so make possible a modern Gaelic literature. Let us say, Dr Douglas Hyde, Mr James Stephens, who is always working at his Irish, and Mr Robin Flower,[311] who is a great scholar and a fine critic. They would not have to do much of the great work themselves, but they could put others to it. Up to, say, ten years old, a child is content with a wild old tale, but from ten years on you must give it something with more of the problems of life in it. I would like to see the great classics, especially of the Catholic Latin nations, translated into Gaelic.

The tendency of the most modern education, that in Italy, let us say, is to begin geography with your native fields, arithmetic by counting the school chairs and measuring the walls, history with local monuments, religion with the local saints, and then to pass on from that to the nation itself. That is but carrying into education principles a group of artists, my father among them, advocated in art teaching. These artists have said: 'Do not put scholars to draw from Greek or Roman casts until they have first drawn from life; only when they have drawn from life can they understand the cast'. That which the child sees—the school—the district—and to a lesser degree the nation—is like the living body: distant countries and everything the child can only read of is like the cold Roman or Greek cast. If your education therefore is efficient in the modern sense, it will be more national than the dreams of politicians. If your education is to be effective you must see to it that your English teaching also begins with what is near and familiar. I suggest therefore another commission or committee to find writers who can create English reading books and history books, which speak of Ireland in simple vivid language. Very few such books exist, indeed I can only think of Mr Standish O'Grady's *Bog of Stars,* published at the suggestion of this Society many years ago.[312] That book is a fine piece of writing, and the books I think of should be fine pieces of writing, written by men of letters, chosen by men of letters; yet I do not think that I would exclude from the children's books any simple masterpiece of English literature. Let them begin with their own, and then pass to the world and the classics of the world.

There are two great classics of the eighteenth century which have deeply influenced modern thought, great Irish classics too difficult to be taught to children of any age, but some day those among us who think that all things should begin with the nation and with the genius of the nation, may press them upon the attention of the State. It is impossible to consider any modern philosophical or political question without being influenced knowingly or unknowingly by movements of thought that originated with Berkeley, who founded the Trinity College Philosophical Society, or with Burke, who founded the Historical.[313] It would be but natural if they and those movements were studied in Irish colleges, perhaps especially in those colleges where our teachers themselves are trained. The Italian Minister of Education has advised his teachers continually to study the great classics, and he adds that those great classics will be as difficult to them as is the lesson to the child, and will therefore help them to understand the mind of a child.

In Gaelic literature we have something that the English-speaking countries have never possessed—a great folk literature. We have in Berkeley and in Burke a philosophy on which it is possible to base the whole life of a nation. That, too, is something which England, great as she is in modern scientific thought and every kind of literature, has not, I think. The modern Irish intellect was born more than two hundred years ago when Berkeley defined in three or four sentences the mechanical philosophy of Newton, Locke and Hobbes, the philosophy of England in his day, and I think of England up to our day, and wrote after each, 'We Irish do not hold with this', or some like sentence.[314]

Feed the immature imagination upon that old folk life, and the mature intellect upon Berkeley and the great modern idealist philosophy created by his influence upon Burke who restored to political thought its sense of history, and Ireland is reborn, potent, armed and wise. Berkeley proved that the world was a vision, and Burke that the State was a tree, no mechanism to be pulled in pieces and put up again, but an oak tree that had grown through centuries.[315]

Teacher after teacher in Ireland has said to me that the young people are anarchic and violent, and that we have to show them what the State is and what they owe to it. All over the world during the Great War the young people became anarchic and violent, but in Ireland it is worse than elsewhere, for we have in a sense been at war for generations, and of late that war has taken the form of burning and destruction under the eyes of the children. They respect nothing, one teacher said to me, 'I cannot take them through Stephen's Green because they would pull up the plants'. Go anywhere in Ireland and you will hear the same complaint. The children, everybody will tell you, are individually intelligent and friendly, yet have so little sense of their duty to community and neighbour that if they meet an empty house in a lonely place they will smash all the windows. Some of the teachers want lessons on 'Civic Duty', but there is much experience to show that such lessons, being of necessity dry and abstract, are turned to mockery. The proper remedy is to teach religion, civic duty and history as all but inseparable. Indeed, the whole curriculum of a school should be as it were one lesson and not a mass of unrelated topics. I recommend Irish teachers to study the attempt now being made in Italy, under the influence of their Minister of Education, the philosopher Gentile, the most profound disciple of our own Berkeley,[316] to so correlate all subjects of study. I would have each religion, Catholic or Protestant, so taught that it permeate the whole school life, and that it may do so, that it may be good education as well as good religion, I would have it taught upon a plan signed, as it is in Italy, by the representative of the Government as well as by the religious authority. For instance, the Italian teachers are directed by the Minister to teach 'no servile fear'. Up to three years ago in Ireland religion could not be taught in school hours, and even now, though that regulation is no longer binding, it is often nothing but a daily lesson in the Catechism. In Italy it takes four forms, that it may not be abstract, and that it may be a part of history and of life itself, a part, as it were, of the foliage of Burke's tree. First, praying, the learning and saying of simple prayers; second, singing, the learning and singing of famous religious songs; third, narration, the reading, or perhaps among the younger children the hearing, and writing out in the child's own words of stories out of the Bible, and stories of the great religious personages of their own country; fourth, contemplation, by which I mean that dogmatic teaching which stirs the mind to religious thought. The prayers and songs for an Irish school exist in abundance. There are, for instance, many religious songs in Gaelic with their traditional music, and they are already published in little books.

Every child in growing from infancy to maturity should pass in imagination through the history of its own race and through something of the history of the world, and the most powerful part in that history is played by religion. Let the child go its own way when maturity comes, but it is our business that it has something of that whole inheritance, and not as a mere thought, an abstract thing like those Graeco-Roman casts upon the shelves in the art-schools, but as a part of its emotional life.

One never knows where one's words carry, and I, in speaking, though I speak to you all, am thinking perhaps of some one young man or some one young girl who may hear my words and bear them in mind years hence. Even he and she may do nothing with my thought, but they may carry it, or some other amongst you may carry it, as a bird will carry a seed clinging to its claws. I am thinking of an Egyptian poem, where there are birds flying from Arabia with spice in their claws.[317] I do not think any of you are millionaires, and yet permit me to dream that my words may reach one that is. If the Government were to do all that I suggest, if after the schools are put in good repair it were to get together the right editors and they find the right authors, if all the textbooks necessary to create a religious and secular culture in Irish and English were published, there would still be much that no Government, certainly no Government of a poor country, can accomplish. England has had great educational endowments for centuries, everyone knows with what lavish generosity the rich men of America have endowed education. Large sums of money have been sent to Ireland for political ends, and rich Irish-Americans have largely contributed, and we all hope, I think, that there is no further need for that money. If societies like this interest themselves in Irish education and spread that interest among the Irish educated classes everywhere, money may be sent to us to cheapen the price of school-books for the poor, or to clothe the poorer children, or to make the school buildings pleasanter to a child's eyes, or in some other way to prepare for an Ireland that will be healthy, vigorous, orderly, and above all, happy.

W. B. Yeats

36

THE NEED FOR
AUDACITY OF THOUGHT[318]

Some weeks ago, a Dublin friend of mine got through the post a circular from the Christian Brothers, headed A Blasphemous Publication and describing how they found 'the Christmas† number of a London publication in the hands of a boy'—in the hands of innocence. It contained 'a horrible insult to God . . . a Christian Carol set to music and ridiculing in blasphemous language the Holy Family'. But the Editor of a Catholic Boys' Paper rose to the situation; he collected petrol, roused the neighbourhood, called the schoolboys about him, probably their parents, wired for a film photographer that all might be displayed in Dublin, and having 'bought up all unsold copies . . . burned them in the public thoroughfare'. However, he first extracted the insult—the burning was to be as it were in effigy—that he might send it here and there with the appeal: 'How long are the parents of Irish children to tolerate such devilish literature coming into the country?'

'The devilish literature' is an old Carol of which Dr Hyde has given us an Irish version in his *Religious Songs of Connacht*.[319] The version enclosed with the circular was taken down by Mr Cecil Sharp,† and differs in a few unessential phrases from that in *The Oxford Book of English Ballads*.[320]

> Then up spake Mary,
> So meek and so mild;
> Oh, gather me cherries Joseph
> For I am with child.

Then up spake Joseph,
With his words so unkind;
Let them gather cherries
That brought thee with child.

Then up spake the little child,
In his Mother's womb;
Bow down you sweet cherry tree,
And give my Mother some.

Then the top spray of the cherry tree,
Bowed down to her knee;
And now you see Joseph
There are cherries for me.

The poem is a masterpiece, because something of great moment is there completely stated; and the poet who wrote the English words—it may exist in every European tongue for all I know—certainly wrote before the Reformation. It has been sung to our own day by English and Irish countrymen, but it shocks the Christian Brothers. Why?

The actual miracle is not in the Bible, but all follows as a matter of course the moment you admit the Incarnation. When Joseph has uttered the doubt which the Bible also has put into his mouth, the Creator of the world, having become flesh, commands from the Virgin's womb, and his creation obeys. There is the whole mystery —God, in the indignity of human birth, all that seemed impossible, blasphemous even, to many early heretical sects, and all set forth in an old 'sing-song' that has yet a mathematical logic. I have thought it out again and again and I can see no reason for the anger of the Christian Brothers, except that they do not believe in the Incarnation. They think they believe in it, but they do not, and its sudden presentation fills them with horror, and to hide that horror they turn upon the poem.

The only thoughts that our age carries to their logical conclusion are deductions from the materialism of the seventeenth century; they fill the newspapers, books, speeches; they are implicit in all that we do and think. The English and Irish countrymen are devout because ignorant of these thoughts, but we, till we have passed our grain through the sieve, are atheists. I do not believe in the Incarnation in the Church's sense of that word, and I know that I do not, and yet seeing that, like most men of my kind these fifty years, I desire belief, the old Carol and all similar Art delight me. But the Christian Brothers think that they believe and, suddenly confronted with the reality of their own thought, cover up their eyes.

Some months ago Mr Lennox Robinson gave to a paper edited by young poets a story written in his youth.[321] A religious young girl in the west of Ireland, her meditations stirred perhaps by her own name of Mary, begins to wonder what would happen if Christ's second coming were in her own village. She thinks first that the people are so wicked they would reject him, and then that they might accept him and grow good. She is pursued by a tramp, becomes unconscious, is ravished, and returns to consciousness in ignorance of what has happened. Presently she finds herself with child and believes, and persuades her parents, that a miracle has taken place, and gradually the neighbours believe also and turn good. At last she dies bringing forth a girl-child; and the tramp arrives in the village knowing nothing of what has happened, gets drunk, and boasts of his crime.

This story roused as much horror as the Cherry Tree Carol. Yet countless obscure Mothers have so dreamed, have been so deceived; some of them born in Protestant communities have become Johanna Southcotts[322] and lost our sympathy, but if we imagine such a mother as a simple country girl living amongst settled opinions, the theme grows emotional and philosophical. I have myself a scenario upon that theme which I shall never turn into a play because I cannot write dialect well enough, and if I were to set it where my kind of speech is possible, it would become unreal or a mere conflict of opinion. Mr. Lennox Robinson and I want to understand the Incarnation, and we think that we cannot understand any historical event till we have set it amidst new circumstance. We grew up with the story of the Bible; the Mother of God is no Catholic possession; she is a part of our imagination.

The Irish Religious Press attacked Mr Lennox Robinson, and a Catholic Ecclesiastic and an Ecclesiastic of the Church of Ireland resigned from the Committee of the Carnegie Library, because it would not censure him. I think that neither the Irish Religious Press nor those Ecclesiastics believe in the Second Coming. I do not believe in it—at least not in its Christian form—and I know that I do not believe, but they think that they do. No minds have belief who, confronted with its consequence—Johanna Southcotts, deluded peasant girls, and all the rest—find those consequences unendurable. The minds that have it grow always more abundant, more imaginative, more full of fantasy even, as its object approaches; and to deny that play of mind is to make belief itself impossible.

I have worked with Mr Lennox Robinson for years and there are times when I see him daily, and I know that his mind plays constantly about the most profound problems, and that especially of late his Art, under the mask of our brisk Dublin comedy, has shown itself akin to that of writers who have created a vision of life Tertullian would have accepted.[323] I think of Strindberg in his *Spook Sonata*, in his *Father*, in his books of autobiography, as mad and as profound as King Lear;[324] of James Joyce in his *Ulysses* lying 'upon his right and left side' like Ezekiel and eating 'dung' that he might raise 'other men to a perception of the infinite';[325] of John Synge, lost to the 'dazzling dark' of his *Well of the Saints* and of the last act of his *Deirdre*. I cannot deny my sympathy to these austere minds though I am of that school of lyric poets that has raised the cry of Ruysbroeck though in vain: 'I must rejoice, I must rejoice without ceasing, even if the world shudder at my joy'.[326]

The intellect of Ireland is irreligious. I doubt if one could select from any Irish writer of the last two hundred years until the present generation a solitary sentence that might be included in a reputable anthology of religious thought. Ireland has produced but two men of religious genius: Johannes Scotus Erigena[327] who lived a long time ago, and Bishop Berkeley who kept his Plato by his Bible; and Ireland has forgotten both; and its moral system, being founded upon habit, not intellectual conviction, has shown of late that it cannot resist the onset of modern life. We are quick to hate and slow to love; and we have never lacked a Press to excite the most evil passions. To some extent Ireland but shows in an acute form the European problem, and must seek a remedy where the best minds of Europe seek it—in audacity of speculation and creation. We must consider anew the foundations of existence, bring to the discussion—diplomacies and prudences put away—all relevant thought. Christianity must meet to-day the criticism, not, as its ecclesiastics seem to imagine, of the school of Voltaire, but of that out of which Christianity itself in part arose, the School of Plato; and there is less occasion for passion.

I do not condemn those who were shocked by the naive faith of the old Carol or by Mr Lennox Robinson's naturalism, but I have a right to condemn those who encourage a Religious Press so discourteous as to accuse a man of Mr Lennox Robinson's eminence of a deliberate insult to the Christian religion, and so reckless as to make that charge without examination of his previous work; and a system which has left the education of Irish children in the hands of men so ignorant that they do not recognise the most famous Carol in the English language.

37

A DEFENCE OF
THE ABBEY THEATRE[328]

Mr Reddin[329] complains that the Abbey Theatre has produced many bad plays; that its Directors and play-writers are a 'cult'; that it cannot be national, not being 'the expression of the entire people'; that it uses the English language; that we Directors, being not only 'Cromwellians', but 'stout Cromwellians', have invented a form of dialect that he who has 'lived with the people of the western south has never heard'; and, on top of all our other offences, that we have neither produced foreign masterpieces nor predominantly religious and political plays.

Now the last matter first. I do most anxiously assure Mr Reddin that the Cromwellian mind has always loved religion and politics. We Cromwellian Directors laid down this principle twenty-five years ago, and have not departed from it: never to accept or reject a play because of its opinions. When we began our work, it was the accepted principle that an artistic or a literary society should have nothing to do with religion or politics. We could have had far greater support—greater financial support—had we made the usual declaration, but we refused to do so, because we considered all thought legitimate dramatic material. A good many years had to pass before people understood that we were sincere, that we were not trying to undermine anybody's political or religious opinions. Indeed that was only understood when many plays of different tendencies had been shown. Our first trouble was with the Unionists, but we have had to fight all parties, and are prepared to go on doing so. *Kathleen ni Houlihan, The Piper, The Rising of the Moon, The Lost Leader, The Plough and the Stars,* Miss Macardle's[†] revolutionary plays,[330] and many others are political, but political in different ways. We have no object but good plays, made out of whatever thought is most exciting to the minds of those who make them.

At first, especially, many of our plays were in dialect, for what first attracted our dramatists was that life of 'folk', which in every country is most obviously national, most obviously historical and ancient. The Norwegian dramatists did precisely the same. 'Understand the saga by the peasant, and the peasant by the saga', that was their phrase.[331] But we are, he says, Cromwellians, and can, therefore, know nothing of the matter. All, at this late day, have mixed strains of blood—even Mr Reddin, I imagine—but I think we Abbey Directors can find strains of our blood that came into this country before Cromwell. I think the first Synges came in the time of Elizabeth; but whatever the date, and whatever their strains of blood, Lady Gregory and John Synge were the first educated man and woman who spoke their whole souls in the dialect of the people; the first to see in that dialect not a vehicle of farce, but of intellect. That dialect—the dialect spoken in the west and south of Ireland—is an ancient form of the English language. It has a history of some hundreds of years, and is derived from two main sources. Its syntax is partly that of Irish, and its vocabulary is partly that of Tudor English. Synge and Lady Gregory had enough Irish to understand the syntax. Synge studied ancient Gaelic under H. d'Arbois de Jubainville and, though always half an invalid, modern Irish in the hardship of an Aran† cottage. Lady Gregory had, in her *Cuchulain of Muirthemne* and her *Gods and Fighting Men,* made the most famous translations ever made from the Irish language, and she had, before writing a word of her plays, filled notebook after notebook with the English of her neighbourhood. Furthermore Synge and Lady Gregory knew Tudor English—Lady Gregory especially, for when I knew her first, the *Morte d'Arthur* was her book of books. I do not believe that Mr Reddin's knowledge equals that of either; but if it does, that is not sufficient for me—the farmer and the sailor have knowledge, but we do not accept their opinion as to the merits of a landscape or a sea-scape. I should want to be certain that he had an equal understanding before I weighed his opinion against that of Lady Gregory and John Synge. Of course, Synge and Lady Gregory no more reproduce dialect like a phonograph than a great painter copies land and sea like a photograph—'art is art because it is not Nature'.[332] They have selected, but selected from a knowledge few dialect writers of any country have equalled. Sir Walter Scott made a single lowland Scottish dialect serve for all Scotland; and the Irish novelists, or the greater number of them, made Munster, Leinster and Connaught talk like a Dublin jarvey.[333] Scott and the Irish novelists did their work according to their knowledge and their purpose, and were justified.

It is a recognised rule of criticism that you should never criticise at all till you have seen or tried to see what your author has done or tried to do. Let Mr Reddin take down some anthology of prose— English, French or German—I care not what the language, and ask himself if he cannot find passages equal to any there of a like species—I do not mean by this in dialect—in Synge's *Playboy,* in the last Act of his *Deirdre,* in Lady Gregory's *Gaol Gate,*[†] or here and there among her comedies, or among the slight dialect of her translations from the Gaelic. He will find that these passages are not only expressed in a way peculiar to this country, but that they are the classic prose of modern Ireland.

But he has more than our dialect against us—there are all those bad plays. Of course we have produced bad plays, some to give their authors experience, and some—and in these there is always good—because they are popular. Until a year ago the Abbey was practically bankrupt. It had survived war and civil war, and I assure you an audience gets very thin when there is firing in the streets. Time and again we Cromwellians had to go to our friends, some of these Cromwellians too, and raise money; but a time came when we could do this no longer. When we were an independent nation, it did not become the dignity of that nation that we should go to London, where we got £2,000 the last time, to save the dramatic movement of Ireland. Then the Government gave us our subsidy, and peace restored our audience. From that moment we began weeding out poor plays, improving our scenery, and bringing into our repertory plays from other countries. We have always played a certain number of foreign masterpieces, and for a long time we guided ourselves in this by the principle that, as our object was to create an Irish theatre, we would translate such foreign masterpieces as threw light upon our Irish plays. Because of their likeness in a part of their method to the work of Synge and Lady Gregory, we have long had plays by Molière in our repertory; and while we still hoped for an Irish religious drama, we produced a number of medieval 'mysteries' and 'moralities'. Lately we have chosen foreign masterpieces without first thinking of our Irish plays, because an Irish school of drama has been created and does not need the same anxious fostering. We have always wished to do more foreign masterpieces than we have been able to, but they seldom succeed with the audience— I think I see signs of a change in that matter, but it will come slowly. It takes even longer to train an audience than a company of actors. You cannot have a national theatre without creating a national audience, and that cannot be done by the theatre alone, for it needs the help of schools and newspapers, and of all teachers of the people. The theatre can go only a little ahead of the people, and it can only continue to do that if Directors and shareholders agree not to take a penny in profits.

But I had forgotten. We play and act in English because we are Cromwellians, and that is the worst charge of all. Mr Reddin is mistaken—we play and act in English because that is the language in which our audience thinks. Years ago Lady Gregory and I persuaded that other Cromwellian, Dr Hyde, to write—I know he will not mind my saying this—those admirable little plays of his, those plays where there is often a humour so beautiful and an eloquence so touching.[334] We thought that we were helping to create a Gaelic theatre in country villages where Gaelic is the language of thought. That theatre almost came into existence, but it was destroyed because subordinated[335] to propaganda, for the natural man is bored by propaganda. But now a new Gaelic theatre has arisen which will not commit that error. We are glad it uses the same stage that we do, and we wish it success.[336] If the mass of the people come to think in Gaelic, it will become the national theatre of Ireland, but not till then. People can only act and sing and write well or enjoy these things well in the language of their thought.

Mr Reddin is too abstract; he has a theatre in his head, a kind of spiritual substance out of time and space. An intellectual movement of any kind moves in narrow limits—a few people, a spot of the earth—and it grows out of the knowledge that it finds and does, not what it should according to any man's theory, but what it can or must. If those few people are interested in the villages, it goes to villages for its vehicle of expression; and if they are interested in slums, it must go there for a vehicle, and when that interest is exhausted it turns to something else, and always the greater the success, the more marked are the limits. A master is known, somebody has said, by the fact that he works within limits. Of one thing we may be quite certain: at no time, neither in the beginning nor in its final maturity, does an intellectual movement express a whole people, or anybody but those who are built into it, as a victim long ago was built into the foundation of a bridge. Sometimes if those few people are great enough, if there is amongst them a Sophocles or a Shakespeare, or even some lesser genius who has the sincerity of the Great Masters, they give their character to the people.

38

MEMORIAL TO THE
LATE T. W. LYSTER[337]

When, after the late Mr Lyster's death in 1922, some friends of his decided to put up a memorial to commemorate his long service in the National Library, it was quite clearly in their minds that the memorial must be in the Library, or, at any rate, just outside its door. For forty-two years Mr Lyster was in the service of the Library, and for thirty-two of those forty-two years in this building. When, as quite a young man, he became a librarian, the reading room was the large room in Leinster House where the Senate now meets.[338] When he was ten years there, the Library was moved into the present building. He became full Librarian in 1895; up to that he had been Assistant Librarian to Mr W. Archer, F.R.S.,[339] who was Head Librarian before him. When Mr Lyster became Head Librarian, he put aside all other work, and made this Library the business of his life—this Library and the municipal libraries of Dublin, to which he was of great service, conducting examinations, for instance.

He also served in connection with the Royal Dublin Society Library. Libraries became his passion—he knew all about them, and how to make them efficient; he read notable papers upon that subject at library congresses. At the same time he was what a librarian was not always—he was a great scholar in books. He read perpetually, and had a vast memory. He read in English literature and in German literature. If he had not entered into the service of this Library, he would have done works of scholarship of very great value.

As it is, we owe to him that very fine translation of Düntzer's *Life of Goethe,* much more readable than the original.[340] I remember that he gave me a copy of it when I was a very young man. I still read it for its exhaustive and vivid account of one of the greatest men who ever lived. He was, I think, something which we have not now in Dublin—a great scholar in literature. We have great scholars in various subjects; but he was our last great scholar in literature for itself. He inherited that passion from a great friend of his youth, Edward Dowden, and from him also his interest in German and in German literature.[341] I myself would like to say that I am deeply indebted to Mr Lyster. When I was a very young man, I read literature in the National Library—at that time it was in Leinster House—and it was Mr Lyster who guided me. He had a great knowledge of Elizabethan literature, and I read that constantly under his guidance in that magnificent eighteenth-century room.

I am indebted to him also for something else. My first published work owed much to his correction. I wrote a long pastoral play, which was accepted by the short-lived *Dublin University Review*.[342] When a young man writes his first poems, there will often be a good line followed by a bad line, and he should always go to a scholar to be advised; and Mr Lyster did that for me. I used to go to his house, and he would go over the manuscript of my play with me, and help me to correct the bad lines.

I have said that we were quite clear in our minds that the memorial must be in this building. He had, I think, strong affection for it, not only because it was the place where he spent his life, but because it was the place where he was surrounded by the young men whom he loved. Many young men owed a great deal to his guidance here. The Library was full of young students. On one occasion some person wished to prevent the students from sitting on the steps outside, and he said: 'No; they must be allowed to sit there, because this is their building'. And that was always his attitude towards the young men who surrounded him.

When we came to think of what kind of memorial we would erect, we sadly gave up some charming schemes because of the difficulty of light. Some of us, for instance, were anxious to have a little mosaic with Mr Lyster in the Library, surrounded by those young men; but the light was too dim for that. Then we thought of some sculptured memorial, and that, too, seemed impossible. We played with the idea of a stained-glass window, because that is one of the things which Dublin artists can produce so beautifully; but it would have been out of keeping with the other windows: so the Committee decided on the simple lettered memorial to Mr Lyster's achievements and his scholarship, and they asked Mr George Atkinson, R.H.A., to carry out that decision; and I will now hand over Mr Atkinson's dignified, simple design to Sir Philip Hanson,[343] who represents the Board of Works.

39

THE CENSORSHIP AND ST THOMAS AQUINAS[344]

I

'The Censorship of Publications Bill' declares in its preliminary section that 'the word "indecent" shall be construed as including "calculated to excite sexual passion".' I know something of the philosophy of St Thomas, the official philosophy of the Catholic Church. Indeed, the new Thomist movement in literary criticism has made such knowledge almost essential to a man of letters,[345] and I am convinced that this definition, ridiculous to a man of letters, must be sacrilegious to a Thomist. I cannot understand how Catholic lawyers, trained in precision of statement and ecclesiastics, who are supposed to be trained in philosophy, could have committed such a blunder. Had Professor Trench[346] made it I would understand, for his sort of evangelical belief, whatever it owes to the ascetic Platonism of the seventeenth century, owes nothing to Aquinas.

II

Cardinal Mercier writes in his *Manual of Modern Scholastic Philosophy*, Vol. 1, p. 314, English Edition: 'Plato and Descartes, who both considered the soul as a substance completely distinct from the body, make it reside in some central part whence, like a pilot at the helm, it can control the movements of the whole organism. By Plato the rational soul is placed in the brain, whilst Descartes relegates it to the minute portion of it called the pineal gland. St Thomas's opinion, to which we adhere, is entirely different; he lays down that the soul is wholly present in the whole body and in all its parts—

anima rationalis est tota in toto corpore et tota in qualibet parte corporis.[347]

For centuries the Platonizing theology of Byzantium had dominated the thought of Europe. Amidst the abstract splendour of its basilicas stood saints with thought-tortured faces and bodies that were but a framework to sustain the patterns and colours of their clothes. The mosaics of the Apse displayed a Christ with face of pitiless intellect, or a pinched, flat-breasted virgin holding a child like a wooden doll. Nobody can stray into that little Byzantium chapel at Palermo, which suggested the chapel of the Grail to Wagner,[348] without for an instant renouncing the body and all its works and sending all thought up into that heaven the pseudo Dionysius, the Areopagite, fashioned out of the Platonic ideas.[349]

III

Within fifty years of the death of St Thomas the art of a vision had faded, and an art of the body, an especial glory of the Catholic Church, had inspired Giotto. The next three centuries changed the likeness of the Virgin from that of a sour ascetic to that of a woman so natural nobody complained when Andrea del Sarto chose for his model his wife, or Raphael his mistress, and represented her with all the patience of his 'sexual passion'. A corresponding change in technique enabled him to imagine her, not as if drawn upon a flat surface, but as though moulded under the hand in bas-relief. Painters liberated from a conviction that only ideas were real, painted, from the time of Orcagna, bodies that seemed more and more tangible till at last Titian saw grow upon his canvas an entirely voluptuous body.[350] 'Anima est in *toto* corpore' (the italics are Cardinal Mercier's).[351] 'The breast's superb abundance where a man might base his head.'[352] The lawyers who drew up the Bill, and any member of the Dáil or Senate who thinks of voting for it, should study in some illustrated history of Art Titian's *Sacred and Profane Love,* and ask themselves if there is no one it could not incite to 'sexual passion', and if they answer, as they are bound to, that there are many ask this further question of themselves. Are we prepared to exclude such art from Ireland and to sail in a ship of fools, fools that dressed bodies Michael Angelo left naked, Town Councillors of Montreal who hid the *Discobolus*† in the cellar?[353]

IV

There is such a thing as immoral painting and immoral litera-ture, and a criticism growing always more profound establishes that they are bad paintings and bad literature, but though it may be said of them that they sin always in some way against 'in *toto* cor-pore', they cannot be defined in a sentence. If you think it necessary to exclude certain books and pictures, leave it to men learned in art and letters, if they will serve you, and, if they will not, to average educated men. Choose what men you may, they will make blunders, but you need not compel them to with a definition.

W. B. Yeats

40

THE IRISH CENSORSHIP[354]

The other night I awoke with a sense of well-being, of recovered health and strength. It took me a moment to understand that it had come to me because our men and women of intellect, long separated by politics, have in the last month found a common enemy and drawn together. Two days before I had gone to see an old friend, from whom I had been separated for years, and was met with the words, 'We are of the same mind at last'.[355] The Free State Government has in a month accomplished what would, I had thought, take years, and this it has done by drafting a Bill which it hates, which must be expounded and defended by Ministers full of contempt for their own words.

Ecclesiastics, who shy at the modern world as horses in my youth shied at motor-cars, have founded a 'Society of Angelic Welfare'. Young men stop trains, armed with automatics and take from the guard's van bundles of English newspapers. Some of these ecclesiastics are of an incredible ignorance. A Christian Brother publicly burnt an English magazine because it contained the Cherry Tree Carol, the lovely celebration of Mary's sanctity and her Child's divinity, a glory of the mediaeval church as popular in Gaelic as in English, because, scandalized by its *naïveté*, he believed it the work of some irreligious modern poet; and this man is so confident in the support of an ignorance even greater than his own, that a year after his exposure in the Press, he permitted, or directed his society to base an appeal for public support, which filled the front page of a principal Dublin newspaper, upon the destruction of this 'infamous' poem.

Then out and spoke that little Babe
Which was within Her womb:
'Bow down, bow down thou cherry tree
And give my Mother some.'[356]

The Bill is called 'Censorship of Publications Bill, 1928', and empowers the Minister of Justice to appoint five persons, removable at his pleasure, who may, if that be his pleasure, remain for three years apiece, and to these persons he may on the complaint of certain 'recognized associations' (The Catholic Truth Society and its like) submit for judgement book or periodical. These five persons must then say whether the book or periodical is 'indecent', which word 'shall be construed as including calculated to excite sexual passions or to suggest or incite to sexual immorality or in any other way to corrupt or deprave', or whether, if it be not 'indecent' it inculcates 'principles contrary to public morality', or 'tends to be injurious or detrimental to or subversive of public morality'. If they decide it is any of these things the Minister may forbid the post to carry it, individual or shop or library to sell or lend it. The police are empowered by another section to go before a magistrate who will be bound by the Bill's definition of the word 'indecent' and obtain, without any reference to the committee or the Minister, a right to seize in a picture-dealer's shop, or at a public exhibition where the pictures are for sale, an Etty, or a Leighton—the police have already objected to *The Bath of Psyche*—and fine or imprison the exhibitor.[357] Another section forbids the sale or distribution of any 'appliance to be used for', or any book or periodical which advocates or contains an advertisement of any book or periodical which advocates 'birth control'. *The Spectator,* the *Nation,* the *New Statesman,* and *Nature,* are, I understand, liable to seizure.[358]

This Bill, if it becomes law, will give one man, the Minister of Justice, control over the substance of our thought, for its definition of 'indecency' and such vague phrases as 'subversive of public morality', permit him to exclude *The Origin of Species,* Karl Marx's *Capital,* the novels of Flaubert, Balzac, Proust, all of which have been objected to somewhere on moral grounds, half the Greek and Roman Classics, Anatole France and everybody else on the Roman index, and all great love poetry.[359] The Government does not intend these things to happen, the Commission on whose report the Bill was founded did not intend these things to happen, the holy gunmen and 'The Society of Angelic Welfare' do not intend all these things to happen; but in legislation intention is nothing, and the letter of the law everything, and no Government has the right, whether to flatter fanatics or in mere vagueness of mind to forge an instrument of tyranny and say that it will never be used. Above all, they have no right to say it here in Ireland, where until the other day the majority of children left school at twelve years old,[360] and where even now, according to its own inspectors, no primary school-master opens a book after school hours.

It will, of course, appoint a 'reasonable committee', and, unless the Minister of Justice decides to remove one or more of its members, four out of five must agree before anything happens. I know those reasonable committee-men who have never served any cause but always make common cause against the solitary man of imagination or intellect. Had such a committee, with even those two Protestant clergymen upon it somebody suggests, censored the stage a while back, my theatre, now the State Theatre, would never have survived its first years. It now performs amid popular applause four plays, of which two, when first performed, caused riots, three had to be protected by the police, while all four had to face the denunciation of Press and pulpit. Speaking from the stage, I told the last rioters—to-day's newspaper burners—that they were not the first to rock the cradle of a man of genius.[361] By such conflict truth, whether in science or in letters, disengages itself from the past. The present Bill does not affect us, but if it passes into law the next will bring the stage under a mob censorship acting through 'recognized associations'.

The well-to-do classes practise 'birth control' in Ireland as elsewhere, and the knowledge is spreading downwards, but the Catholic Church forbids it. If those men of science are right, who say that in a hundred years the population will overtake the food supply, it will doubtless direct the married to live side by side and yet refrain from one another, a test it has not imposed upon monk or nun, and if they do not obey—well, Swift's 'Modest Proposal' remains, and that, at any rate, would make love self-supporting.[362]

Although it was almost certain that Catholic Ireland, thinking 'birth control' wrong in principle, would follow the lead of countries that, being in sore need of soldiers and cheap labour, think it undesirable and legislate against it, those who belong to the Church of Ireland or to neither Church should compel the fullest discussion. The Government is forbidden under the Treaty to favour one religion at the expense of another, which does not mean that they may not propose legislation asked for by one Church alone, but that they must show that the welfare of the State demands it. 'You Mahommedans must not quote your Koran because the Christians do not believe in it, you Christians must not quote your Bible', said the chairman at the religious meeting in ancient Damascus—or was it Baghdad?—which scandalized the Spanish Traveller.[363] Those who think it wrong to bring into the world children they cannot clothe and educate, and yet refuse to renounce that 'on which the soul expands her wing', can say 'no man knows whether the child is for love's sake, the fruit for the flower, or love for the child's sake, the flower for the fruit'; or quote the words of St Thomas: '*Anima est in toto corpore*'.[364]

The enthusiasts who hold up trains are all the better pleased because the newspapers they burn are English, and their best public support has come from a newspaper that wants to exclude its rivals; but their motives may be, in the main, what they say they are, and great numbers of small shopkeepers and station-masters who vaguely disapprove of their methods approve those motives. A Government official said of these station-masters and shopkeepers the other day: 'They are defending their sons and daughters and cannot understand why the good of the nine-tenths, that never open a book, should not prevail over the good of the tenth that does'. Twenty years ago illegitimacy was almost unknown, infanticide unknown, and now both are common and increasing, and they think that if they could exclude English newspapers, with their police-court cases which excite the imagination, their occasional allusions to H. G. Wells which excite the intellect,[365] their advertisements of books upon birth control which imply safety for illicit love, innocence would return. They do not understand that you cannot unscramble eggs, that every country passing out of automatism passes through demoralization, and that it has no choice but to go on into intelligence. I know from plays rejected by the Abbey Theatre that the idealist political movement has, after achieving its purpose, collapsed and left the popular mind to its own lawless vulgarity. Fortunately, the old movement created four or five permanent talents.

There are irresponsible moments when I hope that the Bill will pass in its present form, or be amended by the Republicans, as some foretell, into a still more drastic form, and force all men of intellect, who mean to spend their lives here, into a common understanding. One modern-minded Catholic writer has been hawking a letter round the Press threatening anti-clericalism; but if that come, and I do not expect it in my time, it will not come in the old form. No Irishman wants the fourteenth century, even though most damnably compromised and complicated by modern Rathmines,[366] driven from his back door so long as the front door opens on the twentieth. Our imaginative movement has its energy from just that combination of new and old, of old stories, old poetry, old belief in God and the soul, and a modern technique. A certain implacable and able Irish revolutionary soldier[367] put me to read Berkeley with the phrase: 'There is all the philosophy a man needs'; and I have long held that intellectual Ireland was born when Berkeley wrote in that famous note-book of his after an analysis of contemporary mechanistic thought: 'We Irish do not think so', or some such words.[368] The power to create great character or possess it cannot long survive the certainty that the world is less solid than it looks and the soul much solider—'a spiritual substance' in some sense or other—and our dramatists, when they leave Ireland, or get away from the back door in some other fashion, prefer cause or general idea to characters that are an end to themselves and to each other.[369] Synge's *Playboy* and O'Casey's *Plough and the Stars* were attacked because, like 'The Cherry Tree Carol', they contain what a belief, tamed down into a formula, shudders at, something wild and ancient.

W. B. Yeats

41

OEDIPUS THE KING[370]

Nearly thirty years ago I was at the Catholic University of Notre Dame at Illinois; I had come there to give a lecture about Irish literature and stayed for a couple of days. A certain monk, specially appointed I think to look after the guests, was the best of companions and told me a great many exciting things about his monastery, about the Irish in America, and about his own thoughts. The thing that stayed longest in my memory was that *Oedipus the King* had just been performed under the auspices of his University.[371] *Oedipus the King* was at that time forbidden by the English censor, and I thought that if we could play it at the Abbey Theatre, which was to open on my return, we might make our audience proud of its liberty and take a noble view of the stage and its mission. Some three or four years passed and I began my version with the help of Mr Nugent Monck,† who was at the time helping us at the Abbey and has since established a famous theatre in Norwich;[372] and a young Greek scholar, then one of our actors but now a circuit judge;[373] and half a dozen translations. Sometimes I went on to the stage and spoke a sentence to be sure that it was simple enough and resonant enough to be instantaneously felt and understood in every part of the theatre. I did not want to make a new translation for the reader but something that everybody in the house, scholar or potboy, would understand as easily as he understood a political speech or an article in a newspaper. The subject matter might be strange and sometimes difficult, but no word might be strange or difficult, nor must I tire the ear by putting those words in some unnatural order. I finished my first rough draft and began to look for an actor, but before I had found one the English censorship withdrew its ban and, when the pleasure of mocking it and affirming the freedom of our Irish uncensored stage was taken from me, I lost interest in the play. I put it into the file with my letters and forgot it and then four or five years ago my wife found it and persuaded me to finish it and put it on to the Abbey stage. It was a very great success there. Mr F.[†] J. McCormick showed himself a great tragic actor and, though no other actor had an equal opportunity, the whole performance was powerful and harmonious.[374] Just as I had to put that dialogue into whatever form could be best spoken, so I had to put the choruses into whatever form could be best sung, and sung by singers from the choir of St Patrick's Cathedral. When the play was performed in Athens there was a place in front of the stage like half a circus ring with an altar in the middle, and the chorus had moved in some kind of pantomimic dance round that altar, but in Dublin they would have to stand side by side in the narrow space where the orchestra sits in ordinary plays and sing almost lost in shadow. There were other differences. When the Abbey Company broadcasts the play next week from Belfast these differences, dependent on sight, will not be apparent, and you should try and call up not the little Abbey Theatre but an open-air Greek theatre with its high-pillared stage, and yourselves all sitting tier above tier upon marble seats in some great amphitheatre cut out of a hillside. If the wireless can be got to work, in the country house where I shall be staying,[375] I shall be listening too, and as I have never heard a play broadcasted I do not know whether I shall succeed in calling into my imagination that ancient theatre. Probably the first thing that will seem to you very strange, very unlike anything seen on the English stage, is that every few minutes a number of persons who are called citizens of Thebes sing their comments upon the actors. I never understood the dramatic value of their singing, perhaps the sole reason for its existence from the point of view of a theatrical producer, until I attended a meeting of the Salvation Army in Dublin. They had hired the Abbey Theatre for a Sunday evening, and unnoticed by anybody I went to a little window high up above the stage platform among the pulleys and ropes that lower the stage scenes, and stood there listening. There were, I think, five sermons, all with a single idea—Christ's presence in the world—and between every sermon came a hymn. And I found that, rested by the change of attention made possible by the hymn, the change to a different kind of attention, I listened to the exposition of one idea taken up by speaker after speaker without any sense of monotony. A Greek play, unlike a Shakespearian play, is the exposition of one idea; in the case of *King Oedipus,* fate closing in upon one man who is almost continuously upon the stage. There is no comic relief, no Polonius with his worldly wisdom and his absurdity, no gravedigger taking off, perhaps in accordance to an ancient stage tradition, innumerable waistcoats, no sub-plot, no Fortinbras with his filibustering army, but the chorus is there so that we may sit back and relax our strained attention. Not that we must cease to listen, for the chorus is beautiful—past ages are called up before us, vast emotions are aroused—but our attention is no longer concentrated upon a single spot, a single man.

But what of the play itself? There is a consensus of opinion that *Oedipus the King* is the greatest dramatic masterpiece of antiquity. Sophocles was as voluminous a writer as Shakespeare, but only five of his plays have reached us, probably those that were most often acted and therefore most often copied out, and of these *Oedipus the King* is the most concentrated, the most logical. It has a sequel, *Oedipus at Colonus,* and of that also I have made a version which is finely played at the Abbey Theatre, but it is very long, playing more than two hours, a great length for a Greek play. In the first play, the play which will be broadcasted next week, Oedipus brings upon himself the curse of the gods because of an involuntary sin, but in the second play he wanders an outcast from road to road, a blind old man, attended and protected by his two daughters as Lear was protected by Cordelia. So great has been his suffering that the gods have come over to his side and those that he curses perish and those that he blesses prosper. He becomes to us the representative of human genius. We think perhaps of Jonathan Swift, hating himself first of all and then mankind, until suffering has made him half divine. And then perhaps by a strange freak of imagination we think of our blind Gaelic poet Raftery wandering with his blessings and his cursings from road to road. There is an old thorn tree pointed out on a Galway road to this day that Raftery is said to have withered with a curse. When Oedipus takes refuge in a wood beside the road it is just such a wood as blind Raftery might have found, for it is sacred to certain spirits called Eumenides, which means Good People. I think those great scholars of the last century who translated Sophocles into an English full of Latinised constructions and Latinised habits of thought, were all wrong—and that the schoolmasters are wrong who make us approach Greek through Latin. Nobody ever trembled on a dark road because he was afraid of meeting the nymphs and satyrs of Latin literature, but men have trembled on dark roads in Ireland and in Greece. Latin literature was founded upon documents, but Greek literature came like old Irish literature out of the beliefs of the common people. Because I think this I get great pleasure from the knowledge that my friend, Father Patrick Browne of Maynooth, has translated the Greek text of *Oedipus the King* into Gaelic, and had it played by the Gaelic Theatre in Dublin.[376] Father Patrick Browne may have done very much better than I have with the choruses of Oedipus the King, for Lady Gregory tells me that he has made fine translations of Shelley into Gaelic,[377] and I do not think I did very well with those choruses. I do think, however, that I have made a good translation of the great chorus of *Oedipus at Colonus* where the tragedy of the old wandering man is described and his fate summed up:

> Endure what life God gives and ask no longer span;
> Cease to remember the delights of youth, travel-wearied
>   aged man;
> Delight becomes death-longing if all longing else be vain.
>
> Even from that delight memory treasures so,
> Death, despair, division of families, all entanglements of
>   mankind grow,
> As that old wandering beggar and these God-hated children
>   know.
>
> In the long echoing street the laughing dancers throng,
> The bride is carried to the bridegroom's chamber through
>   torchlight and tumultuous song;
> I celebrate the silent kiss that ends short life or long.
> Never to have lived is best, ancient writers say;
> Never to have drawn the breath of life, never to have looked
>   into the eye of day;
> The second best's a gay goodnight and quickly turn away.[378]

When the Abbey Company broadcast *Oedipus the King* next week, that will be the last time you will hear their voices for many months, for early in October they sail for America. They are going to play the Abbey plays all over the United States as far west as California, as far south as Texas.[379] They want to show our plays to everybody, but are particularly anxious to show them to our own people and to the children of our own people. We are but four and a half millions here in Ireland, but there must be thirty millions of us scattered through the world, of whom a portion are still ready to share our imagination and our discoveries. We are sending them a vision of the new Ireland, so full of curiosity, so full of self-criticism, our new satirical comedy, sometimes so tolerant, sometimes so bitter in its merriment.

42

READING OF POEMS[380]

I am going to read my poems with great emphasis upon their rhythm, and that may seem strange if you are not used to it. I remember the great English poet, William Morris, coming in a[381] rage out of some lecture hall where somebody had recited some passage out of his *Sigurd the Volsung,* 'It gave me a devil of a lot of trouble', said Morris, 'to get that thing into verse'.[382] It gave me the devil of a lot of trouble to get into verse the poems that I am going to read and that is why I will not read them as if they were prose. I am going to begin with a poem of mine called 'The Lake Isle of Innisfree' because, if you know anything about me, you will expect me to begin with it.[383] It is the only poem of mine which is very widely known. When I was a young lad in the town of Sligo I read Thoreau's essays and wanted to live in a hut on an island in Lough Gill called Innisfree, which means[384] Heather Island. I wrote the poem in London when I was about twenty three. One day in the Strand I[385] heard a little tinkle of water and saw in a shop window a little jet of water balancing a ball on the top; it was an advertisement, I think of cooling drinks, but it set me[386] thinking of Sligo and lake water. I think there is only one obscurity in the poem; I speak of noon as a 'purple glow'; I must have meant by that the reflection of heather in the water.

> I will arise and go now, and go to Innisfree,
> And a small cabin build there, of clay and wattles made:
> Nine bean-rows will I have there, a hive for the honey-bee,
> And live alone in the bee-loud glade.

And I shall have some peace there, for peace comes
    dropping slow,
Dropping from the veils of the morning to where the
    cricket sings;
There midnight's all a glimmer, and noon a purple glow,
And evening full of the linnet's wings.

I will arise and go now, for always night and day
I hear lake water lapping with low sounds by the shore;
While I stand on the roadway, or on the pavements grey,
I hear it in the deep heart's core.[387]

A couple of miles from Innisfree [no, four or five miles from Innisfree][388] there is a great rock called Dooney Rock where I often picnicked when a child, and when in my twenty fourth[389] year I made up a poem about a merry fiddler, I called him 'The Fiddler of Dooney' in commemoration of that rock and of all those picnics. The places mentioned in the poem are places near Sligo.

When I play on my fiddle in Dooney,
Folk dance like a wave of the sea;
My cousin is priest in Kilvarnet,
My brother in Mocharabuiee.

I passed my brother and cousin:
They read in their books of prayer;
I read in my book of songs
I bought at the Sligo fair.

When we come at the end of time
To Peter sitting in state,
He will smile on the three old spirits,
But call me first through the gate;

For the good are always the merry,
Save by an evil chance,
And the merry love the fiddle,
And the merry love to dance:

And when the folk there spy me,
They will all come up to me,
With 'Here is the fiddler of Dooney!'
And dance like a wave of the sea.[390]

I used to go a great deal into the cottages when I was a child and listen to the stories of the people, and a great deal both of my prose and my poetry was the retelling of those stories. Presently Galway took the place of Sligo for I had come to spend every summer there. One day I met an old man in the wood who had spent seventy years of life keeping the wood clear for shooters.[391] He talked about the sights and sounds of the wood and the beasts that came there; he told me that hedgehogs used to steal apples by rolling about until they were stuck all over with apples and then going home, and a lot about cats, cats that had gone wild and lived in the wood. He said that every cat in the beginning of the world had ninepence and that it gave threepence to have nine lives, threepence to see in the dark, and threepence that we might leave it a plateful of milk every day. 'Never expect gratitude from a cat', he said, 'for when you leave it a plateful of milk, what are you doing but carrying out the bargain?' But he saw things that were not of this world. Once he saw a beautiful young girl plucking nuts and while he was looking at her she vanished into the ground, and he said, 'I saw her never again, never again'. And that made me think that perhaps quite a number of people may have seen in dreams of the day or the night beautiful forms and been unhappy because they saw them never again, and that thought started me making up a story to express their emotion, and I put that story into a poem called 'The Wandering Aengus'. I associate apple blossom with the woman in it not for the sake of ornament but because in ancient Ireland the apple tree sometimes symbolised a woman whereas a man was symbolised by the yew tree from which bows are made.

> I went out to the hazel wood,
> Because a fire was in my head,
> And cut and peeled a hazel wand,
> And hooked a berry to a thread;
> And when white moths were on the wing,
> And moth-like stars were flickering out,
> I dropped the berry in a stream
> And caught a little silver trout.
>
> When I had laid it on the floor
> I went to blow the fire aflame,
> But something rustled on the floor,

And some one called me by my name:
It had become a glimmering girl
With apple blossom in her hair
Who called me by my name and ran
And faded through the brightening air.

Though I am old with wandering
Through hollow lands and hilly lands,
I will find out where she has gone,
And kiss her lips and take her hands;
And walk among long dappled grass,
And pluck till time and times are done
The silver apples of the moon,
The golden apples of the sun.[392]

The poems which I have read you up to this were written in early life and belong to my more popular work. Of recent years I have ceased writing of legends and country stories and have written mainly of the passing events of life as those events have affected myself. Sometimes I have written of the deaths of friends and acquaintances and such poems are probably the best I have written of recent years. When I was a very young man at Sligo I met two very lovely young girls and when the other day they died as old women I wrote the poem which I am now going to read to you; it is called 'In Memory of Eva Gore-Booth and Con Markiewicz'; both names may be known to you, one will certainly be known.[393]

The light of evening, Lissadell,
Great windows open to the south,
Two girls in silk kimonos, both
Beautiful, one a gazelle.

But a raving autumn shears
Blossom from the summer's wreath;
The older is condemned to death,
Pardoned, drags out lonely years
Conspiring among the ignorant.
I know not what the younger dreams—
Some vague Utopia—and she seems,
When withered old and skeleton-gaunt,
An image of such politics.

Many a time I think to seek
One or the other out and speak
Of that old Georgian mansion, mix
Pictures of the mind, recall
That table and the talk of youth,
Two girls in silk kimonos, both
Beautiful, one a gazelle.

Dear shadows, now you know it all,
All the folly of a fight
With a common wrong or right.
The innocent and the beautiful
Have no enemy but time;
Arise and bid me strike a match
And strike another till time catch;
Should the conflagration climb,
Run till all the sages know.
We the great gazebo built,
They convicted us of guilt;
Bid me strike a match and blow.[394]

Sometimes I have written of my living friends and the poem which I am now going to read you is addressed to Lady Gregory's grandchild Anne Gregory, a girl of twenty who has a great abundance of yellow hair, beautiful hair the colour of a wheatfield. I have in the poem expanded some few words that I once said to her and a word or two that she replied.

'Never shall a young man,
Thrown into despair
By those great honey-coloured
Ramparts at your ear,
Love you for yourself alone
And not your yellow hair.'

'But I can get a hair-dye
And set such colour there,
Brown, or black, or carrot,
That young men in despair
May love me for myself alone
And not my yellow hair.'

'I heard an old religious man
But yesternight declare
That he had found a test to prove
That only God, my dear,
Could love you for yourself alone
And not your yellow hair.'[395]

Twenty years ago when I was lecturing in America and I read a number of my poems to some audience in one of the eastern states, a woman asked from the end of the hall—I found afterwards that she was a professional elocutionist—'Why do you read your poetry in that manner, Mr Yeats?' I said, 'All poets from Homer up to date have read their poetry exactly as I read mine'. She said, 'What is your authority for saying Homer read his poetry in that manner?' and I said, 'The only authority I can give you is the authority that the Scotchman gave when he claimed Shakespeare for his own country. The ability of the man warrants the presumption'.

43

IRELAND, 1921−1931 [396]

I

I walked along the south side of the Dublin quays a couple of years ago; looked at the funnels of certain Dublin steamers and found that something incredible had happened; I had not shuddered with disgust though they were painted green on patriotic grounds; that deep olive green seemed beautiful. I hurried to the Parnell Monument and looked at the harp. Yes, that too was transfigured; it was a most beautiful symbol; it had ascended out of sentimentality, out of insincere rhetoric, out of mob emotion. When I reached home I took from the mantelpiece a bronze medal of myself and studied the little shamrock the American medallist had put after the date.[397] But there there had been no transformation; the disgust that will always keep me from printing that portrait in any book of mine, or forgiving its creator, had increased, as though the ascent of the other symbols had left the shamrock the more alone with its association of drink and jocularity.

II

What had happened to those other symbols? What had gone down into my subconsciousness? What had changed the foundations of my mind? Five or six years ago an old Galway farmer told me that he supported the Government because it had given us the only peace Ireland had known in his lifetime. A month ago a Thomist philosopher who is an experienced politician said to me: 'Nothing can bring Europe to its senses but an epoch of Bolshevism; the people ask the impossible and the governments are afraid to govern'. Our Government has not been afraid to govern, and that has changed the symbols, and not for my eyes only. We are on the edge of a general election and nobody in either party is confident, for it is hard to foretell anything about an election held under a scheme of proportional representation except that neither side will have more than a bare majority.[398] If the Republicans come into power we shall have a few anxious months while they discover where they have asked the impossible, and then they in their turn will govern. An Irishman is wild in speech, the result of centuries of irresponsible opposition, but he casts it off in the grip of fact with a contempt beyond the reach of sober-speaking men.

The Government of the Free State has been proved legitimate by the only effective test; it has been permitted to take life. The British Government, after the Rebellion of 1916, executed some sixteen or seventeen men and it was out of the country in five years. In the middle of our Civil War a Republican prisoner said to his fellow-prisoners: 'We have won. I have news: they have executed their first man'. They executed more than seventy and not a vote changed.[399] These dead cannot share the glory of those earlier dead; their names are not spoken aloud to-day except at those dwindling meetings assembled in O'Connell Street or at some prison gate by almost the sole surviving friend of my early manhood, protesting in sybilline age, as once in youth and beauty, against what seems to her a tyranny.[400]

III

When I think of the legislation of those ten years I think first of the roads which have brought lorry and bus, the newspaper, and here and there books, to remote villages; then of the electrical works at Ardna-crusha. These works are successful; the demand has exceeded the prophecy of the Minister. The Minister and his Board have quarrelled as to whether they should pay their way from the start or sell cheap until the whole power of the Shannon is employed; but of the works themselves there has been no criticism.[401] They were the Government's first great practical success, a first object-lesson in politics. Planned by German engineers, they were attacked in the English Press, and still more vigorously by men and newspapers in Ireland, which the Irish public associated, often mistakenly, with English interests. When the Government seized the

Republican headquarters they found letters from men all over Ireland resigning from Republican posts because such a project, carried against such opposition, proved our economic independence.

Nothing remains the same and there have been few mistakes. My six years in the Irish Senate taught me that no London Parliament could have found the time or the knowledge for that transformation. But I am less grateful to the Government for what it has done than because its mere existence delivered us from obsession. No sooner was it established, the civil war behind it, than the musician, the artist, the dramatist, the poet, the student, found—perhaps for the first time —that he could give his whole heart to his work. Theatre and concert audiences increased, the Royal Dublin Society built a new hall double the size of the old and doubled the number of performances; and this vigorous life stayed unimpaired until the European economic crisis.

IV

Freedom from obsession brought me a transformation akin to religious conversion. I had thought much of my fellow-workers—Synge, Lady Gregory, Lane—but had seen nothing in Protestant Ireland as a whole but its faults, had carried through my projects in face of its opposition or its indifference, had fed my imagination upon the legends of the Catholic villages or upon Irish mediaeval poetry; but now my affection turned to my own people, to my own ancestors, to the books they had read. It seemed we had a part to play at last that might find us allies everywhere, for we alone had not to assume in public discussion of all great issues that we could find in St Mark or St Matthew a shorthand report of the words of Christ attested before a magistrate. We sought religious conviction by a more difficult research:

> How charming is divine philosophy!
> Not harsh and crabbed, as dull fools suppose,
> But musical as is Apollo's lute.[402]

Now that Ireland was substituting traditions of government for the rhetoric of agitation our eighteenth century had regained its importance. An Irish Free State soldier, engaged in dangerous service for his Government, said to me that all the philosophy a man needed was in Berkeley. Stirred by those words I began to read *The Dialogues of Hylas and Philonous*.[†, 403] From Berkeley I went to

Swift, whose hold on Irish imagination is comparable to that of O'Connell. The Protestant representatives in Dáil and Senate were worthy of this past; two or three went in danger of their lives; some had their houses burnt; country gentlemen came from the blackened ruins of their houses to continue without melodrama or complaint some perhaps highly technical debate in the Senate. Month by month their prestige rose. When the censorship of books was proposed certain Protestant Bishops disassociated themselves from it and had the Government persisted with the Bill in its first form and penalized opinion we might have had a declaration, perhaps from the Episcopacy as a whole, that private judgement implied access to the materials of judgement. Then, just when we seemed a public necessity, our Episcopacy lost its head. Without consulting its representatives in Dáil or Senate, without a mandate from anybody, in the teeth of a refusal of support from Trinity College, terrified where none threatened, it appealed, not to the Irish people, but to the Colonial Conference, to keep the Irish Courts in subordination to the Privy Council, thereby seeming to declare that our ancestors made the independence of the legislature and the Courts the foundation of their politics, and of Ireland's from that day, because those Courts and that legislature protected not a nation but a class.[404] When these blind old men turned their backs upon Swift and Grattan, at a moment too when the past actions of the Colonial Conference itself had already decided the issue, they had forgotten, one hopes, or had never learnt, that their predecessors sat in the Irish House of Lords of 1719, when it sent the Irish Court of Exchequer to prison for accepting a decision of that Privy Council.

V

If I were a young man I would start an agitation to show them their task in life. As a beginning I might gather together the descendants of those who had voted with Grattan against the Union that we might ask the British Government to return his body; it lies in Westminster Abbey under a flat plain stone since it was laid there, despite the protests of his followers, less to commemorate his fame than to prevent a shrine and a pilgrimage. Then I would ask the Irish Government to line the streets with soldiers that we might with all befitting pomp open the pavement of St Patrick's for one last burial.

44

POEMS ABOUT WOMEN[405]

I asked a great friend, a very old woman, what I should read to-night.[406] She said, 'Read them poems about women'. I told her of something that happened to me in one of the Southern States of America when I was upon a lecturing tour. I had heard that I would have round me on the platform a great many poets who had been poets before the Civil War. Yes, they were all there, men and women of an incredible age, the survivors from a cultivated and leisurely life long past away. When I had finished my lecture I read some of my poems, and then from various parts of the lecture hall came voices asking for this or that poem of mine and all the poems they asked for were love poems. At last I got cross and said 'I will not read you any poem of mine which any of you can by any possible chance think an expression of my personal feelings, and certainly I will not read you my love poems'. Then there came a voice from one of the old poets at my side, a cracked high female voice—'Quite right, quite right. I shall always say that in future'. I thought that story would convince my old friend that she had suggested an impossible subject, but she merely repeated with an impatient voice 'Read them poems about women'. Then I remembered that I would not be reading to a crowd; you would all be listening singly or in twos and threes; above all that I myself would be alone, speaking to something that looks like a visiting card on a pole; that after all it would be no worse than publishing love poems in a book. Nor do I want to disappoint that old friend of mine for I am sure that she has had her portable wireless brought to her room, that she is at this moment listening to find out if I have taken her advice.

The first poems which I am going to read contain no secrets. They were written when I was a very young man, not yet in love with anybody or troubled about anything but literary style. My generation hated poetic diction and poetic eloquence. We respected Swinburne but were afraid to read him for fear he might lead us astray.[407] If you study Dowson's 'Cynara' or Lionel Johnson's 'King Charles' you will notice that they are before all else good speech, the natural words in the natural order.[408] There is no mere ornament, there is nothing that seems literary or sedentary. So might some actual man have spoken to some one man or woman if greatly moved. When I made my search for simplicity, I went from cottage to cottage in Ireland getting people to tell stories or sing them, and I tried to write like those stories. Perhaps you will think the little verses I am now going to read you rather empty, but they still seem to me good in their unpretending way. In each case it was somebody else's thought that I took up and elaborated. I asked a man who pretended to know Irish to tell me the meaning of the words 'Shule, shule, shularoon'—they are the burden of a well-known Irish ballad. He said they mean 'Shy as a rabbit, helpful and shy'. They meant nothing of the kind, he was a liar, but he gave me the theme of a poem which I call 'To an Isle in the Water'.[409]

Shy one, shy one,
Shy one of my heart,
She moves in the firelight
Pensively apart.

She carries in the dishes,
And lays them in a row.
To an isle in the water
With her would I go.

She carries in the candles,
And lights the curtained room,
Shy in the doorway
And shy in the gloom;

And shy as a rabbit,
Helpful and shy.
To an isle in the water
With her would I fly.

An old woman at Ballisodare sang me a song of which I have forgotten everything except this refrain,

> She bid me take life easy
> As the leaves grow on the tree.

and that suggested to me the following poem which I call 'Down by
the Salley Gardens'.[410] It is well known because an Irish musician
called Hughes set it to a fine air.[411] I wish I could sing it to you instead
of speaking it. A salley garden is a place where willows grow.

> Down by the salley gardens my love and I did meet;
> She passed the salley gardens with little snow-white feet.
> She bid me take love easy, as the leaves grow on the tree;
> But I, being young and foolish, with her would not agree.
>
> In a field by the river my love and I did stand,
> And on my leaning shoulder she laid her snow-white hand.
> She bid me take life easy, as the grass grows on the weirs;
> But I was young and foolish, and now am full of tears.

A year ago, more than forty years after I wrote these poems,
somebody repeated to me a refrain which is all that has survived of
a mediaeval Dublin poem.[412] I founded upon this refrain a poem
that is not yet published. It will show you perhaps how little I have
changed. A dancer is speaking, but I will not explain the poem
which owes what quality it has to its mystery. Who was the dancer,
to whom does she speak? I do not know.

'I AM OF IRELAND'

> *'I am of Ireland,*
> *And the Holy Land of Ireland,*
> *And time runs on,' cried she.*
> *'Come out of charity,*
> *Come dance with me in Ireland.'*
>
> One man, one man alone
> In that outlandish gear,
> One solitary man
> Of all that rambled there
> Had turned his stately head.

'That is a long way off,
And time runs on,' he said,
'And the night grows rough.'

'I am of Ireland,
And the Holy Land of Ireland,
And time runs on,' cried she.
'Come out of charity
Come dance with me in Ireland.'

'The fiddlers are all thumbs,
Or the fiddle-string accursed,
The drums and the kettledrums
And the trumpets all are burst,
And the trombone,' cried he,
'The trumpet and trombone,'
And cocked a malicious eye,
'But time runs on, runs on.'

'I am of Ireland,
And the Holy Land of Ireland,
And time runs on,' cried she.
'Come out of charity
Come dance with me in Ireland.'

Now I am going to read a much longer poem and in the second stanza are the names of famous dancers in Europe before the war, the French dancer Gaby Deslys,[†] the Russian Pavlova, the American Ruth St Denis whose London success was not as great as beauty and skill deserved. I speak also of an American actress but do not name her, her name was Kate Marlow. I call the poem 'His Phoenix'.[413]

There is a queen in China, or maybe it's in Spain,
And birthdays and holidays such praises can be heard
Of her unblemished lineaments, a whiteness with no stain,
That she might be that sprightly girl trodden by a bird;
And there's a score of duchesses, surpassing womankind,
Or who have found a painter to make them so for pay
And smooth out stain and blemish with the elegance of his
    mind:
I knew a phoenix in my youth, so let them have their day.

The young men every night applaud their Gaby's laughing eye,
And Ruth St Denis had more charm although she had poor
    luck;
From nineteen hundred nine or ten, Pavlova's had the cry,
And there's a player in the States who gathers up her cloak
And flings herself out of the room when Juliet would be bride
With all a woman's passion, a child's imperious way,
And there are—but no matter if there are scores beside:
I knew a phoenix in my youth, so let them have their day.

There's Margaret and Marjorie and Dorothy and Nan,
A Daphne and a Mary who live in privacy;
One's had her fill of lovers, another's had but one,
Another boasts, 'I pick and choose and have but two or three.'
If head and limb have beauty and the instep's high and light
They can spread out what sail they please for all I have to say,
Be but the breakers of men's hearts or engines of delight:
I knew a phoenix in my youth, so let them have their day.

There'll be that crowd, that barbarous crowd, through all the
    centuries,
And who can say but some young belle may walk and talk
    men wild
Who is my beauty's equal, though that my heart denies,
But not the exact likeness, the simplicity of a child,
And that proud look as though she had gazed into the
    burning sun,
And all the shapely body no tittle gone astray.
I mourn for that most lonely thing; and yet God's will be
    done:
I knew a phoenix in my youth, so let them have their day.

The next poem is more dramatic, more personal, a definite man
speaking. Like the last poem it was written when I was old enough
to know what I felt, to stand outside myself as it were and look at
myself. It is called 'The Folly of Being Comforted'.[414]

> One that is ever kind said yesterday:
> 'Your well-belovèd's hair has threads of grey,
> And little shadows come about her eyes;
> Time can but make it easier to be wise

Though now it seems impossible, and so
All that you need is patience.'

Heart cries, 'No,
I have not a crumb of comfort, not a grain.
Time can but make her beauty over again:
Because of that great nobleness of hers
The fire that stirs about her, when she stirs,
Burns but more clearly. O she had not these ways
When all the wild summer was in her gaze.'

O heart! O heart! if she'd but turn her head,
You'd know the folly of being comforted.

When we are young we do not know what we feel, we cannot stand outside ourselves and look at ourselves, we live in dreams and express ourselves in a kind of mythology, or at any rate I so lived and so expressed myself. I think what popularity I have had as a poet began when Stevenson praised my poem 'Innisfree', and a great nonconformist editor praised my love poem 'The Cloths of Heaven'.[415]

Had I the heavens' embroidered cloths,
Enwrought with golden and silver light,
The blue and the dim and the dark cloths
Of night and light and the half-light,
I would spread the cloths under your feet:
But I, being poor, have only my dreams;
I have spread my dreams under your feet;
Tread softly because you tread on my dreams.

I pass on to poems that are not love poems.[416] Though they are not love poems I shall find it difficult to read some of them without too much emotion. A little before the war there died a beautiful, distinguished, charming witty lady. Though I had known her but slightly, somebody asked me to visit her upon her deathbed. I had known a member of her family well and she knew my poetry. Every day for many months some friend sat and talked at her bedside. My turn came once in each week I think. During all that time, although dying of a most painful illness, she was always gay, always charming. If one of her visitors had suffered from some slight ailment she never forgot to ask about it, she seemed the only person there who was in perfect health. She was in reality happy. 'I was never happy' she said to me 'until I began to die. Never before had I known that my friends loved me'. Balzac was the moralist of her generation and mine and she died like one of his great ladies.[417] The first poem about her that I am going to read I call 'Her Courtesy'.

> With the old kindness, the old distinguished grace,
> She lies, her lovely piteous head amid dull red hair
> Propped upon pillows, rouge on the pallor of her face.
> She would not have us sad because she is lying there,
> And when she meets our gaze her eyes are laughter-lit,
> Her speech a wicked tale that we may vie with her,
> Matching our broken-hearted wit against her wit,
> Thinking of saints and of Petronius Arbiter.

One day a famous artist brought her some drawings and a set of dolls that he had made for her, caricatures of friends or of enemies. A couple of the dolls represented herself in costumes worn at fancy dress balls. I made a poem upon this theme.[418]

> Bring where our Beauty lies
> A new modelled doll, or drawing,
> With a friend's or an enemy's
> Features, or maybe showing
> Her features when a tress
> Of dull red hair was flowing
> Over some silken dress
> Cut in the Turkish fashion,
> Or, it may be, like a boy's.
> We have given the world our passion,
> We have naught for death but toys.

At Christmas her friend brought her a Christmas tree hung all over with curious little works of art. In the poem I made upon that theme I speak of the great enemy, that great enemy is of course death.[419]

> Pardon, great enemy,
> Without an angry thought
> We've carried in our tree,
> And here and there have bought

Till all the boughs are gay,
And she may look from the bed
On pretty things that may
Please a fantastic head.
Give her a little grace,
What if a laughing eye
Have looked into your face?
It is about to die.

Her brother, a man of genius who died in early manhood, had faced unjust obloquy with great courage. I allude to him at the end of the following poem.[420]

She has not grown uncivil
As narrow natures would
And called the pleasures evil
Happier days thought good;
She knows herself a woman,
No red and white of a face,
Or rank, raised from a common
Unreckonable race;
And how should her heart fail her
Or sickness break her will
With her dead brother's valour
For an example still?

My last poem will be about a very different person. When I was young I stayed constantly at my grandparents' house in Sligo. From the front windows I could see under the slope of Ben Bulben Sir Henry Gore-Booth's great grey house among trees. His daughter Constance lived there, a daring rider and country beauty. I had never spoken to her but I had often seen her upon horseback. I remember one day standing in the window looking at that old grey house[421] and repeating Milton's lines:

Bosomed high in tufted trees,
Where perhaps some beauty lies,
The cynosure of neighbouring eyes.[422]

A queer story comes into my memory. An old Sligo shop-keeper was out riding. He met the Sligo Harriers. Constance Gore-Booth was leading the hunt but another rider was making a great effort to reach a certain gap in the hedge before her. The old shop-keeper deliberately planted himself and his horse in front of the rider and was carried home with a broken leg or arm. Another memory recalls her as she was a good many years later when she had become Madame Markiewicz,[†] the wife of a Polish count. Somebody had given a supper to the Abbey Players, she was one of the guests. Another of the guests, the editor of an evening newspaper, made a sonnet in praise of her beauty, wrote it upon the table cloth, cut out the piece and passed it across the table to her. Next day, I, as one of the directors of the Abbey Theatre, had to face the enraged hotel proprietor and promise him a new table cloth. Ten years later Madame Markiewicz took part in the insurrection of 1916. She was in command of the rebels who had seized and fortified the College of Surgeons. She fought bravely, was condemned to death and pardoned at the last moment. After the Treaty she took part in the rebellion against the Free State Government and was again imprisoned. I heard that while in gaol she tamed a seagull, taught it to come into her cell for food and take the food out of her hand. My memory went back to her youthful days in Sligo and I made a poem which I have called 'To a Political Prisoner'. In the lines of the poem which condemn her politics I was not thinking of her part in two rebellions, but of other matters of quarrel.[423] We had never been on the same side at the same time.

> She that but little patience knew,
> From childhood on, had now so much
> A grey gull lost its fear and flew
> Down to her cell and there alit,
> And there endured her fingers' touch
> And from her fingers ate its bit.
>
> Did she in touching that lone wing
> Recall the years before her mind
> Became a bitter, an abstract thing,
> Her thought some popular enmity:
> Blind and leader of the blind
> Drinking the foul ditch where they lie?

When long ago I saw her ride
Under Ben Bulben to the meet,
The beauty of her country-side
With all youth's lonely wildness stirred,
She seemed to have grown clean and sweet
Like any rock-bred, sea-borne bird:

Sea-borne, or balanced on the air
When first it sprang out of the nest
Upon some lofty rock to stare
Upon the cloudy canopy,
While under its storm-beaten breast
Cried out the hollows of the sea.

I have as far as possible read you my most popular poems. W. E. Henley, the famous poet and journalist, said in my hearing that he never knew whether he had written well or not until other people told him, and added that Cardinal Newman had said much the same about his own poems.[424] I am not as uncertain as that and yet I am best pleased when somebody else's opinion supports mine.

W. B. Y.

45

PLAIN MAN'S *OEDIPUS*[425]

When I first lectured in America thirty years ago I heard at the University of Notre Dame that they had played *Oedipus the King*. That play was forbidden by the English censorship on the ground of its immorality; Oedipus commits incest; but if a Catholic university could perform it in America my own theatre could perform it in Ireland. Ireland had no censorship, and a successful performance might make her proud of her freedom, say even, perhaps, 'I have an old historical religion molded to the body of man like an old suit of clothes and am therefore free'.

A friend of mine used to say that it was all a toss-up whether she seemed good or bad, for a decision firmly made before breakfast lasted three months. When I got back to Dublin I found a young Greek scholar who, unlike myself, had not forgotten his Greek, took out of a pigeonhole at the theatre a manuscript translation of 'Oedipus' too complicated in its syntax for the stage, bought Jebb's translation and a translation published at a few pence for dishonest schoolboys.[426] Whenever I could not understand the precise thoughts behind the translators' half Latin, half Victorian dignity I got a bald translation from my Greek scholar. I spoke out every sentence, very often from the stage, with one sole object that the words should sound natural and fall in their natural order, that every sentence should be a spoken, not a written, sentence. Then when I had finished the dialogue in the rough and was still shrinking at the greater labor of the choruses the English censor withdrew his ban and I lost interest.

About five years ago my wife found the manuscript and set me to work again, and when the dialogue was revised and the choruses

244

written Lady Gregory and I went through it all, altering every sentence that might not be intelligible on the Blasket Islands. Have I made a plain man's 'Oedipus'? The pit and the gallery of the Abbey Theatre think so. When I say intelligible on the Blasket Islands I mean that, being an ignorant man, I may not have gone to Greece through a Latin mist. Greek literature, like old Irish literature, was founded upon belief, not like Latin literature upon documents. No man has ever prayed to or dreaded one of Vergil's nymphs, but when Oedipus at Colonus went into the Wood of the Furies he felt the same creeping in his flesh that an Irish countryman feels in certain haunted woods in Galway and in Sligo. At the Abbey Theatre we play both *Oedipus the King* and *Oedipus at Colonus,* and they seem at home there.

46

THE GREAT BLASKET[427]

Aran was John Synge's first choice. There he thought himself happy for the first time, 'having escaped the squalor of the poor and the nullity of the rich'.[428] There he and Lady Gregory saw one another for the first time, looked at one another with unfriendly eyes without speaking, not knowing that they were in search of the same thing.[429] Then others came and he fled to the Great Blasket. He told me upon his return that he found an old crippled pensioner visiting there, that they had come away together, stayed in the same little hotel in Ventry or Dingle. One morning the pensioner was not to be found. Synge searched for him everywhere, trying to find out if he had gone back to the Island, jealous as if the Island had been a woman. A few years ago the Irish Government, lacking texts for students of modern Irish, asked Mr Robin Flower to persuade one of its oldest inhabitants to write his life. After much toil he got the main facts on to a sheet of notepaper and thought his task at an end. Then Mr Flower read him some chapters of Gorki's reminiscences.[430] Now all was well, for to write like that was to write as he talked, and he was one of the best talkers upon the Island where there is no written literature. Then came a long delay; scholars had to pronounce upon the language, moralists upon the events; but when the book was published the few Gaelic speakers of my acquaintance passionately denied or affirmed that it was a masterpiece.[431] Then a Blasket Islander settled in Dublin began to read out and circulate in manuscript poems that pleased a Gaelic scholar whose judgement I value, but were too Rabelaisian to please the eye of Government.[432] Then Mr Maurice O'Sullivan, a young Civic

Guard, who had lived upon the Island until he reached manhood, wrote his life, called it *Twenty Years A-Growing,* and Chatto and Windus have published a translation.

All this writing comes from the sheep runs and diminishing fisheries of an Island seven or eight miles long and a mile broad, from its hundred and fifty inhabitants who preserve in their little white cottages, roofed with tarred felt, an ancient culture of the song and the spoken word, who consult neither newspaper nor book, but carry all their knowledge in their minds. A few more years and a tradition where Seventeenth Century poets, Mediaeval storytellers, Fathers of the Church, even Neoplatonic philosophers have left their traces in whole poems or fragmentary thoughts and isolated images will have vanished. 'The young people are no use', said an old man to Synge. 'I am not as good a man as my father was and my son is growing up worse than I am'.[433]

Mr Maurice O'Sullivan, by a series of episodes, his first days at school, his first day puffin hunting, a regatta at Ventry, a wake, a shipwreck, a night upon a deserted neighbouring Island, calls up a vision of the sea, dark or bright, creates by the simplest means a sense of mystery, makes us for the moment part of a life that has not changed for thousands of years. And he himself seems unchanging like the life, the same when a little boy playing truant as when a grown man travelling by rail for the first time. It is not a defect that there is no subjectivity, no development; that like Helen during the ten years' siege he is untouched by time. Upon this limitation depend the clarity and the gaiety of his work. Fate has separated his people from all that could not sustain their happiness and their energy, from all that might confuse the soul, given them the protection that monks and nuns find in their traditional rule, aristocrats in their disdain.

Much modern Irish literature is violent, harsh, almost brutal, in its insistence upon the bare facts of life. Again and again I have defended plays or novels unlike anything I have myself attempted, or anything in the work of others that has given me great pleasure, because I have known that they were medicinal to a people struggling against second-hand thought and insincere emotion. Mr O'Sullivan's book is not a great book, the events are too unrelated, but it is perfect of its kind, it has elegance; Mr E. M. Forster compares it with a sea-bird's egg; and I am grateful.[434] He has found admirable translators—Mrs Llewellyn Davies and Professor George Thomson,[†] who teaches Greek through the vehicle of Gaelic in Galway University.[435] They have translated his Gaelic into a dialect that has taken much of its syntax from Gaelic. Dr Douglas Hyde used it in the prose of his *Love Songs of Connaught;* he was the first. Then Lady Gregory, in her translation of old Irish epics; then Synge and she in their plays. In late years it has superseded in the works of our dramatists and novelists the conventional speech nineteenth-century writers put into the mouth of Irish peasants. To Lady Gregory and to Synge it was more than speech, for it implied an attitude towards letters, sometimes even towards life, an attitude Lady Gregory was accustomed to define by a quotation from Aristotle: 'To think like a wise man but to express oneself like the common people'.

47

THE GROWTH OF A POET[436]

When I was a young man poetry had become eloquent and elaborate. Swinburne was the reigning influence and he was very eloquent.[437] A generation came that wanted to be simple, I think I wanted that more than anybody else. I went from cottage to cottage listening to stories, to old songs;[438] sometimes the songs were in English, sometimes they were in Gaelic—then[439] I would get somebody to translate. Some of my best known poems were made in that way. 'Down by the Salley Gardens', for instance, is an elaboration of two lines in English somebody sang to me at Ballysodare,† County Sligo.[440] In my poetry I tried to keep to very simple emotions, to write the natural words, to put them in the natural order. Here is a little poem in which an old peasant woman complains of the young. There is music for it written to what is called the Irish gapped scale. The poem is called 'The Song of the Old Mother':[441]

> I rise in the dawn, and I kneel and blow
> Till the seed of the fire flicker and glow;
> And then I must scrub and bake and sweep
> Till stars are beginning to blink and peep;
> And the young lie long and dream in their bed
> Of the matching of ribbons for bosom and head,
> Their day goes over in idleness,
> And they sigh if the wind but lift a tress:
> While I must work because I am old,
> And the seed of the fire gets feeble and cold.[442]

A poem called 'A Faery Song' was typical of that period. Diarmuid and Grania are[443] the Irish Paris and Helen. Some countryman told me that they slept under the cromlechs.[444] For that reason I called my poem 'A song sung by the people of Faery over Diarmuid and Grania in their bridal sleep under a Cromlech'. I call the people of faery 'old and gay', not 'old and grey' as it is sometimes misprinted. Time cannot touch them.

> We who are old, old and gay,
> O so old!
> Thousands of years, thousands of years,
> If all were told:
>
> Give to these children, new from the world,
> Silence and love;
> And the long dew-dropping hours of the night,
> And the stars above:
>
> Give to these children, new from the world,
> Rest far from men.
> Is anything better, anything better?
> Tell us it then:
>
> Us who are old, old and gay,
> O so old!
> Thousands of years, thousands of years,
> If all were told.

But the best known of these very simple early poems of mine is 'The Fiddler of Dooney'. The places mentioned in the poem are all in County Sligo.[445] Dooney Rock is a great rock on the edge of Lough Gill. I had been to many picnics there and in gratitude called my fiddler by its name:

> When I play on my fiddle in Dooney,
> Folk dance like a wave of the sea;
> My cousin is priest in Kilvarnet,
> My brother in Mocharabuiee.
>
> I passed my brother and cousin:
> They read in their books of prayer;

I read in my book of songs
I bought at the Sligo fair.

When we come at the end of time
To Peter sitting in state,
He will smile on the three old spirits,
But call me first through the gate;

For the good are always the merry,
Save by an evil chance,
And the merry love the fiddle,
And the merry love to dance:

And when the folk there spy me,
They will all come up to me,
With 'Here is the fiddler of Dooney!'
And dance like a wave of the sea.

Years later I tried to return to this early style in 'Running to Paradise'. Some Gaelic book tells of a man running at full speed, who, when asked where he is running, answers 'to Paradise'. I think you will notice the difference in style. The poem is more thoughtful, more packed with little pictures:

As I came over Windy Gap
They threw a halfpenny into my cap,
For I am running to Paradise;
And all that I need do is to wish
And somebody puts his hand in the dish
To throw me a bit of salted fish:
And there the king is but as the beggar.

My brother Mourteen is worn out
With skelping his big brawling lout,
And[446] I am running to Paradise;
A poor life, do what he can,
And though he keep a dog and a gun,
A serving-maid and a serving-man:
And there the king is but as the beggar.

Poor men have grown to be rich men,
And rich men grown to be poor again,

And I am running to Paradise;
And many a darling wit's grown dull
That tossed a bare heel when at school,
Now it has filled an old sock full:
And there the king is but as the beggar.

The wind is old and still at play
While I must hurry upon my way,
For I am running to Paradise;
Yet never have I lit on a friend
To take my fancy like the wind
That nobody can buy or bind:
And there the king is but as the beggar.

In later life I was not satisfied with these simple emotions—
though I tried, and still try, to put the natural words in the natural
order. I had founded Irish literary societies, an Irish Theatre, I had
become associated with the projects of others, I had met much
unreasonable opposition. To overcome it I had to make my
thoughts modern. Modern thought is not simple; I became argumentative, passionate, bitter; when I was very bitter I used to say to
myself, 'I do not write for these people who attack everything that
I value, not for those others who are lukewarm friends, I am writing for a man I have never seen'. I built up in my mind the picture
of a man who lived in the country where I had lived, who fished in
mountain streams where I had fished; I said to myself, 'I do not
know whether he is born yet, but born or unborn it is for him I
write'. I made this poem about him; it is called 'The Fisherman':

Although I can see him still,
The freckled man who goes
To a grey place on a hill
In grey Connemara clothes
At dawn to cast his flies,
It's long since I began
To call up to the eyes
This wise and simple man.
All day I'd looked in the face
What I had hoped 'twould be
To write for my own race

And the reality;
The living men that I hate,
The dead man that I loved,
The craven man in his seat,
The insolent unreproved,
And no knave brought to book
Who has won a drunken cheer,
The witty man and his joke
Aimed at the commonest ear,
The clever man who cries
The catch-cries of the clown,
The beating down of the wise
And great Art beaten down.

Maybe a twelvemonth since
Suddenly I began,
In scorn of this audience,
Imagining a man,
And his sun-freckled face,
And grey Connemara cloth,
Climbing up to a place
Where stone is dark under froth,
And the down-turn of his wrist
When the flies drop in the stream;
A man who does not exist,
A man who is but a dream;
And cried, 'Before I am old
I shall have written him one
Poem maybe as cold
And passionate as the dawn.'[447]

48

THE IRISH
LITERARY MOVEMENT[448]

Mr Yeats, how did the Irish Literary movement begin?

If you had lived at that time you would know that something had to be done. You want the beginning—which do you want, the egg or the owl?

Egg.

Thank you. I was afraid you were going to say owl. Unionist Ireland read inferior English novels. Nationalist Ireland, so far as it read anything at all, read inferior English novels plus *The Spirit of the Nation,* an anthology of mainly bad political verse, then in its fiftieth edition, and partisan histories, where everybody was good or bad, not according to their characters, but according to the side they took. Some young men made up their minds that they wanted a literature occupied with Ireland and without opinions. We thought that our people were not a reading people, outside the towns, but a listening and singing people. Everybody could sing to some tune or other, and everybody listened to interminable speeches.

You thought that plays were what were really wanted?

The songs came first. We started the Irish Literary Society and the National Literary Society as a substitute for the critical press that we lacked. I seem to remember men singing at meetings of the Irish Literary Society; certainly many songs were written: the famous Irish Song Book was published in a series, edited by Gavan Duffy, with a sub-editor from each society. The songs of Graves, Fahy, and

those of Campbell and Colum written a little later, are folklore.[449]
Then came the theatre, with the two Fays directing the acting, and
Synge, Lady Gregory and I its literature.

*An Irish novelist has been saying, Mr Yeats, that Dublin in those
days was more intellectual than it is now.*

My God, does he say that! Dublin was a vile hole. Nationalist
and Unionist never met. One of the first decisions Lady Gregory
and I made was to accept no invitations, but, when we came to live
in Dublin, to live in the Abbey Theatre as in a ship at sea. Unionist
Ireland was a shabby and pretentious England where we would
have met nothing but sneers. Nationalist Ireland was torn with
every kind of political passion and prejudice, wanting, insofar as it
wanted any literature at all, Nationalist propaganda disguised as
literature. We wanted plays about life, not about opinions—Ireland
for their sole theme. A work of art is any piece of life, seen through
the eyes or experienced in the soul, completely expounded. We
insisted, and the Abbey Theatre today still insists, upon every freedom necessary to that exposition. People accused us of all kinds of
things, but we had no axe to grind; our enemies had the axes.

*Is it true that you began your movement in little halls in back
streets of Dublin?*

Little halls certainly, and they were sometimes in back streets.
We could have done nothing without the two Fays. William Fay
directed a little amateur company that played English farces in a
Dublin coffee palace. He put that company at our disposal; and a
patriotic society called The Daughters of Erin joined us, with Miss
Allgood and her sister, Miss O'Neill, among its members. Lady
Gregory, Synge and I wrote or found the plays. There was no
money. The players worked in some office or warehouse during the
day, but had their real life upon the stage. Then rich friends came
forward, especially one rich English friend, and we were established
in the Abbey Theatre.[450]

Some say that your audience was more intelligent in those days.

It was certainly different. There was an intense curiosity about
Irish life. It had never before been put upon the stage with any re-
semblance to reality. When the curtain rose upon a Connacht kitchen

everybody sat up; even the invention of that stage kitchen was a matter of enthusiastic invention. I made the first model, building it in cardboard and tinting it with ochre to show the effect of the turf smoke. That curiosity about Irish life has gone; a Connacht kitchen bores an audience. Any sort of play about Ireland that has reasonable coherence was of interest once; today it must be a good play.

Are you finding it much harder to get plays?

Yes, much harder; and that is why the Abbey Theatre has changed its policy. We feel that if we are to get dramatists we must interest them in the art of the theatre. We must show them what is being done in Europe; we must show them some of the best work of the modern dramatists; and we must show them certain kinds of modern production. A new scenic art has arisen. Our stage management of the past has had only one object, the acting; in that it has been completely successful. We are not going to give up our fine acting, but we wish to add the modern beauty of scene, and there the Gate Theatre has been far ahead of us.[451]

I think one of your difficulties, Mr Yeats, is that the young men have taken to writing novels instead of plays.

That is very acute of you. I remember Lady Gregory saying some twenty years ago: 'Nobody ever writes an Irish novel now. Everybody is writing plays'. If we can only interest the novelists in the art of the theatre, we may get fine plays again. Their art has developed; it is no longer the old realism.

I saw The Village Wooing *at the Abbey the other day.*[452] *Its scenery was certainly not realistic. I thought that cock-eyed deckhouse, deck and funnell charming and amusing.*

Yes, and quite suitable to the play. Mr Shaw has never been a realist. The more improbable his fable the better it pleased him. He was thinking of the debate between the characters, of the quaint lights it threw on life. We had to invent scenery as improbable as his fable. Mr O'Faolain† said the other day that realism was finished, that men wanted to write about what was happening in their own souls. Well, I want Mr O'Faolain† to write plays.[453] So we are going to show him, not always, but now and again, a form of production that makes the mind more important than the fact. Twenty years ago the one idea a producer had was to copy natural objects. I objected to a scene in an enormously expensive New York production of *Parsifal,* and the producer said to me: 'It must be all right, that tree in front of you was copied from a real oak tree, branch by branch; we got an artist to draw it for us'. He couldn't understand that that was exactly what I objected to. *Parsifal* symbolises an action that takes place in the mind alone.[454] The pendulum has swung so far the other way now that a famous Russian producer said the other day: 'You must never paint a scene upon a backcloth unless to give an air of unreality'. That statement goes too far. If your dialogue is realistic, if your characters talk it in a drawingroom or a kitchen, you must represent that drawingroom or that kitchen as accurately as possible. But if the work is fantastic, poetical, mythical, your scenery must be the same. You are playing a game, and you must keep it a game. An acquaintance of mine once put water into a child's toy bath; the child burst into tears; a toy bath, said the child, must have toy water.

I hope you won't mind my saying what I'm going to say, Mr Yeats. A lot of people think the Abbey Theatre is only Anglo-Ireland, and that what we want in this country is Gaelic civilization.

Of course it is Anglo-Irish. When Chaucer was writing and English literature was being founded, there were people the historians call Anglo-Norman; they became the English people. Anglo-Ireland is already Ireland. You may revive the Gaelic language but you cannot revive Gaelic civilization. We have not only English but European thoughts and customs in our heads and in our habits. We could not, if we would, give them up. You may revive the Gaelic language, you cannot revive the Gaelic race. There may be pure Gaels in the Blasket Islands but there are none in the Four Courts, in the College of Surgeons, at the Universities, in the Executive Council, at Mr Cosgrave's headquarters. You may revive the Gaelic language, but if you do Anglo-Ireland will speak it. But I hate all hyphenated words. Anglo-Ireland is your word, not mine.

Oh but I am only talking to make you talk.

All right, but henceforth I shall say the Irish Race. The pure Englishman came to Ireland under Cromwell and married into the mixed Irish race. The pure Gael from the Blasket Islands comes to

Dublin and goes into the civil service; he will marry into that race in his turn. The Irish people are as much a unity as the German, French, or English people, though many strands have gone to the making of it, and any man who says that we are not talks mischievous nonsense.

You said that the Dublin of your youth was a vile place. What do you think of the Dublin of today?

It is incomparably better, gayer, happier, more intelligent, more liberal-minded. The old Dublin, divided into two hereditary parties and separated from action, was malicious, bitter, and intolerant. The people I meet today are ready to discuss their difference without ill-temper; even men who fought against each other twelve years ago can exchange memories without hate. There must be narrow, savage minds somewhere—I occasionally read their letters to the paper—but an educated man no longer meets them. Dublin is now an Irish capital with the vigorous thought of a capital city, to some extent a European capital.

49

ABBEY THEATRE
BROADCAST

Miss Ria Mooney and Mr John Stephenson, two players from the Abbey Theatre, Dublin, are about to sing and speak a group of poems and songs.[455] The fiddle is being played by Miss O'Hart Burke.[456] Mr Stephenson will first sing 'The Ballad of O'Bruadir'.[457] O'Bruadir was a pirate, and Mr Higgins wrote the poem, being a patriotic man, to make people understand that all pirates hadn't been Englishmen. The second poem is called 'A Glass of Beer', and it's a Gaelic poem translated by James Stephens.[458] The poet's name is O'Bruadir, but he wasn't a pirate, but a poor poet, left behind in Ireland by the Catholic gentry when they went into exile, and so sunk in his fortunes that he is turned out of a wayside tavern. Miss Mooney will then sing 'Come on to the Hills of Mourne'[459]—I forget who wrote it—and the other song is called 'The Rivals' by James Stephens. Of what comes after I'll say something later on.

[The Ballad of O'Bruadir]

When O'Bruadir the captain shook a sword across the sea,
 Rolling glory on the water,
I had a mind O'Bruadir would make an Earl of me,
 Rolling glory on the water.
So I shut my eyes on women, forgot their sturdy hips
And yet I stuffed my pockets by playing on their lips
Until I gave the bundle then I quickly took to ships,
 Rolling glory on the water.

Out there we fought with cutlass, with blunderbuss and gun,
  Rolling glory on the water,
With boarding and with broadside we made the Dutchmen run,
  Rolling glory on the water,
Then down among the captains in their green skin shoes,
I sought for Hugh O'Bruadir and got but little news
Till I shook him by the hand in the bay of Santa Cruz,
  Rolling glory on the water.

O'Bruadir said kindly, 'You're a fresh blade from Mayo,
  Rolling glory on the water,
But come among my captains, to Achill back we'll go,[460]
  Rolling glory on the water,
Although those Spanish beauties are dark and not so dear,
I'd rather taste in Mayo, with April on the year,
One bracing virgin female; so swing your canvas here,
  Rolling glory on the water!'

'There's no man', said a stranger, 'whose hand I'd sooner grip
  Rolling glory on the water.'
'Well I'm your man', said Bruadir, 'and you're aboard my ship
  Rolling glory on the water.'
They drank to deeper friendship in ocean roguery;
And rolled ashore together, but between you and me
We found O'Bruadir dangling upon an airy tree,
  Rolling glory on the water![461]

[A Glass of Beer]

That lanky hank of a she at the inn over there
Nearly killed me for asking the loan of a glass of beer;
May the devil grip the whey-faced slut by the hair,
And beat bad manners out of her skin for a year.

That parboiled ape, with the toughest jaw you'll see
On virtue's path, and a voice that would rasp the dead,
Came roaring and raging the minute she looked at me,
And threw me out of the house on the back of my head!

If I asked her master he'd give me a cask a day;
And she, with the beer at hand, not a gill would arrange!
May she marry a ghost and bear him a kitten, and may
The High King of Glory permit her to get the mange.

[Come on to the Hills of Mourne]

HE

Come on to the Hills of Mourne
Come on, come on, my dear.

SHE

O no, O no, O no, O no.
I killed my husband last Saturday night
And tumbled him down the stair.

HE

Come on to the Hills of Mourne
For nobody'll find you there.

SHE

I might kill you, I might kill you,
For I killed my husband last Saturday night
And tumbled him down the stair.

HE

No matter, no matter, no matter
But love me first, my dear.

SHE

Too long I have moped, too long I have moped
Since I killed my husband last Saturday night
And tumbled him down the stair.

HE

Too long she has moped, too long she has moped,
Since she killed her husband last Saturday night

And tumbled him down the stair.

[The Rivals]

I heard a bird at dawn
Singing sweetly on a tree,
That the dew was on the lawn,
And the wind was on the lea;
But I didn't listen to him,
For he didn't sing to me!

I didn't listen to him,
For he didn't sing to me
That the dew was on the lawn,
And the wind was on the lea!
I was singing all the time[462]
Just as prettily as he!

I was singing all the time
Just as prettily as he,
About the dew upon the lawn
And the wind upon the lea!
So I didn't listen to him,
As he sang upon a tree!

Mr Stephenson has two more poems to sing and one more poem to speak. The spoken poem is a beautiful, strange, mysterious poem by James Stephens. One of the poems he shall sing is about Parnell, the other is about Roger Casement. Mr Yeats wrote this poem about Casement after reading a book called *The Forged Casement Diaries,* in which Dr Maloney has proved that certain Diaries were forged and circulated to blacken Casement's memory.[463] Now Mr Stephenson is going to sing the poem about Parnell, and you're to think yourselves old men, old farmers perhaps, accustomed to read newspapers and listen to songs, but not to read books. You are old and decrepit, because you have been to Glasnevin on all the anniversaries of Parnell's death for the last forty years.[464] There are not many of you left, and you're to imagine yourselves sitting in a public house, after you have returned from Glasnevin graveyard.[465]

[Come Gather Round Me Parnellites]

Come gather round me Parnellites
And praise our chosen man,
Stand upright on your legs awhile,
Stand upright while you can
For soon you lie where he is laid
And he lies underground.
Come fill up all those glasses
And pass the bottle round.

And here's a cogent reason
And I have many more,
He fought the might of England
And saved the Irish poor;
Whatever good a farmer's got
He brought it all to pass;
And here's another reason,
That Parnell loved a lass.

And here's a final reason,
He was of such a kind
Every man that sings a song
Keeps Parnell in his mind,
For Parnell was a proud man,
No prouder trod the ground,
And a proud man is a lovely man
So pass the bottle round.

The Bishops and the Party
This tragic story made.
A husband who had sold his wife
And after that betrayed;
But stories that live longest
Are sung above a glass,
And Parnell loved his country
And Parnell loved a lass.

[In the Night][466]

It is the noise of silence, and the noise
Of blindness!

The noise of silence and the noise of blindness
Do frighten me!
They hold me stark and rigid as a tree!

These frighten me!
These hold me stark and rigid as a tree!
Because at last their tumult is more loud
Than thunder!

Because
Their tumult is more loud
Than thunder,
They terrify my soul! They tear
My heart asunder!

[Roger Casement]

I say that Roger Casement
Did what he had to do,
He died upon the gallows
And that is nothing new.

Afraid they would be beaten
Before the bench of Time
They turned a trick by forgery
And blackened his good name.

A perjurer stood ready
To prove their forgery true;
They gave it out to all the world
And that is something new;

For Spring-Rice had to whisper it
Being their Ambassador,
And then the speakers got it
And writers by the score.

Come Alfred Noyes, come all the troop[467]
That cried it far and wide,
Come from the forger and his desk,
Desert the perjurer's side;

Come speak your bit in public
That some amends be made
To this most gallant gentleman
That's in quick-lime laid.

50

IN THE POET'S PUB[468]

I

I asked the B.B.C. people to let me choose certain poems and have them spoken or sung as I like. I want to make a certain experiment.

Some years ago I heard verses spoken by speakers all belonging to a well-known society for the speaking of verse. All spoke well; all knew that lyric poetry must not be spoken as if it were dramatic dialogue, where nothing matters but the two or three words in a line that arise out of the situation; all knew that every word was important and that the whole must be a form of music. Yet when five or six poems came one after another,[469] not only was there an intolerable monotony, but I could not follow the meaning. While I was thinking of one poem, the next had begun. My mind could not move quickly enough.

I thought I knew the reason. All over the world folk singers who[470] sing without accompaniment have tricks to break the monotony and to rest the mind. At the end of each verse, perhaps, they clap their hands to the tune or crack their fingers or whistle or there is a chorus in which many voices may join. Should not the speakers learn from the singers? Both the folk singers and the speaker[471] of verse must keep within the range of the speaking voice and the range of the speaking voice is small. Perhaps the folk singer[472] may go a little beyond it here and there but if he goes far he becomes a bird or a musical instrument, and his proper place is the concert platform.[473] Why not fill up the space between poem and poem with musical notes and so[474] enable the mind to free itself from one group of ideas, while preparing for another group, and yet keep it receptive and dreaming?† Furthermore to rest and vary the attention I

266

have suggested that certain parts of poems should be sung. There is, however, one point on which I have been emphatic. There must be no speaking through music, nothing like Mendelssohn's accompaniment to the *Mid-Summer Night's Dream*,[475] and there must be no accompaniment to what is sung:[476] the words need all our attention.[477]

I want you to imagine yourself[478] in a Poets' Pub. There are such pubs in Dublin and I suppose elsewhere. You are[479] sitting among poets, musicians, farmers and labourers. The fact that we are in a pub reminds somebody of Belloc's poem beginning 'Do you know[480] an inn, Miranda', and then somebody recites the first and more vigorous part of Chesterton's 'Rolling English Drunkard',[481] and then, because everybody in the inn except me is very English and we are all a little drunk, somebody recites De la Mare's 'Three Jolly Farmers' as patter. Patter is singing or speaking very quickly with very marked time, an art known to all old actors in my youth. We are all delighted, and at every pause we want to pound the table with our tankards. As, however, a tankard must be both heard and seen, the B.B.C. has substituted the rolling of a drum.

TARANTELLA[482]

> Do you remember an Inn,
> Miranda?
> Do you remember an Inn?
> And the tedding and the spreading
> Of the straw for a bedding,
> And the fleas that tease in the High Pyrenees,
> And the wine that tasted of the tar?
> And the cheers and the jeers of the young muleteers
> (Under the vine of the dark verandah)?[†]
> Do you remember an Inn, Miranda?
> Do you remember an Inn?
> And the cheers and the jeers of the young muleteers
> Who hadn't got a penny,
> And who weren't paying any,
> And the hammer at the doors and the Din?
> And the Hip! Hop! Hap!
> Of the clap
> Of the hands to the twirl and the swirl
> Of the girl gone chancing,

Glancing,
Dancing,
Backing and advancing,
Snapping of the[483] clapper to the spin
Out and in—
And the Ting, Tong, Tang of the Guitar!
Do you remember an Inn,
Miranda?
Do you remember an Inn?

Never more;
Miranda,
Never more.
Only the high peaks hoar:
And Aragon a torrent at the door.
No sound
In the walls of the Halls where falls
The tread
Of the feet of the dead to the ground.
No sound:
But the boom
Of the far Waterfall like Doom.

THE ROLLING ENGLISH ROAD[484]

Before the Roman came to Rye or out to Severn strode,
The rolling English drunkard made the rolling English road.
A reeling road, a rolling road, that rambles round the shire,
And after him the parson ran, the sexton and the squire;
A merry road, a mazy road, and such as we did tread
The night we went to Birmingham by way of Beachy Head.

I knew no harm of Bonaparte and plenty of the Squire,
And for to fight the Frenchman I did not much desire;
But I did bash their baggonets because they came arrayed
To straighten out the crooked road an English drunkard made,
Where you and I went down the lane with ale-mugs in our
    hands,
The night we went to Glastonbury by way of Goodwin Sands.

OFF THE GROUND[485]

Three jolly Farmers
  Once bet a pound
Each dance the others would
  Off the ground.
Out of their coats
  They slipped right soon,
And neat and nicesome
  Put each his shoon.
One—Two—Three!—
  And away they go,
Not too fast,
  And not too slow;
Out from the elm-tree's
  Noonday shadow,
Into the sun
  And across the meadow.
Past the schoolroom,
  With knees well bent
Fingers a-flicking,
  They dancing went.
Up sides and over,
  And round and round,
They crossed click-clacking,
  The Parish bound,
By Tupman's meadow
  They did their mile,
Tee-to-tum
  On a three-barred stile.
Then straight through Whipham,
  Downhill to Week,
Footing it lightsome,
  But not too quick,
Up fields to Watchet,
  And on through Wye,
Till seven fine churches
  They'd seen skip by—
Seven fine churches,

And five old mills,
Farms in the valley,
  And sheep on the hills;
Old Man's Acre
  And Dead Man's Pool
All left behind,
  As they danced through Wool.
And Wool gone by,
  Like tops that seem
To spin in sleep
  They danced in dream:
Withy—Wellover—
  Wassop—Wo—
Like an old clock
  Their heels did go.
A league and a league
  And a league they went,
And not one weary,
  And not one spent.
And lo, and behold!
  Past Willow-cum-Leigh
Stretched with its waters
  The great green sea.
Says Farmer Bates,
  'I puffs and I blows,
What's under the water,
  Why, no man knows!'
Says Farmer Giles,
  'My wind comes weak,
And a good man drownded
  Is far to seek.'
But Farmer Turvey,
  On twirling toes
Up's with his gaiters,
  And in he goes:
Down where the mermaids
  Pluck and play
On their twangling harps
  In a sea-green day;

Down where the mermaids,
    Finned and fair,
Sleek with their combs
    Their yellow hair. . . .
Bates and Giles—
    On the shingle sat,
Gazing at Turvey's
    Floating hat.
But never a ripple
    Nor bubble told
Where he was supping
    Off plates of gold.
Never an echo
    Rilled through the sea
Of the feasting and dancing
    And minstrelsy.
They called—called—called:
    Came no reply:
Nought but the ripples'
    Sandy sigh.
Then glum and silent
    They sat instead,
Vacantly brooding
    On home and bed,
Till both together
    Stood up and said:—
'Us knows not, dreams not,
    Where you be,
Turvey, unless
    In the deep blue sea;
But excusing silver—
    And it comes most willing—
Here's us two paying
    Our forty shilling;
For it's sartin sure, Turvey,
    Safe and sound,
You danced us square, Turvey,
    Off the ground!'

II

Then come three poems about the sea. One or two sailors have come in and we have been talking about the sea. That has put into somebody's head to recite Newbolt's poem, 'Drake's Drum', one of the few great patriotic poems in English. Then somebody else or is it the same man speaks Sylvia Townsend Warner's charming and amusing 'Sailor', and then just before closing time, he sings to a folk tune 'The Lady and the Shark', translated from the French by Frederick York Powell. York Powell was Regius Professor of History at Oxford at the beginning of the century, a man of incredible learning whose lighter side was known but to a few intimates. I was staying with him at Oxford and[486] somebody asked him to become Proctor. He replied, 'Impossible. The older I grow the less and less difference can I see between right and wrong'. York Powell, when my brother was a lad of twenty, used to take him to prize fights, or perhaps it was my brother who took Powell, and Powell's pockets were always stuffed with the *Licensed Victualler's Gazette,* which in those days reported all prize fights. He would have been at home in just such[487] a pub as I have imagined.

DRAKE'S DRUM[488]

Drake he's in his hammock an' a thousand mile away,
    (Capten, art tha sleepin' there below?),
Slung atween the round shot in Nombre Dios Bay,
    An' dreamin' arl the time o' Plymouth Hoe.
Yarnder lumes the Island, yarnder lie the ships,
    Wi' sailor lads[†] a-dancin' heel-an'-toe,
An' the shore-lights flashin', an' the night-tide dashin',
    He sees et arl so plainly as he saw et long ago.

Drake he was a Devon man, an' ruled the Devon seas,
    (Capten, art tha sleepin' there below?),
Rovin' tho' his death fell, he went wi' heart at ease,
    An' dreamin' arl the time o' Plymouth Hoe.
'Take my drum to England, hang et by the shore,
    Strike et when your powder's runnin' low;
If the Dons sight Devon, I'll quit the port o' Heaven,
    An' drum them up the Channel as we drummed them long
    ago.'

Drake he's in his hammock till the great Armadas come,
 (Capten, art tha sleepin' there below?),
Slung atween the round shot, listenin' for the drum,
 An' dreamin' arl the time o' Plymouth Hoe.
Call him on the deep sea, call him up the Sound,
 Call him when ye sail to meet the foe;
Where the old trade's plyin' an' the old flag flyin'
 They shall find him ware an' wakin', as they found him long
 ago!

THE SAILOR[489]

I have a young love—
A landward lass is she—
And thus she entreated:
'O tell me of the sea
That on thy next voyage
My thoughts may follow thee.'

I took her up a hill
And showed her hills green,
One after other
With valleys between:
So green and gentle, I said,
Are the waves I've seen.

I led her by the hand
Down the grassy way,
And showed her the hedgerows
That were white with May:
So white and fleeting, I said,
Is the salt sea-spray.

I bade her lean her head
Down against my side,
Rising and falling
On my breath to ride:
Thus rode the vessel, I said,
On the rocking tide.

For she so young is, and tender,
I would not have her know

What it is that I go to
When to sea I must go,
Lest she should lie awake and tremble
When the great storm-winds blow.

THE SAILOR AND THE SHARK[490]

There was a queen that fell in love with a jolly sailor bold,
But he shipped to the Indies, where he would seek for gold.
All in a good sea-boat, my boys, we fear no wind that blows!

There was a king that had a fleet of ships both tall and tarred;
He carried off this pretty queen, and she jumped overboard.
All in a good sea-boat, my boys, we fear no wind that blows!

The queen, the queen is overboard! a shark was cruising
    round,
He swallowed up this dainty bit alive and safe and sound.
All in a good sea-boat, my boys, we fear no wind that blows!

Within the belly of this shark it was both dark and cold,
But she was faithful still and true to her jolly sailor bold.
All in a good sea-boat, my boys, we fear no wind that blows!

The shark was sorry for her, and swam away so fast.
In the Indies, where the camels are, he threw her up at last.
All in a good sea-boat, my boys, we fear no wind that blows!

On one of those same goodly beasts, all in a palanquin,
She spied her own true love again—the Emperor of Tonquin.
All in a good sea-boat, my boys, we fear no wind that blows!

She called to him, 'O stay, my love, your queen is come, my
    dear.'
'Oh, I've a thousand queens more fair within my kingdom
    here.'
All in a good sea-boat, my boys, we fear no wind that blows!

'You smell of the grave so strong, my dear,' 'I've sailed in a
    shark' says she.
'It is not of the grave I smell; but I smell of the fish of the sea.'
All in a good sea-boat, my boys, we fear no wind that blows!

'My lady loves they smell so sweet; of rice-powder so fine.
The queen the King of Paris loves no sweeter smells than
   mine,'
All in a good sea-boat, my boys, we fear no wind that blows!

She got aboard the shark again, and weeping went her way;
The shark swam back again so fast to where the tall ships lay.
All in a good sea-boat, my boys, we fear no wind that blows!

The King he got the queen again, the shark away he swam.
The queen was merry as could be, and mild as any lamb.
All in a good sea-boat, my boys, we fear no wind that blows!

Now all you pretty maidens what love a sailor bold,
You'd better ship along with him before his love grows cold.
*All in a good sea-boat, my boys, we fear no wind that
   blows!*[491]

IN THE POET'S PARLOUR[492]

I

When we were in the Poets' Pub I asked you to listen to poems written for everybody, but now you will listen, or so I hope, to poems written for poets, and that is why we are in the Poet's Parlour. Those present are his intimate friends and fellow students. There is a beautiful lady, or two or three beautiful ladies, four or five poets, a couple of musicians and all are devoted to poetry. The method will be the same as before. Where there is a pause—a short pause in the middle of a poem, when the mood is being changed—or the long pause between poem and poem—there will be music to rest and hold your attention and to make it possible to repeat half a dozen lyric poems without monotony. Two or three of the poems will be sung, but without accompaniment. Whether we speak or sing, our sole object is to fix your attention upon the words. We are all lovers and dancers and our first three poems are about dancing. They are all my work. The first I wrote especially for this programme. The second[493] is an expansion of mediaeval dance song. The last[494] describes what I have heard several[495] Irish country people describe, 'an apparition of dancers in an old ruin'.

SWEET DANCER[496]

That girl goes dancing there
On the leaf-sown, new-mown, smooth
Grass plot in the garden;
Escaped from bitter youth
Escaped out of her crowd
Or out of her black cloud.
Ah, dancer, ah, sweet dancer!

If strange men come from the house
To lead her away, do not say
That she is happy being crazy;
Lead them gently astray;
Let her finish her dance,
Let her finish her dance.
Ah, dancer, ah, sweet dancer!

'I AM OF IRELAND'[497]

'I am of Ireland,
And the Holy Land of Ireland,
And time runs on,' cried she.
'Come out of charity,
Come dance with me in Ireland.'

One man, one man alone
In that outlandish gear,
One solitary man
Of all that rambled there
Had turned his stately head.
'That is a long way off,
And time runs on,' he said,
'And the night grows rough.'

'I am of Ireland,
And the Holy Land of Ireland,
And time runs on,' cried she.
'Come out of charity
And dance with me in Ireland.'

'The fiddlers are all thumbs,
Or the fiddle-string accursed,
The drums and the kettledrums
And the trumpets all are burst,
And the trombone,' cried he,
'The trumpet and trombone,'
And cocked a malicious eye,
'But time runs on, runs on.'

'I am of Ireland,
And the Holy Land of Ireland,
And time runs on,' cried she.
'Come out of charity
And dance with me in Ireland.'

THE WICKED HAWTHORN TREE[498]

O, but I saw a solemn sight;
Said the rambling, shambling travelling-man;
Castle Dargan's ruin all lit,
Lovely ladies dancing in it.

What though they dance; those days are gone;
Said the wicked, crooked, hawthorn tree;
Lovely lady and gallant man
Are cold blown dust or a bit of bone.[499]

O, what is life but a mouthful of air;
Said the rambling, shambling travelling-man;
Yet all the lovely things that were
Live, for I saw them dancing there.

Nobody knows what may befall;
Said the wicked, crooked, hawthorn tree;
I have stood so long by a gap in the wall
May be I shall not die at all.

II

The poems you are now about to hear have love for their theme. The first describes a nymph mourning her lover, Alexander, and is I think, the most beautiful of all Flecker's poems. The second is the only love poem Lionel Johnson ever wrote. Y-e-s?[500] Will you pardon me for a moment while I read a note from our stage manager. (I will rustle paper). O—O—I understand.[501] It seems that one or two of the poets present say that our programme is much too melancholy. That they were much more at home when we were in our pub. They insist on taking charge at the end of Lionel Johnson's poem. At the end of his poem their first poem will come[502] about Jezebel† and it will be accompanied upon the clatter bones. It is the work of the Irish poet, F. R. Higgins. Then will come a poem about the pilgrimage to Lough Derg in Donegal, a great pilgrimage for repented drunkards. The poem has never been published and they do not tell me the name of the author. Now Flecker's poem:

SANTORIN[503]
(A LEGEND OF THE AEGEAN)

'Who are you, Sea Lady,
And where in the seas are we?
I have too long been steering
By the flashes in your eyes.
Why drops the moonlight through my heart,
And why so quietly
Go the great engines of my boat
As if their souls were free?'
'Oh ask me not, bold sailor;
Is not your ship a magic ship
That sails without a sail:
Are not these isles the Isles of Greece
And dust upon the sea?
But answer me three questions
And give me answers three.
What is your ship?' 'A British.'
'And where may Britain be?'
'Oh it lies north, dear lady;
It is a small country.'

'Yet you will know my lover,
Though you live far away:
And you will whisper where he has gone,
That lily boy to look upon
And whiter than the spray.'
'How should I know your lover,
Lady of the sea?'

'Alexander, Alexander,
The King of the World was he.'
'Weep not for him, dear lady,
But come aboard my ship.
So many years ago he died,

He's dead as dead can be.'
'O base and brutal sailor
To lie this lie to me.
His mother was the foam-foot
Star-sparkling Aphrodite;
His father was Adonis
Who lives away in Lebanon,
In stony Lebanon, where blooms
His red anemone.
But where is Alexander,
The soldier Alexander,
My golden love of olden days
The King of the World and me?'

To Morfydd[504]

A voice on the winds,
A voice by the waters,
Wanders and cries:
Oh! what are the winds?
And what are the waters?
Mine are your eyes!

Western the winds are,
And western the waters,
Where the light lies:
Oh! what are the winds?
And what are the waters?
Mine are your eyes!

Cold, cold, grow the winds,
And wild grow the waters,
Where the sun dies:
Oh! what are the winds?
And what are the waters?
Mine are your eyes!

And down the night winds,
And down the night waters,
The music flies:

Oh! what are the winds?
And what are the waters?
Cold be the winds,
And wild be the waters,
So mine be your eyes!

SONG FOR THE CLATTER BONES[505]

God rest that Jewy woman,
Queen Jezebel, the witch[506]
Who peeled the clothes from her shoulder-bones
Down to her spent tits[507]
As she stretched out of the window
Among the geraniums, where
She chaffed and laughed like one half daft
Titivating her painted hair—

King Jehu he drove to her,
She tipped him a fancy beck;
But he from his knacky side-car spoke
'Who'll break that dewlapped neck?'
And so she was thrown from the window;
Like Lucifer she fell
Beneath the feet of the horses and they beat
The light out of Jezebel.

That corpse wasn't planted in clover;
Ah, nothing of her was found
Save those grey bones that Hare-foot Mike
Gave me for their lovely sound;
And as once her dancing body
Made star-lit princes sweat
So I'll just clack: though her ghost lack a back[508]
There's music in the old bones yet.

THE PILGRIM[509]

I fasted for some forty days on bread and buttermilk,
For passing round the bottle with girls in rags or silk,
In country shawl or Paris cloak, had put my wits astray,
And what's the good of women, for all that they can say
Is fol de rol de rolly O.

Round Lough Derg's holy island I went upon the stones,
I prayed at all the Stations upon my marrow-bones,
And there I found an old man, and though I prayed all day
That old man beside me, nothing would he say
But fol de rol de rolly O.

All know that all the dead in the world about that place are
    stuck,
And that should mother seek for son she'd have but little luck
Because the fires of Purgatory have ate their shapes away;
I swear to God I questioned them, and all they had to say
Was fol de rol de rolly O.

A great black ragged bird appeared when I was in the boat;
Some twenty feet from tip to tip had its wings stretched rightly
    out,
With their flopping and their flapping it made a great display,
But I never stopped to question, what could the boat man say[510]
But fol de rol de rolly O.

Now I am in the tavern and lean against the wall,
So come in rags or come in silk, in cloak or country shawl,
And come with learned lovers or with what men you may,
For I can put the whole lot down, and all I have to say
Is fol de rol de rolly O.

52

MY OWN POETRY[511]

In 1916 the poet and schoolmaster Pearse, the labour leader Connolly, and others, including those two unknown men, De Valera and Cosgrave, seized certain public buildings in Dublin and held them against the English army for some days.[512] Neither Pearse nor Connolly had any expectation of victory. They went out to die because, as Pearse said in a famous speech, a national movement cannot be kept alive unless blood is shed in every generation.[513] A poem containing this thought will be the first spoken. It will be followed by a poem called 'An Irish Airman Foresees His Death'. The Irish airman was Robert Gregory—Lady Gregory's son. He was a painter of genius who, immediately after the start of the Great War, joined the Air Force. Like many Protestant Irishmen he stood between two nations. He said to me, 'I think I am going out of friendship'. Meaning, I suppose, that so many of his friends had gone. 'The English are not my people. My people are the people of Kiltartan.' Kiltartan is the name of a town land where he had property. Presently his mother asked, 'Why has Robert joined?' I answered, 'I suppose he thought it his duty'. She said, 'It was his duty to stay here. He joined for the same reason I would have, had I been a young man.[514] He could not keep out of it'. She was right. He was a born soldier. He said to Bernard Shaw shortly before his death, that he was never happy until he began to fight. When his 'plane crashed in Italy he was a famous flying man. He had brought down, according to the official record, nineteen German 'planes.[515]

After this comes a third political poem—'The Curse of Cromwell'. Cromwell came to Ireland as a kind of Lenin. He destroyed a whole social order. There is not one of us, unless of a family imported by him or after him, that has not some memory of his tyranny and his cruelty. Irish and English history know of different Cromwells. The best line in my poem—I leave you to find it out—is not mine. It is translated from a Gaelic† poem, where it was used as I have used it.[516] And now for the poem about Pearse and Connolly.[517]

THE ROSE TREE[518]

'O words are lightly spoken,'
Said Pearse to Connolly,
'Maybe a breath of politic words
Has withered our Rose Tree;
Or maybe but a wind that blows
Across the bitter sea.'

'It needs to be but watered,'
James Connolly replied,
'To make the green come out again
And spread on every side,
And shake the blossom from the bud
To be the garden's pride.'

'But where can we draw water,'
Said Pearse to Connolly,
'When all the wells are parched away?
O plain as plain can be
There's nothing but our own red blood
Can make a right Rose Tree.'

AN IRISH AIRMAN FORESEES HIS DEATH[519]

I know that I shall meet my fate
Somewhere among the clouds above;
Those that I fight I do not hate,
Those that I guard I do not love;
My country is Kiltartan Cross,
My countrymen Kiltartan's poor,
No likely end could bring them loss
Or leave them happier than before.
Nor law, nor duty bade me fight,
Nor public men, nor cheering crowds,

A lonely impulse of delight
Drove to this tumult in the clouds;
I balanced all, brought all to mind,
The years to come seemed waste of breath,
A waste of breath the years behind
In balance with this life, this death.

THE CURSE OF CROMWELL[520]

You ask what I have found and far and wide I go
Nothing but Cromwell's house and Cromwell's murderous
   crew,
The lovers and the dancers are beaten into the clay,
And the tall men and the swordsmen and the horsemen where
   are they?†
And there is an old beggar wandering in his pride,
His fathers served their fathers before Christ was crucified.
           O what of that, O what of that
           What is there left to say?

All neighbourly content and easy talk are gone
But there's no good complaining, for money's rant is on;
He that is mounting up must on his neighbour mount
And we and all the Muses are things of no account.
They have schooling of their own but I pass their schooling by,
What can they know that we know that know the time to die?
           O what of that, O what of that
           What is there left to say?

But there's another knowledge that my heart destroys
As the fox in the old fable destroyed the Spartan boy's
Because it proves that things both can and cannot be;†
That the swordsmen† and the ladies can still keep company,
Can pay the poet for a verse and hear the fiddle sound,
That I am still their servant though all are underground.
           O what of that, O what of that
           What is there left to say?

I came on a great house in the middle of the night
Its open lighted doorway and its windows all alight,
And all my friends were there and made me welcome too;

But I woke in an old ruin that the winds howled through;
And when I pay attention I must out and walk
Among the dogs and horses that understand my talk.[†]
    O *what of that, O what of that*
    What is there left to say?

II

You must permit the poet his melancholy. My last two broadcasts had cheerful moments but, being a poet, I cannot keep it up. The poems you have just listened to were political. I consider those that follow religious. The first of these was written when I was recovering from a long illness. I had begun to read great literature again, though I was still very weak. The overwhelming power of every great genius filled me with terror. I was in the midst of a power that would tear the world in pieces; but for the critics, journalists, commonplace men of all kinds, who adapted it to human use. What if they were to suddenly fail us? I called the poem 'Mad as the Mist and Snow'.[521]

This is followed by a poem called 'Running to Paradise'. Some Irish saint met a man running at full speed and asked where he was going, and the man said 'To Paradise'. This is followed by a poem, written when I first felt the infirmity of age. It is called 'Sailing to Byzantium' for reasons too complicated to explain.

I speak of a bird made by Grecian goldsmiths. There is a record of a tree of gold with artificial birds which sang. The tree was somewhere in the Royal Palace of Byzantium. I use it as a symbol of the intellectual joy of eternity, as contrasted with the instinctive joy of human life.

Then my series of poems winds up with 'He and She', wherein the moon and sun symbolise the soul and God. The soul's flight and return. Now comes the poem 'Mad as the Mist and Snow.'[522]

Mad as the Mist and Snow[523]

Bolt and bar the shutter,
For the foul winds blow;
Our minds are at their best this night,
And I seem to know

That everything outside us is
Mad as the mist and snow.

Horace there by Homer stands,
Plato stands below,
And here is Tully's open page.
How many years ago
Were you and I unlettered lads
Mad as the mist and snow?

You ask what makes me sigh, old friend,
What makes me shudder so?
I shudder and I sigh to think
That even Cicero
And many-minded Homer were
Mad as the mist and snow.

RUNNING TO PARADISE

As I came over Windy Gap
They threw a halfpenny into my cap,
For I am running to Paradise;
And all that I need do is to wish
And somebody puts his hand in the dish
To throw me a bit of salted fish:
And there the king is but as the beggar.

My brother Mourteen is worn out
With skelping his big brawling lout,
And I am running to Paradise;
A poor life, do what he can,
And though he keep a dog and a gun,
A serving-maid and a serving-man:
And there the king is but as the beggar.

Poor men have grown to be rich men,
And rich men grown to be poor again,
And I am running to Paradise;
And many a darling wit's grown dull
That tossed a bare heel when at school,

Now it has filled an old sock full:
And there the king is but as the beggar.

The wind is old and still at play
While I must hurry upon my way,
For I am running to Paradise;
Yet never have I lit on a friend
To take my fancy like the wind
That nobody can buy or bind:
And there the king is but as the beggar.

SAILING TO BYZANTIUM[524]

I

Old men should quit a country where the young
In one another's arms, birds in the trees,
—Those dying generations—at their song,
The salmon-falls, the mackerel-crowded seas,
Fish, flesh, or fowl, commend all summer long
Whatever is begotten, born, and dies.
Caught in that sensual music all neglect
Monuments of unageing intellect.

II

An aged man is but a paltry thing,
A tattered coat upon a stick, unless
Soul clap its hands and sing, and louder sing
For every tatter in its mortal dress,
Nor is there singing school but studying
Monuments of its own magnificence;
And therefore I have sailed the seas and come
To the holy city of Byzantium.

III

O sages standing in God's holy fire
As in the gold mosaic of a wall,
Come from the holy fire, perne in a gyre,
And be the singing-masters of my soul.
Consume my heart away; sick with desire
And fastened to a dying animal

It knows not what it is; and gather me
Into the artifice of eternity.

IV

Once out of nature I shall never take
My bodily form from any natural thing,
But such a form as Grecian goldsmiths make
Of hammered gold and gold enamelling
To keep a drowsy Emperor awake;
Or set upon a golden bough to sing
To lords and ladies of Byzantium
Of what is past, or passing, or to come.

HE AND SHE[525]

As the moon sidles up
Must she sidle up,
As trips the scared moon
Away must she trip:
'His light had struck me blind
Dared I stop.'

She sings as the moon sings:
'I am I, am I;
The greater grows my light
The further that I fly.'
All creation shivers
With that sweet cry.

53

MY OWN POETRY AGAIN[526]

I spent a great deal of my time as a child with my grandparents in County Sligo. I remember many picnics on some island in Lough Gill or on a wooded rock on its edge called Dooney Rock. Later on, when I read the American essayist Thoreau, I thought I would some day live on one of those islands.

Presently I went to London and made my living reviewing books. One day when I was walking along the Strand I heard a tinkle of water. It came from a jet of water in a shop window. The jet balanced a little ball upon the top. It was an advertisement of cooling drinks. The sound of that water made me homesick. I wanted to go back to Sligo and live on an island in the lake. Out of that homesickness I made the most popular of my poems, 'The Lake Isle of Innisfree'. I am about to read it. I think there is nothing hard to understand except that I speak of noon as 'a purple glow'. The purple glow is the reflection of the heather. Innisfree means 'heather island'. Perhaps you will think that I go too near singing it. That is because every poet who reads his own poetry gives as much importance to the rhythm as to the sense. A poem without its rhythm is not a poem.

> I will arise and go now, and go to Innisfree,
> And a small cabin build there, of clay and wattles made:
> Nine bean-rows will I have there, a hive for the honeybee,
> And live alone in the bee-loud glade.
>
> And I shall have some peace there, for peace comes dropping
>   slow,

Dropping from the veils of the morning to where the cricket
    sings;
There midnight's all a glimmer, and noon a purple glow,
And evening full of the linnet's wings.

I will arise and go now, for always night and day
I hear lake water lapping with low sounds by the shore;
While I stand on the roadway, or on the pavements grey,
I hear it in the deep heart's core.

I wrote a poem about a merry fiddler and named it, in gratitude
for many picnics, 'The Fiddler of Dooney'.

> When I play on my fiddle in Dooney,
> Folk dance like a wave of the sea;
> My cousin is priest in Kilvarnet,
> My brother in Mocharabuiee.
>
> I passed my brother and cousin:
> They read in their books of prayer;
> I read in my book of songs
> I bought at the Sligo fair.
>
> When we come at the end of time
> To Peter sitting in state,
> He will smile on the three old spirits,
> But call me first through the gate;
>
> For the good are always the merry,
> Save by an evil chance,
> And the merry love the fiddle,
> And the merry love to dance:
>
> And when the folk there spy me,
> They will all come up to me,
> With 'Here is the fiddler of Dooney!'
> And dance like a wave of the sea.

As a child and as a young man I went into country cottages and
heard stories of fairies and spirits. One woman told me that when
she was in chapel a tall grey man sat beside her. She said 'Where are
you from?' and he said 'From Tir-nan-oge', which means the land
of youth and is one of the names of fairyland. Many people are said

to go to that land and never return. I describe such a journey in the poem which I am about to read. I called fairyland 'the world's bane' because I thought of it as that ideal perfection which is the source of all hopeless longing and public tumult. I call the poem 'The Happy Townland'.[527]

There's many a strong farmer
Whose heart would break in two,
If he could see the townland
That we are riding to;
Boughs have their fruit and blossom
At all times of the year;
Rivers are running over
With red beer and brown beer.
An old man plays the bagpipes
In a golden and silver wood;
Queens, their eyes blue like the ice,
Are dancing in a crowd.

The little fox he murmured,
'O what of the world's bane?'
The sun was laughing sweetly,
The moon plucked at my rein;
But the little red fox murmured,
'O do not pluck at his rein,
He is riding to the townland
That is the world's bane.'

When their hearts are so high
That they would come to blows,
They unhook their heavy swords
From golden and silver boughs;
But all that are killed in battle
Awaken to life again.
It is lucky that their story
Is not known among men,
For O, the strong farmers
That would let the spade lie,
Their hearts would be like a cup
That somebody had drunk dry.

The little fox he murmured,
'O what of the world's bane?'
The sun was laughing sweetly,
The moon plucked at my rein;
But the little red fox murmured,
'O do not pluck at his rein,
He is riding to the townland
That is the world's bane.'

Michael will unhook his trumpet
From a bough overhead,
And blow a little noise
When the supper has been spread.
Gabriel will come from the water
With a fish-tail, and talk
Of wonders that have happened
On wet roads where men walk,
And lift up an old horn
Of hammered silver, and drink
Till he has fallen asleep
Upon the starry brink.

The little fox he murmured,
'O what of the world's bane?'
The sun was laughing sweetly,
The moon plucked at my rein;
But the little red fox murmured,
'O do not pluck at his rein,
He is riding to the townland
That is the world's bane.'

I shall ask Margot Ruddock to sing to her own music two of my early poems selected by herself. She is not Irish, but she sings as we sing in Ireland, without accompaniment. If you listen, as a trained musician listens, for the notes only, you will miss the pleasure you are accustomed to and find no other. Her notes cannot be separated from the words. Because her singing gives me great pleasure I am sure it will give pleasure to some others. Her first poem is a poem of longing for the West of Ireland. Some love affair had gone wrong and I have always hated towns. It is called 'Into the Twilight'.[528]

Out-worn heart, in a time out-worn,
Come clear of the nets of wrong and right;
Laugh, heart, again in the grey twilight,
Sigh, heart, again in the dew of the morn.

Your mother Eire is always young,
Dew ever shining and twilight grey;
Though hope fall from you and love decay,
Burning in fires of a slanderous tongue.

Come, heart, where hill is heaped upon hill:
For there the mystical brotherhood
Of sun and moon and hollow and wood
And river and stream work out their will;

And God stands winding His lonely horn,
And time and the world are ever in flight;
And love is less kind than the grey twilight,
And hope is less dear than the dew of the morn.

She will now sing a requiem which I wrote for a play of mine called *The Countess Cathleen,* but omitted in some re-writing of the play. It is called 'The Countess Cathleen in Paradise'.[529]

All the heavy days are over;
Leave the body's coloured pride
Underneath the grass and clover,
With the feet laid side by side.

Bathed in flaming founts of duty
She'll not ask a haughty dress;
Carry all that mournful beauty
To the scented oaken press.

Did the kiss of Mother Mary
Put that music in her face?
Yet she goes with footstep wary,
Full of earth's old timid grace.

'Mong the feet of angels seven
What a dancer, glimmering!

All the heavens bow down to Heaven,
Flame to flame and wing to wing.

From my twenty-seventh year until a few years ago all my public activities were associated with a famous country house in County Galway. In that house my dear friend, that woman of genius, Lady Gregory, gathered from time to time all men of talent, all profound men, in the intellectual life of modern Ireland. I have a house three or four miles from where her gate was, a mediaeval tower whose winding stair I am too old to climb.[530] The river that passed my window sank into the earth in a round pool which the blind, or dark, poet Raftery called a cellar, then rose again and fell into a lake in Lady Gregory's park. The poem I am about to read was written shortly before Lady Gregory's death. It is typical of most of my recent poems, intricate in metaphor, the swan and water both symbols of the soul, not at all a dream, like my earlier poems, but a criticism of life. The poem is called, 'Coole and Ballylee, 1931'.[531]

Under my window-ledge the waters race,
Otters below and moor-hens on the top,
Run for a mile undimmed in Heaven's face
Then darkening through 'dark' Raftery's 'cellar' drop,
Run underground, rise in a rocky place
In Coole demesne, and there to finish up
Spread to a lake and drop into a hole.
What's water but the generated soul?

Upon the border of that lake's a wood
Now all dry sticks under a wintry sun,
And in a copse of beeches there I stood,
For Nature's pulled her tragic buskin on
And all the rant's a mirror of my mood:
At sudden thunder of the mounting swan
I turned about and looked where branches break
The glittering reaches of the flooded lake.

Another emblem there! That stormy white
But seems a concentration of the sky;
And, like the soul, it sails into the sight
And in the morning's gone, no man knows why;

And is so lovely that it sets to right
What knowledge or its lack had set awry,
So arrogantly pure, a child might think
It can be murdered with a spot of ink.
Sound of a stick upon the floor, a sound
From somebody that toils from chair to chair;
Beloved books that famous hands have bound,
Old marble heads, old pictures everywhere;
Great rooms where travelled men and children found
Content or joy; a last inheritor
Where none has reigned that lacked a name and fame
Or out of folly into folly came.

A spot whereon the founders lived and died
Seemed once more dear than life; ancestral trees,
Or gardens rich in memory glorified
Marriages, alliances and families,
And every bride's ambition satisfied.
Where fashion or mere fantasy decrees
We shift about—all that great glory spent—
Like some poor Arab tribesman and his tent.

We were the last romantics—chose for theme
Traditional sanctity and loveliness;
Whatever's written in what poets name
The book of the people; whatever most can bless
The mind of man or elevate a rhyme;
But all is changed, that high horse riderless,
Though mounted in that saddle Homer rode
Where the swan drifts upon a darkening flood.[532]

54

I BECAME AN AUTHOR[533]

How did I begin to write? I have nothing to say that may help young writers, except that I hope they will not begin as I did. I spent longer than most schoolboys preparing the next day's work, and yet learnt nothing, and would always have been at the bottom of my class but for one or two subjects that I hardly had to learn at all. My father would say: 'You cannot fix your mind on anything that does not interest you, and it is to study what does not that you are sent to school'. I did not suffer from the 'poetic temperament', but from some psychological weakness. Greater poets than I have been great scholars. Even today I struggle against a lack of confidence, when among average men, come from that daily humiliation, and because I do not know what they know. I can toil through a little French poetry, but nothing remains of the Greek, Latin and German I tried to learn. I have only one memory of my schooldays that gives me pleasure; though in both my English and Irish schools I was near the bottom of the class, my friends were at the top, for then, as now, I hated fools. When I would find out if some man can be trusted, I ask if he associates with his betters. In the Irish school my chief friend was Charles Johnston, son of the Orange leader. He beat all Ireland in the Intermediate examinations, and when I met him in America years afterwards he said: 'There is nothing I cannot learn and nothing that I want to learn'.[534] Some instinct drew us together, it was to him I used to read my poems. They were all plays—except one long poem in Spenserian stanzas, which some woman of whom I remember nothing, not even if she was pretty, borrowed and lost out of her carriage when shopping. I recall three plays, not of any merit, one vaguely Elizabethan, its scene a German forest, one an imitation of Shelley, its scene a crater in the moon, one of somebody's translations from the Sanscrit, its scene an Indian temple. Charles Johnston admired parts of these poems so much that I doubt if he ever thought I had fulfilled their promise. A fragment, or perhaps all that was written, of the Indian play, I put near the opening of my *Collected Poems* because when I put it there he was still living, and it is still there because I have forgotten to take it out.[535] I have sometimes wondered if I did not write poetry to find a cure for my own ailment, as constipated cats do when they eat valerian. But that will not do, because my interest in proud, confident people began before I had been much humiliated. Some people say I have an affected manner, and if that is true, as it may well be, it is because my father took me when I was ten or eleven to Irving's famous *Hamlet*. Years afterwards I walked the Dublin streets when nobody was looking, or nobody that I knew, with that strut Gordon Craig has compared to a movement in a dance, and made the characters I created speak with his brooding, broken wildness.[536] Two months ago, describing the Second Coming, I wrote this couplet:

> What brushes fly and gnat aside?
> Irving and his plume of pride.[537]

Nobody should think a young poet pathetic and weak, or that he has a lonely struggle. I think some old and famous men may think that they had in their schooldays their most satisfying fame; certainly I had about me a little group whose admiration for work that had no merit justified my immense self-confidence.

When eighteen or nineteen I wrote a pastoral play under the influence of Keats and Shelley, modified by that of Jonson's *Sad Shepherd,* and one of my friends showed it to some Trinity undergraduates who were publishing the *Dublin University Review,* an ambitious political and literary periodical that lasted for a few months—I cannot remember who, except that it was not Charles Johnston, who had passed for the Indian Civil Service, gone to India, and would stay there until he tired of it.[538] I was at the Art Schools because painting was the family trade, and because I did not think I could pass the matriculation examination for Trinity. The undergraduates liked the poem and invited me to read it to a man four or five years older than the rest of us, Bury, in later years a classical historian and editor of Gibbon.[539] I was excited, not merely because he would decide the acceptance or rejection of my play, but because he was a schoolmaster and I had never met a schoolmaster in private life. Once when I was at Edward Dowden's the head of my old school was announced, but I turned so pale or so red that Dowden brought me into another room. Perhaps I could get Bury to explain why I had been told to learn so many things that I had not been able to fix my attention upon anything.

I thought a man brought his convictions into everything he did; I had said to the photographer when he was arranging his piece of iron shaped like a horseshoe to keep my head in position: 'Because you have only white and black paper instead of light and shadow you cannot represent Nature. An artist can, because he employs a kind of symbolism'. To my surprise, instead of showing indignation at my attack upon his trade, he replied: 'A photograph is mechanical'.[540] Even today I have the same habit of thought, but only when thinking of pre-eminent men. A few days ago I read of some University meeting where, when somebody said: 'Nobody today believes in a personal devil', Lord Acton said: 'I do'; and I knew that because the *Cambridge Universal History,* which he had planned, contains nothing about a personal devil's influence upon events, Lord Acton was a picturesque liar.[541] For some reason which I cannot recollect I was left alone with Bury and said, after a great effort to overcome my shyness: 'I know you will defend the ordinary system of education by saying that it strengthens the will, but I am convinced that it only seems to do so because it weakens the impulses'. He smiled and looked embarrassed but said nothing.

My pastoral play *The Island of Statues* appeared in the review. I have not looked at it for many years, but nothing I did at that time had merit. Two lyrics from it are at the beginning of my *Collected Poems,*[542] not because I liked them but because when I put them there friends that had were still living. Immediately after its publication, or just before, I fell under the influence of two men who were to influence deeply the Irish intellectual movement—old John O'Leary the Fenian leader, in whose library I found the poets of Young Ireland and Standish O'Grady, who had re-written in vigorous romantic English certain ancient Irish heroic legends. Because of the talks of these men, and the books the one lent and the other wrote, I turned my back on foreign themes, decided that the race was more important than the individual, and began my *Wanderings of Oisin;* it was published with many shorter poems by subscription, John O'Leary finding almost all the subscribers. Henceforth I was one of the rising poets. I lived in London and had many friends, and when I could not earn the twenty shillings a week which in those days bought bed and board for man or boy, I could stay with my family or a Sligo relative. In this I was more fortunate than Isadora Duncan who was to write of her first London years: 'I had renown and the favour of princes and not enough to eat'.[543] As a professional writer I was clumsy, stiff and sluggish; when I reviewed a book I had to write my own heated thoughts because I did not know how to get thoughts out of my subject; when I wrote a poem half-a-dozen lines sometimes took as many days because I was determined to put the natural words in the natural order, my imagination still full of poetic diction. It was that old difficulty of my school work over again, except that I had now plenty of time.

APPENDIX A

Copy-Texts Used for This Edition

Copy-texts for works which were published in printed form are given below. Textual sources of the radio programme material are noted in the first note to each broadcast.

1. Noble and Ignoble Loyalties: *The United Irishman* (21 April 1900), 5.
2. Irish Fairy Beliefs: *The Speaker* (14 July 1900), 413–14.
3. Irish Witch Doctors: *The Fortnightly Review* (September 1900), 440–56.
4. Irish Language and Irish Literature: *The Leader* (1 September 1900), 13–14.
5. A Postscript to a Forthcoming Book of Essays by Various Writers: *All Ireland Review* (1 December 1900), 6.
6. John Eglinton: *The United Irishman* (9 November 1901), 3.
7. Literature and the Conscience: *The United Irishman* (7 December 1901), 3.
8. Egyptian Plays: *The Star* (23 January 1902), 1.
9. Away: *The Fortnightly Review* (April 1902), 726–40.
10. Mr Yeats's New Play: *The United Irishman* (5 April 1902), 5.
11. An Ancient Conversation: *All Ireland Review* (5 and 12 April 1902), 75, 87.
12. The Acting at St Teresa's Hall: *The United Irishman* (12 April 1902), 3.
13. The Acting at St Teresa's Hall II: *The United Irishman* (26 April 1902), 3.
14. The Freedom of the Theatre: *The United Irishman* (1 November 1902), 5.
15. A Canonical Book: *The Bookman* (May 1903), 67–68.
16. The Irish National Theatre and Three Sorts of Ignorance: *The United Irishman* (24 October 1903), 2.
17. Emmet the Apostle of Irish Liberty: *The Gaelic American,* 1, no. 25 (5 March 1904), 1, 5.
18. America and the Arts: *The Metropolitan Magazine* (April 1905), 53–55.
19. British Association Visit to the Abbey Theatre: *British Association Visit, Abbey Theatre, Special Programme* (4 and 8 September 1908), 1–2, 6–8.
20. The Art of the Theatre: *The New Age* (16 June 1910), 162–63.
21. The Theatre of Beauty: *Harper's Weekly* (11 November 1911), 11.
22. The Story of the Irish Players: *Sunday Record-Herald* (4 February 1912), vii, 1.
23. The Polignac Prize: *Royal Society of Literature, The Academic Committee: Addresses of Reception* (London: Oxford University Press, 1914), 37–42.

24. Thomas Davis: *New Ireland* (17 July 1915), 147–48.
25. Sir Hugh Lane's Pictures: *The Observer* (21 January 1917), 12.
26. Major Robert Gregory: *The Observer* (17 February 1918), 9.
27. The Irish Dramatic Movement: *The Voice of Ireland: A Survey of the Race and Nation from All Angles,* ed. William G. Fitzgerald (Dublin and London: Virtue and Company Ltd, 1923), 460–65.
28. Nobel Prize Acceptance: *Les Prix Nobel en 1923* (Stockholm: Imprimerie Royale, P. A. Norstedt & Soner, 1924), 74.
29. Miss Sara Allgood: *The Irish Times* (19 January 1924), 9.
30. A Memory of Synge: *The Irish Statesman* (5 July 1924), 530–32.
31. Compulsory Gaelic: *The Irish Statesman* (2 August 1924), 649–52.
32. Royal Irish Society Awards at the Tailteann Festival: *The Transatlantic Review* (November 1924), 539–42.
33. An Undelivered Speech: *The Irish Statesman* (14 March 1925), 8–10.
34. Divorce: *The Irish Times* (12 June 1925), 7–8.
35. The Child and the State: *The Irish Statesman* (5 and 12 December 1925), 393–94, 425.
36. The Need for Audacity of Thought: *The Dial* (February 1926), 115–19.
37. A Defence of the Abbey Theatre: *The Dublin Magazine* (April–June 1926), 8–12.
38. Memorial to the Late T. W. Lyster: [pamphlet for subscribers].
39. The Censorship and St Thomas Aquinas: *The Irish Statesman* (22 September 1928), 47–48.
40. The Irish Censorship: *The Spectator* (29 September 1928), 391–92.
43. Ireland, 1921–1931: *The Spectator* (30 January 1932), 137–38.
45. Plain Man's *Oedipus: The New York Times* (15 January 1933), sect. ix, 1.
46. The Great Blasket: *The Spectator* (2 June 1933), 798–99.
47. The Growth of a Poet: *The Listener* (4 April 1934), 591–92.
54. I Became an Author: *The Listener* (4 August 1938), 217–18.

APPENDIX B

Emendations to the Copy-Texts and Broadcast Texts

Changes to the copy-texts are given below, along with the reasons for emendation.

1. Noble and Ignoble Loyalties

	Emendation	Copy-text	Reason
p. 21	Bastille	Bastile	Place name
p. 22	*The Irish*	the *Irish*	Title

4. Irish Language and Irish Literature

	Emendation	Copy-text	Reason
p. 46	*Claidheamh*	*Claideamh*	Title

5. A Postscript to a Forthcoming Book of Essays by Various Writers

	Emendation	Copy-text	Reason
p. 51	subtlest	subtless	Spelling
p. 51	to	to be	Added word
p. 52	fold	fould	Spelling

6. John Eglinton

	Emendation	Copy-text	Reason
p. 58	da	de	Proper name

7. Literature and the Conscience

	Emendation	Copy-text	Reason
p. 61	*Fions*	*Fians*	Title

9. Away

	Emendation	Copy-text	Reason
p. 81	Aran	Arran	Place name

10. Mr Yeats's New Play

	Emendation	Copy-text	Reason
p. 82	Yeats's	Yeats'	Punctuation

11. An Ancient Conversation

	Emendation	Copy-text	Reason
p. 84	conversation	converation	Spelling
p. 85	Nashe's	Nash's	Proper name

12. The Acting at St Teresa's Hall

	Emendation	Copy-text	Reason
p. 88	Renaissance	Rennaisance	Spelling

13. The Acting at St Teresa's Hall II

	Emendation	Copy-text	Reason
p. 89	Martyn	Martin	Proper name
p. 89	Martyn	Martin	Proper name
p. 90	Rossetti	Rosetti	Proper name

17. Emmet the Apostle of Irish Liberty

	Emendation	Copy-text	Reason
p. 102	preferment, if you go	preferment, you go	Sense of sentence

p. 103	hare-brained	hair-brained	Spelling
p. 105	Anne	Ann	Proper name
p. 106	ecstasy	ecstacy	Spelling
p. 108	Young	young	Proper noun
p. 108	Young	young	Proper noun
p. 109	*Young Irelander*	Young Irelander	Sense of sentence
p. 110	county	country	Sense of sentence
p. 111	people through	people, through	Punctuation

18. America and the Arts

	Emendation	Copy-text	Reason
p. 117	Samarkand	Samerkand	Place name
p. 118	mind, fashioned	mind fashioned	Punctuation

19. British Association Visit to the Abbey Theatre

	Emendation	Copy-text	Reason
p. 124	*The Hour-Glass*	The "Hourglass"	Title
p. 124	Myers's	Myers	Punctuation
p. 126	government depends	government, depends	Punctuation

20. The Art of the Theatre

	Emendation	Copy-text	Reason
p. 127	Fortuny	Fortuni	Proper name
p. 127	Appia	Apia	Proper name

21. The Theatre of Beauty

	Emendation	Copy-text	Reason
p. 129	*Canavans*	"Cunavans"	Title

23. The Polignac Prize

	Emendation	Copy-text	Reason
p. 138	Stephens's	Stephens'	Punctuation

24. Thomas Davis

	Emendation	Copy-text	Reason
p. 141	Sidney	Sydney	Proper name
p. 144	*Demi-Gods*	"Demigods"	Title

25. Sir Hugh Lane's Pictures

	Emendation	Copy-text	Reason
p. 147	I		Sense of sentence

26. Major Robert Gregory

	Emendation	Copy-text	Reason
p. 153	*Kincora*	"Kincora"	Title
p. 153	Ricketts's	Ricketts'	Punctuation
p. 154	Leech	Leach	Title

27. The Irish Dramatic Movement

	Emendation	Copy-text	Reason
p. 157	Lewes	Lewis	Proper name
p. 158	Máire	Moira	Proper name
p. 159	'Zozimus'	"Zosimus"	Title
p. 160	Mitchel	Mitchell	Proper name
p. 162	*Whiteheaded Boy*	"White-headed Boy"	Title

29. Miss Sara Allgood

	Emendation	Copy-text	Reason
p. 165	*Spreading the News*	"The Spreading of the News"	Title

30. A Memory of Synge

	Emendation	Copy-text	Reason
p. 167	'a very short-lived	a very short-lived	Proper

| but delightful paper . . . too remote from the world of thought', | but delightful paper '. . . too remote from the world of thought', | quotation |

31. Compulsory Gaelic

	Emendation	Copy-text	Reason
p. 169	Ireland?	Ireland.	Punctuation
p. 173	*Tchekov*	T chekov	Proper name

32. Royal Irish Society Awards at the Tailteann Festival

	Emendation	Copy-text	Reason
p. 178	MacKenna	McKenna	Proper name
p. 180	Stephens's	Stephens'	Punctuation

34. Divorce

	Emendation	Copy-text	Reason
p. 186	fulfilled,	fulfilled;	Punctuation

36. The Need for Audacity of Thought

	Emendation	Copy-text	Reason
p. 198	Christmas	Christian	Sense of sentence
p. 198	Sharp	Sharpe	Proper name

37. A Defence of the Abbey Theatre

	Emendation	Copy-text	Reason
p. 203	Macardle	McArdle	Proper name
p. 204	Aran	Arran	Place name
p. 205	*Gaol Gate*	"Jail Gate"	Title

39. The Censorship and St Thomas Aquinas

	Emendation	Copy-text	Reason
p. 212	*Discobolus*	Discobulus	Title

41. Oedipus the King

	Emendation	Copy-text	Reason
p. 219	Monck	Monk	Proper name
p. 220	Mr F.	Mr P	Proper name

43. Ireland, 1921–1931

	Emendation	Copy-text	Reason
p. 233	*Philonous*	Philonus	Title

44. Poems About Women

	Emendation	Copy-text	Reason
p. 237	Deslys	Delys	Proper name
p. 242	Markiewicz	Marciewicz	Proper name

46. The Great Blasket

	Emendation	Copy-text	Reason
p. 248	Thomson	Thompson	Proper name

47. The Growth of a Poet

	Emendation	Copy-text	Reason
p. 249	Ballysodare	Ballysadare	Place name

48. The Irish Literary Movement

	Emendation	Copy-text	Reason
p. 256	O'Faolain	O'Fallaoin	Proper name
p. 256	O'Faolain	O'Fallaoin	Proper name

50. In the Poet's Pub

	Emendation	Copy-text	Reason
p. 266	dreaming?	dreaming.	Punctuation
p. 267	verandah)?	verandah?)	Punctuation
p. 272	sailor lads	sailor-lads	Format as published

51. In the Poet's Parlour

	Emendation	Copy-text	Reason
p. 278	Jezebel	Jesabel	Proper name

52. My Own Poetry

	Emendation	Copy-text	Reason
p. 284	Gaelic	Gaellic	Spelling
p. 285	they?	they;	Format as published
p. 285	be;	be	Format as published
p. 285	swordsmen	swordsman	Wording as published
p. 286	talk.	talk,	Format as published

APPENDIX C

The Setting of 'My Own Poetry'

A rich textual record exists for the most complex of Yeats's radio programmes, 'My Own Poetry'. In addition to Yeats's words, four textual sources provide valuable information: the scores of the musical settings by Edmund Dulac, Yeats's emendations on the BBC broadcast script, the reader V. C. Clinton-Baddeley's notes on the same copy, and diacritical marks he added to this copy to indicate Yeats's interpretive instructions. The BBC archive offers three supplementary sources of information: the 'programmes as broadcast' file, a note by the BBC producer George Barnes on the programme, and Barnes's account of it in a manuscript essay on his collaborations with Yeats.[544] Letters written by Yeats and Dulac in the two-week period following the programme's broadcast on July 3, 1937, defending and expanding on their several severe skirmishes during the programme's rehearsals, shed further light on the broadcast.

The programme is in two parts, but there is no indication of an actual hiatus in the broadcast. At one point in the programme's preparation, Yeats intended to speak both before and after the poem on Robert Gregory, but his only participation in the actual broadcast was the reading of the introductory material to each part.

Dulac's contributions are of three types: brief musical interludes between poems, accompaniment to recitation or refrains, and two original songs complete with musical scores. His altercations with Yeats resulted in considerable modification of his work as the rehearsals went along.

Barnes's note, in addition to confirming the time and the participants, also indicates the following:

Singer: Olive Groves
Harpist: Marie Goossens
Music: Cymbals with tympani stick and jazz wire broom

The programme began with an announcement:

My Own Poetry: A programme selected and introduced by W. B. Yeats with music composed by Edmund Dulac. The poems are spoken by Margot Ruddock and V. C. Clinton-Baddeley and have been produced by Mr Yeats in accordance with his own ideas. The two songs are produced by Mr Edmund Dulac and are sung by Miss Olive Groves.[545]

Yeats read the introduction to part I:

In 1916 the poet and schoolmaster Pearse, the labour leader Connolly, and others, including those two unknown men, De Valera and Cosgrave, seized certain public buildings in Dublin and held them against the English army for some days. Neither Pearse nor Connolly had any expectation of victory. They went out to die because, as Pearse said in a famous speech, a national movement cannot be kept alive unless blood is shed in every generation. A poem containing this thought will be the first spoken. It will be followed by a poem called 'An Irish Airman Foresees His Death'. The Irish airman was Robert Gregory—Lady Gregory's son. He was a painter of genius who, immediately after the start of the Great War, joined the Air Force. Like many Protestant Irishmen he stood between two nations. He said to me, 'I think I am going out of friendship'. Meaning, I suppose, that so many of his friends had gone. 'The English are not my people. My people are the people of Kiltartan'. Kiltartan is the name of a town land where he had property. Presently his mother asked 'Why has Robert joined?' I answered, 'I suppose he thought it his duty'. She said, 'It was his duty to stay here. He joined for the same reason I would have, had I been a young man. He could not keep out of it'. She was right. He was a born soldier. He said to Bernard Shaw shortly before his death, that he was never happy until he began to fight. When his 'plane crashed in Italy he was a famous flying man. He had brought down, according to the official record, nineteen German 'planes.

After this comes a third political poem—'The Curse of Cromwell'. Cromwell came to Ireland as a kind of Lenin. He destroyed a whole social order. There is not one of us, unless of a family imported by him or after him, that has not some memory of his tyranny and his cruelty. Irish and English history know of different Cromwells. The best line in my poem—I leave you to find it out—is not mine. It is translated from a Gaelic poem, where it was used as I have used it. And now for the poem about Pearse and Connolly.

Clinton-Baddeley read 'The Rose Tree', according to these interpretive notes:

query   (no music)   No 1   V.C.Cb

Read by
Clinton Baddeley

THE ROSE TREE

'O words are lightly spoken,'
Said Pearse to Connolly,
'Maybe a breath of politic words
Has withered our Rose Tree;
Or maybe but a wind that blows
Across the bitter sea.'

'It needs to be but watered,'
James Connolly replied,
'To make the green come out again
And spread on every side,
And shake the blossom from the bud
To be the garden's pride.'

'But where can we draw water,'
Said Pearse to Connolly,
'When all the wells are parched away?
O plain as plain can be
There's nothing but our own red blood
Can make a right Rose Tree.'

(music)

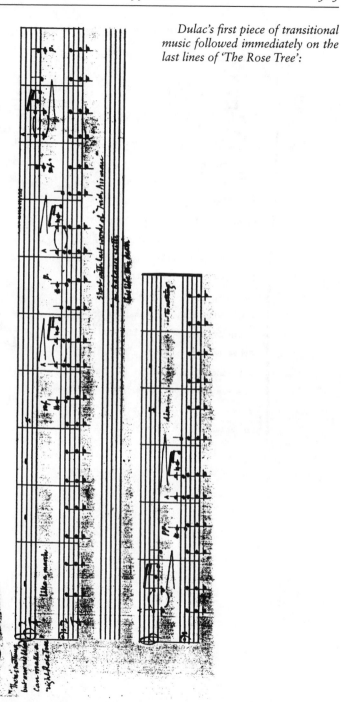

Dulac's first piece of transitional music followed immediately on the last lines of 'The Rose Tree':

Clinton-Baddeley read 'An Irish Airman foresees his Death':

[MUSIC] (harp)   No 2

VCcB
Read by Clinton
Baddeley

AN IRISH AIRMAN FORESEES HIS DEATH

Kristy

I know that I shall meet my fate
Somewhere among the clouds above;
Those that I fight I do not hate,
Those that I guard I do not love;
My country is Kiltartan Cross,
My countrymen Kiltartan's poor,
No likely end could bring them loss
Or leave them happier than before.
Nor law, nor duty bade me fight,
Nor public men, nor cheering crowds,
A lonely impulse of delight
Drove to this tumult in the clouds;
I balanced all, brought all to mind,
The years to come seemed waste of breath
A waste of breath the years behind
In balance with this life, this death.

quicker

Ecstasy

Immediately afterward came the second transitional passage by Dulac:

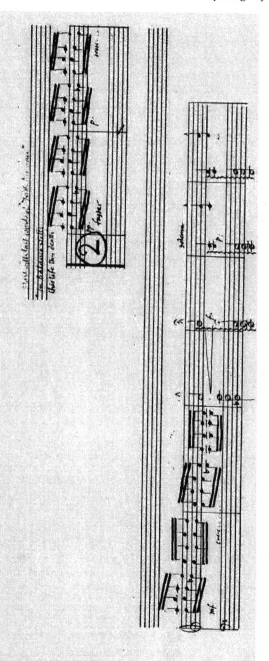

'The Curse of Cromwell' was read by Margot Ruddock:[546]

THE CURSE OF CROMWELL

You ask what I have found and far and wide I go
Nothing but Cromwell's house and Cromwell's murderous crew,
The lovers and the dancers are beaten into the clay,
And the tall men and the swordsmen and the horsemen where
                                        are they;
And there is an old beggar wandering in his pride,
His fathers served their fathers before Christ was crucified.

O what of that, O what of that
What is there left to say?

All neighbourly content and easy talk are gone
But there's no good complaining, for money's rant is on;
He that is mounting up must on his neighbour mount
And we and all the Muses are things of no account.
They have schooling of their own but I pass their schooling by
What can they know that we know that know the time to die?

O what of that, O what of that
What is there left to say?

But there's another knowledge that my heart destroys
As the fox in the old fable destroyed the Spartan boy's
Because it proves that things both can and cannot be
That the swordsman and the ladies can still keep company,
Can pay the poet for a verse and hear the fiddle sound,
That I am still their servant though all are underground.

O what of that, O what of that
What is there left to say?

I came on a great house in the middle of the night
Its open lighted doorway and its windows all alight,
And all my friends were there and made me welcome too;
But I woke in an old ruin that the winds howled through;
And when I pay attention I must out and walk
Among the dogs and horses that understand my talk,

O what of that, O what of that
What is there left to say?

And she sang the first refrain, being joined by Clinton-Baddeley in singing the second, third, and final refrains:

Yeats read the introduction to part II:

You must permit the poet his melancholy. My last two broadcasts had cheerful moments but, being a poet, I cannot keep it up. The poems you have just listened to were political. I consider those that follow religious. The first of these was written when I was recovering from a long illness. I had begun to read great literature again, though I was still very weak. The overwhelming power of every great genius filled me with terror. I was in the midst of a power that would tear the world in pieces; but for the critics, journalists, commonplace men of all kinds, who adapted it to human use. What if they were to suddenly fail us? I called the poem 'Mad as the Mist and Snow'.

This is followed by a poem called 'Running to Paradise'. Some Irish saint met a man running at full speed and asked where he was going, and the man said 'To Paradise'. This is followed by a poem, written when I first felt the infirmity of age. It is called 'Sailing to Byzantium' for reasons too complicated to explain.

I speak of a bird made by Grecian goldsmiths. There is a record of a tree of gold with artificial birds which sang. The tree was somewhere in the Royal Palace of Byzantium. I use it as a symbol of the intellectual joy of eternity, as contrasted with the instinctive joy of human life.

Then my series of poems winds up with 'He and She', wherein the moon and sun symbolise the soul and God. The soul's flight and return. Now comes the poem 'Mad as the Mist and Snow'.

Clinton-Baddeley read 'Mad as the Mist and Snow' to Dulac's harp setting:

Spoken by Clinton Baddeley
with harp between stanzas
No 4
VCB

MAD AS THE MIST AND SNOW
1, 2, 3, 4.
Bolt and bar the shutter,

For the foul winds blow;

Our minds are at their best this night,

And I seem to know

That everything outside us is

Mad as the mist and snow.

[Music] finish run + then
double pluck.

Horace there by Homer stands,

Plato stands below,

And here is Tully's open page.

How many years ago

Were you and I unlettered lads

Mad as the mist and snow?

[Music] 1. 2. 3. 4.

You ask what makes me sigh, old friend,

What makes me shudder so?

I shudder and I sigh to think

That even Cicero

And many-minded Homer were

Mad as the mist and snow.

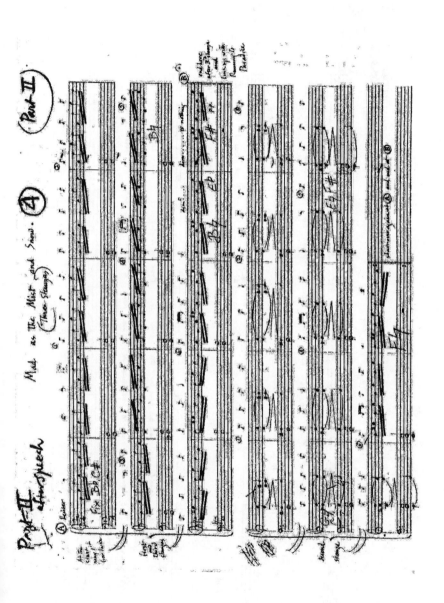

The music accompanying the third stanza of 'Mad as the Mist and Snow' led directly to Olive Groves's singing of 'Running to Paradise':

to Dulac's setting:

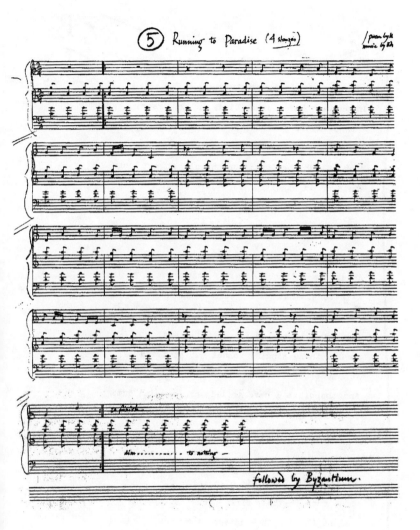

Clinton-Baddeley read 'Sailing to Byzantium' as emended and with interpretive notes by Yeats:

SAILING TO BYZANTIUM   *WCCB*

Old men should quit a country
                                    where
~~That is no country for old men.~~ — The young   *Spoken by*
                                                        Clinton-Baddeley
In one another's arms, birds in the trees,

- Those dying generations - at their song,//

The salmon-falls, the mackerel-crowded seas,,

Fish, flesh, or fowl,//commend all summer long...

Whatever is begotten, born, and dies.,

Caught in that sensual music all neglect

Monuments of unageing intellect.

                        II

An aged man is but a paltry thing,

A tattered coat upon a stick, unless

Soul   clap its hands and sing, and louder sing

For every tatter in its mortal dress,

Nor is there singing school but studying

Monuments of its own magnificence;

And therefore I have sailed the seas and come

To the holy city of Byzantium.

                        III

O sages standing in God's holy fire

As in the gold mosaic of a wall,

Come from the holy fire, perne in a gyre,

And be the singing-masters of my soul.

Consume my heart away; sick with desire

And fastened to a dying animal

It knows not what it is; and gather me

Into the artifice of eternity.

Olive Groves concluded the programme by singing 'He and She':

to Dulac's setting:

NOTES

1. Noble and Ignoble Loyalties

1. Queen Victoria (1819–1901) made her fourth visit to Ireland between April 4 and 25, 1900, in recognition of the service of Irish soldiers in the Boer War (1899–1902). Yeats's account of her generally enthusiastic reception, in the *United Irishman* for April 21, 1900, contrasts with his charge in the *Freeman's Journal,* on March 20, that the Queen's visit was motivated by 'national hatred—hatred of our individual national life' (*L* 336).

2. The French politician and orator Honoré Gabriel Riquetti, Comte de Mirabeau (1749–91), counseled the Constituent Assembly as it awaited Louis XVI's return to Paris from Versailles on July 15, 1789: 'Let a sad respect be the first reception given to the king by the representatives of an unfortunate people: the silence of the people is the lesson of kings'. (F. A. M Mignet, *History of the French Revolution* [London: J. M. Dent, 1915], p. 45.)

3. Victoria's first visit to Ireland, in September of 1849, began at Cork, which she renamed Queenstown in honour of the occasion.

   In 1847, John Mitchel (1815–75), one of the Young Irelanders, founded the *United Irishman,* urging agrarian reform through armed uprising. Convicted of sedition, he was transported in May 1848. Two other Young Irelanders, William Smith O'Brien (1803–64) and Thomas Francis Meagher (1823–67), were subsequently arrested and transported to Van Diemen's Land, an island near Australia.

4. Representatives of various tenant-right societies gathered in Dublin in August of 1850 to found the Tenant League, a short-lived coalition combining agrarian interests of both North and South, which emerged, in the elections of 1852, as the first independent Irish party since the Act of Union dissolved the Irish Parliament in 1801. The multiplicity of goals within the League led to its splintering into political ineffectiveness by 1859.

5. Victoria came again to Ireland, between August 30 and September 8, 1853, to open the International Exhibition of Irish Goods in Dublin.

   On St Patrick's Day, 1858, James Stephens (1824–1901) founded a secret society dedicated to recruiting ten thousand men within three months to establish in Ireland an independent and democratic republic. Although their first attempt at armed rebellion, on March 5, 1867, ended in defeat, arrest, and, in some few cases, execution, the Fenians, as they came to be known, established the model for Republican movements in Ireland.

6. The Queen's Dublin visit, August 21–29, 1861, was ostensibly to visit her son, who was in military training there.

   The *Irish People,* a Fenian paper, was founded in Dublin by James Stephens in 1863. It lasted less than two years. One of the editors, John O'Leary (1830–1907), who was to become Yeats's teacher and friend, spent nine years in prison for subversion.

7. In the title poem of *In the Seven Woods* (1903), Yeats echoes this assessment of Edward VII (1841–1910), whose succession of Victoria in 1901 he terms

   > . . . new commonness
   > Upon the throne and crying about the streets
   > And hanging its paper flowers from post to post (*P* 77).

2. Irish Fairy Beliefs

8. With his own work as a folklorist largely behind him, Yeats reviewed *Peasant Lore from Gaelic Ireland* (1900) by the schoolmaster from Spiddal, Co. Galway, Daniel Deeney (Domhnall O'Duibhne), in the *Speaker* for July 14, 1900.

   Yeats published his *Fairy and Folk Tales of the Irish Peasantry* in 1888. The 'authority' has not been identified.

9. William Larminie (1849–1900) published *West Irish Folk Tales and Romances* in 1893. His essay 'Legends as Materials for Literature' appeared along with pieces by Yeats and several others as *Literary Ideals in Ireland* in 1899.

   Jeremiah Curtin (1835–1906), who translated works on folklore and collected tales and legends, published *Hero-tales of Ireland* in 1894 (O'Shea 459).

   A founder in 1893 of the Gaelic League and its first president, Douglas Hyde (1860–1949) translated Gaelic tales and poetry which, with his own poetry in Gaelic, were primary instances of the revival of the Irish language and literature. Yeats cited Hyde's *The Story of Early Gaelic Literature* (1895) as one of the 'two or three good books' published by the New Irish Library, the publishing venture of the Irish Literary Society (*Au* 228).

10. *Tales of the Fairies and of the Ghost World Collected from Oral Tradition in Southwest Munster* (1895).

11. The collections of Irish tales and legends, in the 1820s and 1830s, by Thomas Crofton Croker (1798–1854) were admired by Sir Walter Scott, among others. Samuel Lover (1797–1868), the Irish ballad-writer and novelist, published his collection of *Songs and Ballads* in 1839 and his comic novel about Irish character, *Handy Andy,* in 1842. 'Croker and Lover', Yeats had written in 1888, 'full of the ideas of harum-scarum Irish gentility, saw everything humorised' (*Fairy and Folk Tales of the Irish Peasantry,* ed. W. B. Yeats [London: Walter Scott, 1888], p. xv).

Yeats, however, drew from Croker's *Fairy Legends and Traditions of the South of Ireland* (1825–28) and Lover's *Legends and Stories of Ireland* (1831) for the *Fairy and Folk Tales*. Lover's 'Barney O'Reirdan' from *Legends and Stories of the Irish Peasantry* appeared in Yeats's list of thirty 'Irish books' which was published in the *Dublin Daily Express* for February 27, 1895.

12. Douglas Hyde's *Beside the Fire* was published in London in 1890.

13. The pre-Norman fishing settlement on the west bank of the Corrib River in Co. Galway, known as the Cladagh, preserved its Irish-speaking traditions well into the twentieth century.

14. Yeats identifies this man as 'Kirwan' on page 26.

15. Deeney's only other published book was a second edition of *Peasant Lore from Gaelic Ireland,* in 1901.

3. Irish Witch Doctors

16. The lifelong friendship and collaboration between Yeats and the Irish playwright and folklorist Augusta, Lady Gregory (1852–1932), began in the summer of 1897, when he first visited Coole Park, her home in Co. Galway. The first products of their collaboration were six long essays on Irish folklore and supernatural experience which Yeats prepared from materials she had collected, with his assistance. The fifth in the series, 'Irish Witch Doctors', appeared in the *Fortnightly Review* for September 1900. The other essays in the series are:

    'The Tribes of Danu' (*New Review,* November 1897)
    'The Prisoners of the Gods' (*Nineteenth Century,* January 1898)
    'The Broken Gates of Death' (*Fortnightly Review,* April 1898)
    'Ireland Bewitched' (*Contemporary Review,* September 1899)
    'Away' (*Fortnightly Review,* April 1902) (see pp. 64–81.)

17. Of the places cited by Yeats in this essay, Gort, Clarenbridge, and Cregg are within twenty miles of each other in Co. Galway on the north-western coast of Ireland near the Co. Clare border. Coole Park, Lady Gregory's home, is about five miles from Gort, as is the Norman tower at Ballylee, which Yeats was later to restore. Bunnahow is in Co. Clare.

18. In 1890, reviewing Sophie Bryant's *Celtic Ireland,* Yeats called the *Táin Bó Cuailgne* (The Cattle Raid of Cooley), the Irish epic of the seventh or eighth century, 'the greatest of all' the bardic tales of Ireland (*UP1* 163).

19. In Lady Gregory's *Visions and Beliefs in the West of Ireland* (New York, 1920), II, 92, this man's name is given as 'Mr Saggarton' (O'Shea 811: vol. I only).

20. In *Autobiographies,* Yeats describes 'AE' (George William Russell, 1867–1935), his early schoolmate, close friend, and frequent collaborator, at the time of this essay: 'Men watched him with awe or with bewilderment; it was known that he saw visions continually, perhaps more continually than any modern man since Swedenborg. . . .' (*Au* 242).

Yeats had grouped AE with William Blake (1757–1827) and the Swedish scientist and mystic Emanuel Swedenborg (1688–1772) in an 1898 review, 'A Symbolic Artist and the Coming of Symbolic Art' (see *UP2* 133).

21. Marie Henri d'Arbois de Jubainville (1827–1910), the pioneer French Celticist, discusses this idea in the second volume, *Le cycle mythologique irlandais et la mythologie celtique* (1884) (O'Shea 1047), of his twelve-volume *Cours de littérature celtique* (1883–1902), which was translated into English by Richard Irvine Best (1872–1959) and published in Dublin in 1903. Jubainville was a friend of Maud Gonne and an early influence on J. M. Synge, who had attended his lectures at the Sorbonne in February and March of 1898.

    The Celtic scholar John Rhys (1840–1915) was the author of *Lectures on the Origin and Growth of Religion as Illustrated by Celtic Heathendom* (Hibbert Lectures, 1886), published in London in 1888 (O'Shea 1741: 2nd ed.), to which Yeats refers in a letter of that year (*L* 92). In the second lecture, 'The Zeus of the Insular Celts', Rhys identifies the 'Bag Men' as the race conquered by the Celts.

22. Although he had met John Millington Synge (1871–1909) in Paris in 1896, Yeats wrote to Lady Gregory in February 1899, suggesting that he was only then becoming acquainted with this 'most excellent man' (*L* 314). At the time of this essay, Synge was at work on the collection of folk material, undertaken partly at Yeats's suggestion, *The Aran Islands,* which he completed in 1901. The Irish National Theatre Society presented Synge's first play, *In the Shadow of the Glen,* cast in a heightened version of the dialect of Synge's native County Wicklow, in the Molesworth Hall, Dublin, on October 8, 1903.

23. Yeats paraphrases a passage from the prefatory letter, 'To the Public', to Blake's *Jerusalem:* 'We who dwell on Earth can do nothing of ourselves; every thing is conducted by Spirits, no less than Digestion or Sleep' (*The Works of William Blake: Poetic, Symbolic and Critical,* ed. Edwin J. Ellis and W. B. Yeats, 3 vols. [London: Bernard Quaritch, 1893] III, pl. 3) (O'Shea 220). In *William Blake's Writings,* ed. G. E. Bentley, Jr., 2 vols. (Oxford: Clarendon Press, 1978), I, 420.

24. Lady Gregory tells this story in the 'Mrs Sheridan' chapter of *Visions and Beliefs* (I, 74–75), where the 'old castle there below' is 'Ballinamantane' (O'Shea 811).

25. Lady Gregory gives this statement in *Visions and Beliefs* (I, 85).

4. Irish Language and Irish Literature

26. Yeats's letter on 'Irish Language and Irish Literature' for the first issue of the *Leader,* on September 1, 1900, was a pause in his quarrel with the paper's editor, David Patrick Moran (1871–1936). In his second issue, Moran agreed to disagree with Yeats, insisting 'that nothing can be Irish literature that is not written in the Irish language'. Moran characterised the Irish literary revival as shallow commercialism, and Yeats's emergence as a representative of the national

renaissance seemed to Moran 'one of the most glaring frauds that the credulous Irish people have ever swallowed' (quoted in *The Shaping of Modern Ireland,* ed. Conor Cruise O'Brien [London: Routledge and Kegan Paul, 1960], p. 111).

27. *An Claidheamh Soluis* (The Sword of Light), edited by Eoin MacNeill (1867–1945) and Padraic Pearse (1879–1916), was the official organ of the Gaelic League. The League sought to preserve Irish as the national language and to extend its spoken use, as well as to promote the study and publication of Gaelic literature and the cultivation of a modern literature in Irish. *An Claideamh Soluis* absorbed the earlier publication *Fainne an Lae* (Dawn), under which name the publication appeared briefly in 1908 and again from 1922 until 1930.

28. The hearings of the Viceregal Commission on Intermediate Education provoked Yeats's letter on 'The Academic Class and the Agrarian Revolution' in the *Dublin Daily Express* on March 11, 1899 (*UP2* 148). In subsequent debate on the commission's report in the House of Commons on July 19, 1900, John Redmond (1856–1917), John Dillon (1851–1927), and T. M. Healy (1855–1931) renewed discussion of the teaching of the Irish language, along with complaints about improper diversion of Irish funds. Their attempts to amend the bill resulted in the expansion of the membership of the controlling board.

29. Sir Charles Gavan Duffy (1816–1903), a leader of the Young Ireland movement in the 1840s, immigrated to Australia in 1855 and did not return to Ireland until 1880. Yeats opposed his leadership of the publishing scheme undertaken by the Irish Literary and the National Literary Societies in 1892, fearing that Duffy, rather than encourage imaginative works by younger writers, 'wanted "to complete the Young Ireland movement"—to do all that had been left undone because of the Famine, or the death of Davis, or his own emigration' (*Au* 226).

30. Yeats's concept of Moran's populist notions of national literature is summed up in his citation of Robert Burns (1759–96) and Charles Dickens (1812–70). While he may well have admired both writers' popularity, he was soon, in 'What is "Popular Poetry"?' (1902) to exclude Burns from the true company: 'Despite his expressive speech which sets him above all other popular poets, he has the triviality of emotion, the poverty of ideas, the imperfect sense of beauty of a poetry whose most typical expression is in Longfellow' (*E&I* 6). Dickens had already been similarly categorised in 1897 when Yeats had defined 'a quotation from Dickens and a quotation from Dr Johnson' as 'unfailing symptoms of popular journalism' (*UP2* 47). Of Moran's obstinacy on this subject, Yeats wrote to Lady Gregory, in January of 1901: 'I think Moran is merely puzzled as so many self taught men are puzzled at finding a mysterious hierarchy, governed by standards they cannot understand. The first result of a man's thinking for himself, when he has no cultivated tradition behind him, is that he values nothing but the obviously useful, the obviously

interesting, the obviously forceful. Such men—I have met a few—commonly judge all poetry by Burns because they can see his effect on Scots men & because he is easy to understand. . . .' (*CL3* 19).

To the conventional poetic triumvirate of William Wordsworth (1770–1850), Percy Bysshe Shelley (1792–1822), and John Keats (1795–1821), Yeats adds a more idiosyncratic prose pantheon, grouping the prodigious novelist and poet George Meredith (1828–1909) and the critic, art historian, and social reformer John Ruskin (1819–1900) with the reluctant leader of the 'aesthetic movement', Walter Pater (1839–94). Yeats had long admired Meredith, whom he exemplified in 1888 as among 'the really great writers of fiction [who] make their readers' minds like sponges' (*L* 94). He documents the influence on him of Ruskin, early and late, from the recollection of the physically violent 'quarrel over Ruskin' with his father in the late 1880s which opens the first draft of his autobiography (*Mem* 19) to his characterisation of *On the Boiler* (1939) as 'a sort of *Fors Clavigera*' (L 900), in reference to Ruskin's eclectic series (1871–78, 1880–84). Of Pater, to whose work and influence he was introduced in the 1890s by Oscar Wilde (1854–1900) and Yeats's fellow 'Rhymer', Lionel Johnson (1867–1902), Yeats recalled, 'we looked consciously to Pater for our philosophy', adding that, on mature rereading, Pater's *Marius the Epicurean* (1885) 'still seemed to me, as I think it seemed to us all, the only great prose in modern English, and yet I began to wonder if it, or the attitude of mind of which it was the noblest expression, had not caused the disaster of my friends' (*Au* 302). Yeats paid tribute to Pater in casting Pater's 'famous passage' on the Mona Lisa in *vers libre* as the opening selection in *The Oxford Book of Modern Verse* (1936) and in citing the Oxford classicist as the 'one writer' who had enjoyed the 'entire uncritical admiration' of his generation of modern poets (*OBMV* viii).

31. The blind Gaelic poet Anthony Raftery (1784–1835) was Yeats's lifelong model of the popular poet. In 1899, he had heard Raftery's verses on Mary Hynes and had begun both the identification of Raftery and Mary with Homer and Helen and the adoption of the tower at Ballylee, near which she had lived and died, as his personal symbol. In his essay on 'Literature and the Living Voice', he described a pilgrimage, probably in 1903, to Raftery's grave in Killeenan, Co. Mayo (see *Ex* 202–21).

32. Yeats contrasts the gentle 'local ballad' 'The Winding Banks of Erne; or, The Emigrant's Adieu to Ballyshanny', by William Allingham (1842–89), to the famous 'ballad' 'The Absent-Minded Beggar', by Rudyard Kipling (1865–1936). After it appeared in the London *Daily Mail* in October 1899, Kipling's poem raised over £250,000 for support of the English expedition against the Boers, through its exhortation to pay up for the girls and families that 'Tommy's left behind him':

> He's an absent-minded beggar, and his weaknesses are great—
> But we and Paul must take him as we find him—

He is out on active service, wiping something off a slate—
And he's left a lot of little things behind him!

Rudyard Kipling, *Rudyard Kipling's Verse: Inclusive Edition, 1885–1918* (New
York and Garden City: Doubleday, 1919), p. 522.

33. Partly through his father's influence, Yeats developed an early affin-
ity to Walt Whitman (1819–92), whom he called, in a letter of 1894,
'the most National' of America's poets (*L* 238).

Saint Columbanus (543–615) was born in Leinster and wrote in
Latin on various subjects. Yeats refers here to his Sermon V which
begins: 'Oh human life, feeble and mortal, how many have you
deceived, beguiled, and blinded! While you fly, you are nothing,
while you are seen, you are a shadow, while you arise, you are but
smoke. . . . You are the roadway of mortals, not their life, beginning
from sin, enduring up till death . . . you have allotted all your trav-
ellers to death' (G. S. M. Walker, *Sancti Columbani Opera* [Dublin,
1957], p. 85).

34. A founding motto of the *Nation* (see note 142, page 349) was 'to create and foster public opinion and make it racy of the soil'.

35. In her diary for December 29, 1900 (Berg NYPL), Lady Gregory
speculated about Moran's attacks on Yeats and others, noting that
Douglas Hyde had told him he shouldn't attack friends: 'whereat M
said: "Your enemies don't mind what you say, but if you attack your
friend, he is the boy that will feel it".'

36. Sharing the platform with Douglas Hyde at a public meeting in Gort
on July 27, 1899, Yeats had foreseen a time when his work in English
would seem foreign in Ireland, invoking the saints and martyrs of the
past who had bequeathed to his and future generations Ireland's
nationhood and its preserver, the Irish language. The essay to which
he refers, 'The Celtic Element in Literature', appeared in *Cosmopolis*
for June 1898. It is the first section of the essay of the same name
which Yeats included in *Ideas of Good and Evil* (1903).

37. Beginning in 1898, two years before his founding of the *Leader*,
Moran's articles appeared in the Dublin monthly the *New Ireland
Review*.

5. A Postscript to a Forthcoming Book of Essays by Various Writers

38. Yeats's first acknowledged contribution to the *All Ireland Review*,
edited by the nationalist Standish O'Grady (1846–1928), appeared
on December 1, 1900. O'Grady's editorial note thanked Yeats for
'the beautiful and eloquent little discourse which you were good
enough to send me', observing that it 'was not written for me or written for Ireland; it was written for London, for all your clever friends
over there, and all your clever enemies, for I know that you are carrying on a sort of war there. . . .' O'Grady resented Yeats's exporta-
tion and explanation of the 'Irish movement'. Nonetheless, excerpts
from his editorials appeared along with pieces by D. P. Moran,

George Moore (1852–1933), Douglas Hyde, and Yeats in Lady Gregory's *Ideals in Ireland* (1901), to which this essay, with minor modifications, is the 'Postscript'.

39. *Ideals in Ireland* reads: 'thrown upward what may seem a passing clamour, to the indifferent and the weary' (p. 105).

6. John Eglinton

40. Yeats had first known 'John Eglinton' (William Kirkpatrick Magee, 1868–1961) as a classmate at Erasmus Smith High School in Dublin and they later were fellow Theosophists. They often concerned themselves with similar issues and generally disagreed about them. An essay by Magee in the Dublin *Daily Express* in 1898 began the controversy which resulted in *Literary Ideals in Ireland* (1899) (O'Shea 606). In this review of Magee's *Pebbles from a Brook* (1901) (O'Shea 605), in the *United Irishman* for November 9, 1901, Yeats pays Magee the tribute of sharp, critical appreciation. This essay is the first of six that Yeats apparently gathered for subsequent publication as 'Some Uncollected Essays and Notes from *The United Irishman: 1901–1903*'. The collection, among Yeats's papers (NLI Ms 30039, SUNY-SB Box 20), was not published.

41. Eglinton's *Two Essays on the Remnant* was published in 1894 (O'Shea 605).

42. Judges 15:4–5.

43. Yeats echoes his review 'Dublin Mystics' in the *Bookman* in 1895, which listed *Two Essays on the Remnant,* along with two editions of a book by AE, as its subjects. There, Yeats briefly characterised Magee's book as 'a passionate and lofty appeal to the "idealists" to come out of the modern world, as the children of Israel came out of Egypt' (*UP1* 357).

44. *Two Essays on the Remnant,* p. 17.

45. *Two Essays,* p. 14, for 'petals fall away' has 'petals were falling'.

46. *Two Essays,* p. 16, has 'violence to his own nature' for 'violence to his nature'.

47. The essay on 'Regenerate Patriotism' in *Pebbles from a Brook* (1901) has on p. 27 'educate, and finally'; p. 81, 'as of days!'

48. In his lecture before the National Literary Society on May 19, 1893, Yeats asserted that 'old nations are like old men and women sitting over the fire gossiping [*sic*] of stars and planets, talking of all things in heaven and earth and in the waters under the earth, and forgetting in a trance of subtlety the flaming heart of man' (*UP1* 272–73).

49. In a note to Yeats's later edition of his writings, Magee regretted his use of the 'metaphor' comparing the plight of the creative remnant of the declining Egyptian and Greco-Roman societies with that of Irish artists at the turn of the century in 'The Chosen People at Work':

'The writer of the following pages would like to say that he has had no hand in the selection, which Mr Yeats has done him the honour to make for the Dun Emer Press Series, and in particular, that if consulted he would hardly have approved of the inclusion of the last essay, written over twelve years ago, in which a metaphor is pressed to the point of being recommended as a gospel' (John Eglinton, *Some Essays and Passages by John Eglinton,* ed. William Butler Yeats [Dundrum: Dun Emer Press, 1905], contents page).

50. In *The Trembling of the Veil,* Yeats associates Oscar Wilde with Cellini, 'who, coming after Michael Angelo, found nothing left to do so satisfactory as to turn bravo and quarrel with the man who broke Michael Angelo's nose' (*Au* 139). Wilde is 'an audacious Italian fifteenth century figure' (ibid., p. 131; cf. *A Vision* [New York: Macmillan, 1956], pp. 148–51), and the *fin de siècle* illustrator Aubrey Beardsley (1872–98) is the tragic saint and victim of the thirteenth phase whose nature is 'on the edge of Unity of Being, the understanding of that Unity by the intellect his one overmastering purpose' (ibid., p. 331; cf. *A Vision,* pp. 129–31).

51. Duc Jean des Esseintes, the hero of *À Rebours* (1884) by J. K. Huysmans (1848–1907), was the model for Dorian Gray, whose creator identified 'Huysmans's over-realistic study of the artistic temperament' (*Letters of Oscar Wilde,* ed. Rupert Hart-Davis [London: Rupert Hart-Davis Ltd, 1962], p. 313) as the book Dorian had read in which the 'things he had dimly dreamed of were suddenly made real to him' (*The Writings of Oscar Wilde, Uniform Edition* [London and New York: A. R. Keller and Co., 1907], p. 229).

52. Romans 14:7.

53. Yeats's admiration for William Morris (1834–96), whom he characterised as 'The Happiest of the Poets' (*E&I* 53–64), began in childhood and intensified when he frequented Morris's Kelmscott House in the late 1880s. Morris's accommodation of magic and fantasy, which qualifies him here as one of 'the Remnant', explains Yeats's observation that Morris's late prose romances 'were the only books I was ever to read slowly that I might not come too quickly to the end' (*Au* 141).

54. Allan Bennett (1872–1923), a chemist and early associate with Yeats in the Order of the Golden Dawn, became a Buddhist and immigrated to Ceylon. In 1907, Yeats had written to Florence Farr (1860–1917) of Bennett's life and work in Burma, where he had by that time settled, noting that 'Bennett was now working on experimental science. . . . The researches are concerned with N Rays. Bennett goes out every morning with his begging bowl as a monk, but always gives the contents of his bowl to some less well-provided-for brother. His own meals are sent in every day to the workshop' (*L* 499). Bennett's *The Wisdom of the Aryas,* a book on Buddhism, was published in London in 1923.

55. The legendary first Anglo-Saxon settlers of Britain, two brothers who, according to Geoffrey of Monmouth, landed in 499.

56. Yeats echoes the yearning of Omar Khayyám which became a motto of Fabian Socialism:

> To grasp this sorry Scheme of Things entire,
>   Would not we shatter it to bits—and then
> Re-mould it nearer to the Heart's Desire!

The Rubáiyát of Omar Khayyám, tr. Edward Fitzgerald (1809–83)
(London: Bernard Quaritch, 1859), p. 16, LXXIII.

57. Yeats had met the exiled Russian geographer and anarchist Prince Peter Kropotkin (1842–1921) 'perhaps but once or twice' at supper at Kelmscott House in the 1880s (*Au* 140).

58. In the first paragraph of his essay on Leonardo da Vinci (1452–1519), Pater says of Leonardo that 'he is so possessed by his genius that he passes unmoved through the most tragic events, overwhelming his country and friends, like one who comes across them by chance on some secret errand' (*The Renaissance: Studies in Art and Poetry* [London: Macmillan, 1910], p. 99).

59. Keats makes this observation in a letter of July 18, 1818, to Benjamin Bailey in which he discusses his fears of not having 'a right feeling towards Women' (John Keats, *The Poetical Works and Other Writings of John Keats,* ed. H. Buxton Forman [New York: Charles Scribner's Sons, 1939], VII, p. 80).

60. In *Henry VI,* part 2, scene ii, the rebel Jack Cade entertains his henchman Dick's suggestion to 'kill all the lawyers':

> Nay, that I mean to do. Is not this a lamentable thing, that of the skin of an innocent lamb should be made parchment? that parchment, being scribbled o'er, should undo a man? Some say the bee stings; but I say, 'tis the bee's wax; for I did but seal once to a thing, and I was never my own man since (ll. 74–79).

61. Yeats's concluding volley at *Pebbles from a Brook* is aimed first at Magee's calling the consideration of beauty, truth, art, and God 'as facts outside experience', the 'beginning of formalism, incredulity, vulgarity, ritual and of all that riff-raff which incumbers the paradise of a true life' (p. 37); the alleged 'phrase' is, in Magee's text, two nouns, separated by a comma. His next targets are Magee's portrayal of the true patriot as one who will turn against his motherland, saying, 'I will persist in seeing thee a virgin mother . . . will still behold thee beautiful and unprofaned, no palsied beldam with whiskey on thy breath and a crucifix in thy hand—two things I never loved' (p. 80) and his assertion that philosophy rarely recognises the heights of 'eternal wisdom' in poetry, having an interest in art which is 'otherwise mainly pathological and perfunctory' (p. 93). Yeats then attacks Magee's declaration that 'The criticism of such ardent but harassed idealists as Shelley and Wagner, who saw in art the refuge from a squalid reality, can hardly satisfy those who have learned from Wordsworth . . . to regard poetry simply as a fact of life' (p. 89). His final allusion is to Magee's praise of Tolstoi's *What Is Art?* (1898),

which lists *Uncle Tom's Cabin* among its 'examples of the highest art flowing from love of God and man' (Leo Tolstoi, *What Is Art?*, tr. Aylmer Maude [London: Oxford University Press, 1959], p. 242).

This final paragraph was probably the major provocation for Eglinton's retort in the *United Irishman* for November 16, that it was 'strange that one who makes so little of modern civilisation as Mr Yeats could think of nothing but fishing and reading Wordsworth as possible occupations for idealists of the school of Rousseau and Tolstoi. . . .'

7. Literature and the Conscience

62. In October of 1901, the Irish Literary Theatre presented *Diarmuid and Grania,* the product of three years' erratic collaboration between Yeats and George Moore. The play drew sharp criticism from Irish nationalists who perceived it as yet another English degradation of an Irish theme. In an interview with the *Freeman's Journal* on November 13, Moore suggested that censorship, perhaps by the church, would be appropriate to a national theatre. Yeats responded in a letter to the *Journal* of November 14 refusing to join Moore in any project which established ecclesiastic censorship. The statements by Moore and Yeats provoked an article which appeared on November 23 in the *United Irishman* by Fred Ryan (1874–1913). An agnostic free-thinker who later became the first secretary of the Irish National Theatre Society, Ryan, under his pseudonym 'Irial', chided both men; Moore's attitude was cowardly, and Yeats had not only failed to 'take the highest ground' in not denouncing censorship but had also betrayed a certain amorality in his elevation of literature as 'the principal voice of the conscience' over 'the special moralities' of churches, governments, and 'peoples' (p. 3). Yeats responded, in a letter on 'Literature and the Conscience' in the *United Irishman* for December 7, 1901.

This is the second of the six essays gathered under the tentative title 'Some Uncollected Essays and Notes from *The United Irishman*: 1901–1903' but ultimately not published.

63. Yeats was introduced to the work of Émile Verhaeren (1855–1916) by Osman Edwards (1864–1936), a close friend and translator of the Belgian poet and dramatist, whose essay on Verhaeren had appeared, along with Yeats's 'The Tables of the Law', in the *Savoy* in November of 1898. Yeats refers to Verhaeren's critical theories in two essays of that year, 'The Celtic Element in Literature' (*E&I* 187) and 'John Eglinton and Spiritual Art' (*UP2* 131). Verhaeren's sentence has not been traced.

64. Yeats had quoted from Shelley's 'A Defence of Poetry' (1821) in a letter to Mrs Patrick Campbell (1865–1940) written shortly before this article (*CL3* 122). John Kelly and Ronald Schuchard (*CL3* 133) speculate that Yeats's specific reference may be to 'Ideas Concerning Intellect' by the German idealist philosopher Arthur Schopenhauer (1788–1860). *The Sense of Beauty,* by the American philosopher

George Santayana (1863–1952), was published in New York and London in 1896.

65. Although the oldest extant manuscript of the Fenian story of Diarmuid and Gráinne, the flight of the betrothed of Finn mac Cúmhail and her lover Diarmuid Ó Duibhne of the white teeth, dates only to the seventeenth century, it is mentioned a thousand years earlier.

66. Just before 'Irial's' note appeared, Yeats wrote to Lady Gregory about the several versions of the story of Diarmuid and Grania, including those in *The Fions* (1891), by John Gregorson Campbell (1836–91), whose work Yeats had admired since the eighties. Noting that Campbell's Grania is 'not very particular in the choice of her lovers' and that 'Finn in one version has her buried alive', Yeats said he was 'half inclined to write for the printed text of the play a preface describing the various versions of the tale—and so dispose of Irish criticism once for all . . .' (*L* 359). Yeats's historical note never appeared, and the play was not printed until 1951, when it was published in the *Dublin Magazine*.

67. In his article, Ryan cited a 'book on the South African War by an Englishman, very nicely written, admirably phrased, the work of a scholar, and yet it was all arguing a lie', concluding that 'fine writing is not by any means always on the side of the true and the just'.

8. Egyptian Plays

68. Yeats reviewed the collaboration of Florence Farr and Olivia Shakespear, both intimate friends, in T. P. O'Connor's London paper, the *Star*, on January 23, 1902. The plays he saw, *The Beloved of Hathor* and *The Shrine of the Golden Hawk,* were produced January 20 and 21, 1902. Wade (*L* 372) says that the texts were on sale at the theatre but that they were never published.

69. Florence Farr, Yeats's fellow student in the Order of the Golden Dawn, had appeared as 'Aleel' in the first production of *The Countess Cathleen* (1899). Subsequently, she and Yeats worked on dramatic productions and readings of his poetry to music. Yeats had met Mrs Shakespear (1863–1938), a novelist and a cousin of Lionel Johnson, in 1894. He wrote of his liaison with her in his posthumously published *Memoirs,* calling her 'Diana Vernon' (*W. B. Yeats: Memoirs,* ed. Denis Donoghue [Macmillan: New York, 1973], p. 74). In 1934, when composing the section of his autobiography which was to become *Dramatis Personae,* he lamented to her that her image, 'the most significant . . . of those years', had to be left out (*L* 820).

70. Yeats had written *The Land of Heart's Desire* for the dramatic debut, in 1894, of Dorothy Paget (1885–1974), Florence Farr's niece. She had read the prologue which Lionel Johnson wrote for the first production of *The Countess Cathleen* by the Irish National Theatre in 1899.

9. *Away*

71. The last of the group of six essays (see note 16, p. 327) which Yeats organized from the folk material gathered with Lady Gregory, this article appeared in the *Fortnightly Review* in April 1902.

72. Most of the places Yeats cites in this essay are on the northwest coast of Ireland near the border between Co. Galway and Co. Clare. Gort, Loughrea, Ardrahan, Kilchreest, Craughwell, Anthry, Kinarva, Ballyvaughan, and Kilfenora are all within thirty miles of one another. The Abbey of Corcomroe is in the Burren hills, a few miles from Ballyvaughan. The Aran Islands, Inisheer, Inishmore, and Inishmaan are off the coast of Galway a few miles from Kilfenora. Knock is farther down the coast in lower Co. Clare.

     Yeats also cites Westport and Moneen, within some twenty miles of each other in Co. Mayo, to the north of Co. Galway.

73. Yeats tells this story in ' "Maive" and Certain Irish Beliefs' (*UP2* 204–7). The story of the 'woman from the North', one of the 'Ingentry', which follows here, is, with minor alteration, taken from the same essay.

74. I.e., earlier in this essay.

75. The apparition, in August 1879, of Mary, Joseph, and St John to two women in the Co. Mayo village of Knock established it, after verification by church authorities, as a primary site for pilgrimage and the seeking of cures.

76. Rhys retells this story in 'The Sun Hero', the fifth of his *Lectures on the Origin and Growth of Religion as Illustrated by Celtic Heathendom* (O'Shea 1741). Yeats used much of the story of Cuchullain 'away', as he recounts it here, in his play *The Only Jealousy of Emer* (1919). *Leabhar na b-Uidhre* (The Book of the Dun Cow), the oldest of the Irish miscellaneous manuscripts, was composed around 1100.

77. In 'The Scapegoat', the ninth volume of *The Golden Bough,* Sir James George Frazer (1854–1941) includes several examples of beating as a purifying process, explaining the 'practice of beating sick people with the leaves of certain plants or with branches in order to rid them of noxious influences. . . . Sometimes it appears that a beating is administered for the purpose of ridding people of a ghost who may be clinging too closely to their persons; in such cases the blows, though they descend on the bodies of the living, are really aimed at the spirit of the dead, and have no other object than to drive it away. . . .' (*The Golden Bough: A Study in Magic and Religion,* 3rd. ed. [London: Macmillan and Company, Limited, 1911], IX, 259–60) (O'Shea 697).

78. 'The Prisoners of the Gods' (*UP2* 74–87).

79. Rhys discusses Cuchullain and the Beetle of Forgetfulness in 'The Culture Hero', the fourth of the Hibbert Lectures.

80. Yeats's text is, with slight emendations, from *The Mabinogion, from the Welsh of the Llyfr coch o Hergest (The Red Book of Hergest) in The Library of Jesus College, Oxford,* tr. Lady Charlotte Guest (London: Bernard Quaritch, 1877), p. 341 (O'Shea 1166).

10. Mr Yeats's New Play

81. The popular success of the first productions of *Deirdre* by AE and
    Yeats's *Cathleen ni Houlihan* in Saint Teresa's Hall, Dublin, on April
    2–5, 1902, led to a brief truce between the National Theatre and
    Arthur Griffith's *United Irishman,* where angry speculation on the
    'failure' or 'betrayal' of national drama had become a regular fea-
    ture. Yeats's brief article in the issue for April 5 reflects this mood, as
    he speaks of his play as 'the call of country'.
82. The unsuccessful rebellion of the Protestant barrister Wolfe Tone
    (1763–98) ended shortly after the landing, late in August 1798, of
    French forces at Killala in Co. Mayo.
83. Richard J. Finneran suggests that the source for Yeats's rendering of
    'Fair-haired Donough' was Lady Gregory, who published her version
    of the poem in an article on 'West Irish Folk Ballads' in the *Monthly
    Review* for October 1902 (*Editing Yeats's Poems: A Reconsideration*
    [New York: St Martin's Press, 1990], pp. 130–31).
84. The 'play about the call of religion' was *The Hour-Glass* which, Yeats
    told Lady Gregory, would not 'offend anybody' but might 'propitiate
    Holy Church' (*L* 370). The edition he speaks of never appeared. The
    text of *Cathleen ni Houlihan* appeared in *Samhain,* the occasional
    publication of the Irish National Theatre Society, in October of 1902
    and was included, along with *The Hour-Glass* and *The Pot of Broth,*
    in the second volume of *Plays for an Irish Theatre* in 1904.

11. An Ancient Conversation

85. Standish O'Grady initiated a series of 'Thoughts on Irish Mythology'
    in his *All Ireland Review* with the issue for December 28, 1901. The
    series continued into the following year, eventually assuming the title
    'The Revival of the Irish Language'. On March 29, 1902, quoting
    from the translation by the German philologist and Celtic scholar
    Kuno Meyer (1858–1919) of a mediaeval dialogue, *King and Hermit*
    (1901), O'Grady noted that the conversation between two charac-
    ters, 'one being King, the other being Hermit', when understood in
    historical perspective, awakens 'a new interest' (p. 61). 'The Revival
    of the Irish Language' concluded in the issue for April 5, 1902. The
    same issue presented Yeats's comments on 'An Ancient Conversa-
    tion' and on the rising controversy over the 'suitability' of Celtic
    myth and Gaelic poetic speech for drama and verse. Yeats's com-
    mentary continued, in the issue for April 12, ending with a section
    from Lady Gregory's *Cuchulain of Muirthemne.*
86. The antiquarian Eugene O'Curry (1796–1862) included two 'copies'
    of this verse in his *Lectures on the Manuscript Materials of Ancient
    Irish History,* both from a manuscript in the British Museum which
    ascribes them to Aibhé, the daughter of Cormac MacArt:

    > 'The apple tree of noble Ailinn,
    > The yew of Bailé,—small inheritance,—
    > Although they are introduced into poem,

They are not understood by unlearned people.'
And [Aibhé] the daughter of Cormac, the grandson of
  Conn, said:—
'What I liken Aluime to,
Is to the yew of Ráith Bailé;
What I liken the other to,
Is to the apple tree of Ailinn. . . .'

Eugene O'Curry, *Lectures on the Manuscript Materials of Ancient Irish History*
(Dublin: William A. Hinch, 1872), pp. 466–67 (O'Shea 1477).

87. In Irish mythology, Brian is one of three sons of the goddess of fertility and poetry, Brigid, by Tuireann, the son of Etain and Ogma. To compensate for killing Cian, father of Lugh Lámhfhada (Lugh of the Long Hand), the ancient King of Ireland, he and his brothers, Iuchar and Iucharba, are ordered to bring to Lugh fabled possessions of several other rulers, in a saga thought of as the Irish equivalent of the voyage of Jason and his quest for the Golden Fleece.

88. Yeats had reviewed Meyer's translation of *The Vision of MacConglinne* in 1893 (see *UP1* 261–63). In 1903, Meyer founded the School of Irish Learning, which was later absorbed into the Royal Irish Academy. The text to which Yeats refers has not been identified.

89. Although both the 'Prose Edda' of Snorri Sturluson (1179–1241) and the anonymous 'Poetic Edda' were written in Iceland in the thirteenth century, the latter was at one time believed to be from the tenth century. Sturluson's work, a handbook of poetics, is complemented in ancient Icelandic tradition by the complex mythological and heroic poems of its anonymous counterpart.

90. Frederick York Powell (1850–1904), Regius Professor of History at Christ Church, Oxford, had been a family friend in Yeats's youth and an early mentor.

York Powell's introduction to volume I of *Corpus Poeticum Boreale,* edited with Gudbrand Vigfusson (1827–89), acknowledges the saga as a 'true child of Iceland', but cites 'the Western Isles', 'when the Irish Church, with her fervent faith, her weird and wild imaginings, and curious half-Eastern legends, was impressing the poetic mind on one side, [and] the rich and splendid court of Eadgar or Canute . . . on the other' as source for its setting and 'curious mythologic fancies' (*Corpus Poeticum Boreale,* 2 vols. [Oxford: Clarendon Press, 1883], I, xiii).

91. Yeats, Hyde, and others had been quarreling with several powerful figures at Trinity College, Dublin, over the aptness of Gaelic and folk materials as literary models. Chief among these critics was Robert Atkinson (1839–1908), professor of Romance languages, Sanskrit, and comparative philology at Trinity. His declarations that ancient Irish texts all contained some elements which were silly or indecent, that Hyde's stories were 'low', and that 'all folklore was at bottom abominable' had provoked Yeats's letter on 'The Academic Class and the Agrarian Revolution' (*UP2* 148) a year earlier as well as Hyde's satiric play *The Bursting of the Bubble* in 1903.

92. This quotation, from 'Adieu, Farewell Earth's Bliss', from *Summer's Last Will and Testament* (1600), by Thomas Nashe (1567–1601), was a favourite of Yeats, who used it as the title of his appreciation of the Gaelic 'Homer', Anthony Raftery.

93. Legendarily, the hair of Berenice (ca. 273–221 B.C.), wife of Ptolemy III of Egypt (ca. 284–221 B.C.), which disappeared after she dedicated it to Venus for her husband's safe return from battle, became the constellation *Coma Berenices*.

    In *The Blind Beggar of Alexandria* (1598), the earliest surviving play of George Chapman (1559–1634), Elimime, a vain countess, lists for her sisters the 'gowns and head-tires', each containing a classical and celestial allusion, in preparation for her:

    > One hath bright Ariadne's crown in it,
    > Even in the figure it presents in heaven;
    > Another hath the fingers of Diana,
    > And Berenice's ever-burning hair;
    > Another hath the bright Andromeda
    > With both her silver wrists bound to a rock.

    > *The Works of George Chapman*, ed. Richard Herne Shepherd (London: Chatto and Windus, 1889), I, 12 (O'Shea 369).

    Yeats alluded to Berenice in 'Veronica's Napkin', and thirty years after writing this essay, he incorporated Chapman's alliteration in 'Her Dream':

    > I dreamed as in my bed I lay,
    > All night's fathomless wisdom come,
    > That I had shorn my locks away
    > And laid them on Love's lettered tomb:
    > But something bore them out of sight
    > In a great tumult of the air,
    > And after nailed upon the night
    > Berenice's burning hair (*P* 263).

94. In Irish mythology, the Tuatha de Dannan defeat the Firbolg at the first Battle of Magh Tuireadh (Moytura) in southern Co. Mayo and achieve dominance over the Fomor at the second Battle of Magh Tuireadh.

95. In Part III, 'Names and Legends', of *The Dolmens of Ireland*, the folklorist William Copeland Borlase (1848–99), speaks of six pigs, the 'Swine of Derbrenn, daughter of Eochaidh Fedlech', her foster-children changed by a spell into pigs and then attacked by Maeve. Borlase adduces this as 'another version of [the story of] the Firbolg. . . . Wherever pigs occur in the Irish legends, I suspect that this same race of people is intended. . . .' (*The Dolmens of Ireland* [London: Chapman & Hall, 1897], III, 867).

96. Immediately following Yeats's essay, O'Grady began quotation from pp. 22–31 of *Cuchulain of Muirthemne,* which continued in the issue for April 19 and concluded in that for April 26.

12. The Acting at St Teresa's Hall

97. Yeats's assessment of the presentation, on April 2, 1902, of AE's *Deirdre* by an all-Irish cast appeared in the *United Irishman* for April 12, 1902. His *Cathleen ni Houlihan* was the other play presented in the 1902 productions of the Irish National Theatre. Privately, Yeats observed to Lady Gregory that, although at the first performance he 'hated' AE's play and 'did not remain in the Theatre because I was so nervous about it', he came to like its 'effect of wall decoration. The absense of character is like the absense of individual expression in wall decoration. . . . The result was curiously dreamlike and gentle' (*CL3* 166–67). This is the third of the six essays gathered under the tentative title 'Some Uncollected Essays and Notes from *The United Irishman:* 1901–1903' but ultimately not published.

98. For the 1901 season of the Irish Literary Theatre, *Diarmuid and Grania* by Yeats and George Moore had been produced by F. R. Benson's English company, and Douglas Hyde's *Casadh an tSugain* (The Twisting of the Rope) had been done in Gaelic by members of the Gaelic League. Nationalist objections and the limited abilities of the League members caused Yeats and his colleagues to invite the Irish National Dramatic Company of W. G. Fay (1872–1947) to stage the 1902 productions. Yeats had praised the company's 'grave acting' in some nationalist tableaux at the Antient Concert Rooms in August of 1901, and he had been corresponding with Fay's brother and collaborator, Frank (1870–1931), since the latter's series of essays on an Irish Theatre had begun appearing in the *United Irishman* in May of 1901. The Fays continued their collaboration with Yeats and Lady Gregory until January 1908.

99. The Bergen Theatre was founded in 1850 by Ole Bull (1810–80). Henrik Ibsen (1828–1906) joined the theatre in 1851 and left it in 1857 to manage the Christiana (Oslo) Norwegian Theatre. He and Bjørnstjerne Bjørnson (1832–1910) founded the Norwegian Society in 1859 to promote national literature and art. Yeats had called this 'theatre of Scandinavia . . . the nearest approach to an ideal theatre in modern Europe', in his address on the 'Ideal Theatre' before the Irish Literary Society on April 23, 1899 (*UP2* 155).

100. In Part II, Book V, of his *William Shakespeare,* entitled 'The Minds and the Masses', Victor Hugo (1802–85) calls the 'transformation of the crowd into the people' the 'profound task' of theatre, where

> . . . the people throw themselves passionately into the beautiful. They pack together, crowd, amalgamate, combine, and knead themselves in the theatre,—a living paste, which the poet is about to mould. . . . The house is crowded; the vast multitude looks, listens, loves; all con-

sciences, deeply moved, throw out their internal fire; all eyes glisten; the huge, thousand-headed beast is there, the Mob of Burke, the Plebs of Titus Livius, the Fex Urbis of Cicero.

William Shakespeare, trans. Melville B. Anderson (New York: Books for Libraries Press, 1970), pp. 297, 308.

John Kelly and Ronald Schuchard (*CL3* 171) speculate that Yeats's reference may be to Chapter 6 of Book IV and cite references to Hugo's book in a review from 1890 and a note from 1934 to 'Three Songs to the Same Tune'.

13. The Acting at St Teresa's Hall II

101. At Yeats's urging, his ally in the Irish Literary Theatre, Edward Martyn (1859–1923), commented on the Irish National Theatre's productions on the front page of the *United Irishman* for April 19, 1902. Praising both *Deirdre* and *Cathleen ni Houlihan* and noting that Maud Gonne (1865–1953) outshone the other players in the title role of Yeats's play, Martyn blamed the audience's laughter during *Cathleen ni Houlihan* on W. G. Fay for playing 'Peter Gillane' as a low-comedy character, irritating Yeats, who had considered modifying the play's beginning to strike 'a tragic note from the start' (*CL3* 167). He responded to Martyn with this brief statement in the *United Irishman* of April 26, 1902.

This note and the preceding one constitute the fourth of the six essays gathered under the tentative title 'Some Uncollected Essays and Notes from *The United Irishman*: 1901–1903' but ultimately not published.

102. An editorial comment on Martyn's criticism defended Fay and asserted that the reaction of the opening night audience had come from the relaxation during Yeats's play of the tensions wrought by AE's solemn drama, noting that, on the following night, 'Peter Gillane's real character impressed the audience and no laughter in the wrong places grated on the ear'.

103. On June 10, 1902, Yeats lectured at Oxford on his notions of dramatic speech set to music, with demonstrations by Florence Farr. His text no doubt resembled his essay on 'Speaking to the Psaltery', which appeared in May and which he reprinted in *Ideas of Good and Evil*.

104. Both founding members of the Pre-Raphaelite Brotherhood in 1848, Sir John Everett Millais (1829–96) and Dante Gabriel Rossetti (1828–82), contrasted sharply in their work and careers. Millais's steady expansion of the Brotherhood's mandate led to a copious output of paintings, illustrations, and, late in his career, distinguished portraits. As a painter, poet, and in his early recognition of the genius of Blake, the erratic Rossetti was a powerful model for Yeats and a representative of the 'neo romantic' giants he faced in the formation of his own career. '. . . I was in all things Pre-Raphaelite', he

recalled in *Autobiographies*. 'When I was fifteen or sixteen my father had told me about Rossetti and Blake and given me their poetry to read . . .' (*Au* 114); and Rossetti's 'conviction that it mattered to nobody whether the sun went round the earth or the earth round the sun' (ibid., p. 89) had aided him in blunting his father's stern objections to his early psychical research.

105. Shortly after he had seen the Purcell Society productions of *Dido and Aeneas* and *The Masque of Love* which Gordon Craig (1872–1966) had staged in London on March 26, 1901, Yeats had written in admiration to the English actor and producer. 'You have created a new art', he wrote on April 2. 'I would like to talk the thing over with you' (*CL3* 53). The following year, in a letter to the *Saturday Review,* he ranked the Purcell productions 'among the important events of our times' (*L* 366), and he subsequently cooperated with Craig on several productions of his plays.

106. Yeats had known of the work of Pedro Calderón de la Barca (1600–81) from the period 1895–96, when he had shared rooms with Arthur Symons (1865–1945), who translated some writings of the Spanish poet and dramatist.

107. *Sakuntalá* is the most famous of the three plays of Kálidása, the great fifth-century Hindu dramatist and poet whom Yeats had grouped with Sophocles, Shakespeare, and Goethe in an 1894 review (*UP1* 322).

14. The Freedom of the Theatre

108. Yeats's article on 'The Freedom of the Theatre', in the *United Irishman* for November 1, 1902, accompanied the text of his play *Where There is Nothing*. The play evolved from a brief and unsuccessful collaboration with George Moore. While his essay accurately anticipated most of the criticisms the play was to provoke, the thin cordiality of Yeats's postscript betrays the strategic purpose it played in the squabble with Moore, who had threatened an injunction should Yeats attempt to publish a work based on their collaboration. This is the fifth of the six essays gathered under the tentative title 'Some Uncollected Essays and Notes from *The United Irishman:* 1901–1903' but ultimately not published.

109. Prior to the presentation, in 1899, of Yeats's *The Countess Cathleen* as the first programme of the Irish Literary Theatre, Frank Hugh O'Donnell (1848–1916) published a pamphlet, *Souls for Gold! Pseudo-Celtic Drama in Dublin* (O'Shea 1479). A politician and onetime member of Parliament who had been expelled from the party by the Irish parliamentary leader Charles Stewart Parnell (1846–91), and who had quarreled with Yeats and Maud Gonne, O'Donnell hoped both to gain in the esteem of conservative Nationalists and to avenge his expulsion from John O'Leary's circle. On the pamphlet's cover were the words of one of the demons in Yeats's play:

> There soon will be no man or woman's soul
> Unbargained for in five-score baronies

followed by the notation 'Mr W. B. Yates [*sic*] on "Celtic Ireland".'

110. Ibsen's *Ghosts* had shocked the public when it was published in 1881. The play was not performed in Norway until 1890 and was banned in several European countries. William Archer (1865–1924) published an English translation in 1890, and the first London production, a single, private—i.e., non-commercial—performance at the Royalty Theatre on March 13, 1891, had brought a torrent of outraged criticism, establishing Ibsen as a *cause célèbre*.

111. After Yeats let the collaborative project lapse, Moore wired him: 'I have written a novel on that scenario we composed together. Will get an injunction if you use it' (*Au* 453). In response, Yeats composed the five acts of *Where There is Nothing* in a fortnight, with the help of Lady Gregory and Douglas Hyde, arranging for its immediate publication in the *United Irishman*.

The choice of the *United Irishman* was calculated to increase Moore's discomfort. Allan Wade (1881–1955) recalled Yeats's telling him he 'knew Moore would not dare to issue an injunction against a Nationalist newspaper for fear of getting his windows broke' (Wade 58). There was no legal action, and the two writers were partially reconciled by the Irish-American attorney John Quinn (1870–1924), then on his first visit to Ireland. Yeats's postscript to the incident came in 1935, two years after Moore's death. In *Dramatis Personae* he looked back with some remorse. 'Had I abandoned my plot and made him write the novel, he might have put beside *Muslin* and *The Lake* a third masterpiece, but I was young, vain, self-righteous, and bent on proving myself a man of action' (*Au* 454).

15. A Canonical Book

112. Yeats followed his review of Lady Gregory's *Poets and Dreamers: Studies and Translations from the Irish* (1903) (O'Shea 807) in the *New Liberal Review* for March 1903, reprinted as 'The Galway Plains' in *Ideas of Good and Evil*, with his praise of her 'canonical book' in the *Bookman* for May 1903.

113. Yeats had begun by 1903 the critical pruning of his Irish propaganda of the mid-nineties. Two of his surviving lists (*L* 246–47 and *UP1* 383–87) include Douglas Hyde's *The Love Songs of Connacht* (1893), which Yeats had praised in the *Bookman* in 1893 (see *UP1* 292–95) and which he continued to cite as exemplary of the early work of the Literary Revival.

114. Lady Gregory; see page 156.

115. The *Spectator* for April 18, 1903, had given *Poets and Dreamers* a generally favourable review. Its reviews of Yeats's own poetry in the nineties, however, spoke in such terms as these: The *Poems* of 1895

were weakened by Yeats's temptation 'to rely on the sound and rush of his words' (January 25, 1896; vol. 75, p. 136). The reviewer of *The Wind Among the Reeds* (1899) had warned that 'a poet, if he is to be a poet of any consequence, has thoughts that he wants to convey; the most that Mr Yeats does is to give us his dreams' (July 8, 1899; vol. 83, p. 54).

116. Lady Gregory reads: 'my mother, give . . .' (*Poets and Dreamers: Studies and Translations from the Irish* [London, John Murray, 1903] p. 65).

117. In section 30 of *Thus Spake Zarathustra*, 'The Famous Wise Ones', Zarathustra charges the hearer with having 'made out of wisdom an alms-house and infirmary for bad poets' (*The Works of Friedrich Nietzsche*, ed. Alexander Tille. Vol. 2: *Thus Spake Zarathustra: A Book for All and None*, tr. Alexander Tille [London: T. Fisher Unwin, 1899], p. 140) (O'Shea 1443: vol. I only).

118. Gregory: 'The swans on the water are nine times blacker than a blackberry since the man died from us that had pleasantness on the tops of his fingers' (*Poets and Dreamers*, p. 32).

119. Gregory: 'In every quarter that he ever knew he would scatter his fill and not gather. He would spend the estate of the Dalys, their beer and their wine' (Ibid.).

120. Gregory: 'And that is the true man, that didn't humble himself or lower himself to the Gall; Anthony O'Daly, O Son of God! He was that with us always, without a lie. But he died a good Irishman; and he never bowed the head to any man. . . . (Ibid., p. 6)' This and the previous two quotations are from poems by Raftery.

121. Lady Gregory included translations of Hyde's plays *The Marriage, The Lost Saint, The Nativity,* and *The Twisting of the Rope,* in the last section of *Poets and Dreamers,* with an introductory essay. Yeats's story 'The Twisting of the Rope', in the *National Observer* for December 24, 1892, is based on the same folktale as Hyde's play.

16. The Irish National Theatre and Three Sorts of Ignorance

122. This essay, which appeared on October 24, 1903, was the third answer by Yeats in the *United Irishman* to an attack on the Irish National Theatre by the *Irish Daily Independent and Nation,* a Nationalist paper founded in 1891 in support of Parnell and the Irish Parliamentary Party and, by 1903, under the control of the Roman Catholic businessman William Martin Murphy (1844–1919). Although Yeats took the high road on October 10 in his first reply, 'An Irish National Theatre' (*Ex* 114–18), he warmed to the growing discussions in the press in his essay on October 17, 'The Theatre, the Pulpit, and the Newspapers' (ibid., pp. 119–23), calling the *Independent* the new 'leader and voice' of 'those enemies of life, the chimeras of the Pulpit and the Press' (ibid., p. 119). In this final article, he categorised the 'obscurantism' against which he was strug-

gling. This is the last of the six essays gathered under the tentative title 'Some Uncollected Essays and Notes from *The United Irishman*: 1901–1903' but ultimately not published.

123. On October 8, a few hours before the opening of Synge's *In the Shadow of the Glen,* the *Independent* had impugned his honesty in attributing the play's theme to peasant sources as well as the motives and judgement of the Theatre's directors, calling 'the eccentricities and extravagances of Mr Yeats and his friends' a 'perversion of the Society's avowed aims' (p. 4).

Yeats had responded in a curtain speech following the presentation of *Cathleen ni Houlihan,* the concluding item on the programme. Joseph Holloway (1861–1944), the tireless Dublin playgoer, noted in his journal that Yeats had made 'a fool of himself in "going" for an article that appeared in this morning's *Independent.* He generally makes a mess of it when he orates' (*Joseph Holloway's Abbey Theatre,* ed. Robert Goode Hogan and Michael J. O'Neill [Carbondale: Southern Illinois University Press, 1967], p. 27).

The *Independent* renewed its attack on Synge, disparaged the first production of Yeats's *The King's Threshold,* and summarised Yeats's speech in the issue for October 9.

124. In the essay of October 17, Yeats described the habitat of ideological conformity, a 'great dim temple where the wooden images sit all round upon thrones, and where the worshippers kneel . . . In the idol-house every god, every demon, every virtue, every vice, has been given its permanent form, its hundred hands, its elephant trunk, its monkey head. The man of letters . . . swings his silver hammer and the keepers of the temple cry out, prophesying evil, but he must not mind their cries and their prophesies, but break the wooden necks in two and throw down the wooden bodies' (*Ex* 120).

125. Douglas Hyde had included two versions of 'The Red Man's Wife' in *The Love Songs of Connacht,* noting that the ballad was 'to be found every place throughout the country'. The verses catalogue the joys to be expected and deeds to be done in order 'to be stretched/For the while of a night by the wife of the Red-haired man' (*Love Songs of Connaught,* ed. Douglas Hyde, 5th ed. [London: T. Fisher Unwin, 1909], pp. 93–97).

126. The outline of Synge's story resembles the tale of the Widow of Ephesus as it occurs in Petronius Arbiter, the first-century satirist, and the Florentine Gian Francesco Poggio Bracciolini (1380–1459), but Synge's direct source is the Aran story-teller Pat Dirane, whose version appears in *The Aran Islands* (*The Works of John M. Synge* [Dublin: Maunsel and Company, 1910], III, 42–46) (O'Shea 2076: vols. I, II, and IV only). Synge's use of the story was the subject of a further controversy in the *United Irishman* in January and February of 1905 (see *UP2* 331–38).

17. Emmet the Apostle of Irish Liberty

127. Yeats agreed to address an estimated four thousand people at the Academy of Music in New York on February 28, 1904, as part of his first American speaking tour, between November 1903 and March 1904. The event, commemorating the 126th anniversary of the birth of the Irish patriot Robert Emmet (1778–1803), was sponsored by the *Clan-na-Gael* (Family of the Gaels), an Irish-American organisation founded in New York in the 1870s and headed by the Irish-American leader John Devoy (1842–1928). An account of Yeats's speech shared the front page of the March 5 issue of Devoy's newspaper, the *Gaelic American,* with a denunciation of the recent alliance of the United States with England in opposition to Russian claims in Manchuria.

    Parts of the address are versions of addresses he had given along the route. But, as the day approached, he had doubted that he could speak his mind before an audience which would include Devoy, the exiled Fenian Jeremiah O'Donovan Rossa (1831–1915), and Yeats's old friend and fellow occult student Charles Johnston (see note 534, page 410), the president of the Irish Literary Society of New York— along with judges, congressmen, members of the Roman Catholic clergy, and 'a delegation of noted Russian ecclesiastics'. 'It is indeed, as you say, a sword dance', he wrote Lady Gregory on February 26, 'and I must give to it every moment. I had no idea until I started on it how completely I have thought myself out of the whole stream of traditional Irish feeling on such subjects. I am just as strenuous a Nationalist as ever, but I have got to express these things all differently' (*L* 432).

    The typescript from which Yeats read, with emendations by Yeats and with the *Gaelic American*'s editor's notations, is in the Berg Collection of the New York Public Library. Minor emendations derived from it are noted in the text, and the texts of the two poems Yeats read, also from the typescript, are supplied in notes.

128. The Irish Parliament, established under the leadership of Henry Grattan (1746–1820) in 1782, was dissolved by the Act of Union (1800), which came into effect January 1, 1801.

129. John Fitzgibbon, first Earl of Clare (1749–1802), was Lord Chancellor of Ireland from 1789 until his death. A stern anti-Catholic, he resisted attempts to weaken Irish ties to England.

130. The Antwerp merchant, historian, and statesman Emanuel Van Meteren (1535–1612) traveled in England in 1575 and was Dutch consul for England from 1583 until his death. In his *History of the Netherlands* (1599), he noted that the Elizabethan English were 'not vindictive, but very inconstant, rash, vain-glorious, light, and deceiving, and very suspicious, especially of foreigners whom they despise' (quoted in William Brenchley Rye, *England as Seen By Foreigners* [London: John Russell Smith, 1865], p. 70).

131. Mitchel's *Jail Journal,* an account of his arrest and his transporta-

tion, originally appeared in his New York newspaper, the *Citizen*, between January 14, 1854, and August 19, 1854, and was published in book form in Dublin in 1913. The 'Jail Journal Introductory', which had not appeared in the serialisation but which had circulated in the Nationalist press in America in 1903, begins with the observation Yeats cites: 'England has been left in possession not only of the soil of Ireland, with all that grows and lives thereon, to her own use, but in possession of the world's ear also. She may pour into it what tale she will: and all mankind will believe her' (*Jail Journal* [1913; rpt. Dublin: Irish University Press, 1982], p. xxxvii).

132. On April 18, 1887, concluding a series of articles on 'Parnellism and Crime', the *Times* had printed a letter, allegedly by Parnell, implicating him and his party in the murders, on May 6, 1882, of the incoming Chief Secretary for Ireland, Lord Frederick Cavendish, and the Under-Secretary T. H. Burke, as they were walking through the Phoenix Park. A Parliamentary Commission in 1889 cleared Parnell and revealed the forger, Richard Pigott (ca. 1828–89), a newspaperman, who fled to Spain and committed suicide. 'Poor Pigott!' Yeats had written to his early friend and confidante Katharine Tynan (1861–1931), 'One really got to like him, there was something so frank about his lies. They were so completely matters of business, not of malice. . . . The poor domestic-minded swindler!' (*L* 112–13).

133. Yeats misquotes Thomas Moore (1779–1852), the author of the *Irish Melodies* (1807–34). In his 'Memoirs of Myself', Moore speaks of Emmet's 'manly daring'. (*Memoirs, Journal and Correspondence of Thomas Moore,* ed. John Russell [London: Longman, Brown, Green, and Longmans, 1853–56], I, 58).

134. Yeats's source for this appreciation and those which follow is, ultimately, the portrait of Emmet in the second edition of *The United Irishmen* (1858–60) by Richard R. Madden (1798–1886). He may, however, have used the condensation of Madden's material by his friend D. J. O'Donoghue (1866–1917), whose *Life of Robert Emmet* had appeared in 1902. This remark is, with some minor changes, that which Madden (2nd ed., p. 287) quotes from the *Recollections of Curran* (1818), by Charles Phillips (1787?–1859).

135. Madden (ibid., p. 269) quotes this passage from a letter by Rev. Archibald Douglas.

136. This quotation, from Moore's *Life and Death of Lord Edward Fitzgerald* (1831), is also in Madden (ibid., p. 266).

137. The Society of United Irishmen, begun in Belfast in 1791 by Wolfe Tone, had grown rapidly until, at the time of the insurrection of May 23, 1798, supporters numbered in the hundreds of thousands. Significant in the failure of 'Wolfe Tone's Rebellion' was the efficiency of the secret service of the English authorities in Dublin Castle.

138. Anne Devlin (ca. 1780–1851), Emmet's housekeeper and a niece of the Wicklow 'mountaineer' Michael Dwyer (1771–1826), steadfastly refused, although tortured by bayonets and subjected to a mock hanging in the courtyard, to reveal his hiding place. She was impris-

oned, along with her father, a partisan of Emmet's, between 1803 and 1806.

139. On December 1, 1640, the 'Sixty Years' Captivity', the union of Portugal with Spain that had begun with its seizure by Philip II (1527–98) in 1581, ended in a bloodless revolution generally accounted successful due to the weakness of the Spanish monarchy and the overextension of its forces.

140. Madden (ibid., p. 466) quotes the account in the *London Chronicle* for September 24–27, 1803, of Emmet's execution: 'He seemed to scoff at the dreadful circumstances attendant on him; at the same time, with all the coolness and complacency that can be possibly imagined—though utterly unlike the calmness of Christian fortitude. Even as it was, I never saw a man die like him; and God forbid I should see many with his principles'.

141. Charles George Gordon (1833–85), known as 'Chinese' Gordon, led the heroic but futile defense of Khartoum during the siege of April 1884–January 1885.

142. The group of writers who gathered around the journalist, poet, and patriot Thomas Davis (1814–45) came to be known as 'Young Ireland' and included Charles Gavan Duffy, John Blake Dillon (1816–66)—co-founders with Davis of the Nationalist newspaper the *Nation*—and James Clarence Mangan (1803–49). 'Young Ireland' disintegrated rapidly after Davis's death and in the face of the Great Famine and the failed insurrection of 1848. Davis edited its major collection of poems, *The Spirit of the Nation* (1843).

143. Yeats had included this anonymous poem, 'By Memory Inspired', in *A Book of Irish Verse* (1895), where it is described as a 'Street Ballad' (pp. 247–49). Yeats's typescript indicates that he read the third, the fourth, and the sixth and final stanzas in his address:

> In 'Ninety-Eight—the month July—
> The informer's pay was high;
> When Reynolds gave the gallows brave MacCann;
> But MacCann was Reynolds' first—
> One could not allay his thirst;
> So he brought up Bond and Byrne, that are gone, boys, gone.
> Here's the memory of the friends that are gone!
>
> We saw a nation's tears,
> Shed for John and Henry Sheares;
> Betrayed by Judas, Captain Armstrong;
> We may forive, but yet
> We never can forget
> The poisoning of Maguire that is gone, boys, gone—
> Our high Star and true Apostle that is gone!
>
> September, Eighteen-three,
> Closed this cruel history,

> When Emmet's blood the scaffold flowed upon;
> O, had their spirits been but wise,
> They might then realize
> Their freedom—but we drink to Mitchell that is gone, boys gone:
> Here's the memory of the friends that are gone!

144. Smith O'Brien led the disastrous and inept insurrection which culminated in confrontation with the constabulary in a cabbage garden in
Co. Tipperary on July 27, 1848, and his subsequent trial and sentence
to death for high treason. Despite his rejection of the commutation
of his sentence, he was transported to Van Diemen's Land, where he
joined Mitchel, Meagher, and other leaders of 'Young Ireland'.

145. Daniel O'Connell (1775–1847), known as 'The Liberator' after his
winning of Catholic emancipation in 1829, had achieved his goal
largely through organisation and political pressure. In later years, he
was a determined and conservative resister to the views on educational reform and revolutionary repeal of the Articles of Union
advanced by the Young Ireland movement.

146. Although re-elected as chairman of the Irish party a week after the
divorce verdict against him on November 17, 1890, Parnell was privately required to resign by Gladstone, the English Prime Minister
and his chief English ally in the cause of Home Rule for Ireland. On
December 1, the Irish representatives, Parnell presiding, met in Committee Room 15 of the House of Commons to reconsider his leadership. On December 6, he was removed from the chairmanship.

147. The National Literary Society, the Dublin organisation founded by
Yeats and John O'Leary in 1892, was allied with the Irish Literary
Society founded by Yeats and T. W. Rolleston (1857–1920) in Lon-
don the same year. The aim of both organisations was to awaken the
Irish-speaking and the English-speaking worlds to Irish literature,
language, and folklore.

148. The political uses of Hyde's Gaelic League became obvious shortly after
its founding in 1893. A collection for the League was taken up during
'Irish Language Week', between March 15 and March 22, 1903, and
the League's campaign for the closing of businesses on 'the Feast Day of
the National Apostle' was largely a success, according to the front page
of the *United Irishman* for March 28, 1903. Padraic Pearse noted, in
1911, that 'the Gaelic League will be recognised in history as the most
revolutionary influence that has ever come into Ireland' (*Political Writings and Speeches* [Dublin: Maunsel and Roberts, 1922], p. 91).

149. Yeats's typescript contains the text of this poem and an introductory
sentence omitted from the *Gaelic American*:

> When the Boer War was at its height this poem that I am about to read
> to you went through Ireland like a fire:
>
> O God, we call to Thee,
> This hour and this day,

Look down on the England
   That has come down in our midst

O God, we call to Thee,
   This day and this hour,
Look down on England,
   And her cold, cold heart.

It is she was a Queen,
   A Queen without sorrow;
But we will take from her,
   Quietly her crown.

That Queen that was beautiful
   Will be tormented and darkened,
For she will get her reward
   In that day, and her wage.

Her wage for the blood
   She poured out on the streams;
Blood of the white man,
   Blood of the black man.

Her wage for those hearts
   That she broke in the end;
Hearts of the white man,
   Hearts of the black man.

Her wage for the bones
   That are whitening to-day;
Bones of the white man,
   Bones of the black man.

Her wage for the hunger
   That she put on foot;
Her wage for the fever,
   That is an old tale with her.

Her wage for the white villages
   She has left without men:
Her wage for the brave men
   She has put to the sword.

Her wage for the orphans
   She has left under pain;
Her wage for the exiles
   She has spent with wandering.

For the people of India
   (Pitiful is their case);

For the people of Africa
   She has put to death.

For the people of Ireland
   Nailed to the cross;
Wage for each people
   Her hand has destroyed.

Her wage for the thousands
   She deceived and she broke;
Her wage for the thousands
   Finding death at this hour.

O Lord, let there fall
   Straight down on her head
The curse of the peoples
   That have fallen with us.

The curse of the mean,
   And the curse of the small,
The curse of the weak,
   And the curse of the low.

The Lord does not listen
   To the curse of the strong,
But he will listen
   To sighs and to tears.

He will always listen
   To the crying of the poor,
And the crying of thousands
   Is abroad tonight.

That crying will rise up
   To God that is above;
It is not long til every curse
   Comes to His ears.

The crying will be put away;
   Tears will be put away,
When they come to God,
   These prayers to His kingdom.

He will make for England
   Strong chains, very heavy;
He will pay her wages,
   With strong, heavy chains.

150. In 1903, Yeats had written in *Samhain,* the journal of the Irish National Theatre Society, of the 'subtle and eloquent words' of appreciation of the Society's 1903 productions from Arthur Bingham Walkley (1855–1926), the influential drama critic in the *Times Literary Supplement* for May 8, 1903.

151. The Gaelic plays presented in Dublin by the Gaelic League on February 12, 13, and 14, 1903, at the 'round room', one of the public spaces in Dublin's eighteenth-century lying-in hospital known as the Rotunda, were among the earliest such events. Included with plays by Douglas Hyde and others was *An Sprid* (The Spirit) by the parish priest from Castlelyons, Cork, Father Peter O'Leary (1839–1920), a vocal force in the Gaelic League and a pioneer Gaelic playwright and translator.

152. Yeats's reference has not been identified.

153. Father Jeremiah O'Donovan (1871–1942), the liberal priest and, from 1897, administrator of Loughrea parish, had been active in the Gaelic League and the agricultural cooperative movement. Interested in the arts, he had been instrumental in inviting the Irish portrait painter Sarah Purser (1848–1943) and Yeats's brother, Jack Yeats (1871–1957), to work on the new cathedral at Loughrea. In 1904, he left the parish and the priesthood and located in London, where he published several novels as 'Gerald O'Donovan'.

154. Patrick Joseph Hannon (1874–1963) had been a colleague of AE's with the Irish Agricultural Organisation Society in the 1890s and is identified in *The Gaelic American's* introductory note as a representative of the Irish Industrial League. A Conservative and Unionist M.P. from 1921 until 1950, he was knighted in 1936.

155. The 'Tower of Glass' *(An Túr Gloine)* stained glass cooperative was established in 1903 by Edward Martyn and Sarah Purser. The windows at Loughrea Cathedral were their first commission.

156. This metaphorical conclusion is no doubt the one Yeats had used in his address on February 2 at Carnegie Hall and in at least one of his less public talks. 'You remember', he wrote to Lady Gregory, 'my old organ peroration, the one I wound up the speech with at the Horace Plunkitt dinner? Well, there is a big organ on the platform at Carnegie Hall. I turn towards it meditatively and then, as if the thought suddenly struck me, speak that old peroration' (*CL3* 506).

18. America and the Arts

157. Yeats's 1903–4 tour included appearances in New York, New Haven, Philadelphia, Chicago, Saint Paul, Saint Louis, and San Francisco, along with a visit to Canada. His discussion, in the *Metropolitan Magazine* for April 1905, of what he had seen of American culture and education during his visit is his only contribution to the New York monthly.

158. To contrast the influence of the patrician James Russell Lowell (1819–91), Yeats gathers the three American writers who perhaps interested him most in his own development, Walt Whitman, Henry

David Thoreau (1817–62), and Edgar Allan Poe (1809–49). Partly
under his father's influence, Yeats had read Whitman in his teens, calling him, in 1887, 'the greatest teacher of these decades' (*L* 32). In an
exchange in *United Ireland* a few years later, Yeats cited Whitman,
'the most National' of America's poets (*L* 238), as an instance of great
nationalism saved from parochial barbarity by international appreciation—as he himself might need to be. Yeats's famous account of the
conception of 'The Lake Isle of Innisfree' credits as a source 'the
ambition, formed in Sligo in my teens, of living in imitation of
Thoreau on Innisfree, a little island in Lough Gill' (*Au* 153). Poe's
example, however, was troubling. 'His fame always puzzles me', he
told his friend and fellow visionary W. T. Horton (1864–1919) in
1899. 'I have to acknowledge that . . . a writer who has had so much
influence on Baudelaire and Villiers de L'Isle Adam has some great
merit' (*L* 325). Still, although granting Poe, in comparison to
Clarence Mangan, 'a personality' (*L* 447), Yeats concluded, in his
Memoirs, that the 'work of some writers, of Edgar Allan Poe for
instance, suggests to the imagination a fever of the personality which
keeps admiration from being ever complete' (*Mem* 167).

159. The effects of the democratic idealism of Ralph Waldo Emerson
(1803–82), the American transcendentalist poet and essayist, and of
Whitman are qualified by Yeats's speculations in *Autobiographies*
about AE:

> I sometimes wonder what he would have been had he not met in early
> life the poetry of Emerson and Walt Whitman, writers who have
> begun to seem superficial precisely because they lack the Vision of
> Evil; and those translations of the Upanishads, which it is so much
> harder to study by the sinking flame of Indian tradition than by the
> serviceable lamp of Emerson and Walt Whitman (*Au* 246).

160. Writing to Lady Gregory from Bryn Mawr College, in Pennsylvania,
on December 8, 1903, Yeats marvelled at the attendance at his talk,
adding, 'Do you know I have not met a single woman here who puts
"tin tacks in the soup"? and I found that the woman who does is recognized as an English type. One teacher explained to me the difference in this way, "We prepare the girls to live their lives but in
England they are making them all teachers" ' (*L* 414).

161. The decorative painter of the United States Capitol, Constantino
Brumildi (1805–80), completed one third of the frescoed frieze on
the interior of the great rotunda before his death. Filippo Costag-
gini's (1839–1904) completion of Brumildi's designs (1880–88) left a
gap of some thirty feet, which, after many efforts to appropriate sufficient money and to find a suitable artist, was completed in 1953 by
Allyn Cox (1896–1982).

162. Yeats had admired the 'patterns and rhythms of colour' (*UP*2 134) in
the paintings of the American James Abbott McNeill Whistler

(1834–1903) since seeing them in his youth in Dublin, in an exhibition partly arranged by his father (*Au* 82). After several years in Paris, Whistler moved to London in 1859, living there for the rest of his life.

163. On January 30, 1904, James Duval Phelan (1861–1930), a former mayor of San Francisco and Yeats's host during his stay there, reported to John Quinn, who had overseen the organisation of Yeats's tour, that during a visit to the University of California at Berkeley on January 27 Yeats 'was much interested in the amphitheater there—made of concrete after a Grecian model—seating 12,000. He is taken with our climate which has been perfect for weeks—brilliant sunshine & clear skies' (quoted in *CL3*, p. 542).

When they met in San Francisco, the poet and translator Agnes Tobin (1864–1939) had given Yeats her first book of translations from Petrarch (1304–74), *Love's Crucifix* (1902). On February 7, on the trip back to New York, he wrote to thank her:

> . . . I delight in your Petrarch. I have read it over & over. It is full of wise delight—a thing of tears & ecstacy—especially that long lyric at the end (*CL3* 545–46).

19. British *Association* Visit to the *Abbey* Theatre

164. On September 4, 1908, the Abbey presented a matinee programme for the British Association for the Advancement of Science, which met that year in Dublin. Yeats supplied a programme note, 'The Abbey Theatre', and followed a presentation of his *Hour-Glass* with an address on 'The Abbey Theatre—Its Aims and Works'. These remarks appeared in a special programme four days later.

165. Annie E. F. Horniman (1861–1937), an English tea heiress, had been a member with Yeats in the 1890s of the mystical Order of the Golden Dawn. Involved throughout her life in theatrical affairs, she had financed a season of plays by Florence Farr in 1894 and, in 1904, bought and restored the Mechanics' Institute in Abbey Street, giving the Irish National Theatre Society its free use. Shortly thereafter, she agreed to underwrite the publication of Yeats's eight-volume *Collected Works,* which appeared in 1908. Her subsidy for players' salaries, established at £600 annually but usually supplemented, was withdrawn in 1906, to expire with its Patent in 1910. Bitterness over the mistaken failure to close the theatre on the occasion of the death of Edward VII in May of 1910 gave her reason to refuse to pay the last installment of her obligation, which in turn led to a dispute finally settled in the Abbey's favour in 1911. She and Yeats were partially reconciled shortly before her death.

166. The Abbey company performed in London, Oxford, and Cambridge in November 1905 and again in June 1907. Yeats's assimilation into

his concept of an Irish literature of such eighteenth-century Anglo-Irish writers as the poet, playwright, novelist, and essayist Oliver Goldsmith (1728–74) and the playwright and politician Richard Brinsley Sheridan (1751–1816) was still some years away. In a letter to the *Daily News* in 1903, he asserted that 'Swift, Burke, and Goldsmith . . . hardly seem to me to have come out of Ireland at all' (*CL3* 593). In 1904, allowing that 'It is sometimes necessary to follow in practical matters some definition which one knows to have but a passing use', he declared that:

> Goldsmith and Sheridan and Burke had become so much a part of English life, were so greatly moulded by the movements that were moulding England, that, despite certain Irish elements that clung about them, we could not think of them as more important to us than any English writer of equal rank. Men told us that we should keep hold of them, as it were, for they were part of our glory; but we did not consider our glory very important (*Ex* 159).

167. The editor has been unable to discover the Transvaal pirates. The Japanese critic is probably Hogetsu Shimamura (1871–1918), who had written an evaluation of Yeats's influence on the Irish revival in the *Tokyo Daily News* in March 1906.

168. W. G. Fay, who resigned from the management of the theatre in 1908, had become an electrician because his brother 'urged electricity was a new motive power that was sure to be used more and more. . . . I was not making my fortune as an actor and I wanted to have some means of living that would leave me free to devote more time to the theatre' (W. G. Fay and Catharine Carswell, *The Fays of the Abbey Theatre* [London: Rich and Cowan, Ltd, 1935], p. 99).

169. The Abbey Theatre had produced adaptations by Lady Gregory into the 'Kiltartan dialect' of two plays by Molière (1622–73), *The Doctor in Spite of Himself* (*Le Médecin Malgré Lui*) and *The Rogueries of Scapin* (*Les Fourberies de Scapin*) in 1906 and 1908, respectively (see O'Shea 1330).

170. Yeats's one-act play *The Hour-Glass,* first produced at the Abbey in March 1903, preceded Yeats's address to the British Association at the special matinee.

171. Yeats's reference should be to the pioneer in psychical research F. W. H. Myers (1843–1901) and his posthumous *Human Personality and Its Survival of Bodily Death* (1903). This study of subliminal consciousness bears more closely on the subject of Yeats's *Hour-Glass* than anything by Myers's brother Ernest (1844–1921), a poet, translator, and editor of Milton. In a 'Preface' to the revised version of the play, in 1913, Yeats claimed he 'began a revision of the words from the moment when the play converted a music hall singer and sent him to mass and confession' (*VPl* 577).

172. Lady Gregory's *The Rising of the Moon* was respectfully received when it was first produced on March 9, 1907, and was to become a staple of the Abbey's repertory. But its theme—the spontaneous generosity of an English constable to a Fenian prisoner in the 1860s—caused frequent political nervousness.

173. At the outset of the Abbey's tour in June 1907, Yeats tried to avert a repetition of the Dublin disturbances in 1907 over Synge's *Playboy of the Western World* by such means as publishing his 'Notes' on the whole affair in the *Arrow* (*UP2* 353–55). However, the Lord Chamberlain's Examiner of Plays licensed the production only after Pegeen Mike's allusion in Act I to the 'loosed kharki cut-throats' was struck out. Yeats omits mention here of his removal of the play from the programme in Glasgow and Birmingham, at the Lord Chamberlain's urging, because, as Yeats explained to Synge, there were 'enough slum Irish in Birmingham to stir up a row' (quoted in David H. Greene and Edward Stephens, *J. M. Synge: 1871–1909* [New York: Macmillan, 1961], p. 269).

174. Yeats refers to the playing of 'the Orange card'—the direct invocation of Irish Protestants against Irish Home Rule—in Belfast on February 22, 1886, by the Tory leader Lord Randolph Churchill (1849–95), immediately following his declaration at Larne that 'Ulster will fight, and Ulster will be right'.

175. The last part of this essay, beginning with this sentence, is reprinted in *Samhain* for 1908 (see *Ex* 241–43).

20. The Art of the Theatre

176. Along with Bernard Shaw (1856–1950), Gordon Craig, and others, Yeats took part in a symposium on 'The Art of the Theatre', which appeared in A. R. Orage's weekly review, the *New Age,* for June 16, 1910. His comments were in answer to three questions: 'Have recent developments, in your opinion, shown any advance in the direction of increasing the beauty of the stage picture? Do you think that managers and producers are yet using to the full all the advantages offered by the modern studio? Would you say that artists are availing themselves as fully as they might of the opportunities open to them in the modern theatre?'

177. Herbert Trench (1865–1923), the poet and playwright, was director of the Haymarket Theatre, a position held earlier by Sir Herbert Beerbohm Tree (1853–1917), the actor-manager, who was at this time the owner and manager of His Majesty's Theatre, London. Yeats frequently cited Tree's stagings as examples of the sort of futile ingenuity which his theatre sought to avoid, as in a footnote to a letter to Lady Gregory in November of the preceding year:

> I have just written to Mrs Pat Campbell refusing to consider Tree in writing my play [*The Player Queen*]. I have described his ideal of beauty as thrice vomited flesh (*L* 539).

178. For Yeats's admiration of Gordon Craig's productions, in 1901, for the Purcell Society, see note 105, p. 343; for his further elaboration of these ideas, after his collaboration with Craig, see chapter 21, 'The Theatre of Beauty', pp. 129–33.

179. Yeats's longtime friend Charles Ricketts (1866–1931), the artist, writer, and book and stage designer, had designed the sets for the Abbey's revival of Synge's *The Well of the Saints,* which opened on May 14, 1908.

180. The Italian theatrical designer Mariano Fortuny y Madrazo (1871–1949) had been experimenting since 1902 with a revolutionary lighting system featuring a movable dome over the stage which allowed for greater illusions of depth and ranges of effect. Fortuny's system was perfected in 1910, coincident with the development in Berlin of a similar system by the Austrian actor Max Reinhardt (1873–1943). Yeats discussed both men's work in greater detail in his address at Harvard, 'The Theatre of Beauty' (see pp. 129–33). Yeats had expressed interest in the experiments of Adolphe Appia (1862–1928), the Swiss set designer, in the essay 'The Play, the Player and the Scene', which had appeared in *Samhain* for December 1904. Yeats admitted that he understood little of Appia's experiments with lighting and staging, but had suggested they were 'seeking, not convention, but a more perfect realism. I cannot persuade myself that the movement of life is flowing that way. . . .' (*Ex* 180). Yeats probably learned more about Appia from his friend T. Sturge Moore (1870–1944), the English poet and designer who designed the covers for many of Yeats's books and whose wife was Appia's cousin.

21. The Theatre of Beauty

181. Casting problems and the prospect of trouble in presenting the still controversial *Playboy of the Western World* to Irish-American audiences convinced Yeats to join the Abbey company on an American tour on September 13, 1911. Lady Gregory followed in a few days and remained with the players until the tour ended in March 1912. Both she and Yeats gave interviews and made personal appearances, particularly at colleges where the Irish plays, especially those of Synge, were already classroom texts. They appeared at Vassar and Wellesley and, on October 5, Yeats spoke before the Dramatic Club at Harvard. The text of his address on 'The Theatre of Beauty' was published in *Harper's Weekly* on November 11, 1911.

182. In Lady Gregory's *The Canavans,* produced at the Abbey Theatre in December 1906, W. G. Fay portrayed Peter Canavan, an Elizabethan miller mistakenly imprisoned as a deserter, who is seen at the opening of Act II awaiting his execution.

183. The Abbey Theatre produced *The Miser,* an adaptation by Lady Gregory of Molière's *L'Avare,* in January 1909.

184. In 'Concerning Humour in Comedy', written in the form of a letter to John Dennis, dated July 19, 1695, William Congreve (1670–1729)

observes: 'I take [humour] to be, *a singular and unavoidable manner of doing, or saying any thing, Peculiar and Natural to one Man only; by which his Speech and Actions are distinguish'd from those of other Men'* (*The Complete Works of William Congreve*, ed. Montague Summer, 4 vols. [Soho: The Nonesuch Press, 1923], III, p. 165). Yeats's further reference is to Congreve's subsequent discussion of the relative powers of passions and humours in men and women: '. . . I have never made an observation of what I Apprehend to be true Humours in Women. Perhaps Passions are too powerful in the Sex, to let Humour have its Course. . . .' (ibid., p. 183).

Yeats's reference to Congreve, to the French classical dramatists Jean-Baptiste Racine (1639–99) and Pierre Corneille (1606–84), along with his citations from Shakespeare, echo his essay 'The Tragic Theatre', which had appeared in the *Mask* in October of 1910 (*UP2* 386–87) and which, revised, is the 'Preface' to *Plays for an Irish Theatre* (1911), included in *The Cutting of an Agate* (1912).

185. The French painter Pierre Puvis de Chavannes (1824–98) began, after about 1860, the career of vast and ambitious murals and decorations of public buildings for which he is known and to which Yeats refers.

In *The Tragic Generation*, Yeats joins Puvis with the French poets Stéphane Mallarmé (1842–98) and Paul Verlaine (1844–96), the French painter Gustave Moreau (1826–98), the English artist Charles Conder (1868–1909), and himself in a common sensibility of 'subtle colour, and nervous rhythm . . . faint mixed tints' which he sees as threatened by the 'growing power' of 'comedy and objectivity' represented by the acclaim given the opening of *Ubu Roi* by Alfred Jarry (1873–1907) (*Au* 348–49).

186. In the penultimate scene of Yeats's *The Green Helmet*, produced in February of the preceding year, he treated the 'Horse Boys and Scullions' as scuffling shadows before a wall. While a printed version of the play had been included in *The Green Helmet and Other Poems* in December 1910, the separate edition of the play was in preparation when this address was being written.

187. Just after the turn of the century, Max Reinhardt had become an experimental producer, creating a stylised theatre with the avowed intention both of freeing the stage from the requirements of realistic literature and of greatly intensifying the contact between actors and audience. In December 1911, Reinhardt and his company had produced Vollmöller's *The Miracle* at the Olympic Theatre, London.

188. The continuous wall which Yeats describes here was one of the innovations introduced by the Hungarian stage designer Jenö Kéméndy (1860–1925), at the National Theatre in Budapest. Piercing the wall to allow for various back-lighting effects, he divided the front half of the stage into three sections and provided for either of the side sections to be rolled off and on stage to allow for set changes.

189. Three of the plays of John Galsworthy (1867–1933), each a realistic

portrayal of a contemporary social problem, had been produced in London and New York at this time. _The Silver Box_ (1906) compared the justice available to rich and poor; _Strife_ (1909) dealt with strikes and lock-outs; and _Justice_ (1910) focused on the prison system.

22. The Story of the Irish Players

190. Under Lady Gregory's direction, the Abbey company concluded its 1911–12 American tour in Chicago in February 1912. Although Yeats had returned to Ireland the previous October, his name continued to be associated with the touring players by such devices as his contribution, subtitled 'What We Try to Do', to a gathering of brief essays by, among others, Lady Gregory and George Moore, on 'The Story of the Irish Players' on the front page of the drama section of Chicago's _Sunday Record-Herald_ on February 4, 1912.

191. In 1909, the New Theater, an experiment in national theatre, had been founded in New York by Winthrop Ames (1871–1937). It was imitative of the European art theatres, and, although it listed many of the country's richest men as its patrons, the project collapsed in 1911, with a deficit of $400,000.

192. Of the two originators of the modern Norwegian theatre, Bjørnson was the more frequent proponent of this linking of the ancient sagas with the _bonde,_ or freehold farmers. A biographer, Harold Larson, quotes Bjørnson's recollection in 1880 of this early aim in the Liberal paper _Dagbladet:_

> I began within the ring of the saga and the _bonde,_ in that I let the one illustrate the other, which at that time was new.
>
> _Bjørstjerne Bjørnson: A Study in Norwegian Nationalism_ (New York: King's Crown Press, 1944), p. 32.

Lady Gregory had rendered the Cuchulain legends into the Kiltartan dialect in _Cuchulain of Muirthemne._ Yeats's declaration, in 1902, that it was 'the best book that has come out of Ireland in my time' (_Ex_ 3), was commended for Stephen Dedalus's imitation, in the 'Library' episode of _Ulysses,_ by Buck Mulligan:

> . . . Couldn't you do the Yeats touch?
> He went on and down, mopping, chanting with waving graceful arms:
>
> —The most beautiful book that has come out of our country in my time. One thinks of Homer.
>
> _James Joyce, Ulysses_ (New York: Random House, 1934), p. 213.

Synge had translated the story of Deirdre and the Sons of Usna from the Gaelic in 1901 and had praised Lady Gregory's rendering of it in Cuchulain of Muirthemne in 1906, as he was beginning work on *Deidre and the Sorrows,* which he was completing at the time of his death in 1909 (Green and Stephens, pp. 222–23).

193. In his *Memoirs,* Yeats recalled having made 'some judge' resign from the Irish Literary Society in the 1890s when 'I had described the dishonest figures of Swift's attack on Wood's half-pence and . . . had argued that, because no sane man is permitted to lie knowing[ly], God made certain men mad, and that it was these men—daimonpossessed as I said—who, possessing truths of passion that were intellectual falsehoods, had created nations' (*Mem* 84). His fascination with Jonathan Swift (1667–1745) culminated in his play about Swift, *The Words Upon the Window-Pane,* which was produced at the Abbey Theatre in 1930.

194. Just after Synge's death in 1909, Yeats linked Synge and Goldsmith in his journal. Distinguishing between two kinds of genius, men with 'finished personalities, active wills and all their faculties at the service of the will', and 'men like Goldsmith, like Wordsworth, like Keats who have little personality, little personal will, but fiery and brooding imagination', he identifies Synge with the latter, as 'a drifting, silent man, full of hidden passion. . . . His strength was in character, not in will, and misfortune shook his physical nature while it left his intellect and moral nature untroubled' (*Mem* 203).

195. Dion Boucicault (1820?–90), born in Dublin as Dionysius Lardner Boursiquot and raised and educated in England, was the most successful playwright in England, Ireland, and America of the mid-nineteenth century. Boucicault wrote some 150 plays—a great number of them adaptations and translations. His three plays based on Irish themes, *The Colleen Bawn* (1860) (O'Shea 264), *Arrah na Pogue* (1864), and *The Shaughraun* (1874), all enjoyed immense success.

196. Synge's *In the Shadow of the Glen* provoked two separate attacks in the Nationalist press, in 1903 (see note 123, p. 346) and again in 1905; the iconoclastic *Well of the Saints* was poorly received at its opening in 1905; a week of riots and performances under police protection followed the opening of *The Playboy of the Western World* in 1907.

23. The Polignac Prize

197. In 1913, Yeats served on a committee of the Academic Committee of the Royal Society of Literature to select the recipient of the Society's annual Edmond de Polignac Prize, a grant of £100 intended to recognise the work of younger writers. He had for some time known the work of James Stephens (1882–1950), his friendship with the younger writer having begun with Stephens's spirited defence of him in a lengthy letter in the *New Age* in 1912. Yeats's remarks at the awarding of the prize to Stephens for *The Crock of Gold* (1912), on November 28, 1913, were published by the Society in *Addresses of Reception* (London: Humphrey Milford/Oxford University Press, 1914), pp. 37–42.

198. 'Improvent [*sic*] makes strait roads, but the crooked roads without Improvement are roads of Genius' ('Proverbs from Hell', in *The Marriage of Heaven and Hell,* Ellis and Yeats, eds., III, pl. 10). In Bentley, ed., I, p. 84.

199. The philosopher and statesman Richard Burdon Haldane, first Viscount of Cloan (1856–1928), was among Yeats's colleagues on the Academic Committee, along with the writers and critics Arthur Christopher Benson (1862–1928), Henry Newbolt (1862–1938), and Edmund Gosse (1849–1928).

200. Yeats had praised a section from Stephens's poem 'To the Tree' in a letter to Stephens in May of 1912:

> . . . I know little of our time that excites me more than that stanza which contains the line "The sea shall tramp with banners on the shore".

> Quoted in Richard J. Finneran, *The Olympian and the Leprechaun* (Dublin: Dolmen Press, 1978), p. 11.

Stephens had published this poem, as well as the one Yeats quotes, 'Wind and Tree', in *The Hill of Vision* (1912) (O'Shea 2002).

24. Thomas Davis

201. In the fall of 1914, the Gaelic Society of Trinity College Dublin asked Yeats, among others, to speak on November 17 at a centenary commemoration of the birth of Thomas Davis. Learning that another of the speakers was to be Patrick Pearse, already identified with the forces of revolution and soon to be shot while serving as president of the provisional government established in the 1916 'rising', and fearing that Pearse would use the occasion to press his current campaign against Irish recruitment for the British Army, Trinity's Vice Provost, John Pentland Mahaffy (1839–1919), ordered the College closed to Pearse and disbanded the Society. Mahaffy, a famous classicist and Yeats's early antagonist in his attempts to elevate Gaelic myth and folklore, was soon to become Provost of Trinity.

The Society reorganised the commemoration at the Antient Concert Rooms, where Yeats offered a careful reappraisal of Davis and of his contribution. The address, published in *New Ireland* for July 17, 1915, was introduced with this note:

> The following speech was delivered by Mr Yeats at a public meeting to celebrate the Thomas Davis Centenary, held in the Antient Concert Rooms, Dublin, on November 20th, 1914, under the auspices of the Students' National Literary Society.

Yeats's address, along with an account of the incident and a long letter on it from AE, was published in 1947 by Denis Gwynn (1893–1972). Gwynn, who was both President of the Students' Literary

Society and editor of *New Ireland* at the time of the Davis commemoration, indicates that Yeats read an opening paragraph, addressing the controversy, although it was not printed in *New Ireland*:

> I am very sorry Professor Mahaffy is not here tonight. I am not more vehemently opposed to the Unionism of Professor Mahaffy than I am to the pro-Germanism of Mr Pearse, but we are here to talk about literature and about history. In Ireland above all nations, where we have so many bitter divisions, it is necessary to keep always unbroken the truce of the Muses. I am sorry the Vice Provost of Trinity should have broken that ancient truce. It would have been a great pleasure to have stood on the same platform with Dr Mahaffy, who has done so much good service for English literature, and with Mr Pearse, who has done such good service to Irish literature (NLI Ms 30603, SUNY-SB Box 18).

202. His own early work in the literary revival was free, as Yeats suggests, of glorification of either the Danish and Norwegian invaders whose violence ravaged Ireland in the ninth and tenth centuries or of 'the Great Demagogue' (*E&I* 375), Oliver Cromwell (1599–1658), the architect both of the suppression of Irish Catholics and of the Protestant plantation which sealed English rule in Ireland in the 1650s. However, another leader of the revival, Yeats's sometime antagonist, Standish O'Grady, praised both the Norse and Cromwell's Puritans in his *Story of Ireland* (London: Methuen, 1894), p. 140 (O'Shea 1493):

> The Puritans were able to conquer Ireland for much the same reason that the Norsemen, and afterwards the Normans, were able to conquer it. They were bolder, sincerer, more true-hearted, more upright, and more united than those whom they overthrew.

In the 1890s, Yeats listed Davis among the movement's forebears, but he frequently noted Davis's failings, as when, in an appreciation in 1896 of Sir Samuel Ferguson (1810–86), he listed Davis first among Irish writers who, by taking 'the popular side in Ireland had ruined a part of [their] work by didactic writing, and . . . had often failed to shake off habits of carelessness and commonness acquired in thinking of the widest rather than of the best audience' (*UP1* 404).

The earliest extant version of this essay has 'picked holes in' for both 'dispraised' and 'found certain flaws in' (NLI Ms 30493, SUNY-SB Box 18).

203. In Davis's 'Lament for the Death of Eoghan Ruadh O'Neill', one of the clansmen of O'Neill (1590–1649), the aristocratic chieftain who commanded the Ulster Rebellion in 1642 and the last who might have prevailed against Oliver Cromwell, speaks with one of his soldiers, announcing his death. Yeats's specific objection is to the curse in the final line of the first stanza of Davis's poem:

May they walk in living death who poisoned Owen Roe!

Mangan's 'O'Hussey's Ode to the Maguire', a verse transliteration from the seventeenth-century Gaelic of Eochaidh O'Hussey, the chief bard of Hugh Maguire of Fermanagh, is based on the prose translation by Ferguson.

204. 'The County of Mayo' by Thomas Flavell, a late seventeenth- or early eighteenth-century native of Bophin, an island off Ireland's west coast, was translated into English by George Fox (?1809–?), a graduate of Trinity College Dublin in 1847 who immigrated to the United States the following year. Yeats quoted from the poem in 1895 when introducing his list of the thirty essential Irish books in the *Daily Express* (*CL1* 440), and he included it, with a slight misattribution, in his *Book of Irish Verse* the same year.

205. Yeats elaborates here on the continuity between the politics of O'Connell and those of Parnell which he established in his speech on Robert Emmet. See pp. 107–8.

206. Although not his only public address, Davis's highly charged speech on 'The Young Irishman of the Middle Classes' before the Trinity College Historical Society in 1840 was one of few and the one which, according to Gavan Duffy, in his *Thomas Davis: The Memoirs of an Irish Patriot, 1840–1846* (1892), launched his public career.

207. Yeats had known Lady Wilde (1826–96), Irish woman of letters and mother of Oscar Wilde, in the 1880s. Her frequent contributions to the *Nation,* under the pseudonym 'Speranza', were often volatile, and one article caused the issue for July 29, 1848, to be suppressed and Gavan Duffy to be prosecuted as the suspected author.

208. O'Leary recalls discovering the poems of Davis while recovering from a fever in 1846 and going 'through a process analogous to what certain classes of Christians call "conversion" ' in his *Recollections of Fenians and Fenianism* (London: Downey and Co., 1896), I, 3.

209. *The Doctrine and Discipline of Divorce* by John Milton (1608–74) appeared anonymously in 1643.

210. The third part of Goethe's *Aus meinem Leben Wahrheit und Dichtung* begins with this motto: 'Care is taken that trees do not grow into the sky' (*Es ist dafür gesorgt, daß die Bäume nicht in den Himmel wachsen*) (*Sämtliche Werke*, ed. Klaus-Detlef Müller [Frankfurt am Main: Deutscher Klassiker Verlag, 1986], XIV, 489).

211. *The Demi-Gods,* Stephens's third novel, was published in 1914 (O'Shea 2000).

25. Sir Hugh Lane's Pictures

212. After the death of her nephew, the art dealer and collector Sir Hugh Lane (1875–1915), in the sinking of the *Lusitania* in May 1915, Lady Gregory, together with Yeats, carried on the attempt to establish a municipal gallery for modern art in Dublin to house his collection of modern French paintings. Lane's will gave the collection to

the National Gallery in London. The argument for its return to Dublin was based on a signed but unwitnessed codicil to his will, found in Lane's desk after his death, which reversed his decision to bequeath the pictures to London.

Lane figures in several of Yeats's poems over the years, and their mutual struggle on behalf of Lane's plans is the basis of Yeats's poem for Lady Gregory, 'To a Friend whose Work has come to Nothing' (1913).

Yeats contributed many letters to the press on Lane's bequest between 1916 and 1926, but his most thorough public statement on the controversy was the essay which appeared in the *Observer* on January 21, 1917.

Yeats's partially edited galley proofs (Berg NYPL) include an introductory paragraph which he deleted:

> The Editor of *The Observer* has granted me the privilege of closing the controversy. Each side has spoken, and I shall best help your readers to a sound judgment if I run through the facts and arguments— and many new ones have come to light—with as much justice to my opponents as I can. I will promise not to leave uncommented a single fact or quotation used by Mr MacColl unless where the issue is merely personal between him and me. If I write in some detail or repeat what is familiar, I ask a busy or careless reader's forgiveness. I must write for those few people who may influence the event, and the issues are important. If I fail to convince, Ireland, where national character is still unformed, may lack a necessary means of education.

213. Dougald Sutherland MacColl (1859–1948), a trustee and former Keeper of the Tate Gallery and Lane's designated biographer, vehemently pressed London's claim to Lane's French paintings and recalled Lane's rejection of their being given to Dublin in a letter in the *Observer* in December of 1916. MacColl abandoned the biography during the controversy over Lane's codicil.

214. Sir Charles Holroyd (1861–1917), the painter and etcher, served as the first Keeper of the Tate Gallery from 1897 until 1906.

215. George Nathaniel, Lord Curzon (1859–1925), the statesman and former Viceroy of India, was a trustee of the National Gallery. Reprinting this essay in *Hugh Lane's Life and Achievement* (London: John Murray, 1921) (O'Shea 796), Lady Gregory annotated Yeats's text at this point:

> Hugh wrote to me on July 31, 1913: 'I am busy taking down my "conditional gift". It is my last trump card. . . . Lord Curzon came to see me—pressed me to give [the French pictures] to London if they got a new building. I refused, but offered to lend them to the National Gallery. This they are considering. If it comes off it may help to bring the [Dublin] Corporation to its senses' (p. 222).

216. Lane's remark, that the removal of his pictures to London might 'lead to . . . the establishment in London of a permanent Collection of modern international art', appeared in an interview in the *Manchester Guardian* on September 9, 1913, the day after the rejection by the Dublin Corporation of Lane's conditions for their remaining in Dublin.

217. MacColl had published excerpts from Lane's correspondence with Lady Gregory in which he had expressed his 'hate' for Dublin: 'the place, the people and the "gallery".'

   In the privately circulated *Poems Written in Discouragement*, printed in October 1913, Yeats had included 'To a Wealthy Man who promised a second Subscription to the Dublin Municipal Gallery if it were proved the People wanted Pictures', 'September 1913', 'To a Friend whose Work has come to Nothing', 'Paudeen', and 'To a Shade'.

218. The testimony of Lane's physician, Dr Haydn Brown (1864–1936), a neurologist and author of books on psychology and spiritualism, as to Lane's strategic reasons for removing the pictures to London is cited in all arguments for their return to Dublin.

219. Yeats's corrected proofs of this essay indicate that the parenthesis should end after 'refusal', rather than 'gallery', as in the published text.

220. The French caricaturist and painter Honoré Daumier (1808–79) painted a number of scenes from *Don Quixote*, of which *Don Quixote and Sancho Panza* (1864–66), in Lane's collection, is considered to be among the finest. The picture is in the National Gallery, London.

221. Ruth Shine was Lane's sister and confidential secretary.

222. Along with D. S. MacColl, Robert Clermont Witt (1872–1952), a lawyer and trustee of the National Gallery, and Charles Aitken (1869–1936), Keeper of the Tate Gallery, were the foremost spokesmen for London's claim to the Lane pictures.

223. Lane was Director of the National Gallery in Dublin from February 1914 until his death.

224. The deposition of Ellen Duncan (1850–1937), dated February 12, 1917, is reprinted as an appendix in the Coole Edition of Lady Gregory's book on Lane, *Sir Hugh Lane: His Life and Legacy* (New York: Oxford University Press, 1973), p. 276.

225. Dedicated to 'Alec Martin, Hugh's Friend and Mine', Lady Gregory's book on Lane reprints the deposition on this point given by the art dealer and, later, Managing Director of Christie's, Alec Martin (1884–1971).

226. Yeats combines several constituencies in linking Shaw and AE with the academic Irish painter and portraitist William Orpen (1878–1931) and Horace Plunkett (1854–1932), the agricultural reformer and statesman.

227. See *UP2* 426–27.

228. In a letter in the *Observer* on January 14, 1917, the English collector and critic Paul George Konody (1872–1933) had maintained that

Quite a number of the pictures and drawings comprised in the Lane Collection were not bought by Sir Hugh Lane, and, indeed, did not belong to him. They were presented by various people, spontaneously or at Sir Hugh's urging, to the Dublin Gallery of Modern Art. This, at least, applies to my own modest gift, and I know of several similar cases (p. 14).

26. Major Robert Gregory

229. In the months immediately following the death in action of Lady Gregory's son, William Robert (1881–1918), on January 23, 1918, Yeats wrote three poems in his memory: 'In Memory of Major Robert Gregory', 'An Irish Airman foresees his Death', and 'Shepherd and Goatherd'. His earliest tribute was the appreciation in the *Observer* for February 17, 1918, which echoes his remark in a letter to John Quinn, written a few days after Gregory's death: 'His paintings had majesty and austerity, and at the same time sweetness. He was the most accomplished man I have ever known; I mean that he could do more things well than any other' (*L* 646). On February 22, 1918, he wrote of this essay to Lady Gregory: '. . . I hope you thought my little essay on Robert was right. I tried to imagine to myself those who knew his pictures a little and what they thought and to write so as to settle and define their admiration' (*L* 646).

A manuscript of this appreciation is signed by Yeats and dated February 10, 1918 (NLI Ms 30498, SUNY-SB Box 20).

230. In 1903, Gregory's drawings were the basis of Sturge Moore's settings for Yeats's *The Hour-Glass*, for which Gregory also designed the costumes.

Of the dress rehearsal of Lady Gregory's *Kincora* on March 24, 1905, Joseph Holloway noted that the 'costumes and scenery harmonised like an exquisite piece of music. I heard Lady Gregory say . . . that it was her son's part in the production that pleased her most, and I don't wonder at it. . . .' (Hogan and O'Neill 54).

The Image was presented on November 11, 1909, and *Deirdre of the Sorrows* on January 13, 1910.

On September 8, 1917, a few months before Gregory's death, Yeats had written to Lady Gregory about her 'Wonder Play', *The Dragon*: 'My only doubt about your dragon play is who, Robert being away, is to stage it. I cannot think of anybody in Dublin who could' (*L* 646). *The Dragon*, designed by Gordon Craig, opened on April 21, 1919.

231. Writing to John Quinn at the time of Gregory's death, Yeats compared Gregory's work to that of his friend James Dickson Innes (1887–1914): 'Certainly no contemporary landscape moved me as much as two or three of his, except perhaps a certain landscape by Innes, from whom he had learnt a great deal' (*L* 646).

232. Yeats had been studying the woodcuts of Edward Calvert (1799–1883) and Samuel Palmer (1805–81) in the Bodleian Library (*L* 646).

Blake rendered seventeen woodcuts—his only work in that medium
—for the edition of Virgil's *Bucolica* (1821) by the English physician,
botanist, and classicist John Robert Thornton (ca. 1758–1837).

Charles Ricketts painted the first of his treatments of the parable
of the wise and foolish virgins (Matthew 25: 1–3) in 1914.

233. Wordsworth's 'Resolution and Independence' (1802) was called by
the Wordsworth family 'The Leech-Gatherer', after the central figure,
an aged peasant. It bears this title in Matthew Arnold's popular edition of Wordsworth, which first appeared in 1879.

234. Bernard Shaw had, with some reluctance, visited the British front in
France between January 28 and February 5, 1917, and had dined with
Robert Gregory in Tirancourt. On February 5, 1918, having just
learned of Gregory's death, he wrote to Lady Gregory: 'When I met
Robert at the flying station on the west front, in abominably cold
weather, with a frost-bite on his face hardly healed, he told me that the
six months he had been there had been the happiest of his life. An amazing thing to say considering his exceptionally fortunate and happy circumstances at home, but he evidently meant it. To a man with his power
of standing up to danger—which must mean enjoying it—war must
have intensified his life as nothing else could; he got a grip of it that he
could not through art or love' (*Collected Letters: 1911–1925,* ed. Dan
H. Laurence [London: Max Reinhardt, 1985], p. 527).

27. The Irish Dramatic Movement

235. In 1923, in observance of the founding of the Irish Free State, William
George Fitzgerald (1872–?), a British political and economic writer
and lecturer, published *The Voice of Ireland,* a collection of essays
subtitled 'A Survey of the Race and Nation from all Angles by the
Foremost Leaders at Home and Abroad'. The volume presented
essays and messages from contributors ranging from Pope Pius XI,
King George V, and Lloyd George to Douglas Hyde, Lady Gregory,
Maud Gonne, AE, and Yeats, who contributed 'The Irish Dramatic
Movement'. Under the pseudonym 'Ignatius Phayre', Fitzgerald contributed 'From "The Terror" to the Truce', an account of events leading to the truce between England and the Irish of July 11, 1921, and
to the treaty granting Ireland Free State status on December 6, 1921.
His closing essay, 'by the editor', called 'Just an Idea', urged the
establishment of a 'New Entente', or 'Anglo-Irish Friendship League'.

Yeats's essay bears the same title of both the early collection of his
writings on the theatre, which he published in the fourth volume of
The Collected Works in Verse and Prose (1908), and of his Nobel
address to the Swedish Academy, published in *The Bounty of Sweden*
(1925), which echoes one passage of this essay. Robert O'Driscoll's
edition of this essay compares the text with Yeats's manuscript.
(*Theatre and nationalism in twentieth-century Ireland,* ed. Robert
O'Driscoll [Toronto: University of Toronto Press, 1971], pp. 79–88).

236. Yeats dined and spoke at Santa Clara College in San Jose on January

29, 1904. He recalled the occasion in the preface to the first volume of *The Poetical Works of William B. Yeats* (1906): 'I remember how strange and foreign all that beauty seemed to me; and yet the lads I spoke to were moved, as I thought, by the imaginative tradition that would have moved them at home. . . . I was able to forget the palm trees, and to say what I would have said to young men in Dublin or in Connacht. As I am looking over the proof sheets of these two books, where I have gathered for the first time all of my poetry I have any liking for, San Jose comes into my head with the thought that I also have been true to that tradition as I understand it' (*VP* 851).

237. Lady Gregory concluded her essay 'West Irish Folk Ballads' in the *Monthly Review* for October 1902, with a complete version of this poem, which was a favourite of Yeats, who quoted it more fully but without attribution in 'What is "Popular Poetry"?' in the *Cornhill Magazine* for March 1903. See also page 96.

238. George Henry Lewes (1817–78), the husband of George Eliot (Mary Ann Evans, 1819–80) and a writer on philosophical and literary subjects, was the first editor (1865–67) of the *Fortnightly Review*.

Between 1801 and 1804, Thomas Bruce, seventh Earl of Elgin (1766–1841) and, at the time, English ambassador to Turkey, removed Greek marbles from Athens to London, including the frieze of the Parthenon and other sculptures from the Acropolis. In 1816, after the publication of his vindicating pamphlet, *Memorandum on the Subject of the Earl of Elgin's Pursuits in Greece* (1810), the marbles were purchased by the British Museum.

239. In a letter to his father, on July 21, 1906, Yeats reviewed his experiences with the poet and influential critic Andrew Lang (1844–1912): 'Andrew Lang was hardly civil when I sent him my first book, and was very uncivil indeed when he reviewed the Rhymers' book. Two years later he wrote a very generous article of apology. He excused himself by saying that new work was very difficult to him, and that when he first read Verlaine's poetry he thought it no better than one finds in the poet's corner of a country newspaper' (*L* 474–75). Lang's 'generous article' has not been identified.

240. See pp. 99–100 for Yeats's quarrel in October 1903 with the *Irish Daily Independent and Nation,* which had attacked the 'dangers' of the nascent Irish National Theatre Society's intention to present 'such dramatic works of foreign authors as would tend to develop an interest in dramatic art' (October 8, 1903, p. 4).

241. This observation, along with the anecdote about 'The Daughters of Erin' and his appreciation of Sara Allgood (1883–1950) and her sister, below, appear, with slight modification, in Yeats's Nobel address. (*The Bounty of Sweden* [Dublin: Cuala Press, 1925], pp. 38–39.)

242. Molly Allgood (Máire O'Neill, 1887–1952) joined her elder sister, Sara, in the Abbey company in 1905 and, within a year, had become a featured player. She was engaged to J. M. Synge and, after his death, assisted Yeats and Lady Gregory in the edition and production, in 1910, of his *Deirdre of the Sorrows,* in which she played the title role.

243. 'The Last Gleeman', Yeats's appreciation of 'Zozimus' (Michael Moran, 1784–1846), Dublin's blind street balladeer, appeared in the *National Observer* on May 6, 1893, and was included in *The Celtic Twilight* (1893).

244. Published in 1907, Synge's *The Tinker's Wedding* was not produced by the Abbey. In a letter in 1906, Synge observed: 'We have never played it here as they say it is too immoral for Dublin!' (*The Collected Letters of J. M. Synge,* ed. Ann Saddlemyer [Oxford: Clarendon Press, 1983], I, p. 148). In 1917, Yeats wrote to Lady Gregory that 'Miss O'Neill gave a wonderful performance yesterday of the old woman in *Tinker's Wedding,* most poetical, and distinguished and yet such an old drunken good for nothing' (Berg NYPL).

245. Lady Gregory's *The Gaol Gate* was first produced at the Abbey on October 20, 1906, and Synge's *The Well of the Saints, The Playboy of the Western World, Riders to the Sea,* and *Deirdre of the Sorrows* appeared on February 4, 1905, January 26, 1907, January 25, 1904, and January 13, 1910, respectively.

246. The Abbey produced *The Country Dressmaker* by George Fitzmaurice (1878–1963) in 1907 and, at the time of this essay, his *Twixt the Giltinans and the Carmodys* was in the company's repertory. Thomas Cornelius Murray (1873–1959) wrote a number of successful, realistic plays for the Abbey, starting with *Birthright* (1910) and including *Autumn Fire,* produced in 1924. The Abbey career of Lennox Robinson (1886–1958) spanned nearly fifty years as playwright, manager (1910–14, 1919–23), and director (1923–56). His *The Clancy Name* was produced there in 1908, the first of some dozen plays over the years. He wrote an early history, *Ireland's Abbey Theatre* (1951), edited *Lady Gregory's Journals* (1947), and was the author of the story 'The Madonna of Slieve Dun', which Yeats defended against censorship (see p. 200). Beginning with *The Building Fund* (1905), several plays by William Boyle (1853–1923) were produced in the Abbey's early years, before his withdrawal of his plays in 1907 over the controversy caused by Synge's *Playboy of the Western World.* Boyle's *Family Failing* was produced by the Abbey in 1912. Daniel Corkery (1878–1964) provoked considerable response with *The Labour Leader* (1919), a realist critique of the exploitation of Irish labourers. He later wrote *Synge and Anglo-Irish Literature* (1931) and an influential study of Gaelic poetry, particularly of the eighteenth century, *The Fortunes of the Irish Language* (1954).

Several of the plays of Seumas O'Kelly (1878?–1918) were first produced by the Theatre of Ireland—a group which had split off from the Abbey in 1908 and which included Edward Martyn, Padraic Colum, and the actress Máire Nic Shiubhlaigh (Máire Walker). After *The Flame on the Hearth* (1908), the Abbey presented four other of O'Kelly's plays. The last, *Meadowsweet,* was produced posthumously in 1919, after O'Kelly's death following a beating by a mob which attacked the headquarters of Sinn Fein, where he had assumed the editorship of *Nationality,* the party journal.

The Abbey had produced *Broken Soil* by Padraic Colum (1881–1972) in 1903 and two other of his plays before his immigration to America in 1914. The 'one of his plays' to which Yeats refers is probably *The Land* (1905), which Yeats had praised in a letter to Florence Farr (*L* 448).

247. From their first meeting in 1902, at the urging of AE, Joyce (1882–1941) and Yeats had been wary that, in addition to having, as AE had promised, 'all the intellectual equipment, culture and education' (*Letters from AE,* ed. Alan Denson [London: Abelard-Schuman, 1961], p. 43), Joyce represented a modernist reaction to Yeats's art. In a rejected introduction to *Ideas of Good and Evil,* Yeats had meditated on their meeting. At its conclusion, Joyce, having asked Yeats's age, declared, 'with a sigh, "I thought as much. I have met you too late. You are too old".' Yeats observes: 'And now I am still undecided as to whether I shall send this book to the Irish papers for review. The younger generation is knocking at my door as well as theirs' (quoted in Richard Ellmann, *James Joyce* [New York: Oxford University Press, 1982], p. 103). Yeats, however, admired Joyce's talent and worked actively to secure him commissions and to promote his work.

248. Verhaeren, see p. 61. O'Driscoll (p. 87) substitutes 'moral' for 'modern' in this phrase, on the authority of Yeats's manuscript.

249. Tony Lumpkin is the idle and mischievous antagonist of Goldsmith's *She Stoops to Conquer* (1773).

250. Robinson's comedy of middle-class family life, *The Whiteheaded Boy,* was produced by the Abbey in December 1916, and marked a turning-point in his career from earlier ironic works to lighter works touched with satire. It was followed by *The Round Table* and *Crabbed Youth and Age,* in January and November of 1922.

In his dedication to Robinson of his *Essays* (1924), dated November 26, 1923, Yeats wrote: 'I dedicate this book to you because I have seen your admirable little play, *Crabbed Youth and Age,* and would greet the future. My friends and I loved symbols, popular beliefs and old scraps of verse that made Ireland romantic to herself, but the new Ireland, overwhelmed by responsibility, begins to long for psychological truth' (*Essays* [London: Macmillan, 1924], dedication page).

251. The editor has not identified this attribution to the Belgian poet and dramatist Maurice Maeterlinck (1862–1949).

28. Nobel Prize Acceptance

252. Yeats's brief remarks, at the banquet on December 10, 1923, as part of the Nobel Prize ceremony, were published in *Les Prix Nobel,* Nobelstiftelsen (Stockholm: Imprimerie Royal, P. A. Norstedt & Soner, 1924).

253. Yeats collaborated with a friend of his father, Edwin John Ellis (1848–1916), on *The Works of William Blake: Poetic, Symbolic and Critical* (1893) (O'Shea 220), the first comprehensive interpretation

of Blake's symbolism. In his unpublished autobiography, Yeats attributes to Ellis 'certain doctrines about the Divine Vision and the nature of God which have protected me for the search for living experience, and . . . perhaps my mastery of verse' (*Mem* 30).

254. In *The Tragic Generation,* Yeats links Samuel Taylor Coleridge (1772–1834), the Romantic poet and essayist, with Rossetti in opposition to other English poets in seeking 'images' that 'grow in beauty as they grow in sterility', noting that they 'sought this new, pure beauty, and suffered in their lives because of it' (*Au* 313).

In 'Swedenborg, Mediums, and the Desolate Places', Yeats characterises Blake's engagement with Swedenborg, 'who to William Blake seemed but an arranger and putter away of the old Church, a Samson shorn by the churches, an author not of a book, but of an index' (*Later Essays,* ed. William H. O'Donnell [New York: Charles Scribner's Sons, 1994], p. 49).

29. Miss Sara Allgood

255. An original member of the Fays' group of Irish amateurs, Sara Allgood first appeared as 'Princess Buan' in the Irish National Theatre Society's production of Yeats's *The King's Threshold* in 1903. Her talents as a singer and an actress were quickly recognised and, for a brief period after the departure of the Fay brothers in 1908, she was a producer at the Abbey. After 1913, her career took her more and more to England, Australia, and America. Her return to the Abbey, late in 1923, to appear in *The Glorious Uncertainty* by Brinsley MacNamara (John Weldon, 1890–1963), and Lady Gregory's poetic monologue, *The Old Woman Remembers,* provoked Yeats's short essay in the *Irish Times* on January 19, 1924, which was accompanied by a portrait sketch by Patrick Tuohy (1894–1930).

256. Sara Allgood appeared not as 'the old woman', Mary Doul, but as the spirited Molly Byrne in the first production of Synge's *The Well of the Saints* on February 4, 1905.

257. On December 27, 1904, the opening night of the Abbey Theatre, Sara Allgood emerged from a series of small roles to great success as Mrs Fallon, the wife and defender of Bartley Fallon, in Lady Gregory's *Spreading the News.* Joseph Holloway pronounced her portrayal 'admirably real' and proclaimed her 'an actress to her fingertips' (Hogan and O'Neill, eds., p. 51).

258. Yeats and Lennox Robinson were primarily responsible for the founding in 1918 of the Dublin Drama League, which until 1929 produced plays by continental writers, using the resources of the Abbey. On February 12, 1924, the League presented *The Two Shepherds* by the prolific Spanish dramatist Gregorio Martinez Sierra (1881–1947) and later in the year, on November 3, his play *The Kingdom of God.* At its opening on November 10, 1910, Sara Allgood portrayed Mary Broderick, the subtle country woman in Lady Gregory's *The Full Moon,* who, aided by her cronies—Shawn, Bart-

ley, Peter, and Cracked Mary—induces the 'madness' of the inter-
loper Hyacinth Halvey.

259. It was Yeats's practice throughout their often troubled relationship
to refer to Sean O'Casey (1880–1964), as he does here, as 'Casey'.
Sara Allgood played the title role in O'Casey's *Juno and the Paycock*
when it opened, on March 3, 1924.

30. A Memory of Synge

260. In 1923, Horace Plunkett revived the *Irish Statesman,* with AE as its
editor. Yeats's brief article 'A Memory of Synge', in the issue for July
5, 1924, introduced 'John Synge as I Knew Him', a short reminiscence
which had been sent to him by Cherrie Matheson Houghton
(1870–1940), one of Synge's early acquaintances. Yeats had written
to her in June: 'I thought it better to send it to *The Irish Statesman* than
some English or American review, because I thought the essential
thing was to put it on record for future use in a paper where it would
be remembered' (quoted in Ronald Ayling, 'Synge's First Love: Some
South African Aspects', *Modern Drama*, VI, no. 4 [Feb. 1964], p. 454).

261. Probably *John Millington Synge and the Irish Theatre,* published in
1913 by Maurice Bourgeois.

262. James Huneker (1860–1921), the American journalist and critic, had
written warmly of Synge just after his death. His essay was reprinted
as part of 'The Celtic Awakening' in *The Pathos of Distance* (New
York: Charles Scribner's Sons, 1913), pp. 228–35.

263. Yeats's reference is to the 'boyish verses' written in 1894 which Synge,
reviewing them in 1908, noted were 'not to be printed under any circumstances' (Greene and Stephens, p. 50). Yeats's edition of Synge's
Poems and Translations was published by the Cuala Press in 1909.

264. Houghton's memoir records Synge's fondness for Patrick Street in
Dublin, 'which runs between the two Cathedrals, and was more like
some queer continental street with little booths all down the centre
of it', and his saying to her, around 1902, ' "You know I am getting
on quite swell; I have a little house of my own now in Paris" ' (*The
Irish Statesman,* July 5, 1924, p. 534).

265. Houghton recalls her last meeting with Synge, in 1904, on a visit to
Ireland from South Africa, where she had lived since her marriage in
1902: 'I remember we talked a little about *Dana* (a short-lived but
delightful paper)'. He said it was too good to get a paying circulation
in Ireland, that Ireland was too remote from the world of thoughts.
(*The Irish Statesman,* p. 534). John Eglinton had founded *Dana; A
Magazine of Independent Thought* in 1904 with Fred Ryan. The
periodical ceased publication in 1905. Of Eglinton's temperament at
this time, AE noted that he was 'still sulking in Wales hiding away
from the world. I think he is cursed by the "Dusk of the Perverse"
which Poe imagined sheer opposition to everybody and everything
ordinary' (Denson, ed., p. 168).

31. Compulsory Gaelic

266. As a Senator, Yeats grappled with problems of establishing the official language of the Free State, having taken the positions of both 'Paul', the proponent of strong governmental insistence on Gaelic, and 'Peter', who resists it, in this essay, which appeared in the *Irish Statesman* on August 2, 1924.

267. *Peg o' My Heart,* by the American dramatist J. Hartley Manners (1870–1928), opened in 1912. By 1922, it had been played over eight thousand times in North America and Great Britain and had been translated into three languages. In addition, over 245,000 copies of the novel based on the play had been sold.

    Among the Irish actresses who played the role of Peg, the Irish girl who inherits a fortune and goes to live in London, was Sara Allgood, who left the Abbey at the end of 1913 and toured in the play throughout 1915 and 1916.

268. Yeats's reference is probably to the legendary Johanne Dybwad (1865–1950), who interrupted her sixty-year career with the Norwegian national theatre, leaving for the 1908–9 season in a dispute largely over increased control over her own work. One condition of her return was that she be hired, during stipulated periods, as a 'guest' player, thus qualifying for exceptional fees.

269. The unification of dynamics and optics by William Rowan Hamilton (1805–65), the Irish mathematician and professor at Trinity College, Dublin, was of lasting influence on mathematical physics.

270. In the *Tractatus Theologico-Politicus,* the Dutch philosopher Benedict Spinoza (1632–77) observes the 'melancholy instance' of the English in support of his notion that 'peoples, though often able to change their tyrants, have never been able to abolish them and replace monarchy by a different form of constitution. . . . They tried to find plausible legal grounds for removing their king; but having removed him, they still found it quite impossible to change the form of the state. Indeed, after much bloodshed they got the length of calling their new king by a different name (as though the name alone had been the whole question at issue!)' (*The Political Works,* ed. A. G. Wernham [Oxford: Clarendon Press, 1958], p. 201).

271. This observation attributed Ruskin has not been identified.

272. Compulsory Gaelic instruction was already established by law, and a Senate Committee which Yeats chaired had reported on June 4, urging that some £5,000 be vested in the Royal Irish Academy for increased activity in seven separate fields of research and recovery of the language. On July 2, however, he had denounced a proposal that railway tickets, signs, and notices be printed bilingually as 'a form of insincerity that is injurious to the general intellect and thought of this country and . . . an irritation against the Gaelic language' (*The Senate Speeches of W. B. Yeats,* ed. Donald R. Pearce [Bloomington: Indiana University Press, 1960], p. 79).

273. Yeats's reference is probably to the productions of An Combar Dra-

muiochta (The Dramatic Union), which had been successful in its presentation of both original works and translations in Gaelic since 1922.

274. Sancho Panza is the companion and earthy counterpoint to the idealistic Don Quixote in Cervantes's masterpiece. The ancient province of Munster, in southwest Ireland, comprises Counties Clare, Tipperary, Limerick, Kerry, Cork, and Waterford.

275. The Platonic Academy of Florence flourished in the last forty years of the fifteenth century under the patronage of the Medici. Modelled by Cosimo de' Medici (1389–1464) on the ancient academy at Athens, the Florentine academy cultivated dialogues on classical thought and supported translations from the Greek and Latin, among them the famous translation of Plato by the academy's chief exponent, Marsilio Ficino (1433–99). One of the academy's themes was opposition of later Pythagorean and Platonist thought to concepts of both Greek and Latin Christianity.

276. Established in 1795, the 'Orange Society'—later known as the 'Orange Order'—had become the embodiment of organised resistance by the Protestants of Ulster to any recognition of the rights of Catholics.

32. Royal Irish Society Awards at the Tailteann Festival

277. In 1924, the Free State government revived the public games according to legend begun at a hill called Tailteann in Co. Meath by Lugh Lámhfhada. The events, which took place annually on the first of August, were said to have begun as funeral sports in honour of Lugh's foster-mother, Tailte, the daughter of a king of Spain, and to have been celebrated nearly continuously from 632 B.C. until A.D. 1169, the year of the Anglo-Norman invasion.

For the first modern Tailteann Games, the 'Aonach Tailteann', August 2 through August 18, Yeats, who chaired the Visitors Entertainment Committee, persuaded the Royal Irish Society to authorise the awarding of medals to the best writers resident in Ireland for the last three years. On behalf of a committee which had included the poet F. R. Higgins (1896–1941), James Stephens, and Lennox Robinson, he presented the awards on August 9, and the text of his remarks was published in the *Transatlantic Review* in November 1924.

278. The translation of Plotinus (205?–270) by Stephen MacKenna (1872–1934) (see O'Shea 1589–94), one of the two works Yeats brought to Thoor Ballylee in the summer of 1926, prompted him to include MacKenna in the group of nine Irish 'men of letters' he proposed that year for addition to the Royal Irish Academy. MacKenna, an implacable Republican who had attempted to join the garrison at the General Post Office in the 'rising' of 1916, had left Ireland for England in 1923, dissatisfied with the establishment of the Free State. Although he was honoured by Yeats's public praise, he refused to accept the gold medal, which was accepted on his behalf by the English author and journalist G. K. Chesterton (1874–1936).

279. John Milton, 'The Doctrine and Discipline of Divorce', *Complete Prose*

Works, ed. Don M. Wolfe (New Haven: Yale University Press, 1953), II, p. 256.

280. Plotinus, *The Ethical Treatises,* tr. Stephen MacKenna (London: Medici Society, 1926), I, p. 86. Quotation marks have been added.

281. Padraic Colum, who had immigrated to America in 1914, had published *Castle Conquer,* the first of his two novels, in 1923.

Joyce's exile from Ireland began in October 1904, and *Ulysses* had been published in Paris in 1922.

Although he had spent most of his early manhood in Paris, George Moore had written prolifically and diversely during his Irish period, between 1895 and 1910. After 1911, he had lived largely in England, where his *Conversations in Ebury Street*—a collection of critical and autobiographical dialogues—was published in 1924.

282. In a letter to Olivia Shakespear in 1933, Yeats contrasted the characters of Joyce and the brilliant French satirist François Rabelais (1490–1553): 'Joyce never escapes from his Catholic sense of sin. Rabelais seems to escape from it by his vast energy' (*L* 807).

283. Although frequently resident in Ireland, either in Co. Meath or in Dublin, and while he had written his first play, *The Glittering Gate* (1909), for the Abbey at Yeats's request, Lord Dunsany (Edward J. M. D. Plunkett, 1878–1957) had not participated significantly in the revival of Irish culture and literature which the Tailteann Awards symbolised. He had refused to contribute to the fund for the Royal Society prizes, noting in a letter to Yeats on July 29, 1924, that his work had not been appreciated in Ireland:

> I am not complaining of this, and I do not think it has been ascertained that recognition in an artist's own country does him any good whatever; but I am ineligible as a subscriber to this fund.

> *Letters to W. B. Yeats,* ed. Richard J. Finneran, George Mills Harper, and William M. Murphy (London: Macmillan, 1977), II, p. 458.

Dunsany's *Chronicles of Rodriguez* was published in 1922, and *The King of Elfland's Daughter* appeared in 1924.

284. When *The Return of the Hero* (1923), a novel by the nationalist politician and man of letters Darrell Figgis (1882–1925), first appeared under the pseudonym 'Michael Ireland', the work was so unlike any other of Figgis's writings that it was widely thought to be the work of James Stephens.

Liam O'Flaherty (1896–1984) had published *Thy Neighbour's Wife* in 1923 and *The Black Soul* the following year. In 1927, Yeats commended O'Flaherty's *The Informer* (1925) and *Mr Gilhooley* (1926) (O'Shea 1487, 1488) to Olivia Shakespear: 'I think they are great novels and too full of abounding natural life to be terrible despite their subjects' (*L* 722).

In the years immediately after the publication of his first novel, *The Valley of the Squinting Windows* (1918), Brinsley MacNamara had published three more, *The Clanking of Chains* (1919), *The Irishman* (1920), and *The Mirror in the Dusk* (1921). *The Irishman* appeared under the pseudonym 'Oliver Blyth'.

Stephens's *Deirdre* (1923) (O'Shea 1999) was one of two completed works in a projected five-volume version of the *Táin Bó Cuailgne*.

285. Yeats quotes from 'Eros and Psyche' by the English poet and essayist Coventry Patmore (1823–96):

> Himself the God let blame
> If all about him bursts to quenchless flame!
> My Darling, know
> Your spotless fairness is not match'd in snow,
> But in the integrity of fire.
> Whate'er you are, Sweet, I require.

> *Poems*, 2 vols. (London: George Bell and Son, 1900), II, p. 86.

He also uses this phrase in a journal entry on the antithesis of 'beauty' and 'character' on March 17, 1909:

> What beautiful woman delights us by her look of character? That shows itself when beauty is gone, being the creation of habit; it's the stalk that remains after the flowers of spring have withered. Beauty consumes character with what Patmore calls 'the integrity of fire' (*Mem* 189).

Its use in this context may also echo Patmore's praise of Robert Bridges's 'Prometheus the Firegiver' in 1895:

> . . . those who have eyes to see with Mr Bridges may discover fire within fire—from that which consumes the heap of sticks upon the altar, through the fires of the senses, the affections, and the will, up to the last ardour of intellectual light.

> *Courage in Politics and Other Essays* (London: Humphrey Milford/Oxford University Press, 1921), p. 146.

286. Yeats's friendship with the physician, writer, and wit Oliver St John Gogarty (1878–1957) began early in the century and continued until Yeats's death. In 1920, Gogarty had removed Yeats's tonsils, discussing literature 'as long as I retained consciousness . . . and continued the discussion when I awoke' (*L* 663). They served together in the first Free State Senate.

Gogarty, whom Yeats later called 'one of the great lyric poets of our age' (*OBMV* xv), published his third collection of poetry, *An Offering of Swans,* at Yeats's sisters' Cuala Press in 1923.

287. In Greek mythology, Zeus appeared in a shower of gold to Danae, who had been imprisoned by her father and who subsequently gave birth to Perseus.

288. 'Non Dolet', the poem quoted here, is the first in Gogarty's volume, where it differs slightly from this version:

Our friends go with us as we go
Down the long path where Beauty wends,
Where all we love foregathers, so
Why should we fear to join our friends?

Who would survive them to outlast
His children; to outwear his fame—
Left when Triumph has gone past—
To win from Age not Time a name?

Then do not shudder at the knife
That Death's indifferent hand drives home;
But with the Strivers leave the Strife,
Nor, after Caesar, skulk in Rome.

289. *We Have Kept the Faith* by Henry Francis Stuart (b. 1902) had been printed privately in 1923 and released in 1924 (O'Shea 2028). Stuart had married Maud Gonne's daughter, Iseult (1895–1954). The poet, playwright, and novelist Austin Clarke (1896–1974) had published his first collection of poems, *The Sword of the West,* in 1921. Yeats, after some hesitation, included him—along with Stuart and Higgins—among the 'Founder Members' of The Irish Academy of Letters when it was at last established in 1932, but his exclusion from the extensive Irish representation in *The Oxford Book of Modern Verse* a few years later was a bitter blow to Clarke. Yeats's library contains an inscribed copy of *The Holy Wells of Orris* (1927) (O'Shea 2286) by the Irish writer Robert N. D. Wilson (1899–1953). Luba Kaftannikoff was born in Glasgow and was an active member of the United Arts Club Dublin.

290. Yeats quotes from 'To the Moon', which appeared in Stuart's *We Have Kept the Faith* (pp. 10–11).

291. From 'Complaint to the Moon' (ibid., p. 32).

33. An Undelivered Speech

292. In the Senate debate on divorce on June 11, 1925, Yeats spoke passionately against legislation which would in effect make laws about divorce impossible to pass, seeing this as the Catholic majority's imposition of its morality on the whole nation and as a great impediment to eventual union with the Northern counties.

Yeats proposed 'a very simple solution, namely, that the Catholic members should remain absent when a Bill of Divorce was brought before the House that concerned Protestants and non-Catholics only, and that it would be left to the Protestant members . . . to be dealt with' (Pearce, ed., p. 91).

He was prepared to speak on this question earlier, in February, when a resolution came to the Senate from the Dáil which requested a rule proscribing even the introduction of any bills dealing with divorce. When the chairman of the Senate ruled this resolution out of order, Yeats published his undelivered speech in the *Irish Statesman* for March 14, 1925.

This note introduced the essay:

> (Expecting a debate upon the problem of Divorce in the Senate on March 4, I had made notes for a speech. As the Message from the Dáil was ruled out of order, debate was impossible. As I think that whoever can should help to inform public opinion before the matter comes round again, I send you my notes.—W. B. Yeats)

293. Inaugurated in 1899 at the Catholic Seminary at Maynooth, the Catholic Truth Society of Ireland was modelled on the Catholic Truth Society founded in London in 1884 by James Britten (1846–1924), whose aims were the production of inexpensive literature expounding Catholic positions and the promotion of conversion to the faith.

294. With the enactment of the Free State constitution, the acting chairman of the Irish provisional government, William T. Cosgrave (1880–1965), became President of the Executive Council, a post he held for ten years.

295. In 'Questions of Divorce', a review of Florence Farr's *Modern Woman: Her Intentions* (1910), G. K. Chesterton, responding to Farr's approval of indissoluble marriage 'for the great mass of mankind', claimed the right 'to impose the Family on everybody if it suits nearly everybody' (*The Uses of Diversity* [New York: Dodd, Mead and Company, 1921], p. 172).

Yeats's devotion to the novels of Honoré de Balzac (1799–1850) began with his father's recounting the French writer's stories in Yeats's youth. In 1905 he acquired a forty-volume set of Balzac's novels which he read over the next few years. This citation has not been identified.

34. Divorce

296. Yeats apparently arranged for his Senate speech on divorce on June 11, 1925, to appear the following day in the *Irish Times*. Senators were not allowed to read their speeches, and Donald R. Pearce's transcript from the official report of the Senate varies considerably from that published in the *Times,* which is, however, nearly identical to the second of two versions of the speech among Yeat's papers (NLI Ms 30080, SUNY-SB Box 18).

Pearce includes an introductory exchange involving Yeats, George Moore's brother, Colonel Maurice Moore (1854–1939), and John Henry Mussen Campbell, first Baron Glenavy (1851–1931), the Senate's *Cathaoirleach*, or Chairman, in which Yeats suggests his intention to publish his remarks:

> Dr Yeats: I speak on this question after long hesitation and with a good deal of anxiety, but it is sometimes one's duty to come down to

absolute fundamentals for the sake of the education of the people. I have no doubt whatever that there will be no divorce in this country for some time. I do not expect to influence a vote in this House. I am not speaking to this House. It is the custom of whose who do address the House to speak sometimes to the Reporters.

Colonel Moore: No, no.

An Cathaoirleach: Perhaps the Senator would please address me. I do not think that Senator Yeats intended to be uncomplimentary to the House, but his observation looked like it.

Dr Yeats: I did not intend to be uncomplimentary. I should have said I do not intend to speak merely to the House (Pearce, ed., p. 91).

297. Although Milton's four tracts on divorce (1643–45) frame much subsequent argument for civil divorce and matrimonial choice and despite the considerable agitation they provoked among Protestants at the time, these concepts were not realised in English law until the Act of 1857.

298. In both his typescript and the published version of this speech, Yeats speaks of and attributes the subsequent quotation to the Most Reverend Dr Edward Byrne (1872–1940), Archbishop of Dublin. He emended his typescript, apparently after the copy had gone to the *Irish Times,* to refer to the Archbishop of Armagh, Patrick O'Donnell (1856–1927), whose name also appears in Pearce's transcript of the speech as Yeats delivered it.

His vacillation may have arisen because the speaker he was citing was neither man, but was instead a Very Reverend J. Byrne. The focus of the twenty-second annual conference of the Catholic Truth Society in October of 1924 had been 'the Christian family'. Divorce and its new advocates were chief among the family's adversaries enumerated by Dr Byrne in his address on October 21 entitled 'The Christian Family and its External Enemies'.

299. The *Irish Times* includes an exchange between Senator Thomas Farren and the Chairman:

Mr Farren: Is it in order to bring in names?

The Chairman: I am not a judge of taste. I cannot say that it is out of order.

300. Yeats had perhaps forgotten the early criticism directed at the Irish theatre by the Reverend Peter Finlay, S.J. (1851–1930), who had denounced Yeats's *Where There is Nothing* when it was published in 1903. Finlay was Professor of Catholic Theology at the National University of Ireland from 1912 until 1923 and retained the same title at the Jesuit House of Studies until his death.

301. The Right Reverend Benjamin John Plunkett (1870–1947) was Protestant Bishop of Meath from 1919 until the end of 1925.

302. Matthew 19:3–9:

The Pharisees also came unto him, tempting him, and saying unto him, Is it lawful for a man to put away his wife for every cause?

And he answered and said unto them, Have ye not read, that he
which made them at the beginning made them male and female,
And said, For this cause shall a man leave father and mother, and
shall cleave to his wife: and they twain shall be one flesh?
Wherefore they are no more twain, but one flesh. What therefore
God hath joined together, let not man put asunder.
They say unto him, Why did Moses then command to give a
writing of divorcement, and to put her away?
He saith unto them, Moses because of the hardness of your
hearts suffered you to put away your wives: but from the beginning it was not so.
And I say unto you, Whosoever shall put away his wife, except
it be for fornication, and shall marry another, committeth adultery: and whoso marrieth her which is put away doth commit
adultery.

303. Yeats's reference has not been identified.
304. These three statues in O'Connell Street, Dublin's main thoroughfare
from the early eighteenth century, are the subjects of Yeats's poem
'The Three Monuments' (1927), in which 'the three old rascals'—each
accused publicly of adultery at the height of his career—'laugh aloud'
at the declaration of 'statesmen' that 'intellect would make us
proud/And pride bring in impurity'. The earliest and tallest, the
monument to the British naval hero Viscount Horatio Nelson
(1758–1805), Nelson's Column (1808), was damaged by a bomb in
1966 and subsequently demolished.
305. The *Irish Times* includes the following:

The Chairman: Do you not think that we might leave the dead alone?
Dr Yeats: I am passing on; I will not dwell long on them.

306. Yeats's reference is probably not to Thomas Aquinas but to the biblical passage from Matthew the historicity of which he questions
above.

35. The Child and the State

307. Yeats spoke to the Irish Literary Society on November 30, 1925,
about his visits to Irish primary schools as a representative of the
Senate. His lecture appeared in two parts in the *Irish Statesman* as
'The Child and the State', on December 5 and 12, 1925.
308. Colonel Fritz Brasé (1875–1940), a German officer, was the first
Director of the Irish Army Music School, serving from 1923 until
shortly before his death.
309. Compulsory attendance at school had been a concern in Ireland at
least since the Irish Education Act of 1896. A scheme for its imple-
mentation, contained in the School Attendance Act of 1926, provided for its enforcement by local 'School Attendance Committees'
and allowed parents to provide 'compulsory' education in the home.

310. See p. 374, note 272.
311. Robin E. W. Flower (1881–1946), the poet and Celticist, was at this time Assistant in the Department of Manuscripts of the British Museum.
312. In *The Trembling of the Veil*, Yeats recalled O'Grady's *The Bog of Stars* (1893) as one of the 'two or three good books' published in Gavan Duffy's series (*Au* 228).
313. Yeats combines two important Anglo-Irish exemplars in noting the founding, in 1705, of the Philosophical Society by Bishop George Berkeley (1685–1753) and that of the Historical Society by Edmund Burke (1729–97) in 1761.
314. In a note, Yeats explicated a favourite passage which occurs towards the end of the penultimate section of the *Commonplace Book,* a collection of notes, observations, and queries written by Berkeley between 1705 and 1708, when he was a student at Trinity College:

> Note—The passage in the *Commonplace Book* is as follows:—'There are men who say there are invisible extensions. There are others who say that the wall is not white, the fire is not hot.' (Meaning that there is a substratum differing from the appearance and outside mind.) 'We Irishmen cannot attain to these truths. The mathematicians think there are insensible lines. About these they harangue: these cut at a point in all angles: these are divisible *ad infinitum*. We Irish can conceive no such lines. The mathematicians talk of what they call a point. This they say is not altogether nothing, nor is it downright something. Now, we Irishmen are apt to think something' (meaning the mathematicians' 'something' which is an abstraction) 'and nothing are near neighbours. . . . I publish this . . . to know whether other men have the same ideas as Irishmen'.

315. This sentence concludes the part of this essay in the *Irish Statesman* for December 5, 1925.
316. Early in 1925, Yeats had discovered the theories of Giovanni Gentile (1875–1944), the Italian metaphysician and Minister of Education. He found in Gentile's *La Riforma dell' Educazione* (see O'Shea 741) the perfect method for the introduction into Irish education of the 'rebirth of European spirituality in the mind of Berkeley, the restoration of European order in the mind of Burke' (quoted in Hone 379–80). Several years after this essay, in a letter to Olivia Shakespear, Yeats recommends Gentile's 'dry difficult beautiful book', *Teoria Generale dello Spirito come Atto Puro* (see O'Shea 742), 'for that founds itself on Berkeley' (*L* 782).
317. 'The Love-lorn Sister', a translation of an Egyptian love song from Harris Papyrus 500 at the British Museum, was published in '*And in the Tomb were Found . . .*' (Cambridge: W. Heffer & Sons, 1923), p. 227, by the writer and theatrical producer Terence Gray (1895–1986):

> I am come to prepare my snare with my hands,
> My cage, and my hiding place, for all the birds of Puanit.

They swoop upon the Black Land, laden with incense.
The first which cometh, he shall seize my worm-bait,
Bearing from Puanit the fragrance which he exhales,
His claws full of sweet-smelling resins.
My heart desires that we take them together,
I with thee alone.

36. The Need for Audacity of Thought

318. Ostensibly provoked by the recent suppression in Ireland of a news-paper which had published a version of 'The Cherry-Tree Carol', Yeats composed a critique for AE's *Irish Statesman* in which thoughts on education, historical speculation, and reflections on his experi-ence in the Senate and elsewhere in public life came together. When AE declined the essay, Yeats published it in the *Dial* for February 1926, with a note:

> Note: The Irish periodical which has hitherto published my occa-sional comments on Irish events explained that this essay would endanger its existence. I have therefore sought publication elsewhere.

319. Hyde's version from the Gaelic, called 'Mary and St Joseph', is in Vol. I of *The Religious Songs of Connacht* (London: T. Fisher Unwin and Dublin: M. H. Gill and Son, 1906), pp. 279–85.

320. Cecil Sharp (1859–1924), the collector of folk music and dances, published several series of collected songs beginning with *A Book of British Songs* (1902). With slight difference, the text Yeats gives of this fifteenth century card is that in Sharp's *English Folk-Carols* (London: Novello and Co., 1911), pp. 7–8.

321. In 1924, Lennox Robinson published 'The Madonna of Slieve Dun', in the first issue of *To-Morrow,* the review edited by Francis Stuart, F. R. Higgins, and the artist Cecil ffrench Salkeld (1901–72), for which Yeats had composed a manifesto (see *UP2* 438–39). Robin-son's story—along with Yeats's 'Leda and the Swan' and a story by the wife of a Trinity professor which concerned miscegenation—caused an uproar in which both Father Thomas Finlay (1848–1940) and John Henry Bernard (1860–1927), the Provost of Trinity, resigned from a Carnegie Library Advisory Committee, of which Robinson was secretary and treasurer. Lady Gregory, who was also on the committee, tells of 'The Carnegie Row' in her *Journals* (pp. 272–82).

322. As early as 1802, Johanna Southcott (1750–1814), an English prophe-tess and fanatic, had proclaimed herself 'the Lamb's wife' and announced that she was to give birth to the second Christ. This prophecy, magnified by her followers, aroused great indignation. While she displayed signs of pregnancy during her last illness, an autopsy revealed nothing.

323. A father of the Roman Catholic Church, Tertullian (ca.160–ca.230)

was, after his conversion to Christianity in early manhood, a vigour-
ous apologist and critic of the Church.

324. Yeats recalled a brief meeting in Paris in the 1890s with August
Strindberg (1849–1912) in *The Bounty of Sweden:* 'I have always
felt a sympathy for that tortured self-torturing man who offered himself to his own soul as Buddha offered himself to the famished tiger.
He and his circle were preoccupied with the deepest problems of
mankind' (*Au* 539).

Both Strindberg's *Fadren* (*The Father*) (1887) and his *Spöksonaten* (1907) were first performed in London in 1927, the latter as
The Spook Sonata. Fadren was translated into English in 1930, and
Spöksonaten appeared as *The Ghost Sonata* in 1929. His autobiography, *Tjänstekvinnans son,* was published as *The Son of a Servant*
in 1913.

325. Ezekiel 4:4–12.

326. Maeterlinck had translated selections from the writings of the Flem-
ish mystic Jan van Ruysbroeck (1293–1381). Yeats's quotation is
untraced.

327. Yeats claimed the prolific and controversial Celtic theologian
Johannes Scotus Erigena (ca.800–ca.877) for Ireland in 1897, when
he had urged Ireland to 'speak again among nations. We gave Christianity to Western Europe; we gave Johannes Scotus Erigena to philosophy. . . . (quoted in D. T. Torchiana, *W. B. Yeats and Georgian
Ireland* [Evanston: Northwestern University Press, 1966], p. 343).

37. A Defence of the Abbey Theatre

328. The controversy over the opening of O'Casey's *The Plough and the
Stars* on February 8, 1926, contained almost every feature of the earlier ones. An Abbey director and one of the actresses threatened to
desert the production, much as Edward Martyn had in the case of
The Countess Cathleen in 1899, and Joseph Holloway was on hand
on February 11 to record Yeats's vain efforts to lecture the crowd
amid a tumult during which 'Some of the players behaved with
uncommon roughness to some ladies who got on the stage, and
threw two of them into the stalls' and 'One young man thrown from
the stage got his side hurt by the piano' (Hogan and O'Neill, p. 254).
As with the first production of the *Playboy,* performances continued
under police surveillance and were accompanied by a raging battle in
the press.

Yeats delivered his major commentary on the disturbances in 'A
Defence of the Abbey Theatre' on February 23 at a meeting of the
Dublin Literary Society, which he published in the *Dublin Magazine*
for April–June 1926, with the following note:

> One cannot recall an impromptu speech with verbal accuracy, nor is
> it necessary that one should. This is, however, the substance of what
> I said. W. B. Y.

329. Yeats apparently shared the platform with the Dublin Solicitor Norman Reddin (?–1942). With his brother, Kenneth (1895–1967), who, under his occasional pen-name, Kenneth Sarr, had written two short plays produced by the Abbey in 1924, Reddin was associated with the Irish Theatre, which had been founded in 1914 as an alternative theatre to the Abbey and which evolved into the Gate Theatre. All that survives of Reddin's remarks is Joseph Holloway's note, in his diary, that they consisted of 'a short paper on the need of a national theatre in which he said a lot of controversial things . . .' (NLI Ms Holloway, 1900, 358).

330. *Cathleen ni Houlihan* (1902), Lady Gregory's *The Rising of the Moon* (1907), and *The Lost Leader* (1918) by Lennox Robinson were popular and artistic successes, but *The Piper* by Norreys Connell (Conal O'Riordan, 1874–1948) had embroiled Yeats in public dispute. *The Old Man* (1925), one of three plays by Dorothy Macardle (1899–1958) produced at the Abbey, was cited as one of its inoffensive political plays in Sean O'Casey's letter to the *Irish Times* on February 19, 1926, at the time of the controversy over *The Plough and the Stars*.

331. See p. 135.

332. Yeats quoted this favourite aphorism, which he attributed to Goethe, in 'At Stratford-on-Avon' (1901) (*E&I* 101) as well as in 'Notes' in *Samhain* for October 1902 (*Ex* 88). Kelly and Schuchard suggest its use in a letter of 1904 may reflect a passage from an 1893 translation of Goethe's reflections:

> . . . the Arts also produce much out of themselves, and . . . add much where Nature fails in perfection, in that they possess beauty in themselves (*CL3* 642).

333. Three of the four ancient provinces of Ireland, Munster, Leinster, and Connacht (Connaught at the time of this essay) contain twenty-three of Ireland's thirty-two counties, including Co. Dublin, in Leinster.

334. The Abbey produced two Gaelic plays by Douglas Hyde in their original form, *Casadh an t-Sugain* (The Twisting of the Rope) in October of 1901 and *An Tinnceur agus an tSidheog* (The Tinker and the Fairy) in February 1912. A third play by Hyde, *An Posadh* (The Marriage), had been produced in November 1911, in a translation by Lady Gregory.

335. Here, Yeats appended a note:

> Subordinated also, as I pointed out in *Samhain* at the time, to bad stage management and worse rehearsal. (See my *Plays and Controversies*, pages 35 and 36, and elsewhere.) The first Gaelic play ever performed in a theatre, *The Twisting of the Rope*, was performed under our management. It had no successor, because it is impossible to specialise in two languages.—W. B. Y.

336. In 1925, *An Combar Dramuiochta* (The Dramatic Union) had been granted a government subsidy to produce plays in Irish, and it was using the Abbey stage at this time.

38. Memorial to the Late T. W. Lyster

337. On March 27, 1926, Yeats spoke at the unveiling in the National Library of the memorial to T. W. Lyster (1855–1922), the 'Quaker librarian' of Joyce's *Ulysses,* who had encouraged both Joyce and Yeats in their early efforts. Yeats had collaborated with Louis Claude Purser (1854–1932) on the simple inscription, and the memorial was designed by George Atkinson (1880–1941), the Director of the National College of Art. Yeats's remarks were published in June 1926, in a pamphlet for the subscribers.

338. Constructed in the early 1740s, the stone mansion which served as the Dublin residence of the Duke of Leinster was later sold to the Royal Dublin Society. It was appropriated by the Free State government as chambers for the Irish Senate. The National Library and the National Museum, facing Kildare Street on either side of Leinster House, were opened in 1890.

339. William Archer (1830–97), a naturalist, had been elected in 1875 as Fellow of the Royal Society for his work on protozoa. He became the first Librarian of the National Library in 1877.

340. Lyster published his translation of *Goethes Leben* (1880) by Heinrich Düntzer (1813–1901) in 1883 (O'Shea 592).

341. The Shakespearean critic and Professor of English at Trinity, Edward Dowden (1845–1913), had been a close friend of Yeats's father and his own early idol. Later, Yeats often personified in Dowden the stultifying influence of Trinity and of Anglo-Irish culture, as in the *Autobiographies,* where Dowden is opposed to Yeats's early nationalist mentor, John O'Leary (pp. 89–101). There, Yeats also notes of Dowden that the 'study of Goethe . . . should have been his life-work' (p. 235).

342. Yeats's *The Island of Statues* appeared in April–June 1885, in the *Dublin University Review,* the journal founded in February 1885 by Charles Hubert Oldham (1860–1926). Many of Yeats's early lyrics and his second published essay appeared in the *Review,* which ceased publication in June 1887.

343. Sir Philip Hanson (1871–1955) was Acting Chairman of the Board of Public Works.

39. The Censorship and St Thomas Aquinas

344. Yeats's health declined toward the end of his term as Senator. His final speech, on July 18, 1928, was a short plea for the priority of personal ability in the selection of Senators, about which he wrote to Lady Gregory: 'Probably I have made my last Senate appearance. A little speech, three sentences, was followed by a minute of great pain.

. . .' (*L* 745). A few weeks later, as the Senate prepared to take up a subject of great importance to him in the 'Censorship of Publications Bill', Yeats presented his views in two essays, 'The Censorship and St Thomas Aquinas' in the *Irish Statesman* on September 22, 1928, and 'The Irish Censorship' in the *Spectator* on September 29 (see pp. 214–18).

345. The system of theological thought of St Thomas Aquinas (1225–74), principally in the *Summa Theologica* (1267–73), was declared the official Catholic philosophy by Pope Leo XIII (1810–1903) in his *Aeterni Patris* (1879).

Yeats refers to the work of such neo-Thomists as Jacques Maritain (1882–1973) and Charles Maurras (1868–1952), which had been appearing in the *Criterion,* and to that of Wyndham Lewis (1894–1957), whose *Time and Western Man* (O'Shea 1126) Yeats had been reading with great enthusiasm at the time of this essay. In November 1927, he wrote to Olivia Shakespear that he wanted to meet Lewis: 'we are in *fundamental* agreement' (*L* 733). And in January of the next year, he wrote, 'You will see from this that *Time and Western Man* still fills my imagination. . . . I read the last chapter again and again. He reminds me of a Father of the Church. . . .' (*L* 734).

346. At the death of Edward Dowden in 1913, Dr Wilbraham Trench (1873–1939) had been appointed to the chair of English Literature at Trinity College, Dublin, for which Yeats had also been considered. In his 'Introduction' to P. A. Ussher's translation of *The Midnight Court* (1926), Yeats had alluded ironically to Trench's solemnity in wishing 'that a Gaelic scholar had been found or, failing that, a man of known sobriety of manner and of mind—Professor Trench of Trinity College, let us say—to introduce to the Irish reading public this vital, extravagant, immoral, preposterous poem' (*Ex* 281).

347. The *Manual of Modern Scholastic Philosophy,* an English version of the *Traité élémentaire de philosophie* of D. F. F. J. Cardinal Mercier (1851–1926), the Archbishop of Malines, Belgium, and founder of the Institute of Philosophy, had been published in 1917 (O'Shea 1305). Yeats set this passage off with parentheses in the copy in his library.

348. Yeats was to be disputed by his estranged friend Annie Horniman on this attribution of the inspiration for the Grail Temple scene in Wagner's Bayreuth production of *Parsifal* to the Byzantine chapel at Palermo (see *UP2* 485–86).

349. The philosopher called Pseudo-Dionysius (ca. 500), because his works were wrongly identified with the first-century martyr, Dionysius the Areopagite, became known in the sixth century. His letters and treatises seek to apply Neoplatonism to Christianity and were influential in Christian theology until the sixteenth century. Yeats refers to the concepts, in his treatises, of earthly and celestial hierarchies and of a 'Mystical Theology', through which knowledge of God and the progressive deification of man may be attained by a process of Neoplatonic abstraction.

Yeats had cited the mystical theologian in 1893 in his review 'The

Ainu' (*UP1* 297) and again in 1895 in his second article on 'Irish National Literature' (*UP1* 367–68).

350. The mosaics at Palermo date from around 1180. St Thomas died in 1274, and the decoration of the Chapel of the Virgin of the Annunciation in Padua by Giotto (ca. 1266–1337) was begun around 1306. Andrea del Sarto lived from 1486 until 1531 and Raphael from 1483 until 1520. Orcagna lived from ca. 1308 until 1368, and Titian (ca. 1477–1576) painted his *Sacred and Profane Love* around 1503.

351. The entire Latin quotation, in Mercier, is italicised.

352. This line is from the fifth section of Browning's 'A Toccata of Galuppi's':

> Was a lady such a lady, cheeks so round and lips so red,—
> On her neck the small face buoyant, like a bell-flower on its bed,
> O'er the breast's superb abundance where a man might base his
> head?

> *The Poetical Works of Robert Browning* (London: John Murray, 1919), I, 266.

353. The relegation of a plaster cast of the *Discobolus* of Myron of Eleutherae (ca. 450 B.C.) to a 'lumber room' in the Montreal Museum of Natural History because of its 'vulgarity' is the inspiration for 'A Psalm of Montreal', written in 1875 and published in 1878, by Samuel Butler (1835–1902).

40. The Irish Censorship

354. Yeats's second article on the proposed censorship in Ireland appeared in the *Spectator* on September 29, 1928.

355. The 'old friend' is probably AE. The estrangement which had become public in his withdrawal from the Abbey in 1904 had been suspended on several occasions, such as William Martin Murphy's lock-out in 1913 (see *UP2* 405) and the Conscription Act of 1918. Yeats's first public statement on the Censorship Bill had appeared in AE's *Irish Statesman* and debate of the bill continued in its columns. On November 9, 1928, AE wrote to Yeats, who was then at Rapallo, sending him the four issues from October 20 through November 10 and adding that Bernard Shaw had sent 'a devastating article on the censorship' which would appear on November 17 (Denson, ed., p. 180).

356. See p. 198.

357. William Etty (1787–1849), the English colourist and history painter, often painted the female nude. *The Bath of Psyche,* by the English portraitist and history painter Sir Frederick Leighton (1830–96), is a representative, sensuously coloured female nude.

358. Despite the efforts of Yeats, AE, Shaw, and many others, the Censorship of Publications Bill which became law in 1929 was, in most particulars, that which Yeats describes here.

359. Yeats cites an observation by the French poet, critic, playwright, and fellow Nobel laureate in literature Anatole France (Jacques Anatole

François Thibault, 1844–1924) in 'Swedenborg, Mediums, and the Desolate Places' (see O'Donnell, ed., p.48).

The earliest *Index Librorum Prohibitorum,* forbidding reading or possession of writings on doctrinal or moral grounds, dates to the fifth century. The first modern Roman index, advanced by Pope Paul IV (1476–1559), underwent gradual modification until the reform in 1897 of Leo XIII.

360. The School Attendance Act (1926) made attendance compulsory for Irish children between the ages of six and fourteen.

361. Rioting less severe than that over *The Playboy of the Western World* in 1907 had broken out during the second performance, on February 9, 1926, of O'Casey's *The Plough and the Stars.* On both occasions —as he had done at the time of the controversy over his *Countess Cathleen* in 1899—Yeats had called for police protection. The fourth disputed play referred to here is probably Synge's *In the Shadow of the Glen,* which Yeats had defended against charges of indecency and plagiarism in 1903 (see pp. 99–100) and again in 1904 (see *UP2* 331–38).

In his speech to the audience of *The Plough and the Stars,* Yeats had declared: 'You have disgraced yourselves again. Is this to be an ever-recurring celebration of the arrival of Irish genius? Once more you have rocked the cradle of genius. The news of what is happening here will go from country to country. You have once more rocked the cradle of reputation. The fame of O'Casey is born tonight' (quoted in *The World of W. B. Yeats,* ed. Robin Skelton and Ann Saddlemyer [Seattle: University of Washington Press, 1965], p. 102).

362. Swift's pamphlet, proposing to cure Ireland's overpopulation and poverty by having the poor sell their children as edible delicacies to the rich, appeared in 1729.

363. Yeats's allusion has not been identified.

364. See Yeats's citation of this passage, p. 212.

365. In the unpublished draft of his *Autobiography,* written some ten years before this essay, Yeats had noted that the English novelist, journalist, and social reformer H. G. Wells (1866–1946) owed his growing popularity to 'the returning seriousness of the public' (*Mem* 89).

366. Rathmines, a large 'urban district council area' since the middle of the nineteenth century, became part of the city of Dublin in 1930.

367. D. T. Torchiana has identified the 'implacable and able Irish revolutionary soldier' as the Reverend Jephson Byrne O'Connell, a Catholic priest (Torchiana, p. 222). Yeats refers to O'Connell's recommendation of Berkeley on p. 232.

368. See p. 195.

369. Yeats's reference is probably to O'Casey, who had published earlier in 1928 Yeats's letter explaining the Abbey's rejection of *The Silver Tassie.* 'The mere greatness of the world war has thwarted you', Yeats wrote. 'Dramatic action is a fire that must burn up everything but itself. . . . The whole history of the world must be reduced to wallpaper in front of which the characters must pose and speak' (*L* 741).

41. Oedipus the King

370. Yeats's first radio broadcast, from BBC Belfast at 7:15 P.M. on Tuesday, September 8, 1931, anticipated a radio performance by the Abbey players of his translation of Sophocles' *King Oedipus,* which was first produced at the Abbey Theatre on December 7, 1926, and published in 1928. Except for the final page, which is taken from an earlier draft, the text of the programme, broadcast in the BBC Belfast Programme only, is transcribed from what remains of the typescript from which Yeats read (NLI Ms 30109, SUNY-SB Box 23).

371. Yeats visited the University of Notre Dame in Notre Dame, Indiana, January 15–17, 1904. Sophocles' play was produced at Notre Dame on May 15, 1899.

372. Yeats had visited the English actor and producer Nugent Monck (1878–1958) on his return from America in October 1911, just before beginning his first version of Sophocles' play. Monck, who had founded the Norwich Players in 1911, followed Yeats to Dublin, where he formed a school of acting at the Abbey. A producer at the Abbey in the 1911–12 season, Monck joined the company on its 1913 American tour. After military service, he returned to Norwich in 1919, reconstructing the Maddermarket Theatre, in 1921, as an Elizabethan playhouse. The Norwich Players' special emphasis was on Shakespearean, Elizabethan, and mystery plays.

373. In *W. B. Yeats, The Writing of Sophocles'* King Oedipus (Philadelphia: American Philosophical Society, 1989), David R. Clark and James B. McGuire suggest that the young scholar was probably Charles Stewart Power (1892–1950), son of John Wyse Power, the partial model for the editor Myles Crawford in *Ulysses,* and a frequent member of Abbey casts at the time of Yeats's early work on his translation in 1912.

374. Peter Judge (1889–1947) joined the Abbey company in 1918 and, under his stage name, F. J. McCormick, became one of its most versatile actors. McCormick's acting of Oedipus in both of Yeats's plays based on the work of Sophocles won great critical acclaim.

375. In the fall of 1931, Yeats was staying with Lady Gregory at Coole.

376. Monsignor Patrick Browne (1889–1947), Professor of Mathematics at St Patrick's College, Maynooth, from 1914 until 1945, published many translations into Gaelic of Plutarch, Dante, Racine and, in 1929, of Sophocles' *Oedipus at Colonus.*

377. Yeats's extant radio script ends at this point.

378. Yeats's typescript: '(read chorus)'. *Sophocles'* Oedipus at Colonus, of which these are lines 1147–58, was first published in *The Collected Plays of W. B. Yeats* in 1934.

379. The Abbey company's American tour lasted more than six months, and the players visited twenty-six states and Canada.

42. Reading of Poems

380. Yeats's first broadcast reading of his poems originated in Belfast on Tuesday, September 8, 1931, the same night as the talk on *Oedipus,* and was broadcast in the BBC National Programme at 9:10 P.M., as part of 'An Irish Programme'. The text in the files of the BBC, Belfast, was burned during the war, and the version given here is taken from Yeats's working typescript, with many manuscript corrections (NLI Ms 30249, SUNY-SB Box 23). Slight emendations have been possible from surviving recorded fragments (BBC #22145) of the broadcast. Yeats may well have made further revisions before broadcasting.

381. Yeats's typed text inserts 'great'.

382. Morris published the great narrative poem based on the Icelandic *Volsunga Saga, The Story of Sigurd the Volsung and the Fall of the Niblungs,* in 1876.

383. In the text: 'to do so'.

384. The text: 'I think'.

385. The text: 'had'.

386. The text inserts: 'to'.

387. 'The Lake Isle of Innisfree' first appeared in the *National Observer* in 1890 and was collected in *The Book of the Rhymers' Club* and *The Countess Kathleen and Various Legends and Lyrics* in 1892.

388. In his broadcast, Yeats added the material set off by brackets.

389. Yeats's typed text: 'or twenty fifth'.

390. 'The Fiddler of Dooney' was first published in the *Bookman* in December 1892. It appeared in *The Second Book of the Rhymers' Club* and, although not included in *Poems* (1895), was collected in *The Wind Among the Reeds* in 1899.

The recorded fragment of this broadcast ends at this point.

391. The text here, after 'wood', is in Yeats's hand in the typescript; lower on the page, a typed insert is crossed out: 'He had spent seventy years of his life keeping the paths clear for shooters in that wood'.

392. 'The Song of the Wandering Aengus' first appeared in the *Sketch* in August of 1897; it was included in *The Wind Among the Reeds.*

393. Yeats had met Constance Gore-Booth (1868–1927), the daughter of a Co. Sligo landlord, Sir Henry William Gore-Booth (1843–1900), in 1893, when she was studying art in London. He was especially drawn to her sister, Eva (1870–1926), a poet, when he visited them at the family seat, Lissadell, near Sligo, the following year. His relationship with Constance proved the more durable.

Condemned to death for having commanded the rebel forces in St Stephen's Green during the 1916 'rising', Constance Gore-Booth, who married the Polish artist Count Casimir Markiewicz (1874–1932) in 1900, became a member of the first Dáil Éireann and, subsequently, an Irish Cabinet minister.

394. Yeats's typescript indicates that the next poem was to be 'An Irish Airman Foresees His Death'. A heavily revised introduction is crossed out, and the poem was evidently omitted from the broadcast.

395. Yeats subsequently published this poem as 'Anne Gregory' in *Words for Music Perhaps* (1932) and as 'For Anne Gregory' in the *Spectator* in December 1932, and *The Winding Stair* (1933).

A reading of 'Sailing to Byzantium', and the following introduction of it, were cancelled by Yeats, according to Curtis Bradford, on the authority of W. H. McMullen, who supervised the programmes for BBC Belfast:

> Now I am trying to write about the state of my soul, for it is right for an old man to make his soul, and some of my thoughts upon that subject I have put into a poem called 'Sailing to Byzantium'. When Irishmen were illuminating the Book of Kells and making the jewelled croziers in the National Museum, Byzantium was the centre of European civilisation and the source of its spiritual philosophy, so I symbolise the search for the spiritual life by a journey to that city.

43. Ireland, 1921–1931

396. As the general elections of February 1932, approached, Yeats was named in the *Irish Press* by the journalist and Republican propagandist Aodh De Blacam (1890–1951) as part of 'the attempt now being made by certain "Anglo-Irish Leaders" to bring back the Irish Eighteenth Century' (*L* 790). A few days earlier, Yeats had compared the 'hold on Irish imagination' of Berkeley and Swift with that of O'Connell in 'Ireland, 1921–1931', which appeared in the *Spectator* for January 30. 'De Blacam's passing mention is valuable', he wrote to Joseph Hone (1882–1959), for whose book on Berkeley (1931) he had supplied an introduction, 'as it conveys an idea that something is happening, and that may get it [into] some undergraduate's head' (*L* 791).

397. In 1922, with help from his friend James Stephens, and possibly through the mediation of Oliver Gogarty, the American artist and medallist Theodore Spicer-Simson (1871–1956), who had, Stephens wrote to Gogarty, 'sculpted everybody except Yeats', made the medal to which Yeats refers (James Stephens, *Letters of James Stephens*, ed. Richard J. Finneran [New York: Macmillan, 1974], p. 277).

398. In the election on February 16, 1932, the Republican Fianna Fail party of Eamon de Valera (1882–1975) defeated the incumbent Cumann na nGaedheal party of W. T. Cosgrave.

399. Seventy-seven Republican 'Irregulars', including the author and statesman Erskine Childers (1870–1922), were executed as a result of the enforcement of the Army Emergency Powers Resolution of September 23, 1922, by Kevin O'Higgins (1892–1927), the Vice-President and Minister for Home Affairs in the Cosgrave government. O'Higgins's assassination by Republican gunmen on July 10, 1927, had prompted Yeats to call him, in a public letter to his widow, 'a martyred intellect' and a 'great builder of a nation' (*UP2* 476).

400. Maud Gonne organised a tireless publicity campaign on behalf of

Republican prisoners during their detention by O'Higgins in 1923–24 and she remained implacably devoted to the Republican cause. 'When Lady Gregory goes', Yeats wrote to Olivia Shakespear in September of 1929, 'and she is now very frail, I too shall have but one old friend left. (M. G. has been estranged by politics this long while.)' (L 769).

401. The 'Shannon Scheme', a massive and spectacularly successful hydro-electric project at Ardnacrusha in Co. Clare, was championed by Patrick McGilligan (1889–1961), Minister for Industry and Commerce from 1924 to 1932.

402. Milton, *Comus*, ll. 472–4.

403. The Free State soldier is J. B. O'Connell. Berkeley's *Three Dialogues between Hylas and Philonous* appeared in 1713.

404. In order to regularise what had become a common practice, a Bill amending the Free State Constitution by abolishing the right of appeal from Free State Courts to the Committee of the Privy Council had been introduced towards the end of the Cosgrave administration. Despite the strong opposition of the Protestant Episcopacy which Yeats cites here, the Bill was enacted shortly after the election of de Valera.

44. Poems About Women

405. Yeats read from his own poetry on the BBC National Programme on April 10, 1932, between 9:05 and 9:30 P.M. Although neither the listing of the programme in the BBC *Radio Times* nor the official 'Programme as Broadcast' record specifically confirms it, much evidence establishes that this is the programme he read, as Wade's bibliography states (Wade, p. 410–11). A manuscript and three typescripts of this broadcast are among his papers. The typescript containing Yeats's late revisions along with manuscript indications of pauses are the source for the present text.

406. The friend was Olivia Shakespear (see *L* 786).

407. Yeats held that the rhetorical poetry of Algernon Charles Swinburne (1837–1909) had partly intimidated Oscar Wilde into assuming an abrasive and combative pose and, in its profusion, had overshadowed the more direct and passionate accomplishment of Swinburne's contemporary William Morris.

408. The best-known poem by Yeats's fellow Rhymer of the 1890s, Ernest Dowson (1867–1900), 'Non sum qualis eram bonae sub regno Cynarae', first appeared in the *Century Guild Hobby Horse* in 1897. Lionel Johnson published 'By the Statue of King Charles the First at Charing Cross' in *The Book of the Rhymers' Club* in 1892. Yeats included both poems in *The Oxford Book of Modern Verse*.

409. The refrain of the eighteenth-century ballad 'Shule Aroon':

> Siubhail, siubhail, siubhail, a rúin!
> Siubhail go cosair, agus siubhail go ciúin,

> Siubhail go d-ti an doras agus eulaigh liom,
> Is go d-teich tu, a mhúrnin, slán!

had been translated by Yeats's early acquaintance George Sigerson (1839–1925) as follows:

> Come, come, come, O Love!
> Quickly come to me, O Love!
> Come to the door, and away we'll flee,
> And safe for aye may my darling be!

> Quoted in *A Treasury of Irish Poetry in the English Tongue*, ed. Stopford A. Brooke and T. W. Rolleston (London: John Murray, 1900), p. 14.

'To an Isle in the Water' first appeared in *The Wanderings of Oisin and Other Poems* in 1889.

410. Yeats had first collected folk materials when visiting the Co. Sligo cottages around Ballisodare and Rosses Point with his Middleton cousins in the 1880s.

When it first appeared in 1889, 'Down by the Salley Gardens' had borne a subtitle, 'An Old Song Re-sung', and, in a footnote, an attribution:

> This is an attempt to reconstruct an old song from three
> lines imperfectly remembered by an old peasant woman in
> the village of Ballysodare, Sligo, who often sings them
> to herself (*VP* 90).

Yeats cited this revivification of a fragment of 'popular poetry' in a letter to his confidante of this period, the English poet Dorothy Wellesley, duchess of Wellington (1889–1956), of September 25, 1935:

> The work of Irish poets, quite deliberately put into circulation with
> its music thirty and more years ago, is now all over the country. The
> Free State Army march to a tune called "Down by the Salley Garden"
> without knowing that the march was first published with words of
> mine, words that are now folklore. Now my plan is to start a new set
> of 12 next Spring with poems by English as well as Irish poets. . . . I
> want to make another attempt to unite literature and music.

> *Letters on Poetry from W. B. Yeats to Dorothy Wellesley,* ed. Dorothy Wellesley (London: Oxford University Press, 1940), p. 32.

In *Editing Yeats's Poems: A Reconsideration,* Richard Finneran cites this attribution as an example of the difficulty in interpreting Yeats's reworking of, particularly, translated sources, drawing on, among others, Michael Yeats (b. 1921) (pp. 109–11).

411. The Irish music critic and composer Herbert Hughes (1882–1937) published his setting of Yeats's poem in *Irish Country Songs* (1909).

412. Yeats published ' "I am of Ireland" ', which is based on a Middle English lyric of the fourteenth century, in *Words for Music Perhaps and Other Poems* later in 1932. Yeats's broadcast substituted 'Come' in the second and third iterations of the refrain for 'And', which appears in all published versions.

413. In addition to Gaby Deslys (1884–1920), the French actress and dancer, the American dancer Ruth St Denis (1879–1968) and the Russian ballerina Anna Pavlova (1885–1931), Yeats identifies here the 'player in the States'. During his 1904 visit to America, he had admired the acting of Julia Marlowe (1866–1950), an English-born actress and friend of both Arthur Symons and Agnes Tobin, who had been raised in America. Yeats had thought of asking her to play the title role in his *Deirdre* (Hone 200).

    'His Phoenix' first appeared in *Poetry* in February of 1916 and was included in *The Wild Swans at Coole* the following year.

414. Yeats first published 'The Folly of Being Comforted' in the *Speaker* in January 1902. It was collected in *In the Seven Woods* the following year.

415. In 1894, Robert Louis Stevenson (1850–94) praised 'The Lake Isle of Innisfree', which appeared in W. E. Henley's *National Observer* in December of 1890. 'It is so quaint and airy', Stevenson wrote, 'simple, artful, and eloquent to the heart—but I seek words in vain' (*The Letters of Robert Louis Stevenson to His Family and Friends,* ed. Sidney Colvin [New York: Charles Scribner's Sons, 1902], p. 386).

    Henley (1849–1903) himself, although his praise of this particular poem hasn't been located, is probably the 'non-conformist editor'. He befriended Yeats in his earliest days as a poet and reviewer, often and to Yeats's discomfort rewriting verses as they were in the process of publication. In *Autobiographies,* Yeats recalls Henley's telling a friend to whom he sent a copy of 'The Man who Dreamed of Fairyland', 'See what a fine thing has been written by one of my lads' (*Au* 129).

    In a note in his transcription of Yeats's typescript, Curtis Bradford speculated that perhaps Yeats omitted this poem, which in its published version is entitled 'He wishes for the Cloths of Heaven', from the broadcast.

416. Yeats apparently altered his reading text just before the broadcast, omitting almost all of a passage which had survived from the earliest manuscript drafts:

    > Before I pass on to poems that are not love poems though they are about women, I want to answer a criticism that may have occurred to somebody. Young men tell me that love poems are no longer written and suggest in some polite indirect way that I wrote them because I belonged to the now obsolete romantic movement. Yes, the romantic

movement is over. They are right to attempt something new but wrong if they think that great movement was a literary error. It is sometimes right to say 'the spring vegetable[s] are over', but never right to say 'they have been refuted'.

417. The series of seven poems about Mabel Beardsley (1871–1916), Aubrey Beardsley's sister, who died of cancer, was first published in the *Little Review* and the *New Statesman* in August 1917. Later that year, Yeats included them, under the title 'Upon a Dying Lady', in *The Wild Swans at Coole*.

418. Yeats's title for this poem is 'Certain Artists Bring Her Dolls and Drawings'.

419. Yeats's title for this poem is 'Her Friends Bring Her a Christmas Tree'.

420. In *Memoirs*, Yeats recalls Aubrey Beardsley's dismissal as art director of the *Yellow Book*, in the wake of Oscar Wilde's downfall, and his own efforts on behalf of the dying artist, whom he greatly admired:

> In Beardsley, I found that noble courage that seems to me at times, whether in man or woman, the greatest of human faculties. I saw it in all he said and did, in the clear logic of speech and in [the] clean swift line of his art. . . . I cannot imagine to myself the profession where he would not have made himself a foremost man. (*Mem* 92)

Yeats's title for this poem is 'Her Race'.

421. This passage echoes Yeats's recollection, in the early draft of his autobiography, of his first visit to Lissadell:

> In my childhood I had seen on clear days from the hill above my grandmother's house or from the carriage if our drive was towards Ben Bulben or from the smooth grass hill of Rosses the grey stone walls of Lissadell among its trees.
>
> . . . I have no memory of when I first met the Gore-Booth girls or how I came to be asked. Con Gore-Booth all through my later boyhood had been romantic to me, and more than once as I looked over to the grey wall and roof I had repeated to myself Milton's lines:
>
> Bosomed deep [*sic*] in tufted trees,
> Where perhaps some beauty lies,
> The cynosure of neighbouring eyes. (*Mem* 77–78)

422. 'L'Allegro', ll. 78–80. This passage is set off in brackets in the copy of the book in Yeats's library (O'Shea 1322).

423. As 'On a Political Prisoner', this poem appeared in the *Dial* in November of 1920 and was included in *Michael Robartes and the Dancer*, which appeared the following year.

424. This observation by the English theologian and author John Henry Newman (1801–1900) has not been located in his writings.

45. Plain Man's *Oedipus*

425. The Abbey Theatre company successfully toured in North America in 1932 and again in 1933, the year of Yeats's last American lecture tour. His article, entitled 'Plain Man's *Oedipus*', which appeared in the *New York Times* on January 15, 1933, reiterates some of his remarks to his radio audience on September 8, 1931 (see p. 219) about the play, by this time a staple with the Abbey company.

426. For the scholar, see note 373, p. 390. Many of the translations from Greek and Latin of the classicist Sir Richard Claverhouse Jebb (1841–1905) were the standard texts of his era. His first translation of *Oedipus* appeared in 1887.

46. The Great Blasket

427. Yeats recognised his appreciation in the *Spectator* for June 2, 1933, of the translation of *Twenty Years A-Growing* (New York: Viking, 1933) by Maurice O'Sullivan (Muiris o Súileabháin) (1904–50), a Civic Guard in Connemara raised in the Blasket Islands off the Dingle Peninsula, as 'the last [review] I shall ever write. I haven't the gift', he wrote on May 21, 'my writings have to germinate out of each other. I spent about ten days on the thing and it's not worth the trouble. It is something else altogether, dressed out to look like a review' (*L* 809). A few days later, however, he commended the autobiography to Olivia Shakespear: 'Read *Twenty Years A-Growing* or some of it', he wrote. 'I once told you that you would be happy if you had twelve children and lived on limpets. There are limpets on the Great Blasket' (*L* 811).

O'Sullivan's book was awarded the Irish Academy of Letters O'Growney Literary Award for a work written in Gaelic in 1934.

428. Near the end of Part I of *The Aran Islands,* Synge describes his feelings when returning from the Arans:

> I have come out of an hotel full of tourists and commercial travellers, to stroll along the edge of Galway Bay, and look out in the direction of the islands. The sort of yearning I feel towards those lonely rocks is indescribably acute. This town, that is usually so full of wild human interest, seems in my present mood a tawdry medley of all that is crudest in modern life. The nullity of the rich and the squalor of the poor give me the same pang of wondering disgust.

> *The Works of John M. Synge* (Dublin: Maunsel and Company, 1910), III, 100–101 (O'Shea 2076: vols. I, II, and IV only).

429. In her essay on Synge, in the *English Review* for March 1913, Lady Gregory recalls first seeing him 'in the North Island of Aran':

> I . . . felt quite angry when I passed another outsider walking here and there, talking also to the people. I was jealous of not being alone on

the island among the fishers and seaweed gatherers. I did not speak to the stranger, nor was he inclined to speak to me; he also looked on me as an intruder, I only heard his name.

'Synge', *The English Review*, 13 (March 1913), p. 556.

430. The Russian writer and revolutionary Maxim Gorki (1868–1936) published his *Reminiscences of my Youth* in 1924.

431. Robin Flower had translated the reminiscences of a Blasket Islander, Tomas O Crohan, as *The Islandman* in 1929.

432. Yeats's reference has not been identified.

433. Synge, *Works*, IV, 90 (O'Shea 2076).

434. In his 'Introductory Note' to O'Sullivan's book, E. M. Forster (1879–1970) notes the author's pleasure that the book will appear in the original Irish, 'because it will be read on the Blasket. They will appreciate it more there than we can, for whom the wit and poetry must be veiled. On the other hand, we are their superiors in astonishment. They cannot possibly be as much surprised as we are, for here is the egg of a sea-bird—lovely, perfect, and laid this very morning' (p. vi).

435. George Derwent Thomson (1903–82) had been Fellow and Assistant Lecturer in Classics at King's College, Cambridge, before taking up a post at Galway University in 1931. His *Greek Lyric Metre* was published in 1929.

Moya Llewellyn Davies (1895–1943), a friend of Forster and a patron of the arts, maintained a home, Watermill, in Raheny, outside of Dublin. Yeats was later to propose a reading there of poems selected by himself and F. R. Higgins.

47. The Growth of a Poet

436. On March 17, 1934, Yeats took part in 'St Patrick's Night', an hour-long broadcast from the Belfast studios of the BBC which also included a number of choirs, orchestral music, and the bells of Armagh Cathedral. His contribution to the programme was published as 'The Growth of a Poet' in the *Listener* on April 4. Of the two typescripts of this broadcast (NLI Ms 30249, SUNY-SB Box 23), the second, mounted on cardboard, is heavily corrected in Yeats's hand and is almost certainly the copy from which he read. Variations in this text from that printed in the *Listener* are noted.

437. See p. 235 for Yeats's concern with Swinburne's dominance. This late reaffirmation of it recalls Yeats's remark to his sister, in April 1909, as favourable reviews of his *Collected Works in Verse and Prose* were appearing on the morrow of Swinburne's death: 'I am King of the Cats' (quoted in Hone 245).

In the script from which he read, Yeats crossed out 'and' in this sentence.

438. Yeats's radio text: '. . . to stories and old songs'.

439. The radio text: '. . . Gaelic and then . . .'

440. Ballisodare, Co. Sligo. See note 410.

Yeats's radio text inserts a sentence: 'I will not read it because it will be sung later on'.

V. C. Clinton-Baddeley (1900–1970), who collaborated with Yeats on his radio broadcasts, identified the song as 'The Rambling Boys of Pleasure', an Anglo-Irish ballad (*Words for Music Perhaps* [Cambridge: Cambridge University Press, 1941], p. 65).

441. Yeats undoubtedly refers to the pentatonic basis of much Gaelic folk music. The five-note scale commonly includes several whole tones that are set off by minor thirds (gaps) in a formation resembling the black notes of the piano keyboard.

'The Song of the Old Mother' was first published in the *Bookman* for April 1894, and was included in *The Second Book of the Rhymers' Club* in the same year. Yeats's note after the text read:

> The 'seed of the fire' is the Irish phrase for the little fragment of burning turf and hot ashes which remains in the hearth from the day before (*VP* 151).

442. The broadcast typescript indicates that Yeats revised lines 5, 7, and 8 in his reading. His omission of 'And' at the beginning of line 7 was retained in the *Listener*. In addition, he substituted 'But' for 'And' at the start of line 5 and he omitted 'And' at the start of line 8, reading 'Their' (l.7) and 'they' (l.8) with great emphasis.

443. Yeats's typescript has 'were'.

444. A cromlech is a prehistoric arrangement of stones, a flat stone resting on three or more stones, often associated with a tomb.

445. Yeats's manuscript emendation for this sentence in his broadcast script: 'There is a rock on the edge of Lough Gill called Dooney Rock'.

446. Yeats wrote 'But' for 'And' in his broadcast script.

447. The final form of Yeats's concluding remarks to this programme, introducing a singing of 'Down by the Salley Gardens' in the setting by Herbert Hughes, is unclear. He struck out the original sentence: 'Mr——will now sing "Down by the Salley Gardens" to the music of Herbert Hughes'. The first manuscript alternate—'now somebody is going to sing my poem "Down by the Salley Gardens" it has been beautifully set to music'—was probably succeeded by the version Yeats wrote in a blank space on the same page of the broadcast script: 'Now you will hear my poem "Down by the Salley Gardens" sung to an old Irish air'.

48. The Irish Literary Movement

448. This dialogue, broadcast on October 12, 1935, on the 'radio Athlone' band of the Irish broadcasting service, was part of a series of radio discussions called 'A Visitor Interviewed on the Radio' which had

begun in June. The 'interviewer', called 'D. McD' in the typescript from which the text of this broadcast is transcribed, has not been identified. Yeats wrote to Dorothy Wellesley on October 9 that he was writing in bed but 'soon must get up to write a broad cast in reply to questions from a journalist' (Kelly). George Yeats's note on the envelope containing it identifies the text as 'WBY & Deirdre Macdonagh', contradicting Curtis Bradford's identification of the interlocutor as the poet and playwright Donagh McDonagh (1912–68), who was a frequent contributor to Irish radio.

The format of the dialogue is modified here from that of the radio script. In place of 'D. McD.' and 'Mr Yeats' in the margins, questions are italicized and answers are in roman type.

449. Alfred Perceval Graves (1846–1931), the father of the poet and novelist Robert Graves and an early member of the Irish Literary Society, wrote popular and humourous verse which was often set to music. *The Irish Song Book* (1894), edited by Graves, was included in the 'List of the Best Irish Books' in the *Bookman* in 1895, at the conclusion of Yeats's essays on 'Irish National Literature' (*UP1* 387).

In the 1880s, Yeats spoke before the Southwark Irish Literary Club, founded in 1883 by Francis A. Fahy (1854–1935), writer of popular songs and ballads. Fahy, Yeats wrote to Katharine Tynan, 'seems a king among his own people and what more does any man want? I hear they—that is, the members of the Club—sing his songs and have quite a Fahy cult' (*L* 64).

In a letter to Katharine Tynan in 1906, Yeats had linked the Belfast poet Joseph Campbell (1879–1944) with Campbell's friend Padraic Colum: 'Colum has written a couple of little poems—'The Ploughman' and 'The Poor Scholar'—which are charming. . . . [Campbell] knows better than the others what a poem is, though not a very interesting sort of poem, but he has not written it yet' (*L* 477). A student of Gaelic culture and literature, Campbell was an early contributor to O'Grady's *All Ireland Review* and Griffith's *United Irishman*.

450. For the involvement of Annie E. F. Horniman in the Abbey Theatre, see p. 121.

451. Founded in 1928 by the Irish playwright and actor Micheál Mac-Liammóir (1899–1978) and his English partner, Hilton Edwards (1903–1982), the Gate Theatre had, after two seasons in the experimental annex to the Abbey Theatre called the Peacock, moved into permanent quarters in the Rotunda, where it was noted for its eclecticism of style and its presentation of works of international origins.

452. *A Village Wooing, A Comediettina for Two Voices,* by Bernard Shaw, was first produced by the Abbey on September 30, 1935.

453. A prolific writer of fiction, Sean O'Faolain (1900–1985) was among several younger writers whom Yeats was encouraging at this time and had been among the founding members of the Irish Academy of Letters in 1932, the year in which his first collection of stories, *Midsummer Night Madness and Other Stories,* appeared. O'Faolain's

only play, *She Had to Do Something: A Comedy in Three Acts,* was produced at the Abbey in December 1937.

454. The production at the Metropolitan Opera in New York of Wagner's *Parsifal* in December 1903, by Heinrich Conried (1848–1909), was the first American production of the work. After Yeats attended the performance on December 31, 1903, he spoke at a reception at the Authors' Club.

49. *Abbey Theatre Broadcast*

455. The day after it was presented, Yeats called the February 1, 1937, broadcast from the Abbey stage 'a fiasco. Every human sound turned into the groans, roars, bellows of a wild [beast]' (*L* 879). Three weeks later, he confessed to the Australian-born music critic Walter James Turner (1889–1946) that:

> . . . what I heard on my wireless-set while my Abbey Theatre arrange-ment of poems was being done was like the roaring of beasts in the jungle. The arrangement had great success on the stage so I have not the least notion what went wrong. I do not know enough (Kelly).

The programme exists only as a recording made in Dublin a few days after the technically disastrous original broadcast and in a typewrit-ten list of contents in the BBC archives, which was compiled consid-erably later. Yeats arranged for the programme, originally broadcast between 8:00 and 8:15 P.M. on the Radio Athlone band of the Irish service, to be recorded for possible use by the BBC producer George Barnes (1904–60), with whom he was planning future radio pro-grammes. He also prepared many influential friends for the 'political' item in the projected broadcast, his poem on Roger Casement; he intended to supplement its appearance at the end of the programme, transmitted directly from Athlone to thousands of English homes, with its nearly simultaneous publication in the *Irish Press* and, he hoped, by dissemination of the recording.

The programme he chose, he told Barnes in a letter of January 23, was 'rough singing of rough songs . . . I think the great thing is to make everybody understand that we don't want professionally trained singers, but the sort of people who sing when they are drunk or in love' (Kelly).

The other poems were Higgins's translation of a Gaelic ballad, 'The Ballad of O'Bruadir', three of James Stephens's poems, Yeats's own 'Come Gather Round Me Parnellites', published a month ear-lier, and his unpublished 'Come on to the Hills of Mourne'.

Yeats evidently did not take part in the actual broadcast. Ria Mooney (1904–73) had appeared in Abbey productions since 1924 and, in 1937, started its Experimental Theatre. In 1948, she was appointed Producer.

John Stephenson (1895–1963) first appeared at the Abbey in O'Casey's *The Plough and the Stars* (1926). He was later a producer of plays for Radio Éireann.

456. The BBC list of contents notes that the music for 'Come on to the Hills of Mourne' and 'The Rivals' was supplied by Art O'Murnaghan, a composer and stage manager for the Gate Theatre. Yeats identifies him in *A Broadside* (December 1937) as the composer of music published there for his poem 'Colonel Martin'.

Nothing further is known about the fiddle player on the recording of this programme.

457. Yeats omits the first stanza of this poem in *The Oxford Book of Modern Verse,* inserting 'When first I took to' for the first five words of the second stanza.

458. Yeats included Stephens's translation, as it appeared in *Collected Poems* (1931) (O'Shea 1997), in *The Oxford Book of Modern Verse.*

459. A manuscript (NLI 30523, 1r) and two typescripts (NLI 30508, 2r, 3r) of this poem were in Yeats's papers, and Ria Mooney's copy, with notations in pencil by Yeats, is in the Berg Collection of the New York Public Library. It is undoubtedly the programme's 'comic song', which, he told Dorothy Wellesley, 'might amuse you' (Wellesley, p. 133).

460. *OBMV* (p. 373) has: 'to Achill back we go'.

461. *OBMV* (p. 373) has: 'Ghosting glory from the water!'

462. *OBMV* (p. 222) has: 'I was singing at the time'.

463. Having retired in 1906 from a notable career in the British consular service, the Ulster nationalist Sir Roger Casement (1864–1916) was active in encouraging the Irish Republicans to ally themselves with Germany and in arranging German arms and, perhaps, troops in support of the Republican cause. Arrested by the British in April 1916, shortly after having returned to the Irish coast aboard a German ship, he was tried for treason and, in August, hanged. The controversy over his treatment was complicated by the release of the 'black diaries', detailed accounts, purportedly, of his homosexual activities.

Through their mutual friend, the Irish-American physician, journalist, and devoted Republican Patrick McCartan (1878–1963), Yeats had for some time followed the progress of *The Forged Casement Diaries* (1936) by William J. M. A. Maloney (1882–1952), a Scots-American neurologist whom he had met in New York. Yeats persistently attempted to interest Bernard Shaw in supplying a preface to the book, and in November 1936, he wrote to the English novelist Ethel Mannin (1900–1984): 'I am in a rage. . . . [Maloney] has proved that the diaries, supposed to prove Casement "a degenerate" and successfully used to prevent an agitation for his reprieve, were forged. . . . I long to break my rule against politics and call these men criminals but I must not. Perhaps a verse may come to me, now or a year hence' (*L* 867).

464. Parnell's monument in Glasnevin cemetery north of Dublin is near that of the cemetery's founder, Daniel O'Connell. It was a principal Republican gathering place from the time of Parnell's death in 1891.

465. In the same letter to Ethel Mannin, Yeats speaks of 'Come Gather Round Me Parnellites': 'I have lately written a song in defence of Parnell (about love and marriage less foul lies were circulated), a drinking song to a popular tune and will have it sung from the Abbey stage at Xmas' (*L* 867–68). It was first published in *A Broadside,* in January 1937.

466. The broadcast omits the first line of Stephens's poem. In *OBMV,* the first line reads: 'There always is a noise when it is dark!' (p. 212)

467. English authorities had shown the Casement diaries to Alfred Noyes (1880–1958), the English poet, at the time of Casement's trial, and Noyes had some responsibility in the circulation of their contents, subsequently citing them in England and America as exemplary of the depravity of Irish rebels. Yeats's attack here and in the published text of the poem the following day provoked from Noyes an immediate and temperate explanation of his involvement with the diaries. Yeats's letter to the *Irish Press* on February 13 (*L* 882) accepts Noyes's explanation and his suggestion that the diaries be reviewed impartially. Substituting 'Come Tom and Dick, come all the troop' for this line, Yeats restated his charge that Sir Cecil Arthur Spring-Rice (1859–1918), the British ambassador to America, 'had to whisper' the imputations against Casement, both to spread them and to avoid their becoming available to Casement's defence for refutation.

50. In the Poet's Pub

468. 'In the Poet's Pub', the first of Yeats's BBC stagings in collaboration with George Barnes, was broadcast on the BBC from London on Friday, April 2, 1937, between 9:20 and 9:40 P.M. The poems were read by V. C. Clinton-Baddeley. Yeats's annotated copy of the text of the broadcast is in the BBC Written Archives Centre, and a manuscript and typescript of his introductions are among his papers. This text is based on the complete recording of the broadcast in the BBC Sound Archive at Broadcasting House in London (BBC #14879-81). It is Yeats's programme as broadcast, with variations from the typescript noted.

469. For 'came one after another', Yeats's BBC script has 'followed one another'.

470. For 'folk singers who', 'those that'.

471. For 'folk singers and the speaker', 'singers of folk songs and the speakers'.

472. For 'folk singer', 'singer of a folk song'.

473. In preparing his broadcast version, Yeats deleted the following from his script, after 'concert platform':

I have suggested to the B.B.C. that it should use some musical instrument to fill up pauses, whether in the middle of a verse or at the end of it, to vary and to rest the attention. When I first produced a play at the Abbey Theatre some thirty years ago I told an actor to pause to mark a change of mood, and the impression he gave me was that of a man who had forgotten his lines. Then I told him to fill up the pause with a significant movement of his body and all was well. But when you are reciting to the wireless and nobody can see your body it seems right to fill up the pauses with musical sounds. They enable . . . (BBC, NLI Ms 30580, SUNY-SB, Box 23).

474. For 'Why not . . . and so', Yeats had written in: 'These tricks of the folk singer'.

475. The incidental music by Felix Mendelssohn-Bartholdy (1809–47) to Shakespeare's *A Midsummer Night's Dream* was first performed in Potsdam in 1843.

476. Yeats's script reads 'the songs'.

477. Yeats deleted from the typescript:

And I have begged them, with all the vehemence of which I am capable, to avoid properly trained singers. Those magnificent people belong to the concert platform, not to us. We are just ordinary people who sing because we are in love or drunk, or because we don't want to think of anything in particular.

478. Yeats's text: 'yourselves'.

479. Yeats's text, after 'Pub': 'there are such pubs in Dublin and I suppose elsewhere, sitting'.

480. This poem's text: 'Do you remember an Inn'.

481. Both Yeats's correspondence and the BBC recording, in which what he calls 'the first and more vigorous part' of Chesterton's 'The Rolling English Road' is followed by drum-rolls, support Barnes's statement that the last two stanzas of Chesterton's 'The Rolling English Road' were not read because Yeats found them 'sentimental and rather disgusting' (Hone 456). According to Barnes, Yeats also pruned poems by Thomas Hardy (1840–1928), Kipling, and Edith Sitwell (1887–1964) in the final preparation of this broadcast.

482. Although they appear in Yeats's typescript, none of the titles of the poems in this broadcast was read.
     'Tarantella', by the English poet Hilaire Belloc (1870–1953), was published in 1923 in *Sonnets and Verse*. Yeats selected it for inclusion in *The Oxford Book of Modern Verse*.
     1.9, *OBMV*: '(Under the dark of the vine verandah)?'
     1.28, *OBMV*: '. . . an Inn!'
     1.39, *OBMV*: 'Only the boom'

483. Yeats's script substitutes 'the' for Belloc's 'a'; 'the' appears in *OBMV*, and it was read this way in the broadcast.

484. 'The Rolling English Road' first appeared in the *Flying Inn* (1914)

and was included in its entirety by Yeats in *The Oxford Book of Modern Verse.*

485. Yeats had met Walter de la Mare (1873–1956) at the home of Lady Ottoline Morrell (1873–1938) in 1930 and had included six of his poems in *The Oxford Book of Modern Verse.* Not among Yeats's selections, De la Mare's 'Off the Ground' first appeared in *Peacock Pie; A Book of Rhymes* in 1913 (O'Shea 508).

486. Yeats's text reads 'when'.

487. Yeats inserted 'just' in his broadcast.

488. 'Drake's Drum', by the English author Henry Newbolt, appeared in *Collected Poems, 1897–1907* (1910) and was included in *The Oxford Book of Modern Verse.*
    l.6, *OBMV: 'sailor-lads'*

489. Sylvia Townsend Warner (1893–1978) first published 'The Sailor' in *The Espalier* (1925).

490. Yeats included two of York Powell's translations from the French of Paul Fort (1872–1960) in *The Oxford Book of Modern Verse,* including this one, which he called in a letter to Dorothy Wellesley 'a song by York Powell which I delight in' (*L* 859).

491. Yeats's text omits the last refrain of York Powell's ballad, but it was sung in the broadcast, with Yeats among the singers, with increasing, feign-drunken rowdiness.

51. In the Poet's Parlour

492. Yeats broadcast 'In the Poet's Parlour' from London on Thursday, April 22, 1937, between 10:20 and 10:40 P.M. The poems were read and sung by the young English actress and poet Margot Ruddock (1907–51), in whom Yeats had become interested a few years earlier, and V. C. Clinton-Baddeley with musical accompaniment. Yeats presented, as he had in his first radio readings, unpublished poems.

    A nearly indecipherable, partial manuscript of the introductions is among Yeats's papers, and it appears that the content and order of the programme was unsettled as the broadcast date approached. The *Radio Times* for April 16 indicated that both Yeats's 'Imitated from the Japanese' and Edith Sitwell's 'The King of China's Daughter' would be included, while Barnes's notes relegate Sitwell's poem in the list of those 'rejected' but retain Yeats's poem, which Clinton-Baddeley recalled rehearsing (Wade 414). The BBC's 'programmes as broadcast' log lists the same contents as Wade and the BBC file copy of the script, but it suggests a different order for the last three poems. The primary source of this text is the BBC file copy, which includes emendations in Yeats's hand.

493. Yeats substituted 'The second' for the typescript's 'One of them'.

494. Yeats struck out 'of the three poems' in the text.

495. Typescript: 'many'.

496. First published in the *London Mercury* in April 1938, 'Sweet Dancer', in the version given here, was spoken by its undoubted subject,

Margot Ruddock, with a 'dance on pipe' accompanying. The titles of poems in this broadcast appear to have been announced.

497. Spoken by Margot Ruddock.

498. Apparently read by Clinton-Baddeley, with pipe accompaniment, in this version, this poem appears without title at the end of the verse version of *The King of the Great Clock Tower* (1934). Yeats first published it in *Life and Letters* in 1934, and it appeared separately as 'The Wicked Hawthorn Tree' in *A Broadside* in February 1935.

499. The BBC text indicates that, in contrast to all printed versions, 'cold' and 'blown' were intentionally reversed in this broadcast.

500. Script: 'Yes, yes.'

501. Inserted by Yeats in the script.

502. Yeats's manuscript alteration changes the text from: 'Their first poem will be . . .'

503. Yeats included 'Santorin' by the English poet James Elroy Flecker (1884–1915) (see O'Shea 683) in *The Oxford Book of Modern Verse*. The poem was spoken by Margot Ruddock, and Yeats may have omitted the final lines, which are stricken from the script, but which appear twice in manuscript, the first time in Yeats's hand, elsewhere on the script.

> She sank into the moonlight
> And the sea was only sea.

504. Johnson's 'To Morfydd' (see O'Shea 1021) first appeared in 1894 in *The Second Book of the Rhymers' Club*. Yeats included the poem the following year in his edition of *A Book of Irish Verse*. It was spoken and chanted by Margot Ruddock, with pipe.

505. Higgins's 'Song for the Clatter Bones', which appeared in *A Broadside* in June 1935, and was included in *The Oxford Book of Modern Verse*, was spoken by Clinton-Baddeley, after an interruption of drums and clatter bones.

506. *OBMV* reads 'bitch'. George Barnes says that Yeats permitted the change 'in the interests of British morals' (see Hone 456).

507. 'Tits' inserted for Higgins's 'teats' in the BBC text.

508. This line reads: 'So I'll just clack: though her ghost lacks a back' in *A Broadside,* and 'So I'll just clack: though her bones lack a back' in *OBMV* (p. 372).

509. Yeats's 'The Pilgrim' subsequently appeared in *A Broadside* in October 1937, and was included in *New Poems* the following year.

Barnes's notes indicate that this poem was not read and that, instead, Yeats's 'Imitated from the Japanese' followed 'Song for the Clatter Bones' and preceded 'To Morfydd'. Both the sense and the contents, however, of the BBC text, along with the BBC's 'Programmes as Broadcast' for this date, support the text as presented here.

510. The format presented here is that of the first published version of this poem. With the exception of a question mark at this end of this line, the BBC typescript contains no punctuation, and the last letter of the

refrain is not capitalised. A manuscript note indicates that the refrain in this and the following stanzas was to be read twice.

52. My Own Poetry

511. After his 1936 broadcast lecture on 'Modern Poetry', included in *Essays 1931 to 1936* (1937), the political experiment of the Abbey Theatre broadcast, and the 'Pub' and 'Parlour' programmes, Yeats moved to further innovation in planning his radio programmes. In his next broadcast, he explored the importance of 'a public theme' to his rekindled interest in the combination of words and music.

Broadcast from London on Saturday, July 3, 1937, between 10:00 and 10:20 P.M., 'My Own Poetry' included readings by V. C. Clinton-Baddeley and Margot Ruddock and musical settings by a friend of many years, the artist Edmund Dulac (1882–1953). Stormy rehearsals eventually reduced Margot Ruddock's participation in the broadcast. Yeats's tactics offended not only Olive Groves (1900–74) and Marie Goossens (1894–1991), the singer and the harpist hired for the occasion, but also Dulac himself, contributing to the cancellation of Yeats's next proposed radio appearance, a simulated artistic argument with Dulac tentatively scheduled for August 5.

The text is from the emended file copy at the BBC and the manuscript of this programme among Yeats's papers. A more complete representation of the programme as broadcast is included in Appendix C.

512. Yeats emended this sentence in the script from which he read, inserting 'those' and moving 'for some days' from after 'held them' to the end.

513. Pearse's powerful eulogy on August 1, 1915, at the graveside of Jeremiah O'Donovan Rossa, a hero of the suppressed insurrection of 1865, was a signal moment in the evolution of the 1916 'rising'. Pearse is eulogised, along with James Connolly (1870–1916), founder of the *Irish Worker*, organiser of the Citizens Army, and martyr in the 1916 'rising', in Yeats's 'Easter, 1916' and 'The Rose Tree'.

514. Yeats emended this sentence in the script from which he read, changing 'if I had been' to 'had I been'.

515. See page 150.

516. At least two passages, line 6 and lines 3 and 4, of 'The Curse of Cromwell' derive from Gaelic sources. Writing about the subjection of Catholic Ireland in the Protestant ascendancy at the turn of the eighteenth century in his historical 'Commentary on "A Parnellite at Parnell's Funeral" ' (1934), Yeats paraphrased a verse from the 'Last Lines' of the Irish poet Egan O'Rahilly (1670–1729):

> At the base of the social structure, but hardly within it, the peasantry dreamed on in their medieval sleep; the Gaelic poets sang of the banished Catholic aristocracy; 'My fathers served their fathers before Christ was crucified' sang one of the most famous (*P* 663).

A more probable referent, however, is a passage in the anonymous Gaelic lament, contemporary with O'Rahilly, for a ruined Butler seat, 'Kilcash':

> The courtyard's filled with water
>   And the great earls where are they?
> The earls, the lady, the people
>   Beaten into the clay.

> *The Penguin Book of Irish Verse,* ed. Brendan Kennelly (Harmondsworth: Penguin
>   Books, 1970), p. 69.

The line and the image are echoed in 'Under Ben Bulben':

> Sing the lords and ladies gay
> That were beaten into the clay
> Through seven heroic centuries (*P* 327).

517. This sentence is in manuscript in the script from which Yeats read.
518. 'The Rose Tree', first published in the *Dial* in November 1920, and included in *Michael Robartes and the Dancer* (1921), was read by V. C. Clinton-Baddeley. Dulac's transitional music at the end of the poem, which apparently was used, is included with the BBC copy of the text.
519. Yeats had first published this elegy to Robert Gregory in *The Wild Swans at Coole* (1919). Transitional music by Dulac is included in the BBC text.
520. First published in *A Broadside* for August 1937, 'The Curse of Cromwell' was included in *New Poems* the following year. The broadcast version of the unpublished poem, given here, was read by Clinton-Baddeley and Margot Ruddock. The first refrain was 'sung', according to the BBC text, by Clinton-Baddeley, and the others by him and Margot Ruddock.
521. Serious respiratory and cardiac illness, exacerbated by profound fatigue, beset Yeats in the fall of 1927, and he spent much of the next two years recuperating in Spain, the South of France, and Italy. For several months, however, starting in early 1929, his health and strength improved dramatically, giving rise to the poems subsequently published in *Words for Music Perhaps and Other Poems* (1932). According to Hone, this poem is among nearly a dozen written in six weeks in February and March (Hone 429).

Yeats's comment here echoes his recollection of that period in his dedication of *The Winding Stair and Other Poems* (1933) to Dulac:

> Then in the spring of 1929 life returned as an impression of the uncontrollable energy and daring of the great creators; it seemed that but for journalism and criticism, all that evasion and explanation, the world would be torn in pieces. I wrote 'Mad as the Mist and Snow', a mechanical little song, and after that almost all that group of poems

called in memory of those exultant weeks 'Words for Music Perhaps' (*VP* 831).

522. This sentence is in manuscript in the script from which Yeats read.
523. As section XVIII of 'Words for Music Perhaps', this poem had first appeared in 1932 in *Words for Music Perhaps and Other Poems*. It was spoken by Clinton-Baddeley with harp music between stanzas.
524. After its first publication in *October Blast* in 1927, 'Sailing to Byzantium' was collected in *The Tower* (1928). In 1949, in the BBC programme 'Broadcasting with W. B. Yeats', Clinton-Baddeley recalled mentioning to Yeats during a rehearsal that the first line, clear enough to the eye, was difficult to read aloud while retaining the sense. Yeats proclaimed the line 'the worst piece of syntax I ever wrote' and later, when they were leaving the studio, presented Clinton-Baddeley with the revised first line which, although broadcast, did not supplant the original in printed versions:

    That is no country for old men. The young . . .

525. 'He and She' first appeared in *Poetry* and the *London Mercury* in December 1934, along with the other poems published the same month under the general title 'Supernatural Songs' in *The King of the Great Clock Tower*. This poem was sung by Olive Groves to music by Edmund Dulac.

53. My Own Poetry Again

526. Yeats's last radio broadcast, 'My Own Poetry Again', was given between 10:45 and 11:05 P.M. on October 29, 1937.
    Broadcasting from BBC London on the National Programme, Yeats selected poems written over a span of forty years, reading all but two himself. 'Into the Twilight' and 'The Old Men admiring Themselves in the Water' were read by Margot Ruddock.
    The text is from Yeats's typescript, marked 'My own copy', which is incomplete. The copy in the BBC files was destroyed during the war, and George Barnes told Mrs Yeats that no recording was made.
527. 'The Happy Townland' first appeared in the *Weekly Critical Review* in June 1903, and was collected in *In the Seven Woods* later that year.
528. Yeats published this poem as 'The Celtic Twilight' in Henley's *National Observer* in 1893 and included it under the present title as the epigraph to a collection of poetry and prose, *The Celtic Twilight*, in the same year.
529. This poem first appeared in the *National Observer* in October of 1891 and was included in *The Countess Kathleen and Various Legends and Lyrics,* which was published the following year.
530. Yeats had written about Thoor Ballylee, the Norman tower near Lady Gregory's Coole Park, since the 1890s; he acquired the prop-

erty in 1916, restoring it after his marriage in 1917. He and his family spent parts of each year there until 1929.

531. First published in 1932, as 'Coole Park and Ballylee 1932', in *Words for Music Perhaps and Other Poems,* this poem is entitled 'Coole and Ballylee, 1931' in all subsequent printings, including Yeats's inclusion of it in OBMV, until the posthumous *Collected Poems of W. B. Yeats* (1950), where it becomes 'Coole Park and Ballylee, 1931'.

532. Yeats's typescript ends at the conclusion of this poem. Notes made by George Barnes, as well as the BBC records of 'Programmes as Broadcast', indicate that Margot Ruddock concluded the programme with a reading of 'The Old Men Admiring Themselves in the Water', with, almost certainly, introductory remarks by Yeats:

> I heard the old, old men say,
> 'Everything alters,
> And one by one we drop away'.
> They had hands like claws, and their knees
> Were twisted like the old thorn-trees
> By the waters.
> I heard the old, old men say,
> 'All that's beautiful drifts away
> Like the waters'.

54. I Became an Author

533. None of the three radio programmes proposed for 1938 was broadcast. Yeats had written the text for one of them, a reminiscence called 'I Became an Author', as part of a BBC series in which contemporary writers discussed 'how they began to write and what obstacles they had to overcome to achieve publication'. 'I Became an Author' appeared in the *Listener* on August 4, 1938, and was Yeats's last publication, with the exception of *The Autobiography of William Butler Yeats,* which appeared on August 30. Yeats died on January 28, 1939.

534. Charles Johnston (1867–1931), later a fellow Theosophist with Yeats, was the founder of the Hermetic Society in Dublin. Johnston was also responsible for Yeats's introduction to Madame Blavatsky (1831–91), Yeats's early spiritualist guide, whose niece Johnston had married in 1888. He entered the Indian Civil Service in the same year and eventually settled in America. In the early 1890s, Yeats had been a visitor at the home in Ballykilbeg, Co. Down, of Johnston's father, William (1829–1902), a Member of Parliament from South Belfast.

535. The 'vaguely Elizabethan play' has not been identified. The 'imitation of Shelley' was a play written in 1886 which, according to Richard Ellmann in *Yeats: The Man and the Masks,* was 'entitled variously *The Blindness, The Epic of the Forest* and *The Equator of Wild Olives*' (pp. 46–47).

The 'fragment . . . of the Indian play' is 'Anashuya and Vijaya'.

Yeats alludes, in his 'Notes' to *Early Poems and Stories* (1925), to Charles Johnston's fondness for these lines. 'Every time I have reprinted them I have considered the leaving out of most, and then remembered an old school friend who has some of them by heart, for no better reason, as I think, than that they remind him of his own youth' (*P* 590).

536. In his biography of the English actor Sir Henry Irving (1828–1905), Gordon Craig notes that 'In dancing a role, Irving went to the extreme limits possible to an actor of the nineteenth century, of preserving the last tingle of a mighty Greek tradition' (*Henry Irving* [New York: Longmans Green and Co., 1930], p. 71).

537. Lines 7–8 of 'A Nativity' (*P* 345).

Yeats's 'Two months ago' is questionable. Jeffares suggests this poem may have been written in August 1936 (*A New Commentary on the Poems of W. B. Yeats* [Stanford: Stanford University Press, 1984], p. 422).

538. The pastoral play was *The Island of Statues* (1885). *The Sad Shepherd, or, A Tale of Robin Hood,* the unfinished last play of Ben Jonson (1572–1637), was published in 1641.

539. John Bagnell Bury (1861–1927), the classical scholar and historian, taught at Trinity College, Dublin, and, later, at Cambridge. His edition of Gibbon's *History of the Decline and Fall of the Roman Empire* appeared between 1896 and 1900 (O'Shea 746).

540. Yeats had been photographed, at W. E. Henley's urging, by the London photographer Frederick Hollyer (1837–1933) in the fall of 1890.

541. The *Cambridge Modern History* (1902–12) (O'Shea 14) was conceived by the Cambridge Professor of Modern History John E. E. D. Acton (1834–1902). Yeats used this example in describing his plans for *On the Boiler* (1939) to Dorothy Wellesley on June 22, 1938, there as here using the popular rather than the actual title (*L* 911).

542. In *Collected Poems* (1933), 'The Song of the Happy Shepherd' and 'The Cloak, the Boat, and the Shoes' survive, with some changes, from *The Island of Statues.*

543. Remembering her Paris days in her autobiography, the dancer Isadora Duncan (1877–1927) notes that 'Neither the appreciation of princes, nor my growing fame, brought us enough to eat' (*My Life* [New York: Boni and Liveright, 1927], p. 86).

Appendix C

544. Barnes's essay, edited by Jeremy Silver, was published in *Yeats Annual No. 5*, pp. 189–94.

545. According to Barnes, this separation of the poet from the musical production reflects Yeats's strenuous disagreements with Dulac and is part of a compromise between them.

546. Dulac's setting for 'The Curse of Cromwell' was evidently simplified as the programme was being rehearsed. The separate line written for the 'reciter' and its musical accompaniment were abandoned.

INDEX

Abbey Theatre, 121–26, 134, 144, 153, 159, 161, 165, 169, 178, 179, 192, 203–7, 217, 219–23, 242, 245, 255, 256, 257, 355, 356, 357, 358, 360, 370, 371, 372, 374, 384, 385, 390, 397, 400, 401

AE. *See* Russell, George William

acting and stagecraft, 62–63, 87–88, 89–91, 123–24, 127–28, 129–33, 220–21, 266–67

Acton, John E. E. D. (1834–1902), 299, 411

Aitken, Charles (1869–1936), 148, 149, 150, 222, 366

Allgood, Molly (Máire O'Neill, 1887–1952), 158, 159, 255, 369

Allgood, Sara (1883–1950), 158, 165, 255, 369, 372–73, 374

Allingham, William (1842–89), 48, 140, 141, 330

All Ireland Review, 331, 338, 400

America, 116–20, 155, 219, 229, 234

Ames, Winthrop (1871–1937), 360

Appia, Adolphe (1862–1928), 127, 358

Aran Islands, 70, 135, 138

Archer, William (1830–97), 208, 386

Aristotle (384–322 B.C.), 177

Arnold, Matthew (1822–1888), 50, 368

art, 90–91, 130–32, 153–54, 212–13

Atkinson, George (1880–1940), 210, 386

Atkinson, Robert (1839–1908), 339

Ballisodare, Co. Sligo, 249, 394, 399

Ballylee, Co. Galway, 35, 327, 375, 409

Balzac, Honoré de (1799–1850), 60, 183, 215, 240, 379

Barnes, George (1904–60), 401, 403, 405, 406, 409, 410, 411

Beardsley, Aubrey (1872–98), 55, 333, 396

Beardsley, Mabel (1871–1916), 239–41, 396

Belloc, Hilaire (1870–1953), 404

Bennett, Allan (1872–1923), 56, 333

Benson, Arthur Christopher (1862–1928), 138, 362

Berenice (ca. 273–221 B.C.), 340

Berkeley, Bishop George (1685–1753), 195, 196, 201, 218, 232, 381, 389, 392; *Three Dialogues between Hylas and Philonous,* 232, 393

Bernard, John Henry (1860–1927), 383

Best, Richard Irvine (1872–1959), 328

Birmingham Repertory Theatre, 159

Bjørnson, Bjørnstjerne (1832–1910), 135, 164, 341, 360

Blake, William (1757–1827), 36, 138, 139, 153, 164, 328, 342–43, 362, 368, 371–72

Blasket Islands, 138, 245, 246, 257

Blavatsky, Madam Helen Petrovna (1831–91), 410

Bookman, The, 332, 344, 391, 399, 400